COMMANDER
in CHIEF

ALSO BY NIGEL HAMILTON

*Royal Greenwich: A Guide and History to London's
Most Historic Borough* (with Olive Hamilton)

*Nigel Hamilton's Guide to Greenwich: A Personal Guide to the Buildings and
Walks of One of England's Most Beautiful and Historic Areas*

*The Brothers Mann: The Lives of Heinrich and Thomas Mann,
1871–1950 and 1875–1955*

Monty: The Making of a General, 1887–1942

Master of the Battlefield: Monty's War Years, 1942–1944

Monty: Final Years of the Field-Marshal, 1944–1976

Monty: The Man Behind the Legend

JFK: Reckless Youth

Monty: The Battles of Field Marshal Bernard Law Montgomery

The Full Monty: Montgomery of Alamein, 1887–1942

Bill Clinton, An American Journey: Great Expectations

Montgomery: D-Day Commander

Bill Clinton: Mastering the Presidency

Biography: A Brief History

How to Do Biography: A Primer

*American Caesars: Lives of the Presidents from
Franklin D. Roosevelt to George W. Bush*

The Mantle of Command: FDR at War, 1941–1942

COMMANDER
in CHIEF

FDR'S BATTLE
WITH CHURCHILL,
1943

Nigel Hamilton

HOUGHTON MIFFLIN HARCOURT

BOSTON · NEW YORK

2016

For information about permission to reproduce selections from this book,
write to trade.permissions@hmhco.com or to Permissions, Houghton Mifflin Harcourt
Publishing Company, 3 Park Avenue, 19th Floor, New York, New York 10016.

www.hmhco.com

Library of Congress Cataloging-in-Publication Data
Names: Hamilton, Nigel.
Title: Commander in chief : FDR's battle with Churchill, 1943 / Nigel Hamilton.
Description: Houghton Mifflin Harcourt : Boston, 2016.
Includes bibliographical references and index.
Identifiers: LCCN 2015037253
ISBN 9780544279117 (hardcover)
ISBN 9780544277441 (ebook)
Subjects: LCSH: World War, 1939–1945 — United States. | Roosevelt, Franklin D. (Franklin
Delano), 1882–1945 | Churchill, Winston, 1874–1965. | World War, 1939–1945 — Diplomatic
history. | Command of troops — Case studies. | World War, 1939–1945—Campaigns. |
Great Britain — Foreign relations — United States. | United States —
Foreign relations — Great Britain.
Classification: LCC D753 .H249 2016 | DDC 940.53/2273 — dc23
LC record available at http://lccn.loc.gov/2015037253

Maps by Mapping Specialists, Ltd.

Printed in the United States of America
DOC 10 9 8 7 6 5 4 3 2 1

The author is grateful for permission to quote from the following: Diary of Lord Halifax,
1941–1942, reprinted by permission of the Borthwick Institute for Archives, University of
York. Letters and diaries of Margaret Lynch Suckley, reprinted by permission of the Wilderstein Preservation, Rhinebeck, N.Y.

For Lady Ray

Contents

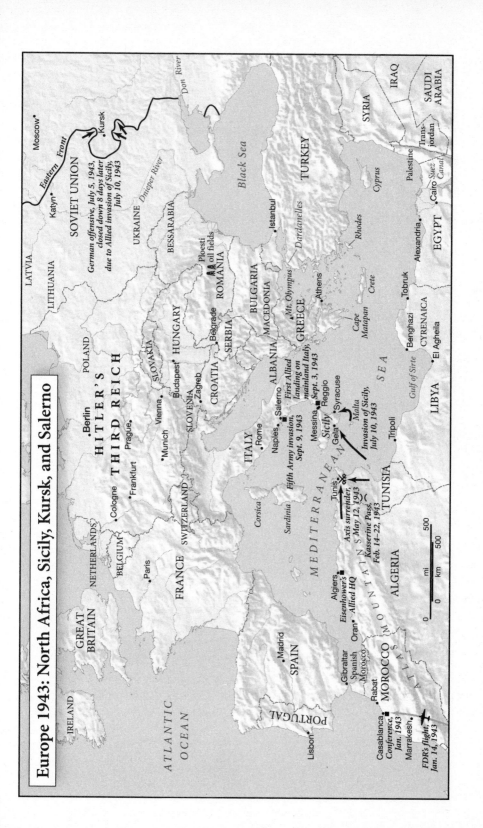

Europe 1943: North Africa, Sicily, Kursk, and Salerno

ATLANTIC OCEAN

IRELAND

GREAT BRITAIN

NETHERLANDS

BELGIUM

•Paris

FRANCE

SWITZERLAND

•Cologne
•Frankfurt
•Munich

Berlin•

HITLER'S
THIRD REICH

•Prague

SLOVENIA

•Vienna
•Budapest

SLOVAKIA

POLAND

LITHUANIA

LATVIA

•Katyn

SOVIET UNION

•Moscow

Eastern Front

•Kursk

German offensive, July 5, 1943,
closed down 8 days later
due to Allied invasion of Sicily,
July 10, 1943

Don River

Dnieper River

UKRAINE

BESSARABIA

Ploesti
▲▲ oil fields

ROMANIA

HUNGARY

CROATIA

Zagreb•
Belgrade•

SERBIA

BULGARIA

Istanbul•

Black Sea

TURKEY

SYRIA

IRAQ

SAUDI ARABIA

Trans-
jordan

Palestine

Cairo• Suez Canal

EGYPT

Alexandria•

Cape
Matapan

Crete

Rhodes

Dardanelles

Athens•

GREECE

•Mt. Olympus

MACEDONIA

ALBANIA

Tobruk•

Benghazi•

CYRENAICA

El Agheila•

Gulf of Sirte

LIBYA

Tripoli•

Malta

Invasion of Sicily,
July 10, 1943

Syracuse
Gela•
Reggio
Messina•

Sicily

Sept. 3, 1943

First Allied
landing on
mainland Italy,

Salerno•
Naples•

Fifth Army invasion,
Sept. 9, 1943

Rome•

ITALY

Corsica

Sardinia

MEDITERRANEAN   SEA

Tunis•

Axis surrender,
May 12, 1943

Kasserine Pass,
Feb. 14–22, 1943

TUNISIA

ALGERIA

MOUNTAINS

Algiers•

Oran•
Eisenhower's
Allied HQ

Gibraltar•

Spanish
Morocco

MOROCCO

Rabat•

Marrakesh•

Casablanca•
Conference, Jan. 1943

FDR's flight,
Jan. 14, 1943

ATLAS

SPAIN

Madrid•

PORTUGAL

Lisbon•

500
mi

500
km

0

0

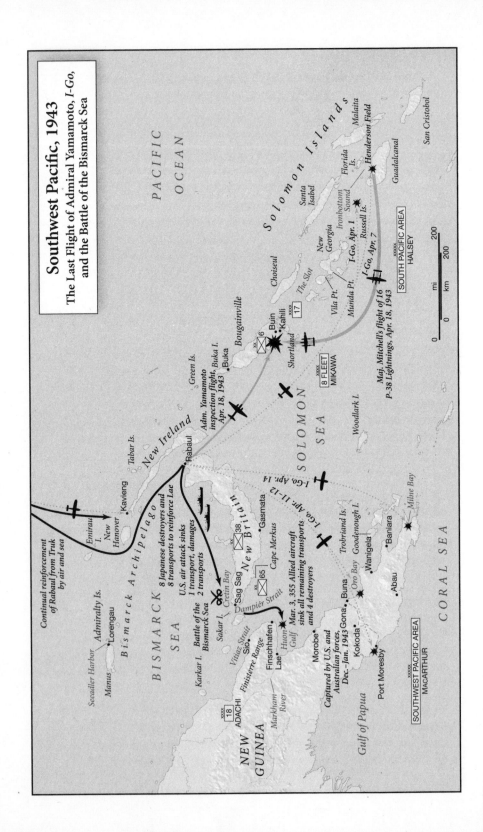

Southwest Pacific, 1943

The Last Flight of Admiral Yamamoto, *I-Go*,
and the Battle of the Bismarck Sea

PACIFIC OCEAN

Solomon Islands

Henderson Field

Malaita

San Cristobol

Guadalcanal

Santa Isabel

Florida Is.

Ironbottom Sound

Russell Is.

I-Go, Apr. 7

New Georgia

Munda Pt.

I-Go, Apr. 1

Vila Pt.

SOUTH PACIFIC AREA
HALSEY

The Slot

Choiseul

Maj. Mitchell's flight of 16
P-38 Lightnings, Apr. 18, 1943

mi   200

km   200

0

17

Bougainville

Buka

Green Is.

Buka I.

Adm. Yamamoto
inspection flight, Buka I.
Apr. 18, 1943

Kahili

Buin

6

Shortland

8 FLEET
MIKAWA

Woodlark I.

SOLOMON SEA

Tabar Is.

New Ireland

Rabaul

I-Go, Apr. 14

Bismarck Archipelago

Continual reinforcement
of Rabaul from Truk
by air and sea

Emirau
I.
New
Hanover

Kavieng

Gasmata

Cape Merkus

New Britain

38

65

Sag Sag

Milne Bay

Trobriand Is.

Goodenough I.

Baniara

I-Go, Apr. 11–12

Mar. 3, 355 Allied aircraft
sink all remaining transports
and 4 destroyers

Admiralty Is.

Seeadler Harbor

Lorengau

Manus

Karkar I.

8 Japanese destroyers and
8 transports to reinforce Lae

U.S. air attack sinks
1 transport, damages
2 transports

Sakar I.

Battle of the
Bismarck Sea

Cretin Bay

Wanigela

Oro Bay

Buna

Gona

Kokoda

Abau

BISMARCK SEA

Dampiér Strait

Vitiaz Strait

Sio

Finisterre Range

Finschhafen

Lae

Huon

Gulf

Morobe

Captured by U.S. and
Australian forces,
Dec.–Jan. 1943

CORAL SEA

Markham
River

18

ADACHI

*NEW
GUINEA*

Port Moresby

Gulf of Papua

SOUTHWEST PACIFIC AREA
MACARTHUR

Prologue

In *THE MANTLE OF COMMAND: FDR AT WAR, 1941–1942*, I described how President Franklin Roosevelt first donned the cloak of commander in chief of the Armed Forces of the United States in war — a world war stretching from disaster at Pearl Harbor to his "great pet scheme," Operation Torch: the triumphant Allied invasion of North Africa in November 1942, which stunned Hitler and signified one of the most extraordinary turnabouts in military history.

Commander in Chief: FDR at War, 1943 addresses the next chapter of President Roosevelt's war service: a year in which, moving to the offensive, the President had not only to direct the efforts of his generals but keep Prime Minister Winston Churchill, his "active and ardent lieutenant," in line. Roosevelt's struggle to keep his U.S. subordinates on track toward victory, without incurring the terrible casualties that would have greeted their military plans and timetable, proved mercifully successful that fateful year, but his assumption that Churchill would abide by the strategic agreements they had made proved illusory. Thus, although Roosevelt's patient, step-by-step direction of the war led to historic victories of the Western Allies in Tunisia in the spring of 1943, and again in Sicily in August of that year — results that assured the President a cross-Channel assault would be decisive when launched, in the spring of 1944 — the British prime minister did not agree. The President's resultant "battle royal" with Churchill — who was in essence commander in chief of all British Empire forces — became one of the most contentious strategic debates in the history of warfare.

This dramatic, repeated struggle forms the centerpiece or core of this volume, for it is not too bold to say that upon its outcome rested the outcome of World War II, and thus the future of humanity. The struggle took most of the year — *das verlorene Jahr,* as German military historians would call it. Had Churchill prevailed in his preferred strategy, the war might well have been lost for the Allies, at least in terms of the defeat of Hitler. Even though the President won out over the impetuous, ever-evasive British prime minister, the fallout from Churchill's obstinacy and military mistakes would be profound. Not only was American trust in British sincerity severely damaged, but the need to keep the Prime Minister sweet, and loyal to the agreements he had only reluctantly made for Operation Overlord, led to dangerously naive plans for the Allied invasion of mainland Italy in September 1943 — plans involving an airborne landing on Rome, and a gravely compromised amphibious landing in the Gulf of Salerno, south of Naples: Avalanche.

The reality was, Winston Churchill had remained a Victorian not only in his colonial-imperialist mindset, as President Roosevelt often remarked, but in his understanding of modern war — and the Wehrmacht. He grievously underestimated the Wehrmacht's determination to hold fast to the last man at the very extremity of the European mainland, giving rise to fantasies of easy Allied victory, and a possible gateway to central Europe that would make Overlord unnecessary.

Fortunately, the President's absolute determination in 1943 to prepare his armies for modern combat and to then stand by the Overlord assault as the decisive battle of the Western world rendered Churchill's opposition powerless. The Prime Minister's strategic blindness would prove tragically expensive in human life, but mercifully it did not lose the war for the Allies. The President may justly be said to have saved civilization — but it was a near-run thing.

To a large extent the facts of this dark saga are well known to military historians. However, because President Roosevelt began to assemble[1] but did not live to write his own account of the war's military direction, and since others did go on to recount their own parts — sometimes with great literary skill — the President's true role and performance as U.S. commander in chief has often gone unappreciated by general readers. Churchill, who was nothing if not magnanimous in victory, certainly attempted in his memoirs to pay tribute to Roosevelt's leadership, but in his concern to regain the prime ministership he had lost in 1945 he could not always bring himself to tell the truth. Nor was he ashamed of this. As he had boasted after the Casablanca Conference, he fully intended to tell the story of the war from his point of view — and where necessary to suborn history to his own agenda: "to wait until the war is over and then to write his impressions so that, if necessary, he could correct or bury his mistakes."[2] During the war itself he had openly and publicly expressed his loyalty to President Roosevelt as the mastermind directing Allied strategy — a surprise even to Joseph Goebbels — but in private he nevertheless let it be known that he himself was the real directing genius. As King George VI's private secretary, Sir Alan Lascelles, noted in his diary on November 10, 1942, though in his Mansion House speech extolling the successful U.S. invasion of Morocco and Algeria the Prime Minister "gave the credit for its original conception to Roosevelt," Sir Alan believed "it belongs more truly to himself."[3] By the time General Eisenhower took the surrender of all Axis forces in North Africa six months later, this notion of the Prime Minister as sole military architect of Allied strategy and performance had grown to ridiculous levels. Not only was Churchill given credit for having "built up the 8th Army into the wonderful fighting machine that it has become" — despite Churchill's original refusal to appoint General Montgomery to command the army, and his opposition to the new military tactics Montgomery was employing — but Lascelles was convinced, like King George, that "Winston is so essentially the father of the North African baby that he deserves any recognition, royal or otherwise, that can be given to him . . . He has himself publicly given the credit for 'Torch' to Roosevelt, but I have little doubt that W. was really its only begetter."[4]

Aided by his "syndicate" of researchers, civil servants, and historian-aides, Churchill was able to have his day in literary court, in his six-volume opus, *The Second World War,* which helped win him the Nobel Prize for Literature in 1953 — a work that, as Professor David Reynolds has shown,[5] was often economical with the truth. For the memory of President Roosevelt — whose funeral Churchill had not even attended — it was, however, near-devastating, since its magisterial narrative placed Churchill at the center of the war's direction and President Roosevelt very much at the periphery.

In many ways, then, this book and its predecessor are a counternarrative, or corrective: my attempt to tell the story of Roosevelt's exercise of high command from his — not Churchill's — perspective.

In my first volume I selected fourteen episodes, centering on President Roosevelt's "great pet scheme": his Torch invasion of Northwest Africa, and the near mutiny of his generals to stop this and plump instead for a suicidal invasion of northern France in 1942. In this new volume I have selected twelve representative episodes of 1943, beginning with the Casablanca Conference in January and ending with the invasion of Salerno in September. While this has entailed omitting many important events and aspects of Roosevelt's presidency as U.S. commander in chief — some of which, like the development of the atom bomb, progress in the Pacific, and questions of saving the Jews in Europe, will be addressed in a final volume — they continue to give us a clearer picture of how President Roosevelt operated when wearing, so to speak, his military mantle in World War II. By following him closely in his study, in the Oval Office and the Map Room at the White House, at his "camp" at Shangri-la and his family home at Hyde Park; on his historic trip abroad to Africa (the first president ever to fly in office, and the first to inspect troops on the battlefield overseas); and on his long inspection tour of military installations and training camps in the United States (during which he authorized the secret air ambush of Admiral Yamamoto), we are able to see him at last as we have previously been able to see so many of his subordinate military officers and officials of World War II — that is to say, from *his* perspective.

It will be noted that, as hostilities approach their climax in the fall of 1943, the political ramifications take on a more urgent role. Churchill may have been completely wrong in his understanding of the Wehrmacht, and a menace to Allied unity in his Mediterranean mania — one that drove even his own chiefs of staff to the brink of resignation. But Churchill's understanding of the deepening rift and rivalry with the Soviets bespoke his greatness as a leader. Many thousands of miles removed from the continent of Europe, President Roosevelt needed the Prime Minister by his side not as military adviser — given that Churchill's judgment and obstinacy were more millstone than help, as Churchill's doctor himself recognized — but as the President's political partner in leading the Western democracies.

As the final pages of this volume demonstrate, Winston Churchill was thus invited to spend long weeks with the President in Washington and at Hyde Park, in a deeply symbolic act of unity — as much in confronting Stalin as Hitler.

The degree to which President Roosevelt began to rely on Churchill's loyal political support and his political acumen in the summer and fall of 1943 — before the Tehran and Yalta Conferences — are thus a testament to the importance of their relationship in world history. Churchill had rattled the unity of the Allies that year to the very brink of collapse by pressing for a military strategy that would arguably have lost the war for the Allies had not President Roosevelt overruled him. In political terms, however, it was to be his steadfast, statesmanlike partnership with the President of the United States that would ensure the democracies, under their combined leadership, had at least a chance of ending World War II with western Europe under safe guardianship in relation to Soviet "Bolshevization."

To better understand FDR's direction of the military is thus to me important not only in terms of a greater appreciation of President Roosevelt's actions, but in understanding the foundations of the world we live in today. From boasting only the world's seventeenth-most-powerful military in 1939, the United States gradually took upon itself the successful leadership of the democratic world under Roosevelt's command — and became the most powerful nation on earth, bar none. How exactly President Roosevelt directed this transformation and the operations of his armed forces across the globe — with what aims, with what challenges, with what lessons — is to me of abiding interest in the world we've inherited. For good or ill, America's military power under a freely elected president remains in large part the basis of the continuing role of the United States in attempting to provide leadership and world security, however imperfect.

This, then, is the record of FDR as U.S. commander in chief in the crucial year 1943 — a year in which the United States went on the offensive both in the West and in the East — as seen from the President's point of view. Upon his leadership depended the outcome of the world war: success or failure.

PART ONE

A Secret Journey

1

A Crazy Idea

IT WAS LATE in the evening of Saturday, January 9, 1943, when a locomotive pulling the *Ferdinand Magellan* and four further carriages[1] departed from a special siding beneath the Bureau of Engraving in Washington, D.C. — the federal government's massive printing house for paper money, and thus a sort of Fort Knox of the capital.

Aboard was the President of the United States, his secretary, his White House chief of staff, his naval aide, his White House counselor, and his doctor, all traveling to Hyde Park for the weekend, as usual. Or so it seemed.

The Secret Service had insisted the President use for the first time the massive new railway carriage reconstructed for him — the first such railcar to be made for the nation's chief executive since Lincoln's presidency. Boasting fifteen-millimeter armored steel plate on the sides, roof, and underside, the carriage had three-inch-thick bulletproof glass in all its windows. Best of all, it had a special elevator to raise the President, in his wheelchair, onto the platform of the car — which weighed 142 tons, the heaviest passenger carriage ever used on U.S. rail track.

The car was "arranged with a sitting room, a dining room for ten or twelve persons, a small but well arranged kitchen, and five state rooms," Admiral William Leahy, the President's military chief of staff, recorded in his diary. "Dr. McIntire, Harry Hopkins, Miss Tully, and I occupied the state rooms, and Captain McCrea joined us in the dining room. Other cars accommodated the Secret Service men, the apothecary, the communications personnel, and the President's valet," Chief Petty Officer Arthur Prettyman.[2]

Their luggage had been taken to the baggage car separately, an hour earlier. But was the President really going to Hyde Park? If so, why the thousand pounds of bottled water? Why clothes for two weeks away? Why the four Filipino members of the crew of the USS *Potomac*, the presidential yacht, replacing the normal Pullman staff? Why Eleanor, the First Lady, and Louise Macy, the new wife of Harry Hopkins, bidding them goodbye at the underground siding?

Something was up — something unique. Even historic.

Among the few who did know of the President's real destination, most had counseled against it. Even the President's naval aide, Captain John McCrea, opposed the idea when the President tricked McCrea into supplying information on the geography, history, and significant towns of the region of North Africa. Following the successful Torch landings in Algeria and Morocco on November 8, 1942, the President had explained to McCrea — whose knowledge of the sea exceeded his knowledge of land — U.S. troops would be fighting in battle, and he'd found himself, as U.S. commander in chief, sadly ignorant of the terrain. "See if you can help me correct that deficiency," he'd instructed McCrea, "by means of travel folders, etcetera, put out by travel agencies."

Travel agencies? As the President had quickly assured McCrea, "in the planning and preparatory stages" of Operation Torch, he hadn't wanted to draw attention to "that area." "But now that the troops are there," he'd added, "that restraint is removed."

Innocent of any ulterior motive, McCrea had assembled a raft of informative material. "The President was pleased with it and confided: 'Just the sort of information I want.'"

Some weeks later, though, "late one afternoon, early in December the President sent for me, sat me down at the corner of his desk and this is about the way it went.

"The Pres: 'John, I want to talk to you in great confidence and the matter about which I am talking is to be known to no one except those who need to know.' Since this was the first time the Pres. had ever spoken to me thus, naturally I was greatly curious," McCrea later narrated in his somewhat stilted literary style. The President had then confided, "'Since the landing of our troops in No[rth] Africa, I have been in touch with Winston by letter. I feel we should meet soon and resolve some things and that that meeting should take place in Africa. Winston has suggested Khartoum — I'm not keen on that suggestion. Marrakech and Rabat have been suggested. I'm inclined to rule out those areas, and settle for Casablanca.' And then to my amazement the President said: 'What do you think of the whole idea?'"

McCrea had been stunned.

"As quickly as I could," McCrea recalled, "I gathered my wits and proceeded about as follows. 'Right off the top of my head Mr. Pres. I do not think well of the idea. I think there is too much risk involved for you.'"

The President had been unmoved. "Our men in that area are taking risks, why shouldn't their Commander in Chief share that risk?"

McCrea was a seasoned sailor — an aspect he thought might be a more effective counter. "'The Atlantic can be greatly boisterous in the winter months,'" he had pointed out, "'and a most uncomfortable passage is a good possibility —'

"'Oh — we wouldn't go by ship. We would fly,' said he."

Fly?

McCrea was shocked. No U.S. president had flown while in office — ever. "This was a great surprise to me because I knew he did not regard flying with any degree of enthusiasm," McCrea recounted. Mr. Roosevelt had not flown in a decade, in fact, since traveling to Chicago from New York before the 1932 election. In terms of the President's safety, waging a world war, it seemed a grave and unnecessary risk — especially in terms of distance, and flight into an active war zone. But the President was the president.

McCrea had therefore softened his objection. "I quickly saw that I was being stymied and I tried to withdraw a bit.

"'Mr. Pres.,' said I, 'you have taken me quite by surprise with this proposal. I would like to give it further thought. Right off the top of my head I wouldn't recommend it.'"

When, the next morning, Captain McCrea went upstairs to the President's Oval Study, carrying with him some of the latest reports, secret signals, decoded enemy signals, and top-secret cables from the Map Room — of which he was the director — he'd recognized the futility of opposing the idea. It was a colossal risk, he still thought, but he knew the President well enough to know that, if Mr. Roosevelt had raised the matter, it was because his mind was probably already made up, and he was simply looking for the sort of reaction he would be likely to meet from others.

"He laughed lightly," McCrea recalled — informing him that Prime

Minister Churchill had already responded positively to the suggestion, in fact was gung ho for such a meeting — "'Winston is all for it.'"

McCrea had remained concerned, though. Security would present a problem not only during the broad Atlantic crossing, he warned, but in North Africa itself. "I still think the risk is great and if you are determined to go I will do all possible to manage that risk," he'd assured the President. But the risks were real. "From what I have read in the despatches and the press," he'd said, for example, "affairs in No[rth] Africa are in a state of much confusion." Casablanca itself was a notorious gathering place for spies and expatriates. And worse. "I would suppose that No[rth] Africa is full of people who would take you on for $10 — "

Assassination?

"Why I said that I'll never know," McCrea later reflected. It was almost rude, " — but I did and at the moment, of course, I felt it. He laughed heartily."

McCrea was not being timorous. Several weeks later his concern was validated — Admiral François Darlan, the new French high commissioner under the Allied commander in chief in the Mediterranean, General Eisenhower, was murdered in broad daylight in Algiers.

By then, however, the trip had been prepared in great detail, and the President would hear no more attempts to dissuade him.

Maintaining secrecy for the trip had not been easy, however. There was, for instance, the problem of idle gossip. The British had been making their own travel arrangements for Prime Minister Churchill. By secret cable from his "bunker" beneath Westminster, in London, Mr. Churchill's office had duly informed the British ambassador in Washington, D.C., Viscount Halifax. Halifax had told his wife.

It had been McCrea who had then taken the telephone call from a distraught, elderly Colonel Edmund Starling, who — going back to the days of President Wilson — was chief of the Secret Service detail responsible for the President's safety at the White House. "The Colonel said it was urgent he see me at once," McCrea recalled. "He came to the Map Room and we went out into the corridor, out of earshot of the Map Room personnel. This is about the way it [went]:

"Col — Is anything going on here about the movements of the President of which I should be apprised?"

McCrea had been noncommittal. "I don't understand what you are driving at, Colonel. Could you be more specific?" he'd responded.

"Col — Well, it is this. A taxi cab driver here in Washington called the W.[hite] H.[ouse] today and told the telephone operator that he wanted to talk to someone in authority who had to do with the movements of the President." On being put through to Colonel Starling, he was asked to come straight to the White House. He'd left "just a few minutes ago. His story was that he had answered a call to the British Embassy this forenoon and there he had picked up a couple of ladies and had driven them in town to a Woodward & Lothrop Dept. store. On the way in they had talked at some length and that one lady had said to the other that the President was going soon to North Africa where he would meet with Mr. Churchill. He, the driver, had no way of knowing whether or not it was so, but nevertheless if it was, he thought it was something that shouldn't be talked about."

This was a serious understatement.

Oh, the British. Often so pompous about rank and privilege — and so casual with regard to high-level gossip shared in the presence of the "servant class."

It hadn't boded well, but there was little McCrea had been able to do; an important summit of wartime leaders could hardly be canceled or reconvened because of an ambassador's wife's shopping trip.

The President was more amused by the incident than concerned. What he worried about was his longtime White House military aide, Major General Edwin "Pa" Watson. The general wouldn't be going, the President had told McCrea. "Pa has suffered a heart attack last spring," the President had explained, "and while he is now back on active duty Ron [McIntire, the President's doctor] thinks he is in no condition to stand the stress and strain of a long air trip across the Atlantic and on to Casablanca. I dread telling Pa that I have decided he should not go with us."

McCrea could only marvel at a president more concerned not to upset his loyal military aide than for his own safety. The President had reason to be concerned, however. "I intentionally put off telling Pa as long as possible and when he brought the appointment list to me this morning," Roosevelt told McCrea on January 7, 1943, "I broke the news to him and told him that on Ron's advice because of the considerable flying involved and his recent heart attack that I was not taking him on this trip. Pa was shocked—slumped in his chair and broke into tears—and remarked perhaps his usefulness around the W.H. was about at an end. I comforted him as best I could but to little avail. After a bit he recovered his composure and withdrew. Now John, I told you last evening I would enter the House Chamber [of Congress, for the upcoming State of the Union address] this noon on your arm. If I do that I think it would be a further shock to Pa. Will you please run Pa down at once and tell him that I neglected to tell him this a.m. that as usual I would enter the House Chamber this noon on his arm. That might soften the blow a bit of his not going to No. Africa with us."[3]

Once again Captain McCrea had been amazed at the President's concern for the feelings of others, while directing the administration of his country in a global war. Also the President's innocence, too: for it would be the President's naval aide who would suffer the full force of General Watson's disappointment at being excluded from the North Africa trip, however much the President wished to sugar the pill.

It had not taken long. In General Watson's room next to the Oval Office, where Pa Watson acted as the President's appointments secretary, guarding all access to the Chief Executive, McCrea had endured a tirade from the general. If he himself was forbidden to travel, Watson said, why should the President—who'd had his own heart problems—go? Watson "thought the Pres. was badly advised about making the trip—the risk was too great for him to take. Why hadn't I informed him about the trip? 'I've always taken you in my confidence,' said he, 'and in this important instance you have not taken me into your confidence.'

"I calmed Pa down as best I could," McCrea related. "I told him of the charge given me by the President that no one, absolutely no one, should know about this trip except those who needed to know—and he [the President] laid great emphasis on that point. That he would tell you himself in due course that you could not make the trip and that he would tell me when he had done so."

This did little to solace the Army general—who was, after all, still the President's military aide. The Navy had trumped him. "There was just no comforting Pa," McCrea recalled. "He was deeply disturbed and repeated over and over again that the Pres. was badly advised in the decision to make this hazardous trip. 'I hope you didn't encourage him in that,'" he'd demanded accusingly. "I told Pa that I had done everything I possibly could to dissuade the President — but to no avail. That insofar as I knew the deal had been made with Mr. Churchill and that was it. And then Pa exclaimed with much emphasis: 'There is only one so and so around here who is crazy enough to promote such a thing, and his name is Hopkins'" — the President's White House counselor.[4]

2

Aboard the Magic Carpet

GENERAL WATSON WAS wrong about Harry Hopkins. Recently married, Hopkins had no great wish to go to Casablanca. His wife said goodbye to him "at the rear door" of the *Ferdinand Magellan,* Hopkins jotted in his diary that night. Eleanor had shown no emotion, but Louise had been a bag of nerves—as was Hopkins, who worried about the weeks he'd be away from Washington. A survivor of stomach cancer and major intestinal surgery before the war began, Hopkins required constant medication. Above all, though, he had no wish to leave his new bride. Over Thanksgiving, at a cast party for S. N. Behrman's new play on Broadway, *The Pirate,* he'd been heard to say to a friend, as he introduced his young consort: "Look, Dyke,—I ought to be dead—and here I am married!"[1]

A charming and pretty gadabout, Louise was a socialite who, to her discomfort, had swiftly found herself accused of impropriety after the wedding, thanks to people envious of Hopkins's proximity to the President—people such as the financier Bernard Baruch, who'd failed to obtain a job in the Roosevelt war administration. "I must say that I didn't like the idea of leaving a little bit," Hopkins confided to his diary before going to sleep, for "Louise had been very unhappy all evening because of the political attacks on us."[2]

For his part, Admiral Bill Leahy—the President's chief of staff at the White House, but also now the chairman of the Combined Chiefs of Staff—was equally reluctant to go. The sailor had suffered a bad bout of flu in recent days, and did not relish the long journey by train and then air. Nor did he savor what was awaiting him at the secret destination:

a continuing international political imbroglio that in his view had been pretty much screwed up by people who didn't understand the military difficulties of the situation.

There were others, too, who were anxious. Daisy Suckley, the President's cousin and longtime confidante, had already said her goodbye the day before, and wasn't therefore at the Bureau of Engraving platform. She'd argued strenuously against such "a long trip," she noted in her own diary, one "with definite risks" that included enemy interception, accidents, even assassination. "But one *can't* and *mustn't* think of that."[3] On the plus side there were, she acknowledged, exotic places the President would get to see. And people, too. "W. Churchill first and foremost, of course," she'd added. Others, however, he would not. He'd asked to meet Stalin, "but Stalin answered that he could not possibly leave Russia now — One can understand that," she allowed, given the great winter battle still being fought to the death at Stalingrad.[4]

Fala, the President's beloved Scottish terrier, was not going, either, Daisy noted. The President had asked his wife if she would look after him. Like Stalin, the First Lady had said she was too busy. The President had therefore asked Daisy, who'd originally given him the terrier, as a gift, and she'd agreed to do so.

"I wished him all the best luck on this secret trip," Daisy recorded the next night, after saying goodbye — more devoted to him than ever. "He is leaving as if to go north to Hyde Park," which was near her own baronial home, Wilderstein. "At a certain siding," though, "the train will be picked up by the regular engine & start south for Miami — He goes with all one's prayers."[5]

At Baltimore the locomotive was, indeed, decoupled. Instead of continuing north, a new locomotive bore it south, toward its destination a thousand miles away: through Virginia, North Carolina, South Carolina, Georgia, and Florida, to the former Pan American Clipper terminus.

For his own part, President Roosevelt was glad to get away. Despite the winter cold, the capital was a cauldron of rumor, gossip, political rivalry, and competitive ambitions. Looked after by his valet, Petty Officer Prettyman, and his Filipino crew from the presidential yacht, the USS *Potomac*, he ate and slept well. Rising late on Sunday, January 10, 1943, he lifted the shades of his compartment. The passengers had been instructed that, in order to maintain absolute secrecy, they were to "keep the shades down all day," as he wrote Daisy that night — confiding that he "found myself waving to an engineer & fear he recognized me."[6]

Minor mishaps always amused FDR.

All day, as the heavy, shaded train bore on, the President went through his White House papers, dictating final letters and memoranda to Grace Tully, his secretary, who would be leaving the train in Florida before they reached Miami. He then said goodnight and retired early, knowing they would all have to rise before first light the following morning.

Woken early on January 11, Hopkins donned a robe and made his way to the President's stateroom, where he "found the President alone." Together they "laughed over the fact that this unbelievable trip was about to begin. I shall always feel that the reason the President wanted to meet Churchill," Hopkins surmised, "was because he wanted to make a trip."[7]

Roosevelt had become "tired of having other people, particularly myself, speak for him around the world. For political reasons he could not go to England," Hopkins noted — despite Eleanor having found her husband a nice potential apartment in London, complete with elevator, where he could stay if he chose to meet Churchill there. But the President had balked at the political ramifications. The new, potentially more hostile, isolationist Congress, elected the previous November, would have a field day, he feared. Certain members of Congress and rich, right-wing newspaper owners would accuse the President either of kowtowing to the British or colluding with foreign allies without first telling members of his visit, let alone getting their consent.

London, then, had been out — and the North African battlefield in. Roosevelt would travel as U.S. commander in chief, not as president — thus permitting him to insist upon absolute secrecy, with no press correspondents following him. He "wanted to go to see our troops," Hopkins noted, and "he was sick of people telling him that it was dangerous to ride in airplanes. He liked the drama of it. But above all, he wanted to make a trip."[8]

Whether Hopkins was right was debatable, but the sheer drama of the President's secret getaway from Washington was — like his "escape" from the press to Newfoundland for the Atlantic Charter meeting in 1941 — undeniable.

Grace Tully duly disembarked to stay with relatives. Then, at Miami, the party detrained and was driven by car to the former Pan American

Airways terminal by the harbor. Two huge flying boats were waiting, bobbing on the water.

"My God! Why, that's the Pres[ident]. Why didn't they let me know he was to be one of my passengers?" the captain of the first boat, the *Dixie Clipper*, exclaimed. "It's somewhat of a shock to know you are flying the Pres. of the U.S."[9]

With its giant 152-feet cantilevered wingspan, four fifteen-hundred-horsepower Wright Twin Cyclone engines, plus sponsons attached to both sides of its hull to provide extra lift and ease of embarkation, the Clipper — leased by the U.S. Navy, and its crew given Navy rank — duly took off from the predawn waters of the harbor and made first for Trinidad, in the Caribbean, fourteen hundred miles away. "The sun came up at about 7:30," Roosevelt wrote to Daisy, "& I have never seen a more lovely sunrise — just your kind. We were up about a mile — above a level of small pure white clouds so we couldn't even see the Bahamas on our left — but soon we saw Cuba on the right & then Haiti."[10]

The President had known she'd continue to worry on his account, and wanted to reassure her — not only the first president to fly abroad while in office, but the first since Lincoln to visit a battlefield in war. Taking a celestial fix of sun and moon, the captain turned the forty-four-ton behemoth, like a flying carpet, southeastward. "Then out over the Caribbean — high up — I felt the altitude at 8 or 9,000 feet — and so did Harry and Ad. Leahy — The cumulus white clouds were amazingly beautiful but every once in a while we could not go over them & had to go through one —

"At last — 5 p.m. — we saw the N.E. Coast of Venezuela & then the islands of the Dragon's Mouth with Trinidad on the left — The skipper made a beautiful soft landing & Ad. Oldendorf came out & took us ashore to the U.S. Naval Base — one of 'my' eight which we got for the 50 destroyers in 1940. It is not yet finished but operating smoothly."[11]

The U.S. naval base at Trinidad had come with a hotel, situated at Macqueripe on the north coast, "& thither we went for the night," the President related. However, there had then occurred a serious hiccup, unrelated to the dinner he was served. "Ad. Leahy felt quite ill — he had flu ten days ago — Ross McI[ntire] is worried as he is 68 & his temp. is over 100 — we will decide in the a.m."[12]

In the morning, on January 12, the doctor found Admiral Leahy still feverish. "Up at 4 a.m. This is not civilized," the President joked in his letter to Daisy. However, "Leahy seemed no better & we had to leave him behind — He hated to stay but was a good soldier & will go to the Naval Hospital & get good care — I hope he won't get pneumonia — I shall miss him as he is such an old friend & a wise counselor."[13]

If the President was concerned, though, he did not show it, for he never mentioned Leahy again in his letters to Daisy, despite the fact that Leahy was to have chaired daily meetings not only of the U.S. chiefs of staff but the British chiefs of staff, in their role as the Combined Chiefs of Staff, in Casablanca. The President was on top form: confident he could manage the summit quite successfully on his own, even without Leahy's wisdom.

Thus the *Dixie Clipper* flew on a further thousand miles to Brazil, filled its tanks with fuel at Belém, and set off for its great "hop" across the Atlantic, carrying its august passenger and small, slightly diminished entourage — followed closely by the backup Clipper, lest the *Dixie Clipper* experience engine trouble and have need to ditch.

Reflecting their earlier days as transoceanic first-class passenger planes, each Clipper boasted a lounge, a fourteen-seat dining room, changing rooms, and beds normally for thirty-six passengers — with a honeymoon suite at the rear. They required considerable piloting skills, however — takeoffs and landings in choppy, windswept water always an especial concern. The *Dixie Clipper*'s sister plane, *Yankee Clipper,* for example, would snag its wing several weeks later in Lisbon Harbor, with the loss of twenty-four lives.

Meantime, landing smoothly at the old British trading post of Bathurst (later renamed Banjul) on the Gambia River on January 13, after a twenty-eight-hour flight, the *Dixie Clipper* moored offshore. Arrangements had been made for the President to transfer to the light cruiser USS *Memphis,* ordered up from Natal by FDR's chief of naval operations, Admiral King — there to provide the President with a secure overnight stay where he would not be exposed to tsetse fly. As it was still light, however, he took the opportunity to tour the waterfront — the President seated in a whaleboat as the local British naval commander acted as his guide during a forty-minute cruise amid dozens of tenders and oil tankers. Loading and unloading beneath the evening sun, their crews seemed oblivious to the fact that the upright figure seated in the midst of the whaleboat party, in his civilian clothes and hat, together with Hopkins, McIntire, and McCrea, was the President of the United States.

Finally, hoisted aboard the USS *Memphis,* the President was given the flagship admiral's stateroom, "where I've had a good supper & am about to go to bed," he described, delighted to be in African waters.[14]

Given Roosevelt's childhood dream of going to naval college instead of Harvard (a hope dashed by his mother),[15] his long love of naval history, and his nearly eight years as assistant secretary of the Navy, being piped aboard an American warship as commander in chief for the first time in World War II was inspiring for the President. Yet the sentiment paled beside thoughts of what was to come. The next morning would see him embark for a further "1,200 mile hop in an Army plane," this time overland, as he wrote to Daisy — bound for "that well known spot 'Somewhere in North Africa.' *I* don't know just where," he added, in self-censoring mode. "But don't worry — All is well & I'm getting a wonderful rest." He felt positively refreshed. "It's funny about geography — Washington seems the other side of the world but not Another Place — That is way off," he wrote of Hyde Park, "& also very close to — "[16]

There Roosevelt left the sentence, however — unwilling to give hostage to fortune, lest prying eyes open, or see, his letter to the distant cousin whose romantic adoration he'd encouraged, especially after his mother's death two years earlier. "Lots of love — Bless you," he ended.[17]

To his wife, Eleanor, he meanwhile wrote in a similarly informative, if less tender, vein — telling her he'd be seeing their son Elliott when he arrived, and signing off: "Ever so much love and don't do too much — and I'll see you soon. Devotedly, F."[18]

He was almost there: not only the journey of a lifetime, but bringing the agenda of a lifetime. At Casablanca the President wished not only to map the defeat of the Axis powers in World War II, but commence discussions of the world to follow.

PART TWO

Total War

3

The United Nations

EVEN BEFORE THE war began for the United States, the President had been thinking of the postwar world.

Enlisting the help of his protégé, Assistant Secretary of State Sumner Welles, the President had begun drafting ideas immediately after drawing up the Atlantic Charter, in August 1941. What he wanted to create, he'd told Welles, was a postwar organization that the Americans, British, and Russians would embrace as military guardians, and that all sovereign democratic nations could subscribe to. The Japanese attack on Pearl Harbor several months later had made the need for a viable postwar system all the more urgent: a new world order that would make such wars of imperial conquest difficult if not impossible. He'd therefore charged Welles with modeling the project on the twenty-six countries whose representatives he'd assembled over Christmas 1941 in Washington — a group the President had decided, in a moment of inspiration, to announce to the world as "the United Nations."[1]

Properly constituted, the United Nations authority would, the President determined, avoid the disaster of the League of Nations — which neither the United States nor the Soviet Union had joined when it was formed. Building on the "Declaration of the United Nations," which had been signed in Washington on January 1, 1942, the United Nations would, this time, have teeth: the world's "Four Policemen," as the President called them.[2]

First, the Germans and Japanese would have to be defeated — but the military might of the three foremost antifascist fighting nations could then be turned into a global peacekeeping coalition: the United States, the Soviet Union, and Britain. He had then added China, a nation that had been fighting the Japanese since 1937 — thereby forcing the Japanese to keep an army of more than a million men on the Chinese mainland. Once the war was won, the President proposed, this same group of the world's major military powers could be employed not only to disarm the Axis nations for all time, but to police the world thereafter on behalf of the United Nations authority, ensuring that no Hitler or Mussolini or Hirohito would ever again upset global security by force of arms or conquest.

With laudable dedication, Welles — running the U.S. State Department under the sickly secretary of state, Cordell Hull — had thereupon set about the business, leaving the President to focus, meantime, on the best military strategy to defeat the Axis powers.

Under the aegis of the State Department, Welles had quietly set up a host of secret committees and subcommittees, asking members to think ahead on the President's behalf and produce for Mr. Roosevelt at the White House their specific recommendations and alternatives, on a regular basis.[3] "What I expect you to do," Roosevelt had instructed Welles, "is to have prepared for me the necessary number of baskets so that when the time comes all I have to do is to reach into a basket and fish out a number of solutions that I am sure are sound and from which I can make my own choice."[4]

Welles had done as ordered — magnificently, in retrospect. As historians would later note, neither Britain nor the Soviet Union, the other two primary nations conducting the war against Hitler, did anything in 1942 to address the needs or opportunities of the postwar world on an international scale — a "disastrous blockage at the top" in the case of the British.[5] By contrast, bringing together an extraordinary cross section of the nation's foremost minds and political figures in once-weekly meetings in Washington, Welles had single-handedly, in the midst of a global war being fought from Archangel to Australia, gotten his various teams working on the political, military, economic, labor, and even social (health, drug trafficking, refugees, nutrition, etc.) blueprints the President wanted for his vision of the democratic postwar world.

An extraordinary bipartisan group of Democratic and Republican senators and congressmen from the Capitol — including the chairman of the House Foreign Affairs Committee, the ranking minority member of the House Foreign Affairs Committee, a former chairman of the Senate Foreign Relations Committee, the current chairman of the Senate Foreign Relations Committee, and a senior current Republican member of the Senate Foreign Relations Committee — had joined with Welles's hand-picked, representative minds from the State Department, the Agriculture Department, and the Board of Economic Warfare, as well as members outside government, including individuals from the press, the Council on Foreign Relations, and the academy, to provide the President with the necessary guideposts and alternatives he wanted at hand.

Though at first Welles had assumed the issues would be handled by the President in a peace conference after the conclusion of the war, as had been the case in the aftermath of World War I, the President had soon changed his mind — reckoning that if the postwar system could be settled before the war's end, it could avoid the unfortunate fate of the Versailles conference of 1919. Instead, the President had asked the committees to report their interim findings, via Welles, as swiftly as possible: concerned that America's allies, too, should help him address the challenge *before,* rather than after, the end of hostilities. By October 1942, therefore, as American troops readied for the Torch invasion of Northwest Africa — a draft outline of the postwar UN organization had begun to take shape.

Welles's teams, the President found, had done a grand job — indeed, Welles suggested that the putative "United Nations authoritative body" could already start functioning during the war itself. It would comprise a General Assembly of United Nations, seating representatives of all eligible countries of the world. It would also have a small Executive Council, incorporating the four major powers to arm and lead the organization with strength and simplicity. By April 1942, in fact, after discussing the matter with Mr. Roosevelt, Welles (who had made himself chairman of the Subcommittee on Political Problems, an international organization) had suggested the way the Executive Council should be set up: the President's Four Policemen — the United States, Britain, the Soviet Union, and China — being given permanent seats on an Executive Council together with a small number of further, rotating seats reserved for members elected by the full United Nations authority, in order to give the council more balance and connection with the main Assembly.[6]

As Welles's committees had advanced their confidential proposals in Washington, British Foreign Office officials in London had become anxious lest Churchill's lack of interest in postwar planning leave Great Britain out on a limb. "His Majesty's Government have not yet defined their views on questions or made any response to Mr. Welles's expression of opinion," the head of the British Economic and Reconstruction Department had complained as late as September 3, 1942, only weeks before Torch.[7]

Little was done to rectify this failure, however, in view of the Prime Minister's full-time preoccupation with Britain's military operations, and his aversion to postwar planning—which would inevitably involve the continuing transformation of the British Empire into a Commonwealth of Nations rather than a colonial enterprise directed by Parliament in London.[8] "I hope these speculative studies will be entrusted mainly to those on whose hands time hangs heavy," Churchill had mocked his foreign minister's attempt to produce a British version of Welles's work, "and that we shall not overlook Mrs. Glass's Cookery Book recipe for Jugged Hare—'First catch your hare.'"[9]

In Moscow, too, there had been a complete lack of interest in planning for a democratic future—Stalin's Soviet government simply refusing to comment on or respond to cables from its Russian ambassador in Washington, imploring the USSR to get involved in international postwar proposals.

For FDR, the failure of Joseph Stalin to participate in discussions about the postwar world was galling if perhaps inevitable, given the history of the Soviet Union since the Russian Revolution: its protracted civil war, Stalin's Great Terror and purge trials, and its ever-darkening development as a communist police state based on intimidation, arrest, torture, imprisonment, deportation, and execution. Nevertheless, as president of the world's biggest and most advanced economy, Roosevelt wanted to give the Russians—who were bearing in blood the brunt of Hitler's war of conquest—at least the chance to be a party to his proposals. And if Stalin, the absolute dictator of the Soviet Union, would not sit down to discuss them, then the President would begin the discussions without him—in Casablanca.

Hitler had declared that democracy was a relic of the past. The President, working with Winston Churchill, would now show him he was wrong: that democracy was, in fact, on the move.

Casablanca, then, was to be much more than a military powwow. Weeks before he left the White House on his secret journey, the President had begun to rehearse his developing vision with other world leaders such as Jan Christiaan Smuts, the prime minister of South Africa, whom he'd known since the summer of 1918.

Then, too, the end of the world war had seemed at hand. Twenty-four years later, Roosevelt was "drawing up plans now for the victorious peace

which will surely come" and hoped to discuss them with the former guerilla leader of the anti-British Boers, if Smuts could see his way to come to
Washington. A more durable and effective outcome was necessary than
the ill-fated Versailles Treaty. "As you know," the President explained, "I
dream dreams but am, at the same time, an intensely practical person,
and I am convinced that disarmament of the aggressor nations is an essential first step, followed up for a good many years to come by a day and
night inspection of that disarmament and a police power to stop at its
source any attempted evasion of the rules."[10]

This time, then, postwar peace would not be guaranteed by treaties
that could be broken with impunity, but by irresistible force — on behalf
of the community of nations. There were "many other things to be worked
out," Roosevelt had added in his letter to Smuts, such as decolonization,
effected over time, but with no backsliding by the old European powers,
as after World War I — whether by the British, the Dutch, the French,
the Belgians, the Spanish, or the Portuguese. "Perhaps Winston has told
you of my thought of certain trusteeships to be exercised by the United
Nations where stability of government for one reason or another cannot
at once be assured. I am inclined to think that the [colonial] mandate system" — instituted in the wake of the Versailles Treaty and the League of
Nations — "is no longer the right approach, for the nation which is given
the mandate soon comes to believe that it carries sovereignty with it."[11]

Colonialism, in other words, was to be gradually but responsibly
phased out in the aftermath of World War II, and a new postcolonial
world ushered in.

As prime minister of a former British colony now enjoying self-
government and Dominion status within the British Commonwealth,
Smuts's reaction was important as Roosevelt sought to picture a viable
postwar world and the problems he might encounter in getting international agreement.

Smuts — whose Boer countrymen had, like the Americans, risen up
against British colonial rule — understood the President's strong feelings
on that score, but was facing a new election and could not travel. The
prime minister of Canada, Mackenzie King, could, however — and once
more the President had asked if King could come spend a few days with
him at the White House, after the Torch invasion, so that he could rehearse his notions of what would, effectively, be the endgame.

Arriving from Ottawa by train, King had thus made his way to 1600

Pennsylvania Avenue on the morning of December 4, 1942, three weeks after Torch. Alert to the dangers of premature leaks, rumor, and outright hostility among Republican politicians and newspaper owners who still hated him for his New Deal program, the President was chary of committing thoughts to paper lest they be used against him. Thankfully, the Canadian prime minister dictated each night a careful record of his day — and it is to this diary we owe our most authentic account of the President's military and political strategy for ending the war, and the peace he hoped to mold thereafter, before leaving for Africa.

The President, King had found on arrival, was "sitting up in his bed" on the second floor of the White House mansion, "wearing a gray sweater," smoking. He'd been "reading newspapers. Gave me a very hearty welcome. Began at once by saying he was having a [hard] time with the new Congress," given the loss of so many Democratic seats in the November midterm elections, "but hoped that would go by."[12]

Senator Robert Taft of Ohio, the leading isolationist opponent of the New Deal in Congress and eldest son of Republican president William Howard Taft, was a particular sore, the President had remarked — quoting to King an account in that day's paper. Taft was reported to be opposing the President's attempt to make a new deal with the Panamanian government over the Panama Canal area.

The President had smiled mischievously. "Asked me," King recorded, "if I knew the U.S. owned the largest red-light district anywhere."[13]

Mackenzie King — a staunch, Bible-obsessed Presbyterian who had forsworn alcohol for the duration of the war — was well aware how much Roosevelt enjoyed teasing him. When King confessed his ignorance, the President had "described how one of his ancestors," William H. Aspinwall, had given up hope of building a transcontinental railway across "the isthmus of Panama, having mortgaged [his] homes in the States." Then suddenly he'd heard gold had been "discovered in California. He knew at once that his railway would be a success and half a dozen offers were immediately made by wealthy men to complete his road. Later, when De Lesseps came to develop the canal, the red-light district developed in that area. The U.S. are now wishing to get control of certain parts and had to purchase this area . . ."[14]

It was typical of Roosevelt to use the irony of a vexing situation to render it less frustrating — U.S. senators "querulous about different things" such as this while the President struggled to win a global war and create the basis for subsequent peace.

Beneath African palms, in complete privacy and in secret, the President would soon, he told Mackenzie King, be able to discuss his vision for the world that would follow war: especially his idea of a United Nations Security Council led by the four powers.

First, however, the war had to be won by the United Nations. Roosevelt had already explained his current strategy to the supreme commander of the Soviet Armies, Joseph Stalin, in a cable he'd dispatched from the White House on November 19, 1942. "American and British Staffs are now studying further moves in the event that we secure the whole south shore of the Mediterranean from Gibraltar to Syria," the President had informed Stalin. "Before any further step is taken, both Churchill and I want to consult with you and your Staff because whatever we do next in the Mediterranean will have a definite bearing on your magnificent campaign and your proposed moves this coming Winter." U.S. and British armies were not only forcing Hitler to keep substantial numbers of troops, artillery, tanks, and planes in Norway, the Netherlands, Belgium, and northern France to defend against the threat of Allied invasion in the West, but were forcing Hitler to do so in the Mediterranean now, in order to keep Italy fighting as a primary Axis partner; this would make it difficult, if not impossible, for Hitler to achieve unilateral military victory against the Russians.[15]

Stalin had not immediately responded to the request, however, as the President confided to King — the Russian dictator's focus having been on the Russian counteroffensive that began that day at Stalingrad. A week later, on November 25, Roosevelt cabled again. The President had congratulated Stalin on the Russian breakthrough west of Stalingrad, which threatened to cut off the German salient stretching as far east as the Volga. In order to remind his Russian counterpart that the United States was fighting a *global,* not simply regional, war, however, he'd informed Stalin of a similar U.S. game changer in the Pacific, where the U.S. Navy had decimated the Japanese fleet attempting to reinforce the Japanese army on Guadalcanal. The Japanese had been compelled to evacuate the island, and U.S. forces were now "sinking far more Jap ships and destroying more planes than they can build."[16]

This time Stalin *had* responded. "As regards operations in the Mediterranean, which are developing so favorably, and may influence the whole military situation in Europe, I share your view that appropriate consultations between the Staffs of the United States, Great Britain and the USSR have become desirable," the Russian premier wired back to the White House on November 27, 1942. But beyond this — and his congratulations on the U.S. Navy's success in the Pacific as well as American-British operations in North Africa — he declined to be specific. In particular he had ignored the idea of a meeting of national leaders, not even according it a mention.[17]

Finally, on December 2, the President had decided to get to the point. In yet another cable sent from the Map Room at the White House, he'd urged Stalin to address "the necessity for reaching early strategic decisions" through "an early meeting." This was not simply because military staffs, conferring on their own, would be unable to reach decisions "without our approval," but because Roosevelt felt "we should come to some tentative understanding about the procedures which should be adopted in the event of a German collapse" — i.e., the postwar.

For this, it would be vital to meet in person, the President had emphasized. "My most compelling reason is that I am very anxious to have a talk with you," he'd written. "My suggestion would be that we meet secretly in some secure place in Africa that is convenient to all three of us. The time, about January fifteenth to twentieth [1943]. We would each of us bring a very small staff of our top Army, Air and Naval commanders." He thought a rendezvous in "southern Algeria or at or near Khartoum," in Egypt, would fit the bill.[18]

Mackenzie King had been awed and delighted by the President's initiative — touched that Roosevelt would share with him both the background and his confidential intentions: his game plan.

Still waiting for Stalin's response, the President had the next day discussed with King the problem of Churchill and Great Britain — to which Canada, as a Dominion of the British Empire, was constitutionally tethered. The President still deplored Churchill's stand over India and unwillingness to abide by the terms of the Atlantic Charter he'd signed up to; also Churchill's dislike of the Beveridge Plan for postwar social security in Britain. Churchill's obstinacy in pursuing the postwar revival of the "British Empire," rather than inspiring and leading a new, postcolonial "British Commonwealth of Nations," came under the President's caustic fire — as well as Churchill's aversion to the notion of postwar United Nations trusteeships. "When I asked him about Churchill's attitude, he said the reply which he [Churchill] had made in discussing these things was a rather sad one," King recorded that night. "It was to the effect that he [Churchill] would not have anything to do with any of these questions. That when the war was over he [Churchill] would be through with public life," and would turn to "writing."[19]

That evening, December 5, 1942, there had been cocktails at 7:30 p.m., mixed by the President himself. ("The President said: we will not ask Mackenzie to take any cocktails tonight. I appreciated," the wartime tee-totaler noted, "his anticipating my refusal.")[20] There was then dinner with Harry Hopkins and his wife, Louise. And several short documentary and newsreel films, in black and white and in color.

Looking at the documentary footage that had been spliced together — some of it "going back to the days of his governorship in the N.Y. state," as well as events like Roosevelt's "flight to Chicago at the time of the [1932] Convention" — "reviews of troops, etcetera" — King had found himself amazed. "It made me marvel how a man had ever stood what he did in dealing with crowds over so many years," the quiet Canadian had noted, given the President's physical disability and the demands of America's almost continuous electoral process, compared to the Canadian parliamentary system. "What was the most interesting was the way in which he, from the outset, had stood for the new deal and the rights of the common man in all his addresses," King dictated. "It was a real recreation and most pleasant," he'd added. "As it was getting on toward 10, I asked the President if he did not think he should retire and let him rest. He said no, we want to have a talk about another matter. He had said earlier in the day: 'I want to speak particularly about Stalin tonight.'"[21]

In the President's Oval Study (or "chart room," as King called it in the nightly diary he dictated), "the President sat on the sofa and told me to come and sit beside him there, to get his good ear, the right ear.

"He then ordered a horse's neck for each of us: ginger ale and the rind of an orange. Harry Hopkins came in and sat down for a few minutes and then retired. The President then started in at once on what he has in mind as a post-war programme. I looked up at the clock at that moment. The hands were exactly at 10 to 10."[22]

A fervent believer in spiritualism as well as Christianity, King was forever watching the hands of the clock for signs of significance. Given the magnitude of the President's global problems — war in the Pacific, war in China and Asia, war in the Soviet Union, war in the Mediterranean, war in the Atlantic, war in the Aleutians, preparations for eventual cross-Channel landings — it had seemed extraordinary to Mackenzie King that the President of the United States could set these concerns aside, in his mind, and share his thinking on the world that would come *after* the war was won.

Before addressing the matter of Stalin, the President had given his own views on the objectives or principles that should guide the victorious nations. "We talked of the 4 freedoms. Two of which," the President remarked, "we cannot do much about." Freedom of religion, Roosevelt had explained, was "something that the people have to work out for themselves. The State cannot impose anything. The freedom of speech: that too is something that will take care of itself" — though the President wished something could be done "to prevent exaggerated and untrue statements" from being broadcast or printed, especially the near-treasonable articles constantly being published by "sensational papers," such as Colonel McCormick's right-wing, isolationist *Chicago Tribune.*

This left "the other two" freedoms, which were perhaps more crucial, at least in planning a postwar universe: "freedom from fear and freedom from want."[23]

Of the two, the President told King, "the first is necessarily the most important, as the second depends on it. As respects freedom from fear," the President had continued, "that can only be brought about when we put an end to arming nations against each other." In the case of Germany and Japan, the arms treaties signed after World War I had proven useless. The German and Japanese capacity for making war must therefore be completely and irrevocably destroyed, once and for all time, he felt. This was something that could not be secured by negotiation, à la Versailles Treaty, but only achieved by a policy of "unconditional surrender" to the Allies, the President explained.

It was the first time King had heard President Roosevelt use the term, and he listened most carefully as the President explained.[24]

"My great hero in all of this today," Roosevelt remarked, "is General Grant. In bringing the civil war to an end, Grant demanded to Lee unconditional surrender. He would make no agreements, no negotiated peace."[25] Repeating the point, the President said: "I think there should be no negotiated peace" at all with the Germans and Japanese. "It should be an unconditional surrender. After Grant had gathered in all the guns, ammunition, etc., there were quantities of horses remaining. Grant turned to Lee and said to let the horses go back to the field. For the people to use them in the cultivation of the soil, get back to the art of peace. That I think at present is what we should do with Germany. Deprive her of all right to make planes, tanks, guns, etc., but not take away any of her territories nor prevent her development in any way."[26]

King had asked if the President was confident of dictating unconditional surrender to the forces of the Third Reich on that basis. "He replied: 'yes'" — with Japan to follow: "that he thought what should be done was to defeat Germany first; demand unconditional surrender and then for the 3 powers: Britain, U.S. and Russia to turn to Japan and say: now we demand the same of you. If you want to save human life, you must surrender unconditionally at once. If not, the 3 of us will bring all our forces to bear, and will fight till we destroy you. Russia would then be persuaded to attack Japan. It would not take a year to bring about her defeat. He was not sure the Japanese would accept any unconditional surrender, and would probably seek to fight on. However that plan of campaign would bring its results" — the world finally and definitively spared the possibility of a renascence of German or Japanese militarism — ever. "If the Japanese did not accept unconditional surrender," he added in a remark that would have immense significance later, "then they should be bombed till they were brought to their knees."

Thinking of the ever-burgeoning size of America's air forces as well as the terrifying new bomb — using vital Canadian minerals such as radium and uranium[27] — that he'd ordered to be developed, the President confided to King how the United States would have to push its forces to within bombing distance of Japan, while the war in Europe went on. "At present, Russia is too busy to attack Japan, and Japan is too busy to attack Russia."[28]

Unconditional surrender it was, then, as the President's war aim — not to placate or encourage the Russians, as some subsequently assumed, nor in punitive revenge against the Germans or the Japanese, as others did. And especially not to mollify liberals in America, who were complaining that the United States was installing former fascists, like Admiral Darlan, to administer liberated territories, instead of getting rid of them, as still others later speculated. Rather, the President saw unconditional surrender quite clearly at that moment as the basis for lasting postwar security — leading to a postwar peace to be overseen by the United Nations, using the four most powerful antifascist nations: the United States, Russia, and Britain, together with China (which the United States was supporting as the most populous and potentially important nation in the Pacific) — acting as the world's "international police" on the UN's behalf: the basis of the UN Security Council.

Each of the policing powers would have its "own air force" to enforce the disarmament of Germany and Japan, the President explained to King — able thereby to cauterize any attempt by such nations to step out of line and make war on others. Colonialist imperialism would, over time, become a thing of the past, with nations reverting to their original boundaries after Hitler's war. "Keep everything as it was" was how the President explained his vision — territorial changes agreed only by democratic plebiscite, not war. "Russia to develop Russia but to make an agreement not to take any territory. Not to try to change system of government of other countries by propaganda."[29]

Was all this a pipe dream?

"The President then said: 'to effect all this, of course, [we] would have to get Stalin to agree,'" King recorded, careful to note Roosevelt's actual words.

Stalin was a dictator — but a dictator more concerned with absolute rule over his own vast territory, stretching from Archangel to Vladivostok, than elsewhere: especially in a world revolution that he would find less easy to control. "He said that he believed he [Stalin] would. That he thought Molotov was an Imperialist but he believed Stalin was less and less on those lines."

However abhorrent Russian communism was, one had to be realistic. Since "it was clear that the U.S., Britain, China could not defeat Russia" by force of arms — something even Hitler was failing to do, with more than two hundred Wehrmacht divisions and his Luftwaffe — it would be futile to try. Better, he thought, to see if the Soviets could be drawn into an international system that guaranteed Russia would never be attacked by the Germans or another Hitler. Quoting a former Republican Senate leader, Jim Watson, the President said to King: "If you cannot beat him, join him. The thing to do was to get them all working on the same lines," under the aegis of a supranational United Nations.

Communist or not, the President had continued, Russia was going to be, after the war, "very powerful. The thing to do now was to get plans definitely made for disarmament" of Germany and Japan, with Russia onboard[30] — hence his attempt to set up a secret summit with Stalin and Churchill.

The Canadian prime minister, in his diary, had acknowledged being thrilled. It was clear that, in sharing his notion of unconditional surrender both of the Third Reich and the Empire of Japan, the President was speaking without vengeance or rancor, but almost as a surgeon might, prior to taking out a tumor.

Postoperatively, in the case of the Third Reich after the war's end, "there should be put into Germany immediately a committee or commission of inspectors," Roosevelt said to him, "say 3 — one to be chosen from Canada; one from South America, and one from China," on behalf of the United Nations. "They should have their staffs, and their business would be to inspect day after day, year in and year out, all the factories of Germany to see that no war material should be manufactured. If any such were discovered, the Germans were to be told that unless that stopped within a week's time, that certain of their cities would be bombed. The cities would be named: Frankfurt, Cologne, and probably the cities where the manufacturing is taking place. If they went ahead, despite this threat, they might then be told that from now on, all imports and exports in and out of Germany would be stopped. That no trains passed out of their countries. Persons would be stopped at the borders."[31] Blockaded, in other words, or "ostracized," as King had reflected.

Yet if Mackenzie King had been impressed by the President's visionary thinking early in December, 1942 — less than twelve months after Pearl Harbor — he'd been equally moved by the depth of Roosevelt's *moral and social* purpose. In Britain, Winston Churchill had dismissed the Beveridge Report, which outlined possible future British social and health policies — as pie in the sky:[32] a dismissive view that was echoed by the British ambassador on Mackenzie King's visit to Washington, when King met with him. Americans were "all much excited about the Beveridge Report," Lord Halifax had confided in his own diary. "I told them all that, just as with the Malvern Conference Report, so with this, they [Americans] always know much more about it than I do!"[33]

The President of the United States certainly knew more than the British ambassador about the postwar social blueprint for Britain. "The President said the Beveridge report has made a real impression in this country," King recorded.[34] "The thought of [medical and employment] insurance from the cradle to the grave. 'That seems to be a line that will appeal,'" Roosevelt had said to King at dinner. "You and I should take that up strongly. It will help us politically as well as being on the right lines in the way of reform" — a remark King correctly interpreted as meaning "the President has in mind a fourth term and that he feels it will come as a result of winning the war, and the social programme to be launched."[35]

As president of the United States, Mr. Roosevelt "did not think the country will stand for socialism," King recorded the President's caution, but he did make clear that improving the condition of America's working people was as much a part of his vision of the postwar world as would be international security achieved through unconditional surrender of the Axis warrior nations, and disarmament closely monitored by the United Nations. "I felt in listening to the President that he was naturally anxious to be responsible for planning the new order," King reflected[36] — a new order that would snatch the wind from the sails of those idly or idealistically espousing communism, since it would guarantee the well-being and security of the majority of ordinary people, without communist barbarity or oppression.

As a deeply devout Christian who read the New Testament first thing in the morning and last thing at night, Mackenzie King had thus listened to the President's *tour d'horizon* with growing "relief," he admitted — the opportunity to discuss with the President of the United States "social questions and reform, instead of these problems of war and destruction. I felt tremendously pleased. It may be that when the war is over, new force and energy will come forward toward the furtherance of these larger social aims. It was midnight when I got to bed . . . From the moment I turned out the light until waking I slept very soundly."[37]

The world, after this war, was clearly going to be very different from the one bequeathed by the victors of World War I.

4

What Next?

WHAT HAD MOST moved Mackenzie King on his stay at the White House early in December, 1942, were the little details that went hand in hand with his discussions with the President.

After lunch in the small dining room upstairs in the White House mansion one day, King noticed "on the President's desk" among the bric-a-brac, "a little bronze of his mother," which touched him deeply.[1] Fresh from her trip to England, the President's wife, the First Lady, had been present — the President proud, King had happily noted, of what Eleanor had accomplished there as a spokesperson, so to speak, of American idealism.

The President's health, though, was another matter. On the afternoon of December 4, 1942, for example, King had been somewhat alarmed by Roosevelt's physical condition. "Had tea alone with the President at 5:20 in his circular chart room [the Oval Study]. The President poured tea himself."[2] The two leaders had spoken of manpower and mobilization — problems common to both countries. However, "I noticed that his hand was very, very shaky," King had dictated — the tea in danger of spilling. The President looked "rather tired," but as they talked he'd "brightened up."

Here again Prime Minister Mackenzie King's testimony, in the detailed diary he was keeping, would offer the most intimate clues to the President's mind in late 1942. No other war leader was exploring a postwar vision such as the President was doing; Churchill could only dream of the past; Hitler, only of the German *Volk* and of ruthless conquest. And who knew what Stalin dreamed of? Would the President be well enough, however, to get his allies to cooperate and carry out his grand vision of the postwar world? Would Congress and the American public embrace it, or go back to isolationism? And what of the war itself?

Turning to confront the President on the sofa, King had therefore asked him, face to face: "What are the immediate plans, supposing you get complete possession of North Africa, what next?"[3]

From the point of view of military strategy in order to achieve political ends, it was a most interesting question.

The President seemed glad that King had raised it. "That of course is the next problem," Roosevelt replied. "I wanted to speak of it."[4] To his great disappointment, despite the success of the President's Torch operation, which they'd opposed almost to the point of mutiny, his U.S. generals and admirals were still out of sync with their commander in chief. In fact his generals and admirals were now out of sync with each other, and the British.

"For some time past," Roosevelt confided to the Canadian prime minister — whose country was supplying a vast amount of war material to the Allied effort, as well as significant numbers of troops, and the crucial materials for development of an atomic bomb in the United States — "we have had the Chiefs of Staff both here and in England working on the strategic side of things." There were "at least 10 different places" where the Allies *could* advance, from northern Norway to the Balkans. "No decision was reached as yet," though, Mackenzie King recorded the President's lament, since "it was very hard," the President said, "to get the different Chiefs of Staff to agree on a plan."[5]

Harry Hopkins had been little help in this respect. Hopkins was by nature and ability a "fixer" — a highly intelligent man, brilliant at absorbing reports, and able to see beyond hurdles. Never having fired a gun or seen war at close quarters, however, Hopkins had erratic military judgment, to say the least. He had urged the President to declare war early in 1941, before the nation was ready to fight a one-ocean war, let alone two.[6] Then — having become convinced the Russians were not going to be defeated by the Germans in 1941 — he had urged throughout 1942 a cross-Channel invasion of France rather than the President's "great pet scheme" of Torch, believing the North African operation might actually fail. Even if successful, it would be a diversion of decisive American effort, he felt.

Hopkins, as a civilian, could at least be forgiven for his ignorance of military realities — especially the lack of American experience in fighting an enemy as battle-hardened, ideologically driven, and professional as German troops marching to Hitler's triumphant tune. However, Hopkins's military innocence had been mirrored by most senior, professional desk generals and admirals in the U.S. War and Navy Departments in Washington. Despite the success of Torch, the U.S. chiefs were *once again* urging, early in December, that a cross-Channel Allied invasion be mounted in the spring of 1943, or latest by the summer of '43 — without American soldiers or their field commanders having seen more than a few days of battle, and that only against conflicted Vichy French forces.

Mackenzie King was as skeptical of the chances of a cross-Channel attack succeeding in 1943 as the President — indeed, more so given the "fiasco" of the Canadian raid on Dieppe three months earlier. Still mourning the loss of so many thousands of Canadian soldiers killed or wounded and captured on the beaches of the little French seaport on August 19, 1942 — almost all of them brave volunteers, sacrificed to no real purpose other than to demonstrate the futility of a premature cross-Channel assault — the Canadian prime minister had been alarmed by Hopkins's views the day he arrived at the White House. The President's counselor had shared with him "the need of a decision being fairly quickly made as to what the campaign for next year [1943] was to be. He said the military heads could not yet make up their mind but he thought that decision would have to be made at once if supplies were to be gotten in to the right place. It would seem to him it would probably have to be from England on Europe" — i.e., for a cross-Channel assault in 1943 — "and that great quantity of supplies would have to be gotten across immediately."[7]

The notion that Allied forces could defeat the Wehrmacht simply by *supplies* had seemed to the Canadian premier unbelievably optimistic. To King's profound relief the President, however, declared he didn't agree with Hopkins — or with his U.S. War Department staff. He reminded King how it was only through his own and Churchill's combined efforts that the Allied war against Hitler had been saved from disaster that year, 1942, by insisting on Operation Gymnast (which was then renamed Torch). "It is a good thing Winston and I kept it out [on the table] as we did," the President had remarked of the invasion of Northwest Africa — for "during early 1941, army and navy were all for direct attack across the Channel in the spring of 1942." The plans for a Second Front invasion "kept taking longer and longer, after spring of 1942. Then it was to be on in the summer." Again, this had proved impossible, at least in sufficient force to assure success. "Could not get ships, etc. Then the next plan was that they would try in the spring of 1943." At that prospect, the President had, in the summer of 1942, finally drawn the line as U.S. commander in chief, convinced that U.S. forces would have to gain actual combat experience fighting the Wehrmacht if a difficult cross-Channel invasion were to have any chance of success. "The President then said that he and Winston [had decided they] would get together in June" of 1942, to work out a new strategy. Tobruk's fall, and the failure of the British to halt Rommel's advance in Libya, had put the kibosh on any hopes of British-American success across the English Channel, where twenty-five German divisions were awaiting their arrival. "The President then said he had told Churchill: 'I go back to my first love, which is to attack via North Africa.'" Such a strategic blow would secure the Atlantic port of Dakar and, in terms of lines of communication and resupply, enable the Allies to use "the short route from Britain to Africa, and short route from U.S. to Africa." Torch would coincide with the British, reinforced with U.S. tanks and air groups, getting "control of North Egypt and with good luck" lead to "control of the Mediterranean."[8]

"I felt the soft place was Southern Europe," Roosevelt had reminded King — who'd been staying with him at the White House the previous spring, when the strategic debate had burned fiercely. Side by side with that southern European/North African strategy, the President had meanwhile wanted "a strong hitting force pointed at Germany from the North" as a permanent threat[9] — forcing Hitler to keep his twenty-five or thirty German divisions stationed along the North Sea and Atlantic coasts of Europe, well away from Russia.

It was in the Mediterranean, however, that U.S. forces could best actually fight and gain crucial command and battle experience, the President had explained to King — at the very extremity of German lines of communication and resupply. The campaign in Northwest Africa was already drawing huge Axis military forces to the Southern Front, across the Mediterranean, forcing Germany and Italy to meet the Allies in combat there — the Germans using vital, battle-hardened and battle-worthy troops, planes, and military resources that could not, as a result, be sent to reinforce their war on the Eastern Front.

The Mediterranean thus offered the U.S. Army, Air Forces, and Navy a priceless opportunity: namely to rehearse and perfect the command and combat skills they would need in fighting ruthless, highly disciplined, strongly motivated German forces in Europe, *before* being expected to undertake anything as daunting as a contested cross-Channel invasion —

an operation of war that had not been successfully attempted, after all, in almost a thousand years, since the time of William the Conqueror.

Battle experience, then, was the crux of the matter: the reason why the President so profoundly disagreed with Hopkins; with Secretary of War Henry Stimson; with General George Marshall, U.S. Army chief of staff; and with all the voices in Washington baying again for an immediate cross-Channel Second Front. As U.S. commander in chief he, President Roosevelt, had a responsibility to ensure the nation did not embark on a course of military action that would fail — especially when there was no need to do so, as he confided to Mackenzie King in another talk on December 6, 1942, as King prepared to return to Canada. He had, "this afternoon, sent word to the Chiefs of Staff in Washington and also to the joint staffs in England to ask exactly what they had thus far decided about the next moves, and what were the points they were still debating. He said when you think it took from January till June before we settled on Africa and definite plans for the campaign, you see it is time we get the next step settled or next move determined." As president and commander in chief, however, he had his own view — which he now shared with King.

"In many ways," the President confided, "he wished for nothing more than let the fighting continue in Africa indefinitely. We are able to get supplies across, so much easier to Africa than to any other place. We can wear down the Germans there by a process of attrition" — just as U.S. forces were doing in the Pacific, in the Solomon Islands, while learning the art of modern combat. "He said: I feel the same about the Japs. As long as we can go on the wearing down in the one place, we are coming nearer to certain victory in the end."[10]

Mackenzie King, as prime minister of Canada, had breathed a sigh of relief. When asked by the President if his Canadian generals were also pressing for an immediate Second Front, King responded that, unlike the generals in Washington, the Canadian generals "felt it was better to keep a strong hitting force pointed at Germany from the North," but *not* to launch such an actual invasion before there was a reasonable chance it would succeed. The President "said he felt that very strongly" too, King recorded.

"It would be a great mistake," Roosevelt had remarked, "to do anything which would take away the German armies that are now concentrated in occupied France and in the North — anything which would make them less fearful of an enemy invasion," in terms of threat. Beyond that potent menace, however, the President had explained to King, he had no actual wish to launch a D-day landing any time soon across the English Channel, with forces and commanders still inexperienced in combat. "He thought that what the Canadians had done at Dieppe" — where almost a thousand men were slaughtered in a matter of a few hours, and two-thirds of their forces were killed, wounded, or captured by the Germans, without even getting off the beaches — "was a very necessary part of the campaign," for it had "made clear how terribly dangerous the whole business of invasion across the Channel was."[11]

These had been the President's own words. They explained why the President was so determined to stop his top military staff from insisting upon a suicidal assault in the wrong place, at the wrong time. The Second Front should be kept as a *threat* — but no actual cross-Channel invasion be launched until 1944, when U.S. mass production could ensure superiority in arms; more important still, it would be a time by which Allied forces in Africa and the Mediterranean would have learned the lessons of modern combat: how to defeat the Germans in battle. Only then would it be fair to ask huge numbers of American sons — perhaps two million — to land across the defended beaches of northern France and fight their way to Berlin.

Mackenzie King thus set off to return to Ottawa that evening, December 6, 1942, deeply relieved: knowing the President would do nothing rash before the military forces of the Western Allies — Canada, the United States, and Britain — had proven themselves in combat and were ready: preferably in 1944, unless by some miracle the Germans collapsed. In the meantime, the President hoped, he confided to King, that Stalin would cease parrying his appeals for a summit, and would help start an international dialogue on the postwar world — with history at stake.

5

Stalin's *Nyet*

FINALLY, ON DECEMBER 6, 1942, shortly after Mackenzie King left Washington, the President heard back from Stalin. Although the Russian dictator "welcomed the idea of a meeting of the leaders of the Governments of the three countries to determine a common line of military strategy," he himself would "not be able to leave the Soviet Union. I must say that we are having now such a strenuous time that I cannot go away even for a day." Around Stalingrad, he explained, "we are keeping encircled a group of German troops and hope to finish them off."[1]

The question of postwar agreements was not even mentioned.

Given the amount of aid — more than 10 percent of Russia's war needs — that the United States was supplying the Russians, the President cabled back that he was "deeply disappointed that you feel you cannot get away for a conference with me in January." Stalin was known never to have gone near the Russian front.

The President urged Stalin to reconsider. The date proposed was still five weeks in the future. "There are many matters of vital importance to be discussed between us. These relate not only to vital strategic decisions but also to things we should talk over in a tentative way in regard to emergency policies we should be ready with if and when conditions in Germany permit. These would include also other matters relating to future policies about North Africa and the Far East which cannot be discussed by our military people alone." If Stalin could not see a way to leave Moscow in January, what about "meeting in North Africa about March first"?[2]

To this plea, however, there was no response from Moscow for a week. When the reply came, it was only to say Stalin regretted "it is impossible for me to leave the Soviet Union either in the near future or even at the beginning of March. Front business absolutely prevents it, demanding my constant presence near our troops."[3]

About this patent untruth the President could only shake his head, knowing Stalin never went anywhere near his brave Russian troops. The rest of Stalin's message — asking what exactly were the "problems which you, Mr. President, and Mr. Churchill intended to discuss at our joint conference," and wondering if these could not be dealt with "by correspondence" — had been similarly disappointing, despite the Russian dictator's assurance "there will be no disagreement between us."[4]

The chances of that, Roosevelt knew, were slim — especially given Stalin's hope that "the promises about the opening of a second front in Europe given by you, Mr. President, and by Mr. Churchill in regard of 1942 and in any case in regard of the spring of 1943, will be fulfilled, and that a second front in Europe will be actually opened by the joint forces of Great Britain and the United States of America in the spring of next year."[5]

That hope — as the President had confided to Prime Minister Mackenzie King — was pie in the sky. Unless the Germans showed signs of collapse in 1943, he was simply not going to approve such a strategy until U.S. forces and commanders were battle-hardened in the Mediterranean that year — just as was taking place in New Guinea and the Solomon Islands in the South Pacific, at the extremity of Japanese lines of communication.

It was Stalin who would inevitably be disappointed, then, once he learned of Roosevelt's implacable decision. Though the President's own generals and admirals, his war secretary, his counselor Hopkins, and even his ambassador to London, John Winant, might echo Stalin's appeals for an immediate cross-Channel assault, the President was simply not going to authorize mass American — and Canadian — suicide. Each day, by contrast, the President was more confident of "certain victory in the end" — if the Allies made no more mistakes.

With Stalin still saying *nyet* to a summit meeting, however — whether in January or in March, 1943 — the President had cabled Churchill on December 14, 1942, to say they should go ahead without him. In Casablanca, as he confided to Captain McCrea.

Before he left, however, the President decided he must do two important things. First, get the nation behind him. And second, his generals.

6

Addressing Congress

As the seventy-eighth Congress prepared to reassemble with a much-diminished Democratic majority, the President decided to use his annual State of the Union address, on January 7, 1943, not only to review the past year but to share something of his vision of the future.

The speech went through no fewer than nine full iterations over "many days," starting before Christmas and extending beyond the New Year, Judge Rosenman (the President's primary speechwriter, together with the playwright Robert Sherwood and Harry Hopkins) later recalled.[1] Finally, at noon on January 7, the President was driven to the Capitol to deliver his "sermon."

"The past year," the President began boldly, "was perhaps the most crucial for modern civilization. The Axis powers knew that they must win the war in 1942 — or eventually lose everything. I do not need to tell you," he added to loud cheers, "that our enemies did not win the war in 1942."

Step by step the President reminded members of Congress and those listening on radios at work, or in their homes, of the year's most significant military actions. "In the Pacific area our most important victory in 1942 was the air and naval battle off Midway Island. That action is historically important because it secured for our use communication lines stretching thousands of miles in every direction. In placing this emphasis on the Battle of Midway, I am not unmindful of other successful actions in the Pacific, in the air and on land and afloat, especially those on the Coral Sea and New Guinea and in the Solomon Islands. But these actions were essentially defensive. They were part of the delaying strategy that characterized this phase of the war. During this period we inflicted steady losses upon the enemy — great losses of Japanese planes and naval vessels, transports and cargo ships. As early as one year ago, we set as a primary task in the war of the Pacific a day-by-day and week-by-week and month-by-month destruction of more Japanese war materials than Japanese industry could replace. Most certainly, that task has been and is being performed by our fighting ships and planes. And a large part of this task has been accomplished by the gallant crews of our American submarines who strike on the other side of the Pacific at Japanese ships — right up at the very mouth of the harbor of Yokohama. We know that as each day goes by, Japanese strength in ships and planes is going down and down, and American strength in ships and planes is going up and up. And so I sometimes feel that the eventual outcome can now be put on a mathematical basis. That will become evident to the Japanese people themselves when we strike at their own home islands, and bomb them constantly from the air" — just as Japan had begun the war with aerial bombing.

Japan was not the nation's first priority, however. Nazi Germany was — and would remain so, in terms of global American strategy, as long as Roosevelt remained president. "Turning now to the European theater of war," the President explained, "during this past year it was clear that our first task was to lessen the concentrated pressure on the Russian front by compelling Germany to divert part of her manpower and equipment to another theater of war. After months of secret planning and preparation in the utmost detail, an enormous amphibious expedition was embarked for French North Africa from the United States and the United Kingdom in literally hundreds of ships. It reached its objectives with very small losses, and has already produced an important effect upon the whole situation of the war. It has opened to attack what Mr. Churchill well described as 'the underbelly of the Axis,' and it has removed the always dangerous threat of an Axis attack through West Africa against the South Atlantic Ocean and the continent of South America itself. The well-timed and splendidly executed offensive from Egypt by the British 8th Army was a part of the same major strategy of the United Nations. Great rains and appalling mud and very limited communications have delayed the final battles of Tunisia. The Axis is reinforcing its strong positions. But I am confident that though the fighting will be tough, when the final Allied assault is made, the last vestige of Axis power will be driven from the whole of the south shores of the Mediterranean.

"I cannot prophesy," he added sternly. "I cannot tell you when or where the United Nations are going to strike next in Europe. But we are going to strike — and strike hard. I cannot tell you whether we are going to hit them in Norway, or through the Low Countries, or in France, or through Sardinia or Sicily, or through the Balkans, or through Poland — or at several points simultaneously. But I can tell you that no matter where and when we strike by land, we and the British and the Russians will hit them from the air heavily and relentlessly. Day in and day out we shall heap tons upon tons of high explosives on their war factories and utilities and seaports. Hitler and Mussolini will understand now the enormity of their miscalculations — that the Nazis would always have the advantage of superior air power as they did when they bombed Warsaw, and Rotterdam, and London and Coventry. That superiority has gone forever. Yes," he concluded his strategic survey, "the Nazis and the Fascists have asked for it — and they are going to get it."

To reinforce this message the President announced with pride that, "after only a few years of preparation and only one year of warfare, we are able to engage, spiritually as well as physically, in the total waging of a total war."

The phrase, for the United States, meant complete focus on war production on a scale that dwarfed anything ever done before — exceeding the production figures of America's enemies combined. In the past year the United States had manufactured "48,000 military planes — more than the airplane production of Germany, Italy, and Japan put together," as well as "56,000 combat vehicles, such as tanks and self-propelled artillery" — figures that would double again in 1943. "I think the arsenal of democracy is making good," the President congratulated America. "These facts and figures that I have given will give no great aid and comfort to the enemy," he explained his reason for releasing such numbers. "On the contrary, I can imagine that they will give him considerable discomfort. I suspect that Hitler and Tojo will find it difficult to explain to the German and Japanese people just why it is that 'decadent, inefficient democracy' can produce such phenomenal quantities of weapons and munitions — and fighting men." For, along with the "miracle of production, during the past year our armed forces have grown from a little over 2,000,000 to 7,000,000" men in uniform.

Seven *million?* And that figure rising?

Though the figures were astounding, and though the strategic initiative was now in the President's hands (his personal secretary noting how the "President becomes more and more the central figure in the global war,

the source of initiative and authority in action, and, of course, responsibility"[2]), the President was clearly unwilling, it became clear, to leave
matters there. "In this war of survival we must keep before our minds not
only the evil things we fight against," he asked his audience, "but the good
things we are fighting *for*. We fight to retain a great past — and we fight
to gain a greater future." With that, he proceeded to outline the terms on
which he proposed to end the war. And what to do after the war was won.

"We, and all the United Nations, want a decent peace and a durable
peace. In the years between the end of the first World War and the beginning of the second World War, we were not living under a decent or a
durable peace. I have reason to know that our boys at the front are concerned with two broad aims beyond the winning of the war; and their
thinking and their opinion coincide with what most Americans here back
home are mulling over. They know, and we know, that it would be inconceivable — it would, indeed, be sacrilegious — if this nation and the world
did not attain some real, lasting good out of all these efforts and sufferings
and bloodshed and death."

The good he wanted was, he proceeded to explain, a sort of renewed
New Deal:

> The men in our armed forces want a lasting peace, and, equally, they
> want permanent employment for themselves, their families, and their
> neighbors when they are mustered out at the end of the war.
>
> Two years ago I spoke in my annual message of four freedoms. The
> blessings of two of them — freedom of speech and freedom of religion —
> are an essential part of the very life of this nation; and we hope that these
> blessings will be granted to all men everywhere.
>
> The people at home, and the people at the front, are wondering a little
> about the third freedom — freedom from want. To them it means that
> when they are mustered out, when war production is converted to the
> economy of peace, they will have the right to expect full employment —
> full employment for themselves and for all able-bodied men and women
> in America who want to work.
>
> They expect the opportunity to work, to run their farms, their stores,
> to earn decent wages. They are eager to face the risks inherent in our
> system of free enterprise,

the President allowed. On the other hand,

They do not want a postwar America which suffers from undernourishment or slums — or the dole. They want no get-rich-quick era of bogus "prosperity" which will end for them in selling apples on a street corner, as happened after the bursting of the boom in 1929.

When you talk with our young men and our young women, you will find they want to work for themselves and for their families; they consider that they have the right to work; and they know that after the last war their fathers did not gain that right.

When you talk with our young men and women, you will find that with the opportunity for employment they want assurance against the evils of all major economic hazards — assurance that will extend from the cradle to the grave. And this great government can and must provide this assurance.

I have been told that this is no time to speak of a better America after the war. I am told it is a grave error on my part.

I dissent.

And if the security of the individual citizen, or the family, should become a subject of national debate, the country knows where I stand.

I say this now to this 78th Congress, because it is wholly possible that freedom from want — the right of employment, the right of assurance against life's hazards — will loom very large as a task of America during the coming two years.

I trust it will not be regarded as an issue — but rather as a task for all of us to study sympathetically, to work out with a constant regard for the attainment of the objective, with fairness to all and with injustice to none.

These were the fighting words of a president who, quite clearly, was intending to stand for a fourth term, as Mackenzie King had inferred.

Not content with this domestic sally, however, the President then waded into national security on an international scale — national security that would require the end of American isolationism. "We cannot make America an island in either a military or an economic sense," he pointed out. "Hitlerism, like any other form of crime or disease, can grow from the evil seeds of economic as well as military feudalism. Victory in this war is the first and greatest goal before us. Victory in the peace is the next. That means striving toward the enlargement of the security of man here and throughout the world — and, finally, striving for the fourth freedom — freedom from fear." However, to attain freedom from fear meant taking a new role as peacekeeper in a "shrinking" globe, thanks to the "conquest of the air." It was fruitless to imagine the clock could be turned back, once the war was won.

> Undoubtedly a few Americans, even now, think that this nation can end this war comfortably and then climb back into an American hole and pull the hole in after them.
>
> But we have learned that we can never dig a hole so deep that it would be safe against predatory animals. We have also learned that if we do not pull the fangs of the predatory animals of this world, they will multiply and grow in strength — and they will be at our throats again once more in a short generation.
>
> Most Americans realize more clearly than ever before that modern war equipment in the hands of aggressor nations can bring danger overnight to our own national existence or to that of any other nation — or island — or continent.
>
> It is clear to us that if Germany and Italy and Japan — or any one of them — remain armed at the end of this war, or are permitted to rearm, they will again, and inevitably, embark upon an ambitious career of world conquest. They must be disarmed and kept disarmed, and they must abandon the philosophy, and the teaching of that philosophy, which has brought so much suffering to the world.

Step by step the President was leading his audience, and radio listeners, toward his notion of a United Nations authority.

> After the first World War we tried to achieve a formula for permanent peace, based on a magnificent idealism. We failed. But, by our failure, we have learned that we cannot maintain peace at this stage of human development by good intentions alone.
>
> Today the United Nations are the mightiest military coalition in all history. They represent an overwhelming majority of the population of the world. Bound together in solemn agreement that they themselves will not commit acts of aggression or conquest against any of their neighbors, the United Nations can and must remain united for the maintenance of peace by preventing any attempt to rearm in Germany, in Japan, in Italy, or in any other nation which seeks to violate the Tenth Commandment — "Thou shalt not covet."[3]

The President's words, clearly, were not only directed against isolationists in America, but were a preview of what he would announce internationally in the next few weeks. An announcement, to be given from the podium of a global stage, that would make public the fact that the United States was stepping up to the plate; would not this time back off, following victory, but was going to embrace a new, world-historical role as a leader of the democratic nations — if he could get those nations to support his vision.

7

A Fool's Paradise

REACTION TO ROOSEVELT'S ambitious State of the Union address was, somewhat to the President's surprise, decidedly positive.

The British ambassador, certainly, was impressed. Viscount Halifax had spent almost an hour at the dentist before going to the Capitol, where he was "herded on to the floor" with other diplomats "where we had good places. The President's speech was forceful and well-delivered and well-received," he recorded that night in his diary, remarking on the "very warm personal reception both at the beginning and end. The warmth of applause for China as compared with Russia and ourselves was very noticeable," he'd added — with understandable concern. The President, however, had spoken "with great confidence. I thought what he said on the domestic side was pretty strong and likely to be provoking to his domestic critics, as it seemed to be 'Let us have as much unity as we can, but I am going to go ahead with my social policy, and if you don't like it, let the country judge, and I know what their verdict will be,' but the general impression of it seems to have been that it was conciliatory. The informality of all Congress proceedings on these occasions is striking," he'd reflected, "by contrast with our affairs at home" — the ambassador amazed when, in reelecting its Speaker, Sam Rayburn, the day before, "the House [of Representatives] sang 'Happy birthday to you'!"[1]

If the President was delighted by the reception, however, he had little time to bask in it. Following a quick lunch at the Capitol, he returned to the White House — there to face in the Oval Office a smaller but equally critical audience he'd summoned: the U.S. Joint Chiefs of Staff, who would be flying to Casablanca that very evening, ahead of the President, aboard C-54 transport planes.

• • •

Admiral Leahy had warned the President that there had been no break-through in the Joint Chiefs' continuing dissension over U.S. global strategy. They were at loggerheads not only about whether to launch a cross-Channel invasion that year, but what to do in the Pacific.

The ringleaders of the continuing argument against a Mediterranean strategy in 1943 were — as had been the case throughout the previous year — the President's Republican secretary of war, Henry Stimson, and General Marshall. Colonel Stimson had openly bet the President that his "great pet scheme" — the Torch invasion — would fail. When it didn't — in fact proved a triumphant success — Stimson had found himself embarrassed. On November 20, 1942, for example, former ambassador William Bullitt, who had been U.S. envoy to Russia and France and who was currently working for Secretary Frank Knox at the Navy Department on Constitution Avenue, had rubbed salt in Stimson's wounded pride. He'd asked Stimson "how I liked to be a mere housekeeper of the War Department now that the President had taken over all relations with the military men."

Stimson had been infuriated by the remark. "I told him that so long as I was constitutional adviser to the President, he would not do it," Stimson had countered. "But Bullitt's remark," he confessed in the privacy of his diary, "irritated and annoyed me."[2]

Fortunately the President was nothing if not sensitive to people's feelings. Some days later he'd spoken with Stimson on the phone. They'd had "a talk on the situation and on my duties as Secretary of War. I told him then of Bill Bullitt's recent fresh visit to me and his remark asking me how I liked being merely a housekeeper for the Army. The President said 'What!' and made it very clear that he was going to use me for a great deal more than that. He said Bullitt was always a problem child." This was "very reassuring and satisfactory and balm to my soul after the troubles and suspicions," Stimson had confessed, "that I had been through for the last two or three days."[3]

The President's solace, however, hadn't stopped the elderly war secretary from working behind the scenes to question the President's military strategy in the Mediterranean — which he still thought utterly misguided.

On December 12, 1942, for example, Stimson had recorded he'd had a "long talk" with General Marshall and also Jack McCloy, the assistant secretary of war, as to "what we are going to do after the North African campaign and what it is going to lead to; and from this talk and other talks that I have had with Marshall and particularly the talk which I had with the President last evening, I am very much more relieved because the trend is now to get back onto the sound line of an attack up in the originally planned route" — namely the possibility of a cross-Channel attack "next summer."[4]

Summer '43?

As the President had confided to Mackenzie King, as president and commander in chief he did not favor a cross-Channel attack until U.S. forces had had ample time, in the Mediterranean, to first learn the arduous business of how to defeat the Wehrmacht in combat — which might well take all of 1943, given that the English Channel became too rough to cross by September.

Clearly the secretary was not listening. Inviting General Stanley Embick, the former deputy U.S. Army chief of staff, to his office at the Pentagon two days later, on December 14, 1942, Stimson had been determined not to be seen as a mere War Department housekeeper. Embick had been requested to report not to General Marshall but directly to Stimson on "the question of what we shall do after the African adventure."

The relationship between the two men went back decades — Embick having attended the Command and General Staff College with Stimson in World War I. At age sixty-four, he was now "head of our elder statesmen in military matters and has been made the head of a board of strategy together with Admiral Wilson of the Navy," Stimson noted. "I knew that he had always been very skeptical about the North African adventure," the war secretary added — anxious to know if the general had changed his mind.

Embick hadn't. "His position was very much the same as mine," Stimson had recorded with satisfaction in his diary, "and I found it was confirmed today. We both feel that the North African adventure has done a great deal of good," he allowed — though only because of luck, he maintained. As a result, "we have thus far gotten through without being knocked out by a great many of the perils that we might very well have had fall upon us and spoil the whole expedition." Among these "perils" was German forces being ordered to invade or granted passage through Spain and shipped across the Mediterranean into Spanish Morocco — there to strike American forces in the flank. "Embick laid great stress on keeping the gate open [to Tunisia] and not impairing the forces that were under George Patton in Casablanca for that [defensive] purpose"[5] — i.e., denying Patton the chance to fight in Tunisia rather than guarding U.S. lines of communication running back from Tunisia to Casablanca. Morocco, both Stimson and Embick felt, should be kept well supplied and protected by large numbers of U.S. troops, to guard against a mythical German riposte through Spain, across the Mediterranean, and then across Spanish Morocco. "We regard that as the sine qua non of the whole adventure," Stimson dictated in his diary.[6]

"Embick was strongly of the opinion that it would be impossible to go any further in adventures in Sardinia or Sicily after we are successful in Tunis," Stimson noted frankly—though making sure to exclude such passages from his later memoirs.[7] "Our shipping absolutely forbids that," he asserted, "and the line of supplies has become so long that it would be intolerable. So his thought is that after Tunis is cleaned out, if it is, if there is any surplus of American troops left over, we should send them up to Great Britain to be ready for the next attack there," Stimson recorded, together with his own approval. In fact the secretary had called in the head of the War Department's Operations Division, General John Hull, to join the discussion; "I found that he was in complete accord with both Embick and myself."[8]

Interrupted by visitors—a senator and governor from Idaho there to discuss the equipping of the National Guard in Idaho—Stimson had then returned to his office, where talk of the "next attack" across the English Channel in the summer of 1943 moved yet deeper into fantasy—in fact, seemed even more reckless than what Stimson had promoted in 1942. "Both Embick and Hull feel that the next step after we get back on the rails again up in Great Britain," he'd confided in his diary, "and are prepared to go forward, is not an attack on one of the peninsulas"—i.e., Brittany or Normandy—"but an attack on the flat coast near Havre and the port of Calais, landing in a large number of places."[9]

The problem of first gaining experience in battle and amphibious operations against the German Wehrmacht—the President's main objection to launching a cross-Channel attack prematurely—was thus simply ignored by Stimson and the senior officers of the War Department. The name Dieppe was simply never mentioned in Stimson's diary. Or the savage lessons of the 1942 disaster, only four months earlier.

Stimson was seventy-five years old; Embick, sixty-five.

In younger men, such ill-considered ardor could perhaps have been forgiven. But for two individuals who had enjoyed distinguished military careers and had themselves served in war, albeit in a different age, to task tens of thousands of inexperienced U.S. servicemen and their field commanders with a perilous invasion across the English Channel, at the most heavily defended area — the Pas-de-Calais — was willful fixation. The tragic slaughter of so many Canadian troops at Dieppe was well known in Washington professional military circles, despite attempts by the British to cover up the appalling number of Canadian casualties.[10] To imagine U.S. forces would, without more experience in amphibious operations, do better than brave Canadians in invading the fortified Pas-de-Calais area of northern France was pure hubris — the secretary and his colleagues at the Pentagon steadfastly refusing to see the Mediterranean as a necessary proving ground for the armed forces of the United States.

The first serious encounter-battles after Torch had, after all, begun to take place already in the last days of November and early in December, 1942, in the Medjerda Valley, outside Tunis. There, Eisenhower's U.S. and British forces, including amphibious units and paratroopers, had gotten a rude shock. The sheer professionalism of German armored and infantry units, backed by Mark IV panzers with long-barreled 75mm guns as well as deadly 88mm antiaircraft artillery used in an antitank role, had stunned the inexperienced Allied forces. Aware it could take months before he could break through to Tunis — especially since General Marshall insisted that a whole U.S. army be kept back, guarding against the improbable threat of a German attack out of Spanish Morocco — General Eisenhower had therefore begun plotting an alternative end-run further south, which in theory could strike through the thinly held German flank in Tunisia. If successful this would, the young commander in chief of Allied forces in the western Mediterranean hoped, reach the Mediterranean coast, east of Tunis, before the Germans could be reinforced by Rommel's Panzerarmee Afrika, retreating from Libya. Eisenhower had wanted to use George Patton for the job. He was overruled by General Marshall, who, with Secretary Stimson, remained obsessed with Patton being kept in the rear, defending the Allied flank.

Quite how, if Stimson, Marshall, and Embick, together with a whole cohort of planners and operations officers at the Pentagon, so feared a German counteroffensive via Spain, they could seriously imagine a cross-Channel invasion by virgin U.S. troops against twenty-five or thirty German divisions in northern France would magically succeed was something the President found hard to comprehend.

For the moment, however, the President had not interfered: trusting that, as American troops met German forces in Tunisia and the penny dropped, they would see sense. The British, after all, had taken three years of war to find a combat commander and the troops who could, at Alamein, defeat the Wehrmacht in battle. How on earth did Marshall, Stimson, Hull, and Embick imagine American forces would do so overnight?

Not even reports of mounting casualties and the need for reinforcements in Tunisia — not Morocco — seemed to dent Stimson's obsession, however. Indeed, by early January, 1943, Stimson seemed to be living in a fool's paradise in his huge new office suite inside the vast 2.3-million-square-foot Pentagon building, on the south side of the Potomac River, completed only a week after the Torch landings.[11]

Stimson had not been invited to the Casablanca meeting, but learning that the President wanted the Joint Chiefs of Staff to assemble for a briefing at the White House after his State of the Union address on January 7, 1943, before they left for Africa by plane, Stimson had decided he must have a "long talk with General Marshall this morning on the subject of the future strategy of the war. There are some conferences impending between the war leaders of America and Britain," he anxiously noted in his diary — wisely withholding the location.

Stimson was relieved to hear that Marshall and the senior officers of the War Department opposed further operations in the Mediterranean that year, once Tunis was reached. "Our people are adhering to their old [cross-Channel] line — the one I have approved throughout — and Marshall said that thus far they had the backing of the President," he noted — erroneously. "In a word, it is that just as soon as the Germans are turned out of Tunisia and the north coast of Africa is safely in the hands of the Allies we shall accumulate our forces in the north and prepare for an attack this year upon the north coast of France — preferably one of the two northwest peninsulas" — Cherbourg and Brittany.

At least the notion of landings in the Pas-de-Calais had been dropped — even the War Department's most gung ho planners conceding that the Pas-de-Calais might be tough. "The one is selected," Stimson noted of Brittany, "but I do not care to mention it yet. We think that we can probably hold such a lodgment but even if we don't, even if our forces should be finally dislodged, it would be at such a terrible cost to Germany as to cripple her resistance for the following year."[12]

An amphibious cross-Channel invasion of France — the Brittany peninsula — in the summer of 1943, on the open acceptance it might fail and require its survivors to be evacuated, like the British at Dunkirk in 1940? An invasion that would nevertheless "cripple" the Germans, in order to facilitate a United States relaunch of the invasion the following year, 1944?

It was small wonder Admiral Leahy had noted that "no agreement could be reached by the opposing elements"[13] on December 28, 1942 — Stimson and Marshall's discussions at the Pentagon epitomizing, sadly, the complete lack of realism exhibited in the higher echelons of the U.S. War Department, only hours before the U.S. chiefs were due to leave to meet their British opposite numbers in Casablanca.

The President, however, was not of like mind. And was about to correct them, in the nicest way he knew how.

8

Facing the Joint Chiefs of Staff

AT 3:00 P.M. on January 7, 1943, Admiral Leahy and the U.S. Joint Chiefs of Staff, as well as the secretary of the Joint Chiefs, General John Deane, sat down beside the President in the Oval Office to discuss the strategic impasse.

Mr. Roosevelt proceeded to run the two-hour meeting in his inimitable manner: refusing to follow an agenda but rather, with the greatest friendliness, asking each of the chiefs to present the case as they saw it: once Tunis was secured, where next? "At the conference the British will have a plan, and stick to it,"[1] the President warned. Were they all, he asked innocently, "agreed that we should meet the British united in advocating a cross-Channel operation?"[2]

They were, they said. But *when?* And *where?*

To his credit, General Marshall, on behalf of the chiefs, was too honest to lie. All were not agreed about the timing, he confessed. Somewhat sheepishly, he explained to the Commander in Chief "that there was not a united front on that subject, particularly among our planners" — especially his own chief Army planning officer, Brigadier General Albert Wedemeyer.

"The Chiefs of Staff themselves regarded an operation in the north" — i.e., across the English Channel — "more favorably than one in the Mediterranean" once Tunis was secured, "but the question was still an open one," he admitted. "He said that to him the issue was purely one of logistics; that he was perfectly willing to take some tactical hazards or risks but that he felt we had no right to take logistical hazards. He said that the British were determined to start operations," after Tunisia, "in the Mediterranean" — leaving "Bolero [an early code name for a cross-Channel invasion] for a later date. He said the British pressed the point that we must keep the Germans moving. They lay great stress on accomplishing the collapse of Italy which would result in Germany having to commit divisions not only to Italy but also to replace Italian divisions now in other occupied countries," regions such as southern France, Corsica, the Balkans, and the Eastern Front.

The advantage for the British, Marshall continued, would be a secure Allied sea route to Suez and India, and a base for major operations in southern Europe — not only knocking Italy out of the war but holding out the possibility that Turkey might abandon its neutrality and join the United Nations. In this scenario, were it to be selected, the island of Sicily, Marshall said, was considered by him to be the best target of assault, once the campaign in Tunisia was completed: "a more desirable objective" than Sardinia, he explained, but one that, in terms of amphibious assault, "would be similar to an operation across the Channel," since the "Germans have been in Sicily longer," and "there were many more and much better airfields for them than in Sardinia."[3]

Sicily, then, was the British preference. An amphibious assault on the island dominating the Mediterranean would offer a kind of rehearsal for a future cross-Channel invasion — certainly a better one than Sardinia. But should the United States consent to further operations in the Mediterranean at all? By continuing offensive operations in the northern Mediterranean, whether in assaulting Sardinia or Sicily, Allied forces would be subject to "air attack from Italy, southern France, Corsica, possibly Greece, as well as a concentrated submarine attack," Marshall argued, which could lead to a loss of 20 percent of Allied ships. To this logistical nightmare the general "also pointed out the danger of [neutral] Spain becoming hostile, in which case we would have an enemy in possession of a defile [across the Mediterranean] on our line of communications."[4]

Fear of superior German forces in the Mediterranean and scarcity of Allied shipping thus led General Marshall to "personally favor," instead of further difficult operations in the Mediterranean, "an operation against the Brest peninsula" — i.e., the Brittany coast of northern France, across the widest part of the English Channel. "The losses there will be in troops," Marshall acknowledged, according to the minutes of the meeting, taken by General Deane, the secretary of the committee, "but he said that, to state it cruelly, we could replace troops whereas a heavy loss in shipping" incurred in further operations in the Mediterranean against Sardinia or Sicily, "might completely destroy any opportunity for successful operations against the enemy [across the English Channel] in the near future."[5]

The President was shocked—as historians would be, years later, when the minutes of the meeting were published. Taking vast U.S. casualties in order to hit the ports or beaches of northern France that year, rather than waiting until commanders and men had successful battle experience in the Mediterranean?

What was the hurry? Landing as yet completely inexperienced U.S. forces—commanders and infantry—across the widest part of the English Channel, to be set upon by upwards of twenty-five German divisions? Why invite such a potential disaster when they did not have to? Very politely, the President "then asked General Marshall what he thought the losses would be in an operation against the Brest Peninsula."[6]

Marshall, placed on the spot, had "replied that there would of course be losses but that there were no narrow straits on our lines of communication" like Gibraltar—both in terms of reinforcement or evacuation—"and we could operate with fighter protection from the United Kingdom."[7]

The President could only rub his eyes. No mention of the *two hundred miles* that Allied fighters would have to fly before they, like the assault ships, even reached the heavily defended invasion points, nor the proximity of twenty-five all-German infantry and armored divisions already stationed in western France, waiting and in constant training to repel an assault on its Atlantic coast, as they had done at Dieppe. No mention of the ease with which Germans could reinforce their Wehrmacht troops there, using short lines of communication from the Reich—and further armored forces they could quickly commit to battle. No mention, either, of the Luftwaffe's ability to use French airfields to attack the invading forces. Above all, no mention of the Canadian catastrophe at Dieppe the previous August, only four months ago. Merely a heartless disdain for the U.S. casualties that would be suffered, in comparison with landing craft— and a deeply, deeply questionable assumption that the invasion would, as Marshall had assured Stimson that morning, be at such "terrible cost to Germany as to cripple her resistance for the following year."

Marshall's presentation of the strategy he recommended the United States should best adopt, as chief of staff of the U.S. Army, was thus lamentable — as even Marshall himself seemed aware, once forced to defend his position.

The President, however, was a model of tact — unwilling to humble Marshall before his fellow chiefs. How, exactly, he then questioned Marshall, was such a landing at Brest to be actually mounted by U.S. forces — and how did Marshall expect the Germans to respond?

Marshall twisted in the wind. "The President had questioned the practicability of a landing on the Brest Peninsula," General Deane noted in the minutes of the meeting; "General Marshall replied that he thought the landing could be effected but the difficulties would come later in fighting off attacks from German armored units" — though "U.S. airplanes, flown from the United States, could give the troops help."[8]

Again, the President was amazed. U.S. air power such as U.S. Army Air Forces were giving U.S. and British ground forces in Tunisia, in the battles of Medjez-el-Bab and Longstop Hill — where American casualties were reported as heavy, and the Allies were just beginning to learn how tough it was to defeat the Germans in battle? Tellingly, the President therefore "asked why," if Marshall thought a cross-Channel invasion was the best course, "the British opposed the Brest Peninsula operation?"[9]

Embarrassed, Marshall had to concede "he thought they feared that the German strength would make such an operation impracticable."[10]

To Admiral Leahy's equally direct question as to when Marshall thought such a U.S. invasion of the Brest Peninsula could be "undertaken," Marshall had responded: "some time in August."[11]

August 1943.

It was clear to both President Roosevelt and Admiral Leahy that General Marshall had not done his homework. Above all, the Army chief of staff had no practical idea how a U.S. cross-Channel assault could possibly succeed that very year — in six months' time.

American armed forces currently had only eight weeks' battlefield experience — and most of this fighting ill-armed Vichy French forces, not German troops. How, then, were they to miraculously produce by August of that year the commanders and warriors capable of mounting a successful contested Allied landing in German-occupied Brittany, so close to the German Reich, and then hold out against — let alone defeat — Hitler's concentration of dozens of German infantry and panzer divisions stationed in northern France? And was Marshall really contemplating — as he'd said to Stimson that morning — the possible, even likely, defeat of

U.S. armies on the field of battle, and a Dunkirk-like evacuation from Brest? How would the public at home in America—who in any case favored winning the war against Japan over the difficulties of war in Europe—react to that?

The President had not been impressed. Choosing, by contrast, to back further operations in the Mediterranean, where the Allies had "800,000 or 900,000 men" and were currently in the ascendant, would furnish U.S. forces with a good opportunity to gain tough, amphibious battle experience against retreating German troops, far from the Reich, and in a relatively safe theater of war. U.S. operations in the South Pacific were, after all, providing such experience at the very extremity of Japanese lines of communication and resupply, on the other side of the world. With half a million troops that "might be built up in the United Kingdom for an attack on either Brest or Cherbourg," in Normandy, there was certainly every reason to consider a plan for their commitment to battle, if the Germans showed signs of collapse—but the President saw no reason to rush such a decision. He therefore asked whether "it wouldn't be possible for us to build a large force in England and leave the actual decision" as to its use "in abeyance for a month or two."

General Marshall took the point—saying he "would have a study prepared as to the limiting dates before which a decision must be made."[12]

General Henry "Hap" Arnold, the Army Air Forces commanding officer, did not dare say a word—and Admiral King, embarrassed, very few.

There would, then, be no immediate decision on a U.S. Second Front in France that year—leaving the chiefs ample opportunity to discuss, with the British at Casablanca, the question of whether to assault Sardinia or Sicily if they crossed the Mediterranean after securing Tunis.

This left only the overall politico-military strategy of the war to be addressed. Which, without further ado, the President now rehearsed. "The President said he was going to speak to Mr. Churchill about the advisability of informing Mr. Stalin that the United Nations were to continue on until they reach Berlin," the minutes of the meeting recorded, "and that their only terms would be unconditional surrender."[13]

In the months and years that followed, wild claims would be made that, at Casablanca, the President had thoughtlessly and unilaterally announced a misguided war policy that "naturally increased the enemy's will to resist and forced even Hitler's worst enemies to continue fighting to save their country," as the chief planner on Marshall's team at Casablanca put it.[14]

Moreover, that it was a policy his own staff vainly disagreed with,[15] and that neither Churchill, his staff, nor his government had had any idea of it, prior to the President's announcement.[16]

Like so much popular history, this allegation lacked substance. Not only had the President discussed the matter with Prime Minister Mackenzie King a month prior to the White House meeting with the U.S. Chiefs of Staff, but the President's determination to pursue unconditional surrender of the Axis powers had been widely discussed by Sumner Welles's committees when conceptualizing the United Nations authority and end-of-war requirements — which were in turn shared with senior British government officers. In speaking of it to his generals on January 7, 1943, the President made clear his wish that the chiefs factor this objective into their discussions on military strategy with the British at Casablanca. Thanks to Torch, the war against Germany and Japan was no longer one of defense against Axis attack, but of Allied offense — offense that would not stop until Berlin was reached, and then Tokyo.

No negotiations. No ifs and buts. No concessions, or anything that could later be revoked. Nothing but *complete and unconditional* surrender of the Germans and Japanese, and their "disarmament after the war," as the President put it to his Joint Chiefs of Staff, sharing with them as well his notion of a four-nation postwar policing force on behalf of the United Nations, which they, as the U.S. Joint Chiefs of Staff, would have to lead.[17]

As for the cross-Channel invasion, he would, the President said, follow the Combined Chiefs' advice on the timing "as they thought best." For himself, he was anxious to hammer out with America's allies not only the matter of German and Japanese postwar disarmament but other "political questions" that he would discuss with Mr. Churchill at Casablanca — and hopefully then at another "meeting between Mr. Churchill, the Generalissimo [Chiang Kai-shek], Mr. Stalin and himself some time next summer," perhaps at the port of Nome, in Alaska, which was also the final stop for planes flying Lend-Lease supplies to the Soviet Union.

The Joint Chiefs did not demur. With that — save for a brief discussion of planes for Russia, and French sovereignty versus U.S. military government in North Africa — the meeting ended. The Commander in Chief had spoken, and the chiefs had been given their orders. They would depart that very evening for North Africa, where the President was to join them on January 14, if all went well.

PART THREE

Casablanca

9

The House of Happiness

EARLY ON THE morning of January 14, 1943, the President and his party boarded a four-engine Douglas C-54 Skymaster of U.S. Air Transport Command about twenty miles outside Bathurst. "Normally, the air route from Bathurst to Casablanca would be entirely over land," Captain Mc-Crea later recalled. "On this occasion," however, "a swing to seaward was made in order to afford the President an aerial view of Dakar and St. Louis, Senegal, French West Africa."[1]

The route would allow the President to see the coastline he'd studied for over a year, when thinking about a possible U.S. invasion of Northwest Africa — especially Dakar. First occupied by tribal Africans, then Portuguese, Dutch, British, and finally French slave traders, Dakar was a fabled port. Following the French surrender at Compiègne in 1940, it had posed the danger that, if occupied by the Germans, it could become an impregnable African base for German naval and U-boat operations in the southern Atlantic. Thanks to Torch, however, it was now under American control — the port and fortress having been ceded by its governor-general to General Eisenhower and his French commissioner, Admiral Darlan, on December 7, 1942.

Passing over Dakar, "the French Battleship *Richelieu* was clearly observed alongside a seawall as were several other ships at anchor in the harbor," McCrea noted. There was a special reason, also, that Roosevelt wished to see the battleship, for it symbolized both the challenge and the success of Torch. With its eight fifteen-inch guns, eighty-five-hundred-mile cruising range, and fifteen-hundred-man crew, the *Richelieu* had been the first modern battleship built by the French since the 1922 Naval Treaty. Completed in 1940, too late to defend France against the Nazis, it had nevertheless helped defeat France's former allies and anti-Nazis—

Major General Charles de Gaulle's ill-fated attempt to seize the seaport on behalf of the Free French having been ignominiously repelled that year. For two years the *Richelieu* had then stood sentinel against the Allies, on behalf of the Vichy government and in accordance with the terms of Maréchal Philippe Pétain's capitulation to the Third Reich.

An hour later, two hundred miles further north, at the mouth of the Senegal River, the C-54 flew over "the very old French port" of Saint-Louis as well — giving the Allies two American-controlled ports which, thanks to their strategic importance on the Atlantic seaboard, were to be of inestimable significance to the Allies for the remainder of the war. "Then inland over the desert," the President described his route in a letter he penned that night to Daisy.

On the early-morning drive to the Bathurst airfield, Roosevelt had been upset by the extreme poverty of the people — which said very little for the British and their colonial rule over Gambia, despite having suppressed the slave trade in 1833. Now, over the West African desert, there were no people at all. "Never saw it before — worse than our Western Desert — Not flat at all & not as light as I had thought," he described to Daisy, " — more a brown yellow, with lots of rocks and wind erosion."[2]

The Skymaster, with its wingspan of 117 feet and space for forty-nine troops, was not nearly as luxurious as the Pan American Clipper. For five hours they flew at six thousand feet, until at last they caught sight, inland, of "a great chain of mountains — snowy top," Roosevelt recorded — explaining that the "Atlas run from the Coast in Southern Morocco East and North, then East again till they lose themselves in Tunis": the goal of General Eisenhower's current campaign.

"In approaching the Atlas mountains the cruising altitude was gradually increased from 8,000 feet to 12,000 feet," Captain McCrea remembered the flight — adding his own vivid recollection of how he'd persuaded the President to take oxygen for the first time. "The President was seated amidships, on the starboard side of the plane," he recalled — ever the naval officer. "I was seated directly across the aisle from him, & Ron McIntire was seated immediately in front of me. Harry Hopkins was seated well forward in the plane. Both Ron and I were quickly aware that the pilot was increasing altitude gradually. Ron suggested that I enquire from our pilot as to how much altitude he was going to level off at. This I did." Told that the pilot expected to cruise at about twelve thousand feet, "I squared away in my seat," and the President's doctor, "turning outboard, addressed me in a low tone of voice over his shoulder. 'John,' said he, 'how about putting on your oxygen mask? I want the President to put his on but if I suggest it to him he will no doubt make a fuss. If he sees you put on your mask he no doubt will follow.' In a few seconds I reached for my mask and proceeded to adjust it. Sure enough when the Pres. saw me putting on my mask he started to fumble with his. I promptly moved across the aisle, straightened out his mask harness and adjusted it for him." The doctor then put his own mask on, as did Hopkins — "And thus we were all set when shortly thereafter we reached 12,000 feet — an altitude which [was] maintained while crossing the Atlas Mountains."[3]

"We flew over a pass at 10,000 ft. & I tried a few whiffs of oxygen," the President wrote that night to Daisy. In truth he was more interested in the terrain than the air. "North of the Mts. we suddenly descended over the first oasis of Marrakesh — a great city going back to the Berbers even before the Arabs came — We may go there if Casablanca is bombed."[4]

They were approaching the battlefield.

In Washington the President had done his homework on the Berbers — Lieutenant George Elsey, in the Map Room, managing to get Lieutenant Commander S. E. Morison, a distinguished naval scholar from Harvard, a fifteen-minute interview with the President, "who asked questions I was unable to answer," as Morison subsequently wrote Elsey. Morison had therefore researched a "brief memorandum" on the subject of the Berbers for the President.[5] In this, the historian had pointed out that the Berbers, according to Egyptian inscriptions, dated as far back as 1700 B.C., and were "an entirely distinct race from the Phoenecian [*sic*] Carthaginians, who are comparative newcomers in Africa." The Berbers, by contrast, were "the aborigines of North Africa, with a distinct language and writing," and possibly the original inhabitants of the Iberian Peninsula. "They are a 'white' or 'Nordic' race, brown or hazel eyed, and no darker than the North American Indians in complexion."[6]

Morison's report had only whetted the President's curiosity aboard the C-54 Skymaster as they approached Casablanca — which, despite air raid sirens going off at various times, was not in fact targeted by long-range German bombers from Tunisia. For all their vaunted efficiency, it seemed the Germans had no idea the President was planning to meet Churchill there, let alone intending to stay almost two weeks — Goebbels recording, afterward, his near-disbelief that the *Sicherheitsdienst* of the great Third Reich had actually intercepted enemy phone calls, yet had taken the name Casablanca to be Casa Blanca, or White House, Washington, D.C.[7]

Those "in the know" at the real White House, however, had remained on tenterhooks lest the President, whose leadership of the Allies seemed so crucial to winning the war, fall victim to accident or assassination.

In particular, Mike Reilly, head of the White House Secret Service detail, had furiously objected to the idea of such a well-known venue — fears that had only increased when he arrived in Casablanca in advance of the President. Concerned the city was full of agents, assassins, and former Vichy officials of dubious reliability, Reilly had instantly tried to have the summit moved to Marrakesh, several hours' drive further south. Told that only the President could order this, he'd nevertheless persuaded the U.S. Joint Chiefs of Staff, who'd arrived on January 12, not to go meet the U.S. Commander in Chief in person on his arrival at Medouina airport on the afternoon of January 14, lest they attract unwarranted attention.

Landing at the airfield, the President was not in the least put out. Filming of a new Hollywood movie called *Casablanca* had, by complete coincidence, recently been completed in Los Angeles, and had been flown to Washington and shown to the President at the White House on Christmas Eve. The film — starring Humphrey Bogart, Paul Henreid, and Ingrid Bergman — had charmed him, and the climax at the faux-Medouina airport ("Round up the usual suspects!") had made him much more interested in the fabled city, its kasbah, its émigrés and spies, than in presidential protocol. "At last at 4 p.m. Casablanca & the ocean came in sight — I was landed at a field 22 miles from the town," he recorded in his letter to Daisy. "Who do you suppose was at the airport?" he wrote rhetorically. Not the U.S. chiefs but Lieutenant Colonel Elliott Roosevelt, his second son, standing beside Mike Reilly! And "looking very fit & mighty proud of his D.F.C. [Distinguished Flying Cross]"[8] — awarded for dangerous low-level reconnaissance missions, flown both before and during the Torch invasion.

As Roosevelt proudly told his son when they got into the camouflaged car, this trip marked the first time he'd flown in a decade. And with that the President shared with Elliott his amazement at the progress in air travel in only a few decades. There had been some flights in his early career that had been positively hair-raising, he recounted, when he was assistant secretary from 1913 to 1920. "In naval airplanes. Inspection trips.

The kind of flying," he chuckled, thinking of the open biplane cockpits, "*you'll* never know." By contrast, this, his first transatlantic trip, had given him a dramatic idea of "what so many of our flyers are doing, the sort of thing aviation's going through these days, and developments of flying. Gives me," he'd told Elliott — who knew this far better than his father — "a perspective."[9]

Father and son were then "driven under heavy guard & in a car with soaped windows" not to Rick's Café, the President wrote Daisy, but to "this delightful villa belonging to a Mme. Bessan whose army husband is a prisoner in France — She & her child were ejected as were the other cottage owners & sent to the hotel in town."[10]

He had, in short, arrived.

Selection of the villa, indeed of the city, had only been made a few weeks earlier by Eisenhower's chief of staff, Walter Bedell Smith, and Churchill's military assistant, Brigadier Ian Jacob.

Jacob had judged Casablanca a far better location than Fedala, further north and also on the ocean. The Villa Dar es Saada, in particular, had "the most magnificent drawing room leading out on to a large verandah," plus a dining room at one end, and a "principal bedroom complete with private bathroom" at the other, on the same floor. There were two further rooms upstairs. Along with thirteen other villas it was situated in a "garden suburb" of Casablanca known as Anfa: an area a mile wide, built "on a knoll about a mile inland and 5 miles south-west of the center of town." There was a large forty-room hotel nearby for the Combined Chiefs of Staff and their staffs, with a "view out over the Atlantic, or overland to Casablanca" that was "truly magnificent," as Jacob noted in an account he wrote at the time. "The dazzling blue of the water, the white of the buildings in Casablanca, and the red soil dotted with green palms and bougainvillea and begonia," he recorded, "made a beautiful picture in the sunlight"[11] — bounded, by the time the President arrived, with hastily erected barbed wire, antiaircraft guns, and an entire U.S. infantry battalion restricting all access to a single checkpoint.

Although elaborate steps, Elliott Roosevelt later recalled, had been taken to keep news of the President's impending arrival quiet, the heavily guarded compound could have fooled no one — least of all the "French fascists" left behind by the hastily departing French-German 1940 armistice team. Such individuals were armed, as Elliott caustically put it, "with German money in their pockets."[12] After several air raid alarms — though no German planes — Mike Reilly had certainly had enough, however. Having persuaded the U.S. Chiefs of Staff not to greet the President at the airport, or even at his villa, he now begged them to use their collective military influence, once they did see the President, to get him to change his plans and move south to safer quarters in Marrakesh.

Warned of this, Roosevelt dismissed the very idea. As president he was U.S. commander in chief. He felt on top form — even without his chief of staff, who he'd counted on to keep his Joint Chiefs of Staff in line. Casablanca was the scene of recent battle, and one of the largest artificial ports in the world. Having spent four days and nights getting to the city in a succession of trains, floatplanes, tenders, transport aircraft, and limousines, he was "'agin' it," and "said so, often enough and forcefully enough," Elliott remembered, "to carry the day."[13]

In the meantime he wanted to see where he'd sleep.

"When Father got his first look," Elliott remembered, "he whistled."[14]

The bedroom's décor reminded the President of a French brothel. "Now all we need is the madam of the house," he laughed, throwing back his head. "Plenty of drapes, plenty of frills," Elliott recalled. "And a bed that was — well, perhaps not all wool, but at least three yards wide. And his bathroom featured one of those sunken bathtubs, in black marble."[15]

The plumbing, too, worked fine. Wheeling his father around the house, Elliott found him more at home than he could have imagined possible. Guarded by a battalion of U.S. troops, in an area of Morocco under American rather than French or British military command, the Villa Dar es Saada — meaning "House of Happiness" — was the finest private residence in the suburb. It boasted almost twenty-eight-foot-high ceilings, steel-shuttered windows, and looked out over a beautifully terraced garden with vine-covered trellis. The two rooms upstairs could be used as bedrooms — one for Hopkins, and one for Elliott.

Another of the President's sons, Lieutenant Franklin Roosevelt Jr., would also be coming — unannounced. His destroyer, the USS *Mayrant*, had covered the Torch invasion and was still stationed offshore. Learning of this and having once served as a midshipman with the regional naval commander (the brilliant Rear Admiral John L. Hall), Captain McCrea immediately arranged for FDR Jr. to be brought the next day to Anfa, without being told the reason. "He sighted me and burst out 'My God, Captain, is Pa here?'" McCrea recalled humorously. "I told him his suspicion was correct and I took him across the street" — telling him to be "prepared for a surprised parent. The Pres. indeed was surprised, and father and son indulged in fond embrace" — followed by "an invitation to stay for lunch which, of course, Franklin did."[16]

All in all the Villa Dar es Saada was a house of happiness, thanks to Brigadier Jacob: the President's pro tempore White House and his family residence, established in an American realm, guarded by American soldiers — not a British colony or quasi-colony, such as Khartoum or Cairo, the two cities Churchill had recommended.

Once installed, the President asked Harry Hopkins to go fetch Churchill, whose villa, the Mirador, was only "fifty yards away," as Hopkins recorded.[17] It would be the first time they'd seen each other since Churchill's fateful visit to Washington at the time of the British surrender of Tobruk, seven months before. The President could only marvel at how times had changed.

Churchill, for his part, was equally excited — in fact had arrived two days early to prepare for the arrival of the "Boss." In his speech at the Mansion House in London on November 10, 1942, announcing the success of Torch, Churchill had openly revealed that the "President of the United States, who is Commander in Chief of the armed forces of America, is the author of this mighty undertaking and in all of it I have been his active and ardent lieutenant."[18]

Reading the text of the speech, Hitler's Reichsminister für Propaganda had been fascinated. Churchill, Goebbels had noted in his diary, was not only openly ascribing the Allied victories to the huge superiority now enjoyed by American arms, but "he also admits that the whole invasion plan came from Roosevelt's brain, and that he is only a loyal servant to Roosevelt's plans."[19]

Hitherto, Goebbels had assumed from British newspaper articles that Churchill was the brains behind Allied operations in the European theater — something he'd found "comforting," as he'd noted cynically, "since all previous military operations he's been behind have ended up as disasters."[20] Churchill's public acknowledgment that the U.S. president was now in charge heralded something different — indeed, alarming.

"The Americans are now out of the starter's block. Their next target is Tripoli," Goebbels had recorded; in fact, idle armchair strategists in America and England were assuming the Allies would soon clear Axis forces from North Africa entirely. "They already imagine themselves invading Italy and foresee themselves invading Germany via the Brenner

Pass. All this, of course, a very simple and plausible calculation," Goebbels had added sarcastically, " — if it weren't for us being there!"[21]

This was the crux of the matter — for the quality of armed German
resistance was something the prognosticators of whom Goebbels spoke,
whether in the United States or Britain, seemed incapable of appreciating.
Tunisia was to be the key to thwarting Allied strategic ambitions, Goebbels had been told by the Führer — who saw the battle for Tunis becoming a new Verdun. "If we hang on to Tunis, then nothing is lost in North
Africa," he'd recorded. And already, as General Eisenhower and his invasion forces attempted to come to terms with the business of real combat
with real Germans — as opposed to ill-armed Vichy defenders — Hitler
was being proven right, on the field of battle rather than in the print of
newspaper columnists.[22]

Winston Churchill had been educated as a soldier at Sandhurst and
boasted a lifetime's military experience, from the North-West Frontier to
the Sudan and South Africa. Like so many commentators in the press, he
had visualized a swift Allied advance — by Montgomery's Eighth Army
marching from the east and by Eisenhower's First Army from the west.
"I never meant the Anglo-American Army to be stuck in North Africa,"
the Prime Minister had chided his British chiefs of staff on November
15, 1942, only a week after the Torch invasion — irritated by the celerity
with which Hitler had reinforced his meager forces in Tunisia by air, and
the slowness of British and American ground troops spearheading Eisenhower's thrust from Algeria. In one of his instantly memorable turns of
phrase, the Prime Minister had berated them, saying the Torch invasion
was "a springboard, and not a sofa."[23]

It became a classic Churchillian metaphor, oft repeated. In truth,
though, it masked a huge difference between Allied and German soldiery.
For the simple fact was, whether volunteers or conscripts, Allied soldiers
were not like the Germans or the Japanese. As Roosevelt had confided
in 1942 to Field Marshal John Dill, the British liaison to the Joint Chiefs
of Staff, Allied troops did not have, for the most part, the kind of ruthless, even fanatical obedience to orders and discipline that characterized
German and Japanese forces. Only by adopting a careful, step-by-step
approach to war, evading ventures that posed unnecessary risks; only by
undertaking offensive operations within the capabilities of Allied troops;
only by applying the advantages of U.S. mass production; and only by

pursuing global military strategies that built upon Allied strengths — fusing air, naval, and ground forces — could the Allies actually defeat the Wehrmacht and the Japanese. Not by prime ministerial exhortation, however inspiring.

Churchill's bon mot reflected an aging yet still wonderfully indefatigable English leader. At heart he remained a dashing young cavalryman, as on the North-West Frontier in his early days of service, or in the Sudan fighting the self-proclaimed Mahdi at the turn of the century, in 1898. Half a century later, his "Action this day" tags — the red stickers he would attach to his brilliantly written memos demanding immediate response by his staff — were a tribute to his abiding energy as he approached seventy: spearing lethargy and electrifying traditional British bureaucratic penpushers, sclerotic after centuries of imperial paperwork. However, they masked a profound flaw in the Prime Minister's makeup as his country's quasi–commander in chief in 1943: the irreconcilable difference between his grand strategic ideas and his too-often ill-considered opportunism — a difference affecting tens of thousands of soldiers' lives.

After the war the former prime minister would go to great lengths to cast himself, in his six-volume epic *The Second World War,* not only as a lonely oracle but architect of war. Inasmuch as he saw better than any of his contemporaries the ebb and flow of military history, necessitating that Britain withstand the predations of Hitler's Third Reich until it could be rescued, he was by 1943 being proven right. He had, after all, lost every battle against the Germans since 1940, yet with his U.S. partner in war was helping to force Hitler, thanks to Torch, onto the defensive. Once Tunis fell, the Allies would possess a springboard for eventual victory in Europe, he felt — provided the Russians continued to face the brunt of Hitler's Wehrmacht in the East. But beyond that his military strategy did not go, since he did not believe a cross-Channel attack could possibly succeed. In reality he had no idea how, in fact, the Third Reich could be defeated, beyond constant peripheral pressure and air attack.

As the two Allied leaders met at 6:00 p.m. at the President's villa on January 14, 1943, there was thus, behind the bonhomie and goodwill, a distinct divergence of opinion. The Prime Minister's agenda was how to placate the United States, defer operations against Japan, and by "closing the ring" around the Third Reich — sheering off its allies, such as Italy, as they went, and hoping to get the peoples of occupied Europe to rise up against the Germans — engender Hitler's fall, followed by that of Hirohito. Thence to return the world, as he saw it, to its former European imperialist setup, before the Führer, the Duce, and Tojo's gang of admirals and generals had upset the balance of power.

The President, for his part, had a quite different vision. Not only a vision of the future, but how to achieve that future: the endgame. Their clash of objectives in Casablanca, behind the scenes, thus promised to be historic.

10

Hot Water

Knowing via Field Marshal Dill, in Washington, that the U.S. chiefs of staff did not favor a delay in launching a Second Front that year, Churchill had told his British chiefs they would have to do again what they had done the previous spring: show willing, while stringing the Americans along, in order to pursue a more opportunistic course in the Mediterranean. The chiefs of staff were thus merely to pretend to be agreeable to closing down "the Mediterranean activities by the end of June with a view to 'Round-up'"—an Allied 1943 cross-Channel invasion—"in August." The final decision on a Second Front, however, would be made, he instructed them, "on the highest levels"—i.e., by himself and the President.[1] For Mr. Roosevelt, he was sure, would agree with him it was impossible: the Germans, in northern France, were just too strong in the number of divisions they had there.

With this in mind Churchill had made haste to set off for Casablanca on January 11, together with a huge retinue of staff officers and clerks. Bad weather threatened to vitiate his plan—but had not stopped it.

Serving as Churchill's military assistant, Brigadier Ian Jacob had been wary of the contingent the Prime Minister was taking, instead of the small staff the President had requested. "I was rather horrified at the size of the party which had been gotten together," Jacob wrote in his contemporary account. "The whole added up to a pretty formidable total."[2] Some members of the party could, of course, be concealed and housed onboard the communications ship that was being sent out, HMS *Bulolo*, he recognized. "But knowing as I did from conversations with Beetle [Bedell] Smith that the Americans would bring a very modest team, I was rather afraid that the President or the Chiefs of Staff might take offense at the size of our party, & that the success of the conference might be endangered. I put this point to the P.M. on Sunday morning before I left Chequers [the prime ministerial retreat], & he said the party was to be cut down. However, when we went into the question on Monday with the Chiefs of Staff we found that there were few if any people who could be discarded, & it was decided that the best policy would be to take a full bag of clubs, leaving some of them concealed as it were in the locker — i.e. the ship."[3]

Despite bad weather delaying the takeoff of the main Boeing Clipper, Churchill had insisted the primary team fly still on January 13 using land-based aircraft. The staff were thus farmed out among four RAF American-built Liberator (B-24) planes, each of which could normally take only seven "passengers." As a result the Prime Minister had found himself cramped in a bomb bay bunk, flying without heat, which had not left him in the best of moods. This had not improved when, after asking his man-servant, Sawyers, to run him a bath on arrival at the Villa Mirador, he had found it neither hot nor deep enough. "You might have thought the end of the world had come," Jacob described. "Everyone was sent for in turn, all were fools, and finally the P.M. said he wouldn't stay a moment longer, & would move into the hotel [Anfa] or to Marrakesh" — where he'd spent a pleasant month in 1932.[4]

In the event, food and drink — drink especially — had "had its mellow-ing influence," as the Prime Minister lunched with General Marshall and the Fifth U.S. Army commander, Lieutenant General Mark Clark, and "the excitement died down. Plumbers were assembled from all directions, and somehow or other the water was kept hot in the future."[5]

Bath or no bath, Churchill did, however, take great pains to be amenable to Marshall and Clark — reporting to the British chiefs of staff on the eve-ning of their first day's work in Casablanca, on January 13, that "some kind" of cross-Channel "Sledgehammer" operation in Brittany would have to be undertaken that very year, if only to support U.S. efforts. "Only in this way should we be taking our fair share of the burden of the war," he'd told them at their first meeting with him, at 4.30 p.m.[6]

Brigadier Jacob also noted, however, the Prime Minister's openness to undertaking different operations. The son of a field marshal, Jacob was a first-class administrator, with a crystal-clear mind, fair judgment, loyalty to his superiors, and a talent for lucid exposition, which the Prime Min-ister particularly valued. A U.S. agenda had been lined up and sent from Washington, which "contained a list of every topic under the sun, but the most important thing," the military assistant noted, "was to get settled in broad outline our combined strategy for 1943, and then to get down to brass tacks and decide how exactly to carry it out. One couldn't decide in detail what to do unless one knew what one's strategic aim was to be. At the same time one could hardly fix one's strategic aims unless one examined in detail what operations we were capable of carrying out and what we were not."[7]

"Not" meant a cross-Channel invasion that year.

Jacob did try to see the problem from a U.S. perspective, however, asking Sir John Dill's view as the British representative on the Combined Chiefs of Staff in Washington — and was not surprised when Dill warned that there was a "general fear of commitments in the Mediterranean, and secondly, a suspicion that we did not understand the Pacific problem and would not put our backs into the work there once Germany had been defeated. Thus although the Americans were honestly of the opinion that Germany was the primary enemy, they did not see how quite to deal with her, especially as they felt there were urgent and great tasks to be done in Burma and the Pacific." These tasks involved logistical and operational struggles between General MacArthur and Admiral Nimitz — the Army versus the Navy in terms of distribution of resources — and the right combination of those forces and campaign strategy. They had already led to much infighting, as well as uneven effort, such as at Guadalcanal, "where the U.S. Marines were thrown ashore, and then it was found that there was no follow-up, no maintenance organization, and no transport."[8]

Along with the British chiefs of staff, the Prime Minister also interrogated Dill, who repeated his assessment of U.S. positions and problems. Delighted that he'd come early to the conference, Churchill was sure he could handle the President. The Prime Minister's "view was clear," Jacob recorded Churchill's approach, expressed now in front of Dill and the British chiefs of staff. "He wanted to take plenty of time. Full discussion, no impatience — the dripping of water on a stone." The big British contingent was to methodically wean the small American team away from its fixation on a major cross-Channel assault that year to more gradual, peripheral operations in the Mediterranean, with a smaller operation in Brittany, perhaps, to get a toehold at least on the continent. "In the meantime," while the chiefs met their opposite numbers in the daily Combined Chiefs of Staff meetings at the Anfa Hotel, "he would be working on the President, and in ten days or a fortnight," Churchill was confident, "everything would fall into place. He also made no secret of the fact that he was out to get agreement on a programme of operations for 1943 which the Military people might well think beyond our powers, but which he felt was the least that could be thought worthy of two great powers."[9]

To the alarm of the British chiefs, then, the Prime Minister was all for action, on multiple fronts. To start with, he "wanted the cleansing of the North African shore to be followed by the capture of Sicily. He wanted the reconquest of Burma, and he wanted the invasion of Northern France, on a moderate scale perhaps. Operations in the Pacific should not be such as to prevent fulfilment of his programme. The Chiefs of Staff were dismissed on this note, and the rest of the evening," before the President's arrival the next day, "was given up to ice-breaking dinner parties."[10]

11

A Wonderful Picture

PRESIDENT ROOSEVELT, for his part, was all for icebreaking. "I marveled at the way the Army just moved in and took charge and ran the whole operation," even Captain McCrea later noted — speaking as a sailor.[1]

Brigadier Jacob, who had reconnoitered and recommended the venue, was equally delighted by the U.S. Army's efforts, especially the catering: "certainly excellent, mostly U.S. Army rations, too. Of course it was supplemented with local produce," including oranges, which — "large and juicy, with the best flavor of any oranges in the world" — formed "a part of every meal." The "cooking too was good, and as again the whole thing was free, a genial warmth spread over our souls," he recorded.[2]

McCrea agreed. "So well was this done that on the first evening of our arrival the President was able to entertain at dinner Prime Minister Churchill and the Combined Chiefs of Staff (both the U.S. Joint Chiefs and British Chiefs of Staff), plus Col. Roosevelt and Averell Harriman — some twelve persons in all."[3]

Churchill had hurried over with Hopkins at around 7:00 p.m. No formal notes were made of what was said between the President and Prime Minister, but the "three of us had a long talk over the military situation," Hopkins wrote in his notes that night.[4] The winter weather in the mountains had slowed the campaign in Tunisia, and Montgomery had yet to take Tripoli and advance toward Tunisia, but the plan of campaign was that the two Allied pincers would eventually trap the German and Italian forces in the Cape Bon Peninsula: forcing them either to attempt a Dunkirk-style evacuation or surrender. It was what would happen thereafter — locally, regionally, and internationally — that was the biggest problem to be resolved in the coming days.

The Combined Chiefs of Staff had been having cocktails at the Anfa Hotel when Hopkins arrived with the presidential summons. Dutifully, the bevy of generals and admirals — Generals Marshall and Arnold, Admiral King, General Alan Brooke, Admiral Dudley Pound, Air Marshal Charles Portal, Admiral Louis Mountbatten, as well as the Lend-Lease administrator, Averell Harriman — trooped over.

The dinner, in the President's villa, went rather well. "People were tired, that first night," Elliott recalled, "but it didn't stop anybody from enjoying himself" — particularly as there was no attempt to limit the consumption of wine or liquor.[5] General Hap Arnold recounted how he had just been down to the harbor to see the damage inflicted on the brand-new French battleship *Jean Bart* during the Torch invasion — the airman delighted to see that American thousand-pound bombs had smashed "holes in bow and stern large enough to take a small bungalow."[6] Others gave their own impressions of the city and its kasbah.

Admiral King "became nicely lit up towards the end of the evening," Brooke scrawled in his diary that night. "As a result" the admiral became "more and more pompous, and with a thick voice and many gesticulations explained to the President the best way to organize the Political French organization for control of North Africa!" — something King would never have dared do when sober. "This led to arguments with PM who failed to appreciate fully the condition King was in. Most amusing to watch."[7]

The dinner was certainly a far cry from life at Hitler's headquarters in East Prussia, where the Führer had ceased to dine with his senior military staff. He'd stopped listening even to music at night, refused to go near the battle front or to make any public pronouncements — and was still demanding that no mention be made in the Nazi media of the increasingly catastrophic situation around Stalingrad.

"I busied myself filling glasses," Elliott Roosevelt later recalled. "After dinner, Father and Churchill sat down on a big, comfortable couch that had been set back to the big windows. The steel shutters were closed. The rest of us pulled up chairs in a semicircle in front of the two on the couch."[8] "Many things discussed," Arnold noted in his diary — including their leaders' safety. "Everyone tried to keep President and Prime Minister from making plans to get too near front," given that both men "seemed determined" to go, and "could see no real danger."[9]

"We have come many miles and must stay long enough to solve very important problems," Arnold finished his nightly jotting — aware how much responsibility the President carried, for good or ill. And he quoted the British prime minister, whose words had the sober ring of history, despite the immense quantity of alcohol the Prime Minister had imbibed. "Churchill: 'This is the most important meeting so far. We must not relinquish initiative now that we have it. You men are the ones who have the facts and who will make plans for the future.'"[10]

An air raid siren then wailed, bringing the postprandial get-together almost to a close. "At about 1:30 a.m. an alarm was received," General Brooke noted in green ink in his own leather-bound diary, "lights were put out, and we sat around the table with faces lit by 6 candles. The PM and President in that light and surroundings would have made," he scribbled, "a wonderful picture."[11]

Rembrandt might have painted it, but sadly, no photographs were taken that evening — though other, iconic photos would be, at the climax of the conference, ten days later. None could fail to be aware, however, just how symbolic was the meeting: the leaders of the two main Western democracies, gathering together with their chiefs of staff on the still-scarred battlefield of a foreign land, there to plan the further strategy and military operations against Hitler's Germany, Mussolini's Italy, and Hirohito's Japan. There would clearly be problems, especially political; but the new, dominating role of the United States was unmistakable — visible not only in the planes, tanks, artillery, and equipment factories were churning out at an ever-increasing rate across North America but their presence now in Northwest Africa, thousands of miles from American shores, barely eight weeks since the huge and successful amphibious U.S. invasion.

Not all was positive in the House of Happiness, however.

"Well after midnight, the P.M. took his leave," Elliott later recalled. The President "was tired but still in a talkative mood" — and talk he did to his son. To Elliott the President confided his continuing distrust not only of the French, in regard to their tottering colonial empire, but of Churchill, too, in that respect. This might well complicate his dream of a United Nations authority committed to the principles of the Atlantic Charter, after the war. "The English mean to maintain their hold on their colonies. They mean to help the French maintain *their* hold on *their* colonies. Winnie is a great man for the status quo," the President said sadly to Elliott. "He even *looks* like the status quo, doesn't he?"[12]

Elliott's version of events was considered suspect by some, but Prime Minister Mackenzie King's contemporary record of his stay at the White House the previous month, as well as the diary kept by Daisy Suckley, the President's cousin, would lend credence to the overall veracity of Elliott's account, published immediately after the war's end. The President had disliked Admiral Darlan — but that did not mean he approved of de Gaulle, who harbored dictatorial ambitions. "Elliott," the President said to his son, "de Gaulle is out to achieve one-man government in France" — and was committed to the revival of its colonial empire. "I can't imagine a man I would distrust more. His whole Free French movement is honeycombed with police spies — he has agents spying on his own people. To him, freedom of speech means freedom from criticism . . . of him."[13]

Which led the President to turn to "the problem of the colonies and the colonial markets, the problem of which he felt was at the core of all chances for future peace" across the globe. "'The thing is,' he remarked thoughtfully, replacing a smoked cigarette in his holder with a fresh one, 'the colonial system means war. Exploit the resources of an India, a Burma, a Java; take all the wealth out of those countries, but never put anything back into them, things like education, decent standards of living, minimum health requirements — all you're doing is storing up the kind of trouble that leads to war. All you're doing is negating the value of any kind of organizational structure for peace before it begins." And with that he'd chortled: "The look that Churchill gets on his face when you mention India!"[14]

To Elliott the President then explained his notion of trusteeships: that "France should be restored as a world power, then to be entrusted with her former colonies as a trustee. As trustee, she was to report each year on the progress of her stewardship, how the literacy rate was improving, how the death rate declining, how disease being stamped out, how . . ."[15]

Phased decolonization, under the aegis of the United Nations, in other words.

"Wait a minute," Elliott had countered, "Who's she going to report all this to?"

And with that his father had set out — to Elliott's amazement — his vision of the "United Nations" postwar "organization." Also his notion of policemen: the "big Four — ourselves, Britain, China, the Soviet Union —

we'll be responsible for the peace of the world" — once the war was won. "It's already high time for us to be thinking of the future, building for it," Roosevelt remarked.[16]

"Three-thirty, Pop," his son pointed out.

"Yes. Now I *am* tired," the President acknowledged. "Get some sleep yourself, Elliott."[17]

And with that the eve of the defining conference of World War II came to a close.

12

In the President's Boudoir

ELLIOTT OVERSLEPT. When he staggered downstairs for breakfast on January 15, it was to find the U.S. Joint Chiefs of Staff already assembled in his father's boudoir.

It was 10:00 a.m. — and the President was listening to what had transpired at the preliminary Combined Chiefs of Staff meeting the previous day, at the Anfa Hotel.

In insisting the conference take place in American-held Morocco, the President had chosen wisely — for it was vital the U.S. chiefs be exposed to the actual Torch battlefield in Northwest Africa. Instead of concocting strategy and operations thousands of miles away, in the safety and comfort of the Pentagon and the Mall, they would have a chance to meet the men and commanders on the ground who were fighting Germans now, not Vichy French troops. It was also crucial that the U.S. chiefs be separated for a time from their dangerously irresponsible planners, who had very little idea of modern hostilities in facing the Wehrmacht — or the fanatical Japanese. In the many documents accumulating in his Map Room at the White House — U.S. Joint Chiefs of Staff minutes, Combined Chiefs of Staff minutes, Joint Strategic Survey minutes, Joint Intelligence Committee minutes, Joint Staff Planners Reports, recommendations and analyses of the differences between British and U.S. strategic views since November 1942 — he had never seen a single mention of the need for American combat experience.

The plethora of paper evinced dutiful, unstinting research and statistical evidence gathered in Washington — but no common sense. That the Western Allies were holding half of the Luftwaffe's entire operational strength on the Western and Mediterranean Fronts was calculated down to the nearest plane; the number of Wehrmacht divisions capable of offensive and defensive operations was tallied and enumerated; the amount of German naval vessels and U-boats estimated. Yet the need for American battle *experience* — and lessons — in matching up to professional German foes had seemed a closed book to such bureaucrats and staffers.

At the time of Casablanca — as well as after the war — there would thus be righteous indignation over the President's decision to allow only a handful of staff officers to accompany the U.S. chiefs on the trip to North Africa. Led by the War Office's chief planning officer, Brigadier General Albert Wedemeyer — who was one of the few permitted to travel with General Marshall to Casablanca — these men would complain they had been thrown to English wolves: a British prime minister taking with him a vast retinue of planners and operations officers and clerks committed to a vague British, rather than an Allied, military strategy for 1943.

Wedemeyer, in particular, would complain they'd been duped; that the President had made a terrible mistake; had through naiveté brought a military team simply too small to confront the host of staff officers accompanying the wily Churchill. Moreover, that the British had tricked the American contingent into abandoning their preferred Second Front invasion that summer, 1943. The British staff officers, Wedemeyer would complain, had been backed by yet *more* staffers aboard HMS *Bulolo*, anchored for their special use in Casablanca Harbor. Using this communications ship, the British planners were able to cable London and put their hands on any fact or figure they needed to support their alternative British plans, and thus defeat American counterproposals; whereas the U.S. contingent, despite being in a U.S. compound in a U.S. military area guarded by U.S. artillery and antiaircraft guns, was virtually captive in terms of British bureaucratic firepower.

"They swarmed upon us all like locusts," Wedemeyer lamented in a letter from North Africa to General Thomas Handy, the assistant chief of staff in the War Department's Operations Division (OPD) in Washington, and "had us on the defensive practically all the time" — backed by "a plentiful supply of planners and various other assistants, with prepared plans to insure that they not only accomplished their purpose but did so in stride and with fair promise of continuing in the role of directing strategy the whole course of the war."[1]

General Wedemeyer was certainly not alone in perceiving a British conspiracy to subvert the swifter course of World War II. General Handy, who received Wedemeyer's letter in Washington and passed it on to other generals at the Pentagon, was of like mind, bewailing afterward that "the British on the planning level just snowed them under."[2]

Yet another U.S. planner later recalled how "we were overwhelmed by the large British staff."

Brigadier General J. E. Hull, heading up the OPD at the Pentagon, was even more embarrassed than Wedemeyer and Handy by the U.S. unpreparedness for paper battle. "The British had come down there in droves," he later recalled, "and every one of them had written a paper about something that was submitted by the British Chiefs of Staff to the American chiefs of Staff for agreement."[3]

In sum, "We came, we listened," Wedemeyer recoined Caesar's famous epigram, "and we were conquered."[4]

All this was true — bearing out Brigadier Jacob's nervousness at the size of the British team Churchill insisted should be flown to Casablanca. Yet in terms of the Allied strategy that President Roosevelt was now to lay down at Casablanca, it completely missed the point. For the reality was: Wedemeyer and his colleagues were still living in a fool's paradise. And the moment of truth — not only the President's truth, but truth on the ground — had arrived.

Inexperienced U.S. planning officers like Brigadier General Wedemeyer were the real problem — not the British.

The U.S. War Department's final planning document, produced by the Joint Strategic Survey Committee and sent over to the White House Map Room for the President to review before he departed from Washington, had said it all: stating baldly that once Tunisia and Libya were secured, the Allies' Mediterranean Front should be closed down. Mussolini's Italy, in the planning committee's view, could be forced to surrender by air bombing alone. All U.S. Army forces should be switched to Britain "for a land offensive against Germany in 1943" — without gaining any further amphibious experience, or campaign lessons in facing and fighting German forces.[5]

Thankfully the President had confided to Mackenzie King, in early December, his unwillingness to tackle a cross-Channel invasion before American commanders and troops were blooded and had the measure of their opponents — which could best be done in the Mediterranean, where this could be achieved, as he said, without risking a major setback. His interrogation of General Marshall at the White House before the chiefs left for Casablanca on January 7 had only convinced him more deeply that a premature invasion of northern France would be a disaster — and he had insisted no decision should therefore be made for several months. It was thus with decided relief that President Roosevelt found, at midmorning in his bedroom on his first full day in Casablanca, January 15, 1943, that the penny had finally dropped, at least among his chiefs of staff.

Making his chiefs fly to Casablanca had, he found, already worked — without British intervention. Once in Morocco, Marshall had finally talked to Allied commanders on the battlefield. As Marshall now confessed in the villa's bordello-like bedroom, he had spoken not only to Admiral Mountbatten — the British chief of Combined Operations, who'd been responsible for the disastrous Dieppe landings — but at great length with General Mark Clark. Clark had been Eisenhower's deputy in the Torch invasion, and had just been promoted to command the U.S. Fifth Army in Morocco, both to defend against mythical German invasion across the Mediterranean and prepare for future offensive operations. General Clark had informed the chief of staff of the U.S. Army that there was no chance of a cross-Channel operation succeeding in the summer of 1943.

No chance whatever.

This was music to the President's ears — for he had half-expected to have to do battle once again against his own team, lest in the interval since their meeting in the Oval Office on January 7 they revert to their insistence on a cross-Channel invasion in 1943.

General Clark's battlefield testimony, however, had applied the necessary dose of cold reality. Clark — a man who certainly did not lack courage, having fetched General Henri Giraud from Vichy-held southern France in person by submarine to assist in the Torch invasion — had been emphatic. To Marshall he'd explained that "there must be a long period of training before any attempt is made to land against determined resistance" — especially Wehrmacht resistance of the kind that would meet a cross-Channel invasion. In particular he'd "pointed out many of the mishaps that occurred in the landing in North Africa which would have been fatal had the resistance been more determined," as Marshall now relayed to the President.[6] In fact, General Clark had himself undergone a Pauline conversion. In London, the previous summer, he'd deplored the idea of landings in Northwest Africa as an unnecessary "sideshow."

Now, however, he felt American amphibious operations in 1943 "could be mounted more efficiently from North Africa" — and certainly with less loss of life — than from the British Isles and the United States, across the English Channel.[7]

Hitler's Atlantic Wall, the fighting general had made clear to Marshall, was no joke. The American military was not up to such a gargantuan task, he'd realized — and was backed by the latest British planning reports. The British, it seemed, had done the numbers that Marshall's team had failed to appreciate in Washington. They looked formidable. As General Brooke had pointed out in his first presentation on January 14, the day before, at the Anfa Hotel, "the rail net in Europe would permit the movement of seven [German] divisions a day from east to west which would enable them to reinforce their defenses of the northern coast of France rapidly."

A day?

By contrast, Marshall now acknowledged to the President, in the Mediterranean theater the Germans "can only move one division from north to south each day, in order to reinforce their defense of southern Europe."[8]

If the U.S. armies were to acquire the combat experience necessary to assault Hitler's Atlantic Wall, then it would best be gained in the Mediterranean, at the extremity of German lines of communication. Northern France was, by contrast, the very closest to the German border. General Clark thus favored a continuation of the war in the Mediterranean, Marshall admitted to the President, where "the lines of communication" for the Allies would be "shorter," and where the "troops in North Africa have had experience in landing operations." Not only did the Allies already possess sufficient American and British forces in the Mediterranean — naval, air, and ground — to knock Italy out of the war that year by invading Sardinia or Sicily "once the Axis had been forced out of Tunisia," but, as Clark had pointed out, the Mediterranean offered the opportunity for U.S. units to gain the battle exposure they needed, in a relatively secure environment where even local setbacks would not be disastrous to Allied strategy. This was something that could not be said for a premature cross-Channel assault.

Lest there be any misunderstanding, the necessary "training" for eventual combat against tough German defenders of the West Wall, Clark had repeated to Marshall, would be infinitely "more effective if undertaken in close contact with the enemy," in current combat. Not in the United States or Britain, Clark had insisted, but in real time, in the Mediterranean.[9]

In the strangest of venues, then, reality had finally set in. The Mediterranean, not northern France, should be the proving ground for as-yet-untested U.S. troops, Marshall now agreed — not only in terms of combat but in developing effective coalition command in 1943 — operations involving British, Canadian, French, and other forces, on a front where the Allies could steadily improve their fighting skills, however much the Russians would, doubtless, complain. Not to mention Marshall's Pentagon team.

Headed by Brigadier General Wedemeyer, Marshall's operations planners would be devastated, the President was aware — as would the secretary of war, Mr. Stimson. But Wedemeyer and Stimson were suffering from delusion — dangerous delusion. However doggedly they urged a cross-Channel attack that year, it was not their lives that would be on the line, but the lives of tens of thousands of Americans — facing a Wehrmacht whose true fighting ability they had not even begun to measure.

It was, as Captain McCrea recalled, a "long conference in the President's bed room" and one that only "broke up well past noon."[10]

This was, in retrospect, the turning point of the war, in terms of the Allied military struggle against the Axis powers — clinching not only the strategy but the timing of America's game plan in conducting World War II. Mass American suicide in a premature Second Front would once again be avoided that year, thanks to the President's military realism. Instead, mercifully, the United States military would back only those operations that promised success: success that would boost morale at home and validate the President's step-by-step strategy for prosecuting the war.

Victory rather than disaster: this would now be the order of the day.

As General Clark had now recommended, U.S. forces would be instructed to learn their deadly trade on the periphery of Europe that year, before meeting the deadliest challenge in 1944: one that even Hitler had balked at attempting in 1940, when Britain was on its knees: a massive cross-Channel invasion. Finally, after thirteen months of war, the Commander in Chief and his chiefs of staff were on the same page.

General Marshall's belated recognition, on January 15, that the President's strategy was probably right would now cement the methodical, stone-by-stone U.S. progress in World War II. The question of "What next?" after Tunisia was, effectively, over — before the first plenary session of the Combined Chiefs of Staff meetings began at the Anfa Hotel that afternoon.

American grand strategy for 1943 was clear: attritional warfare at the extremity of the enemy's lines of communication, enabling U.S. forces to learn how to defeat the Wehrmacht in battle.

And to make sure this policy had a good chance of succeeding, the President said he wanted to see the general commanding the Allies in the Mediterranean from his headquarters in Algiers: young General Dwight D. Eisenhower.

Eisenhower seemed to the President to be a bit "jittery" as, shortly before 4:00 p.m. on January 15, the two men sat down by the picture window in the President's villa, Dar es Saada.

It was for a good reason. General Dwight Eisenhower, or Ike, as he was familiarly known, had undergone a hair-raising flight from Algiers to see the President and the chiefs of staff. Two of his Flying Fortress's engines had conked out, and he'd been told he must get ready to parachute from the aircraft. This he'd begun to do — chiding, as he did so, his naval aide for the time it was taking him to refasten one of his general's shoulder pins, which had been accidentally knocked out. "Haven't you ever fastened a star before?" Ike had barked at the hapless officer, whose hands were shaking uncontrollably. "Yes, sir, but never with a parachute on," the aide had squeaked.[11]

Fortunately the pilot had nursed the surviving two engines long enough to land at Medouina airport, and Eisenhower had immediately been driven to the Anfa Hotel to appear before the Combined Chiefs of Staff.

Dissatisfied by Allied progress — or lack of progress — in Tunisia, the Combined Chiefs of Staff had treated the young general roughly, expressing frank disappointment at his failure to seize Tunis at the very start of the campaign, and also at the German rebuff given to his second attempt, earlier that month.

Eisenhower's logistical excuses had seemed somewhat lame to the chiefs, more than two months after the Torch landings. On paper, after all, he possessed more than three hundred thousand soldiers under his command in Northwest Africa, ranged against "only" sixty-five thousand

German troops in Tunisia. His latest plan for an end run — an armored right-hook thrusting out of the Tunisian mountains toward the sea at Sfax, designed to carve a wedge between von Arnim's army in Tunisia and Rommel's retreating army in Libya — sounded ill-conceived to General Brooke, who'd had actual battle experience against German forces in the spring and summer of 1940. Ultra decrypts that very day had shown Rommel to be dispatching the veteran Twenty-First Panzer Division from Libya to deal with just such an Allied threat. Instead of dividing and conquering the German forces in North Africa, the Anglo-American forces might themselves be split apart. Where was the doctrine of concentration of force rather than dispersion of effort — dispersion that could only encourage the Germans to see their chance to counterattack and defeat the Allies in detail?[12]

"Eisenhower is hopeless!" Brooke had noted in frustration in his diary, in late December, reflecting that the American general "submerges himself in politics and neglects his military duties, partly, I'm afraid, because he knows little if anything about military matters."[13]

Brooke was not alone in his criticism of Eisenhower. While "spying out the land" for the President and Prime Minister's visit, Brigadier Jacob, too, had been appalled by Eisenhower's Allied headquarters. "The chief impression I got was of a general air of restless confusion, with everyone trying their best in unnatural conditions. I was assured on all sides that there was no Anglo-American friction at all. But the simple fact of having a mixed staff is quite enough to reduce the overall efficiency by at least a half . . . The British members of the staff, who occupy many of the key positions, have to work with U.S. officers who are entirely ignorant and inexperienced, and have to operate on a system which is quite different from the one to which they are accustomed. They find their task harassing and irritating in the extreme. Many are inclined to doubt whether a combined Allied Staff is a practical arrangement, and think the experiment should not be repeated, and should be brought to an end as soon as possible."[14]

Emerging from his interrogation by the chiefs at the Anfa Hotel, Eisenhower suspected his number might be up as coalition commander in chief in the theater. "His neck is on the noose, and he knows it," even his naval aide, Lieutenant Commander Harry Butcher, noted in his diary.[15] At his headquarters in town General Patton recorded the same. "He thinks his thread is about to be cut," Patton would scribble, after talking with Ike — urging Eisenhower to "go to the front" instead of returning to the huge Allied headquarters in Algeria, many hundreds of miles behind the fighting.[16]

Roosevelt, however, saw things differently — very differently. From the President's point of view, Eisenhower had done extremely well — indeed, given the friction that would arise between de Gaulle and General Giraud over control of French anti-Vichy forces, Ike had achieved miracles in planting the American flag across Vichy-held Algeria and Morocco in only a few weeks, leaving no real chance the Germans could strike the Allies in the flank, as Secretary Stimson and General Marshall feared.

The fact remained: whether General Brooke liked it or not, only an American supreme commander was going to be able to direct the campaign. For good or ill, a system of workable coalition command, in combat, had still to be developed — and it was a blessing that the President had journeyed, as U.S. commander in chief, to see Eisenhower in person, in the active theater of war, whatever might be the disappointments of the British and American chiefs of staff.

Having first put the young general at ease, the President thus listened with interest as Dwight Eisenhower explained what the Allies were up against in advancing across the same mountain range the President had overflown in Morocco, as well as the atrocious mud and winter weather conditions in Tunisia. Hitler had managed to get sixty-five thousand German troops across the Mediterranean from Italy, together with high-quality equipment, including new Panther and Tiger tanks — the latter armed with 88mm guns — but he had been aided, too, by French pusillanimity, the French forces in Tunisia failing to fire a single shot to delay, let alone stop, the Germans.

Even that French timidity had been outweighed by the political and military leadership problems with which the French had confronted Eisenhower as Allied commander in chief in Northwest Africa. General Giraud had succeeded Admiral Darlan as French commissioner, but was proving a disappointment — a "good Division Commander," possibly, but wholly lacking in "political sense" and with "no idea of administration. He was dictatorial by nature and seemed to suffer from megalomania," Eisenhower had already explained to the chiefs — a view he now repeated to the President. "In addition," Giraud "was very sensitive and always ready to take offense. He did not seem to be a big enough man to carry the burden of civil government in any way. It had been far easier," Eisenhower remarked candidly, "to deal with Admiral Darlan," despite Darlan's record as a Pétainite Nazi appeaser.[17]

The President laughed. If only his many critics in America knew! Feckless French troops were deserting by the hundreds, in the field, rather than risk their lives against the ruthless Wehrmacht. So much for coalition fighting. Getting the French to stop squabbling amongst themselves over currency, supplies, pensions, and administrative aspects of the U.S. occupation had also proven a minefield — permitting Eisenhower, as the general himself acknowledged, too little time to focus properly on the battlefront, where progress had been painfully slow. The Wehrmacht forces facing U.S. troops in the Gafsa and Tébessa sectors were, Eisenhower made clear, first class. The "opposition was tough," Elliott Roosevelt — who was acting as his father's aide-de-camp — recorded, "while we were just beginning to learn about war first hand."[18]

This was exactly the kind of honest appraisal the President wanted to hear, from the lips of the top U.S. commander in the theater — confirming what General Clark had told General Marshall.

"No excuses, I take it," the President commented.

"No, sir. Just hard work." Or fighting.

In which case, the President raised the next question, what was the general's estimate of how long it would take to clear North Africa of Axis forces?

At the White House in late November, 1942, General Bedell Smith, Eisenhower's chief of staff, had personally assured the President that fighting would be over by mid-January 1943. It was now mid-January.

"What about it? What's your guess?" the President pressed Ike. "How long'll it take to finish the job?"

"Can I have one 'if,' sir?"

The President chuckled, Elliott remembered, and bade him give his best estimate.

"With any kind of break in the weather, sir, we'll have 'em all either in the bag or in the sea by late spring."

"What's late spring mean? June?"

"Maybe as early as the middle of May. June at the latest."[19]

Elliott recalled being surprised by the young general's cautious estimate, as this — five months of further campaigning — would make a switch of naval, air, and army forces to England, in order to mount a massive amphibious invasion of France across the English Channel that summer, almost impossible. The notorious fall weather would preclude a late-summer amphibious assault — as Hitler, too, had similarly decided in the summer of 1940, after the Luftwaffe had been rebuffed in the Battle of Britain.

"Father looked satisfied," Elliott clearly remembered[20] — and summoned the Combined Chiefs of Staff, once again, to his villa, at 5:30 p.m.

The President asked Winston Churchill to attend the meeting at the Villa Dar es Saada, too — for the session would be, in effect, a presidential briefing, backed by the President's "active and ardent lieutenant."

One by one the generals and admirals — Marshall, King, Arnold, Brooke, Pound, Dill — entered, together with Air Marshal Arthur Tedder, Admiral Mountbatten, General Hastings Ismay, and Harry Hopkins. Once seated, the President asked General Eisenhower to give yet another presentation of "the situation on his front"[21] — an indication that, as President, he was fully behind his protégé.

The President then briefly reviewed the outlook with the assembled chieftains — and made clear to them his own preference. As Brooke noted in his diary, "we did little except that President expressed views favouring operations in the Mediterranean."[22]

Aware that General Marshall might feel he'd lost face among the Combined Chiefs of Staff after arguing so hard for an end to Mediterranean operations and a switch to the U.K. for a cross-Channel attack that year, the President asked Marshall to stay behind and have dinner with him. He also invited Eisenhower.

Elliott made old-fashioneds (sugar, bitters, and whiskey) for the generals — and, joined by Franklin Jr., the five men sat down in the President's dining room for a first-class Moroccan meal.

Typically, Roosevelt wanted Marshall to feel he was respected, even if his advice had been wrong. He therefore deliberately raised again his wish to inspect troops not only in Morocco but closer to the frontline, near the Tunisian border.

"Out of the question, sir," Marshall stated unequivocally.[23] Even with a fighter escort, the President's slow C-54 could be attacked by Luftwaffe planes — "it would just draw attackers," Eisenhower added frankly, "like flies to honey."[24]

The President reluctantly backed off the idea — allowing Marshall to feel he had won at least a tactical victory.

Satisfied, Marshall and Eisenhower departed the villa after dinner and the President then spent quality time with his sons, talking about the family. "Father got to bed early that night: before midnight," Elliott recalled.[25]

The President had cause to feel the conference was off to a good start. The flight to North Africa had been historic. But so, too, had been the President's first full day in Casablanca. By its end he'd ensured that the great Allied military conference would result in compromise and cooperation, *not contention* — thus injecting not only unity of Allied military purpose but a transfusion of realism into the veins of the U.S. Joint Chiefs of Staff, who were, in all truth, more green regarding modern warfare than Eisenhower.

Instead of insisting upon mass American slaughter on the beaches of northern France that August, the U.S. chiefs could now set about mapping a detailed course of operations that year that would, above all, be *within the capabilities* of the Western Allies — whatever Stalin might plead, when eventually informed.

Besides: if the Russian dictator had wanted to argue for a Second Front in Europe that year, he should have taken the trouble to show up.

With that, having bidden his guests goodnight, the President retired and went to sleep, confident that, though the Allies had much to learn in combat, they would do so in the coming months, and that all would be well — with 1944 the year when the coup de grâce could be given and the Third Reich brought to an ignominious end.

How difficult it would be to steer his coalition partners, however, remained to be seen. If the British were difficult, how much more so were the French. Moreover, how to keep the Russians happy with such a timetable, when they were facing two-thirds of the Wehrmacht on the Eastern Front, would be tougher still.

PART FOUR

Unconditional Surrender

13

Stimson Is Aghast

At the Pentagon, Secretary Stimson was aghast on hearing the "bad news" from General McNarney.

Joseph McNarney was the U.S. Army deputy chief of staff, standing in for General Marshall. His news related to "how the British were forcing us to do some more in the Mediterranean" after Tunis, rather than switching U.S. forces to a cross-Channel invasion, to be launched from England that year.[1] In Washington, D.C., however, the secretary of war could do nothing.

Two days later Stimson's heart sank still further with the "somber news that I had been getting yesterday from the conference in Africa where it seems to be clear that the British are getting away with their own theories," he recorded, "and that the President must be yielding to their views as against those of our own General Staff and the Chief of Staff. So it looks as if we were in for further entanglements in the Mediterranean, and this seems to me a pretty serious situation unless the Germans are very much less strong than I think we should assume."[2]

Stimson's continuing lack of realism was deplorable, given the lack of U.S. experience in mounting an operation as vast and serious as a cross-Channel invasion would be, if undertaken that year. At the same time, the war secretary's fear of "perfidious Albion" was well warranted. Could British assurances they would eventually participate in a Second Front honestly be believed? The answer was clearly no.

For all their criticisms of Eisenhower's tardiness in Tunisia, the British were not actually willing or able to say how the Third Reich could be *defeated*, rather than surrounded. As Admiral King reported to the President when the U.S. chiefs of staff came to the Villa Dar es Saada the following evening, January 16, for a two-hour session with Mr. Roosevelt, "the Joint Chiefs of Staff have been attempting to obtain the British Chiefs of Staff concept of how the war should be *won*"[3] — and had had little luck. It seemed the British had no idea.

In his diary General Sir Alan Brooke, after his own experience in battle against German forces in 1940, remained implacably opposed to a cross-Channel attack unless the Wehrmacht was first weakened and brought to its knees elsewhere. He complained, in his diary, at the "slow tedious process" it was to get the U.S. team to accept his "proposed policy." In a postwar annotation to the diary, he would even pen a diatribe against General Marshall. Among "Marshall's very high qualities he did not possess those of a strategist," Brooke (by then Lord Alanbrooke of Brooke-borough) would claim. "It was almost impossible to make him grasp the true concepts of a strategic situation. He was unable to argue out a strategic situation and preferred to hedge and defer decisions until such time as he had to consult his assistants" — assistants who were "not of the required calibre."[4]

Brooke was being disingenuous — for Marshall, like Admiral King, was an excellent strategist; what he lacked was the ability to see how important it was to match U.S. strategy to reality. Neither general properly understood the need to create armies and army commanders who could defeat the Wehrmacht *in battle* — irrespective of wearing down German forces on other fronts.

Hour after hour Marshall thus pressed Brooke and the British to explain how exactly a further campaign in the Mediterranean would, in itself, *defeat the Third Reich* — something neither Brooke nor his colleagues Admiral Pound (who was suffering from an undiagnosed brain tumor) and Air Marshal Portal could answer. Brooke's assertions that the Germans would thereby be "worn down" to a point where they could not send reinforcements to northern France seemed particularly lame, given the likelihood that, if the Allies fought on in Italy, as Brooke envisioned, it would be the Allies who would be worn down rather than the Germans.

Marshall and Brooke thus went at each other hammer and tongs. Almost five hours of discussion at the Anfa Hotel — however irritating to Brooke — did at least permit the American team to challenge and rehearse the different possible military alternatives for 1943 with relentless honesty within the framework of overall war strategy.

The result was a consensus: there were no alternatives. If forced to fight on that year in the relative safety of the Mediterranean theater, the U.S. chiefs accepted, then it would be best to tackle Sicily, once North Africa was cleared — giving the Allies the amphibious-assault-landing experience necessary for a 1944 cross-Channel invasion.

The President had been right, they reluctantly agreed as they went over the requirements for a successful Second Front with their British opposite numbers. General Brooke had pointed to forty German divisions available in or close to France — and a Luftwaffe that was still a potent weapon of war. By contrast, after the expected capture of Tunis in the spring of 1943, the Allies would have but twenty-one to twenty-four divisions ready to assault northern France even by the fall — and as Admiral Pound, the British navy chief, pointed out, "this was too late since the weather was liable to break in the third week of September and it was essential to have a port by then." August 15, 1943, would be the cutoff date, weatherwise, were a cross-Channel invasion to be undertaken that year — moreover, according to the commander of the British amphibious forces, Vice Admiral Mountbatten, it would take all of three months to get the necessary landing craft from the Mediterranean to the United Kingdom. Any hope that the RAF or USAAF could interdict German air forces over Brest were scotched by Air Marshal Portal, the RAF chief, "since it was out of range." Even if the Cherbourg-Normandy area was chosen, "with limited air facilities in the [Cherbourg] Peninsula we should possibly find ourselves pinned down at the neck of the Peninsula by ground forces whose superiority we should be unable to offset by the use of air," Portal pointed out. And once the Germans realized the Allies were not actually going to attack Italy and southern Europe from North Africa, they would "quickly bring up their air forces from the Mediterranean, realizing that we could not undertake amphibious operations on a considerable scale both across the Channel *and* in the Mediterranean."

The simple fact, then, was: "no Continental operations on any scale were in prospect before the spring of 1944," General Arnold concluded.[5]

If the Combined Chiefs were agreed on 1944 for a major cross-Channel assault, at what point should "further operations" in the Mediterranean be halted, though? How exploit Allied strength in the Mediterranean, once achieved, without risking stalemate requiring more and more reinforcements — thus vitiating the success of the cross-Channel campaign planned for 1944? As General Marshall memorably put it, the Mediterranean could become a dangerous "suction pump" on American manpower and arms. What Marshall therefore wanted from Brooke, Pound, and Portal, as a strategist, was an acknowledgment of that danger: an agreement that, if operations in the Mediterranean became stalled or an expensive dead end, the very combat experience the Allies were seeking would thereby be wasted, and a successful cross-Channel invasion in 1944 be rendered impossible.

This danger General Brooke refused to validate, as only an owl-eyed, intelligent, but obstinate Ulsterman could — while paying lip service to the notion of an eventual cross-Channel attack in 1944.[6]

Would Brooke keep his word, though, the U.S. team wondered? Would the British even undertake an offensive to reopen the Burma Road they had lost to the Japanese in 1942, which was vital in order to supply United Nations forces in China?

Marshall had to hope they would. The British, after all, were America's primary allies in the global war. At the Villa Dar es Saada Marshall therefore reported to the President on January 16 his understanding that, after the amphibious invasion of Sicily that summer, "the British were not interested in occupying Italy, inasmuch as this would add to our burdens without commensurate returns."[7]

These were famous last words — or hopes.

The President was as concerned as Marshall over getting bogged down in Italy, and "expressed his agreement with this view."[8] Between them, however, they would have to make the British back off such a potential dead end — the President working on Churchill, Marshall on Brooke. Neither of them had any idea of the nightmares ahead, though, in this regard.

In the meantime, crediting British good faith, the chiefs moved on to other strategic concerns. By Monday, January 18, in fact, Roosevelt had been able to get outline agreement on pretty much all he had wanted at Casablanca. The Combined Chiefs had agreed to his strategy for 1943: further operations in the Mediterranean, after the capture of Tunis, targeted on Sicily, with simultaneous preparations for a cross-Channel assault to be made earliest in late 1943, if there were signs of sudden German collapse; otherwise a full-scale assault early in 1944 on the Cherbourg Peninsula, targeted on Berlin. In Asia there was to be a 1943 British offensive in Burma to open the overland supply route to China. And in the Pacific,

further advances that would take the Allies closer to the Japanese mainland—which would be ultimately bombed into submission, or subjected
to land assault if required, after the defeat of Nazi Germany.

In this respect the President had invited Churchill to lunch with him
privately at the Villa Dar es Saada on the eighteenth, before the afternoon
meeting he'd convened with the chiefs of staff—for he wanted something
of major importance from Churchill: formal agreement to his "unconditional surrender" policy.

Churchill raised no objection whatever—in fact the Prime Minister
found himself positively inspired by the President's proposals for prosecuting the war to the bitter end, gaily promising not only that the British would launch their offensive into Burma (Operation Anakim) under
General Wavell that year but would "enter into a treaty," if necessary, to
assure him that Britain would fight alongside the United States to ensure
the ultimate "defeat of Japan." In reporting the day's deliberations to his
cabinet that night, Churchill informed his colleagues in London that the
Combined Chiefs of Staff in Casablanca were "now I think unanimous in
essentials about the conduct of the war in 1943," and that in respect of the
strategy decided upon at the meeting held in the President's villa with the
Combined Chiefs, "Admiral Q [FDR] and I were in complete agreement."
Moreover, Churchill cabled, he and the President were in agreement that,
at the conclusion of the conference, there would be a public "declaration
of firm intention of the United States and the British Empire to continue
the war relentlessly until we have brought about the 'unconditional surrender' of Germany and Japan."[9]

Historians would later argue over the merits and demerits of such a war
policy,[10] but the fact that neither the U.S. chiefs of staff nor the British
prime minister and his War Cabinet in London opposed the President's
"unconditional surrender" policy gives some idea of how much in control
of such war strategies was the President. Time would tell how it would go
down once announced to the world, but in the meantime Mr. Roosevelt
had come too far to remain closeted in the Anfa camp. He had chosen
as his *nom de plume* Admiral Q, in prior secret communications with
Churchill—a humorous reference to his Spanish literary hero, Don
Quixote. (Hopkins was "Mr. P." for Sancho Panza.) Whether he was tilting at windmills in seeking unconditional surrender of the Axis nations
would only become clear in the fullness of time—and war. In the mean-

while he wanted to get out and visit with his commanders and the troops in the field, like Lincoln.

On the evening of January 19, the President went to dine with General Patton at his palatial headquarters in Casablanca — listening with fascination and amusement to the cavalryman as, in his distinctive high-pitched voice, he described his recent landings under French fire, and expounded upon the primacy of the tank in modern warfare.

Two days later, at 9:20 a.m., the President left Casablanca by car with Patton "for an inspection of the United States Army forces stationed in the vicinity of Rabat, some 85 miles to the northeast," as Captain McCrea recorded.[11] U.S. troops lined the entire route as the fifteen cars in the cavalcade made their way north, covered by a U.S. Air Force umbrella.

Recalled General Clark, the President "started asking questions, and I don't think he stopped all day. He transferred to a jeep at Rabat, where Major-General E. N. Harmon, commanding the Second Armored Division, was introduced and joined us for that part of the trip. The President was driven within a few feet of the front rank of the troops, which were lined with their vehicles." Then on to review the men of the Third Infantry Division. "A stiff wind made the flags and banners stand out smartly, and the outfits were polished and alert, so that the President had a fine time, seemed pleased with what he saw, and showed his pride for what they had accomplished."[12] And in the afternoon, the Ninth U.S. Infantry Division, commanded by Major-General Manton Eddy.

"I went 'up the line' this a.m. beyond Rabat," the President wrote Daisy that night, and "reviewed about 30,000 Am[erican]. Troops," followed by a visit to Fort Mehdia — "a very stirring day for me & a complete surprise to the Troops."[13]

Given his paralysis, driving in an army jeep caused the President intense pain, but he bore it with equanimity: pleased as punch to review combat-readying soldiers on the battlefield — the brim of his soft Panama hat turned up as he held onto the jeep's guardrail.

One British staffer, witnessing the inspection, later recalled how "fortunate" he was "in being invited by an American colonel to watch President Roosevelt inspecting an American battalion. I was the only British officer present and I was told it was an historic occasion — the first time a President of the United States had ever inspected an American unit on foreign soil. Instead of the parade receiving the visiting officer with a general salute, being inspected and then marching past, the President arrived first and took up his seat (in his jeep because of course he was paralyzed) at the saluting base. Then the photographers got busy, taking him from all angles, from above and below" — the brigadier disgusted by the photographers "who buzzed round the commanding officer and the leading ranks like flies round a horse's ears. They put down wooden boxes to stand on and photographed the leading ranks from above; they lay on the ground and photographed them from the snake's eye view, rolling out of the way to avoid being kicked. Even I, on the touch line, wanted to kick them. The proceedings were most undignified. Then the battalion formed up in line and the President, with two fierce and heavily armed detectives on his jeep and four others, one looking to each point of the compass, in a following jeep, drove down the line. Finally he decorated a soldier and then drove off."[14]

Brigadier Davy had been a highly decorated commander and then staff officer in Egypt, but like so many British colleagues he had simply no understanding of America: of its immigrant history, or the miracle by which ethnically and socially disparate citizens were being molded into a world power based on democratic principles and the President's four freedoms. No picture was ever taken indicating the President's paralysis, but press photographers were aware the whole nation would respond to images of the U.S. commander in chief out in Africa, inspecting his troops. Moreover, from the point of view of public opinion in America, where the majority of people favored dealing with Japan before Germany, such patriotic images were of inestimable importance.

Telling his son Elliott about the trip that evening, the President certainly brimmed with pride and excitement. "I wish you could have seen the expression on the faces of some of those men in the infantry division. You could hear 'em say, 'Gosh — it's the old man himself!' And Father roared with laughter," Elliott recalled. He'd eaten field rations there with Generals Clark and Patton. And Harry Hopkins. "Harry!" he now called upstairs. "How'd you like that lunch in the field, hunh?"[15]

Hopkins, running a bath, thought for a moment. Then he called back down that, although the food had been somewhat Spartan, he'd loved the music. "'Oh yes,' said Father. '*Chattanooga Choo-Choo, Alexander's Rag-Time Band,* and that one about Texas, where they clap their hands, *you know . . .*'

"'*Deep in the Heart of Texas?*'

"'That's right. And some waltzes.'" The President paused. "'Elliott, tell me,'" he continued: "'Would any army in the world but the American army have a regimental band playing songs like that while the Commander-in-Chief ate ham and sweet potatoes and green beans right near by? Hmmm?" He even showed Elliott the mess kit he'd eaten lunch out of, which he'd brought back with him. When Elliott said he would surely have been able to obtain one in America, if he wanted, the President was appalled. "But I *ate* out of *this* one, at Rabat," he told his son with childlike pride, "the day I saw three divisions of American soldiers, who are fighting a tough war. It's a good souvenir. I'll take it home with me."[16]

The President had also visited Port Lyautey, he told Elliott, and seen the sunken warships. He'd laid a wreath at the American section of the local cemetery — and had looked at the graves of the French who'd opposed them.

In a world at war, the Commander in Chief wanted to do right by those men — and if it was hubris to imagine he could in person get America's allies to combine in effecting his two-part vision of the world war and the postwar, then that was a designation the "Emperor of the West" — as Eisenhower's British political adviser, Harold Macmillan, described him[17] — accepted. Inspecting three entire U.S. divisions in the theater of combat, he felt his vision was at least grounded in America's burgeoning emergence as a world power: a power that would soon become capable, with its allies, of slaying the Nazi monster, *unconditionally* — and the Japanese demon thereafter. For this he would need, however, not only the Prime Minister, but the Emperor of the East: Joseph Stalin. Also, probably, the two rivals for leadership of the French empire: Generals Henri Giraud and Charles de Gaulle — the latter due to arrive the next day.

14

De Gaulle

GETTING Major General de Gaulle to appear in Casablanca had been a trial from the start. "On our arrival at Casablanca at the first military meeting with the Pres.," Captain McCrea later recalled, "the Prime Minister informed the Pres. that General De Gaulle, despite his invitation to the Casablanca conference by the P.M., had decided not to attend."[1]

Since Major General de Gaulle was the leader of the Free French movement in London, it was considered vital to get him and General Giraud, the French high commissioner under Eisenhower, to meld the forces under one authority, if they were to contribute to the liberation not only of North Africa and France but of Europe.

De Gaulle's refusal to come to Casablanca had thus been a nasty shot across the President's bows. Roosevelt was "greatly" annoyed, McCrea recalled. "The Pres. told the P.M. rather sternly, I thought, that it was up to the P.M. to get De Gaulle there. At this the P.M. took off on De Gaulle about as follows: 'I tell you Mr. President, Gen. De Gaulle is most difficult to handle. We house him. We feed him. We pay him and he refuses to raise a finger in support of our war effort. He states vigorously every time he gets a chance to do it that he is entitled to military command. I ask you Mr. President what sort of a military command could either of us give him?'

"The Pres. acknowledged that no doubt De Gaulle was hard to handle and there continued about as follows: 'Winston, this is a shotgun marriage' — referring of course to the hoped-for collaboration between De Gaulle and Giraud — and continued, 'We have our party here, referring to Giraud, and I feel it is up to you to get *your* party here.' I inwardly squirmed a bit," McCrea confessed, "at the bluntness of the Pres. remarks, but he, of course, put a light touch on the proceedings with a hearty laugh. I felt easier."[2]

This was typical FDR. Whether it was wise was another matter. It bespoke, however, Roosevelt's urgency — for it was vital, in his mind, for the Western Allies to retain the cohesion of their military coalition if they were to persuade the Soviets to go on fighting the Wehrmacht on the Eastern Front. Especially once the time came to inform Stalin that the Allies were *not* going to launch a Second Front in 1943 unless the Germans collapsed that summer — which seemed unlikely.

Day after day Churchill had duly attempted to get de Gaulle to fly out to Casablanca. "De Gaulle refused Churchill's invitation to come from London," the President himself wrote Daisy with a mixture of amusement and irritation. "He has declined a second invitation — says he will not be 'duressed' by W.S.C. & especially by the American President — Today I asked W.S.C. who paid De Gaulle's salary — W.S.C. beamed — good idea — no come — no pay!"[3]

The next day Roosevelt heard that de Gaulle had finally consented. "De Gaulle will come! Tomorrow!" the President wrote Daisy in excitement on January 21.[4] But if the President thought that by bringing de Gaulle and Giraud together, he could achieve a genuine marriage, he was to be profoundly mistaken. By contrast Winston Churchill, who had been dealing with the quirky, proud, and imperious Major General de Gaulle for two and a half years, knew exactly what was to be expected.

Quite why the President would take personal charge of negotiations with the senior French leaders and officials was a mystery to the British prime minister — who possessed a far deeper understanding of political realities on the European side of the Atlantic than the President.

American political policy in Northwest Africa seemed disastrously amateur, even the U.S. vice consul at Marrakesh acknowledged. From public relations to economics and intelligence, the various Washington agencies "who came to North Africa were at loggerheads with State Department policy," Kenneth Pendar afterward recorded. "The heads of all the agencies cooperated, but their subordinates left the French feeling that we, as Americans, had no clear policy or ideology of any kind."[5]

This was all too true. It was also inevitable, perhaps, as the United States emerged from its long isolationist slumber and felt its way as the world's foremost military power. Early in the twentieth century the United States had considered, then balked at, becoming an empire; now, however, it had little alternative, whether that empire was to be territorial or post-territorial. And this exposed a major weakness in the American system of government—for though the President might make military decisions as U.S. commander in chief, political decisions were another matter. Not only Congress but the free media of the country were entitled to "weigh in"—making unity of approach virtually impossible. Secretary Hull was even more skeptical of de Gaulle than the President. He was equally opposed to the restoration of France's colonial empire in the postwar world save as trusteeships—for how could American sons be expected to give their lives merely to reestablish a colonial yoke they themselves had thrown off in 1783?

The President—like General Eisenhower—was thus faced with an awkward military task: harnessing British and French forces to the yoke of the Western Allies, without committing the United States to restitution of their colonial empires.

Not even Roosevelt's personal representative at Eisenhower's headquarters, Robert Murphy, had had any idea of the President's long-range political plans when preparing the Torch invasion: namely, that "Roosevelt was planning to encourage extensive reductions in the French empire," as the diplomat delicately put it in his memoirs. Once he met with the President at the Villa Dar es Saada, however, Murphy had been quickly brought up to speed—and recognized the postwar agenda the President was seeking. Having congratulated Murphy on the "Darlan deal" that had brought such quick Vichy surrender, the President had then looked reproachfully at his emissary. "But you overdid things a bit in one of the letters you wrote to Giraud before the landings, pledging the United States Government to guarantee the return to France of every part of her empire. Your letter may make trouble for me after the war."[6] Without further ado, the President had gone on to discuss "with several people, including Eisenhower and me, the transfer of control of Dakar, Indochina, and other French possessions, and he did not seem fully aware how abhorrent his attitude would be to all empire-minded French including De Gaulle and also those with whom I had negotiated agreements."[7]

It was the President's long-term political agenda that set the cat among the pigeons, rather than his modest military expectations. And late on the evening of Friday, January 22, 1943, after a delightful meal with the Sultan of Morocco at the Villa Dar es Saada, the President realized he was playing with fire.

• • •

Captain McCrea remembered the fateful night in Casablanca vividly. He had hand-delivered the President's invitation to the Sultan at his palace near Rabat the day before. "No Hollywood director could have put on a more colorful spectacle," McCrea recalled. "The Court Yard ankle deep in white sand," the cavalry "dressed in colorful costumes, the white horses draped in red blankets"[8] — and the Sultan asking if he might bring with him his young teenage son, the Crown Prince, to meet the President.

At 7:40 p.m. on the twenty-second, the Sultan had duly arrived with his "entourage" — "magnificently attired in white silk robes" and "bearing several presents — a gold-mounted dagger for the President in a beautiful inlaid teakwood case, and two golden bracelets and high golden tiara for Mrs. Roosevelt."[9] In return, the Sultan was given a signed photograph of the President in a heavy silver frame, engraved with the presidential seal.

It was hardly a fair exchange — yet the Sultan of Morocco and his son were delighted, for the evening was historic: it was the first time the Sultan had ever been allowed to meet the head of any foreign state other than France.

Seating the Sultan on his right, the President had proceeded to lay out, verbally over dinner, a magic table of postcolonial dreams for the country. Morocco, after all, had only been colonized by the French early in the twentieth century, becoming a "protectorate" in 1912; it could become a sovereign country once again, in the war's aftermath.

Churchill, seated on the President's left, had grown "more and more disgruntled," Elliott Roosevelt recalled, as the President discussed living standards for the nation's Muslims, better education, and "possible oil deposits" in the country. "The Sultan eagerly pounced on this; declared himself decidedly in favor of developing any such potentialities, retaining the income therefrom; then sadly shook his head as he deplored the lack of trained scientists and engineers among his countrymen, technicians who would be able to develop such fields unaided," Elliott wrote. "Father suggested mildly that Moroccan engineers and scientists could of course be educated and trained under some sort of reciprocal educational program with, for instance, some of our leading universities in the United States."[10]

General Charles Noguès, who as the French resident general had also been invited to the dinner but had been placed further down the table, "had devoted his career to fortifying the French position in Morocco," according to Robert Murphy's account, and "could not conceal his outraged feelings" at Roosevelt's talk of postcolonial development and American investment.[11] At the end of dinner "the Sultan assured Father," Elliott re-called, "he would petition the United States for aid in the development of his country. His face glowed. 'A new future for my country!'"[12]

It was also a new approach to decolonization: discussion, both at table and beyond. As word spread, in the days and weeks afterward, the story of the dinner would become legendary among Moroccans as a "proof of our sincerity in the Atlantic Charter," another American official remem-bered — almost every Arab in Morocco feeling "he knew the whole story of this *diffa* and everything that was said, just as if he had been there."[13]

"It was a delightful dinner, everybody — with one exception — enjoy-ing himself immensely," Elliott later recalled.

The exception was not General Noguès, however; Elliott meant Mr. Churchill. For his part, Robert Murphy remembered the Prime Minister, thanks to his "rare abstinence," being "unnaturally glum throughout the evening" — as well as uncomfortable at the mention of the end of colonial empires. Captain McCrea, however, recalled Churchill's clever solution to the alcohol problem.

"As to no alcoholic beverage being served [in deference to the Sultan]," the President's naval aide recalled, "the P.M. I think was taken by surprise. At any rate he started to glower, the glower being more pronounced dur-ing the small talk which preceded the dinner. The Pres. noted this and I think was rather amused." In the meantime, "directly dinner was an-nounced seats were taken," and shortly after dinner started, an "amusing incident took place. One of our Secret Service men entered the dining area and whispered to me that a Royal Marine, the P.M.'s orderly, wanted to speak to me . . . He informed me that a most important message had been received at the P.M.'s nearby villa which required immediate at-tention. I indicated where the P.M. was seated and told the Marine to so inform the P.M." This he did. "The P.M. after a word with the Pres, withdrew. In about twenty minutes or thereabouts the P.M. returned. No doubt the message referred to was urgent," McCrea allowed, "but on his return it was evident that the P.M. had taken time out to have a quickie or so while handling the urgent dispatch. After dinner and when the guests had departed the Pres. had a good laugh about it all, remarking 'Winston did not tell me what the message was about. Do you suppose he can have arranged it?'"[14]

It was already 10:00 p.m. "The Sultan obviously wanted to stay and discuss more specifically and with loving emphasis some of the points Father had raised during the dinner," Elliott recounted, "but Father's work for the evening was cut out for him. A signal to Captain McCrea then, to stay and take notes; one to Robert Murphy and Harry Hopkins; one to me to hold myself in readiness to act as Ganymede — and all the others left. The stage was set for Charles de Gaulle."[15]

It had been Theodore Roosevelt's dictum — using a supposed West African proverb — that a successful leader should "speak softly and carry a big stick." Franklin Roosevelt preferred, however, to keep his stick well concealed, relying on the force of his personality, his high intelligence, his self-confidence, and his passionate interest in the future to steer people in what he considered the right direction. Even the generally dismissive General Patton, who despised politicians, had been won over by him.

General Marshall had disappointed Patton when dining with him at Casablanca on arrival — "Never asked a question," Patton had noted in his diary.[16] The President, by contrast, never stopped asking questions. Patton had spent one and a half hours with him on January 16 — the President (whom Patton referred to as A-1) "most affable and interested. We got on fine." The next day Patton had seen the President again, and "we all talked over one and one-quarter hours, then went to see B-1" — Churchill.

Churchill, the general had sniffed in his diary, "speaks the worst French I have ever heard, his eyes run, and he is not at all impressive."[17] On January 18 Patton had again ridden in the President's car for an inspection of the battalion guarding the Anfa enclave. Then on January 19 he'd invited the President to dinner at his headquarters — the President afterward asking Patton to sit and talk with him, alone, "in car while P.M waited, for about 30 minutes. He really appeared as a great statesman," Patton jotted in his diary[18] — and on January 21 the President asked Patton once again to ride with him in his car, together with General Clark, following lunch and his inspection of the three U.S. divisions at Rabat. "Coming back we talked history and armor about which he knows a lot," Patton recorded. "F.D.R. says that in Georgia," in the Soviet Union, "there are Crusaders' Castles intact and that hundreds of suits of armor exist. Then he got on to politics"[19] — with somewhat withering remarks about Vice President Henry Wallace as his potential heir, or even Harry Hopkins; "neither of them had any personality," he claimed, which would rule out any hope of their winning election. Even Churchill drew the President's less-than-complimentary appraisal in terms of empire and future global security. "He also discussed the P.M. to his disadvantage. Says India is lost and that Germany and Japan must be destroyed."[20] Above all, however, the President listened — especially to Patton's military judgment. The general pointed out how green American forces still were, in terms of fighting. "People speak of Germany and Japan as defeated," the general warned sagely, but "we have never even attacked them with more than a division."[21]

Churchill's ill grace at dinner with the Sultan particularly irritated Patton — who claimed the Sultan had "especially asked" to see the President in private, "before Churchill arrived," as he did not seem to like the Prime Minister. Already on arrival the Prime Minister appeared, it had seemed to Patton, "in a very bad temper . . . No wine, only orange juice and water. Churchill was very rude, the President was great, talking volubly in bad French and really doing his stuff," Patton recorded that night. The tanker had personally driven the Sultan home. "On way Sultan said, 'Truly your President is a very great man and a true friend of myself and my people. He shines by comparison with the other one" — the "boor" Churchill.[22]

Patton was being unfair, however — for neither he nor Captain McCrea had any idea of the real cause of Churchill's distemper.

The President did. After the Sultan's departure, the Prime Minister quickly explained. De Gaulle had just visited him, before dinner, at the Villa Mirador — and had scotched any prospect that his arrival would lead to the unification of the Free French movement in London and the French Imperial Council in Algiers, under Giraud.

De Gaulle had been not only intransigent, but rude to the point of insult — "a very stony interview," as Churchill described it to the President. The Prime Minister thus begged the President not to see de Gaulle that night, but to put off the meeting to the next day, when de Gaulle would have had more time to simmer down.

The President, however, insisted de Gaulle be brought straight to him. Thus did the Free French major general arrive at the Villa Dar es Saada, along with two aides, at 10:20 p.m., "with black clouds swirling around his high head and with very poor grace" according to the President's son:[23] there to meet the U.S. commander in chief whose troops had "liberated" Algeria and Morocco.

15

An Acerbic Interview

IN A CABLE to his secretary of state, the President had explained just why he was attempting to accomplish a "shotgun" wedding of the Free French leader from London, where anti-Vichy feeling was high, and the French high commissioner under General Eisenhower from Algiers, where former Vichy administrators and officers still predominated. Though Roosevelt claimed it to be for unity of the French cause, the truth was, the President felt he must give critics of his use of former Vichy personnel in North Africa a sign—a symbol not just of reconciliation but proof that though the United States had acted out of expedience, it was fully resolved to defeat fascism in all its forms.

De Gaulle, unhappily, was loath to oblige—raising serious questions about what kind of "liberation" the Americans were intending to bring to Europe. "It had been my hope that we could avoid political discussions at this time," the President cabled to Hull, in part to explain why he hadn't thought to bring the secretary of state to Casablanca, "but I found on arrival that American and British newspapers had made such a mountain out of a rather small hill that I should not return to Washington without having achieved settlement of this matter."[1]

Knocking de Gaulle's and Giraud's heads together, he imagined with presidential hubris, he would show the free world there was a good, just, fair, and effective alternative to Nazi rule, illustrated by men of goodwill coming together to make democracy work once again, as the Nazis were forced to retreat.

Sitting on the large sofa in the villa's drawing room, the President thus bade de Gaulle sit beside him, and attempted, in his best conversational French, to apply salve to the major general's wounded pride as a Frenchman summoned to appear before an American on what de Gaulle had always thought of as French soil: the President beginning by explaining how he'd come to Casablanca, as U.S. commander in chief, to discuss military operations against the Axis powers in the Mediterranean for the coming year. Mr. Stalin had been invited, but had been unable to leave the Stalingrad front. The purpose of the Casablanca meeting was, therefore, to "get on with the war," and answer the question "Where do we go from here?"

In this context, the President elaborated, he appreciated there were different political views on how North Africa, once liberated from the Nazi yoke, should fare, but the war was not yet won; the "problem of North Africa should be regarded," therefore, "as a military one and that the political situation should be entirely incident to the military situation." How to bring "as much pressure as possible to bear on the enemy at the earliest possible moment" in Tunisia was the order of the day, he claimed;[2] Admiral Darlan, for all his faults, had done his best to make this happen, and General Giraud, his successor, was doing the same. Surely, by moving his London Free French committee to Algiers and fusing it with Giraud's organization, the war could be won more swiftly than if the French war effort were to be hobbled, right at the beginning, by political dissension?

De Gaulle, however, seemed to be a man from a different planet. That American forces had come thousands of miles, and suffered a thousand deaths at the hands of French troops while attempting to roll back the Axis tide and evict the Germans in North Africa as the first step toward the defeat of Hitler was — at least at that moment — a matter of complete indifference to the French general. He'd hoped, rather, for an invitation to come to Washington to meet with the President as the leader of the Free French movement, and for security reasons (Free French headquarters was reputed to leak like a proverbial sieve) had not been told of the Casablanca Conference — just as he had not been told beforehand of the Torch invasion. Feeling insulted, he'd therefore resisted Churchill's invitation to fly out to Casablanca, not only out of pique, but because he foresaw matters of political importance being decided and would have no time to prepare for such discussions, he claimed. Forced nevertheless to present himself, on pain of the Free French movement being stripped of all funds and support in London, he'd reluctantly agreed to travel — promising nothing, however. His arrival at Medouina airport had then given him an indication how low he was on the American totem pole: no band playing

"La Marseillaise"; the windows of the car taking him to Anfa soaped lest he be recognized; American troops and sentries everywhere — and in a country he considered a part of France, not a protectorate.

Interrupting Roosevelt, de Gaulle "made some remark to the President with reference to the sovereignty of French Morocco," Captain McCrea wrote in his notes of the meeting that night — having been asked to stand outside while the President and the general talked. It was, he added, "a relatively poor point of vantage — a crack in a door slightly ajar," and with the Frenchman's voice so low "as to be inaudible to me."[3]

Moroccan sovereignty was not what the President was prepared to discuss with the somewhat mad major general from London, however — especially after spending the evening with Morocco's rightful ruler. Morocco had become a French protectorate only in 1912, barely thirty years ago; it could not by any stretch of the imagination be considered "French" soil, in the President's eyes, and de Gaulle's assumption that the country was to be reestablished as part of the "French Empire," thanks to American blood and courage, aroused Roosevelt's deepest anticolonial feelings.

Reestablishing imperial French sovereignty over colonized peoples promised a hiding to nothing, whereas the opportunity to get "advanced" Western nations to embrace the notion of responsible development in former colonies, encouraging global trade and education, would offer, he felt, mutual benefits. Above all, it would give moral *purpose* to the postwar democracies, especially if the struggle between capitalism and communism worsened. The President therefore dismissed de Gaulle's remarks over French sovereignty over Morocco, "stating that the sovereignty of the occupied territories" — territories occupied now by U.S. forces of liberation — "was not under consideration." Moreover, he stated, it would be up to the occupied countries — like mainland France, once liberated — to elect their own postwar governments to help decide such matters, not jump the gun and be saddled with decisions made by warring factions in exile; in fact, "none of the contenders for power in North Africa had the right to say that he, and only he, represented the sovereignty of France," Roosevelt claimed — neither Giraud nor de Gaulle. "The President pointed out," McCrea recorded, "that the sovereignty of France, as in our country, rested with the people, but that unfortunately the people of France were not now in a position to exercise that sovereignty. It was, therefore, necessary for the military commander in the area [General Eisenhower] to accept the political situation as he found it and to collaborate with those in authority in the country at the time that the occupation took place so long as those in authority chose to be of assistance to the military commander. The President stated that any other course of action would have been indefensible."[4]

Nor did Roosevelt stop there. It was not, he said, simply a matter of temporary accommodation and practicality. With the whole of mainland France now under German occupation[5] and no legitimate or elected French government in exile, it was the task of the Allies — the United Nations — "to resort to the legal analogy of 'trusteeship,'" not committees of self-appointed exiles. It was the President's view "that the Allied Nations fighting in French territory at the moment were fighting for the liberation of France and that they should hold the political situation in 'trusteeship' for the French people. In other words, the President stated that France is in the position of a little child unable to look out and fend for itself and that in such a case, a court would appoint a trustee to do the necessary." He pointed out that General Giraud understood this very well, and wanted only "to get on with the war" — namely, the "urgent task of freeing French territory of the enemy." Only then could questions of sovereignty, empire, and the like be addressed. "The President stated that following the Civil War in our home country, there was conflict of political thought and that while many mistakes were made, nevertheless, the people realized that personal pride and personal prejudices must often be subordinated for the good of the country as a whole, and the contending French leaders could well follow such a program. The only course of action that could save France, said the President, was for all her loyal sons to unite to defeat the enemy, and that when the war was ended, victorious France could once again assert the political sovereignty which was hers over her homeland and her empire. At such time all political considerations would be laid before the sovereign people themselves and that by the use of the democratic processes inherent throughout France and its empire, political differences would be resolved."[6]

De Gaulle looked stunned by such paternalistic American arrogance. He'd endured, he felt, one insult after another that day. "No troops presented honors," he later recalled of his arrival at Medouina, "although American sentries maintained a wide periphery around us." Instead, some American cars had driven up to the plane. "I stepped into the first one," he recorded — as well as his shame when Brigadier General William Wilbur, "before getting in with me, dipped a rag in the mud and smeared all the windows. These precautions were taken in order to conceal the presence of General de Gaulle and his colleagues in Morocco," de Gaulle lamented, using the third person. Once inside the barbed-wire compound, moreover, he'd felt even more insulted. "In short, it was captivity," he remembered feeling—a giraffe incarcerated in an American zoo. "I had no objection to the Anglo-American leaders' imposing it on themselves, but the fact that they were applying it to me, and furthermore on territory under French sovereignty, seemed to me a flagrant insult." Meeting five-star General Giraud, his former commander from 1940, that afternoon, de Gaulle—though a mere major general—blamed Giraud for not feeling similarly aggrieved. "What's this? I ask you for an interview four times over and we have to meet in a barbed-wire encampment among foreign powers? Don't you realize," de Gaulle sneered, "how odious this is from a purely national point of view?"[7]

Giraud didn't. In fact, given that U.S. troops had now liberated Morocco from Nazi control, as laid down under the 1940 armistice agreement, he considered de Gaulle the one who was odious and insulting, especially when de Gaulle had pulled from his pocket a copy of Giraud's letter of loyalty to Marshal Pétain, written the previous spring after his escape from a German prison in Germany and seeking safety from the Nazis in Vichy France.[8] Once Hitler had ordered the occupation of the whole of metropolitan France, Giraud had immediately revoked his letter, and had consented to be brought by Allied submarine to Algeria to take military command of the anti-Axis forces. He'd found it typical of de Gaulle to commence discussions of French unity by producing a copy of such a past document from his pocket; with de Gaulle, you were either subordinate to him or against him. Worst of all, de Gaulle's main opponent seemed neither Hitler nor even Giraud, but the U.S. president.

"Franklin Roosevelt was governed by the loftiest ambitions," de Gaulle allowed later — but not the sort of ambitions of which de Gaulle approved. "His intelligence, his knowledge and his audacity gave him the ability, the powerful state of which he was the leader afforded him the means, and the war offered him the occasion to realize them. If the great nation he directed had long been inclined to isolate itself from distant enterprises and to mistrust a Europe ceaselessly lacerated by wars and revolutions, a kind of messianic impulse now swelled the American spirit and oriented it toward vast undertakings," the major general described in his haughty prose — undertakings, at any rate, that were antithetical to de Gaulle and to the reconstitution of the French Empire under him. Once America had "yielded" to "that taste for intervention in which the instinct for domination cloaked itself," he recorded — ignoring France's capitulation to Hitler, Japan's attack at Pearl Harbor, and Hitler's declaration of war on the United States — "from the moment America entered the war, Roosevelt meant the peace to be an American peace, convinced that he must be the one to dictate its structure, that the states that had been overrun should be subject to his judgment, and that France in particular should recognize him as its savior and arbiter."[9]

This was not far from the truth. The fact that Americans, not Frenchmen, were being asked by their president and commander in chief to die, if necessary, to liberate de Gaulle's country — a country that had put up the most feeble fight against the Germans in 1940, and had submitted to an abject armistice with almost no protest ever since, indeed had attempted to prevent U.S. forces from landing in Morocco and Algeria while not lifting a finger to stop the Germans from occupying Tunisia — was of zero interest to de Gaulle, who deprecated Roosevelt as "a star actor" unwilling to share the limelight de Gaulle craved. "In short, beneath his patrician mask of courtesy," de Gaulle wrote, "Roosevelt regarded me without benevolence."[10]

At 10:55 p.m. the interview came to an end. The "Frenchman unfolded his complete height," Elliott recalled, "and marched with formality and no backward glance to the door."[11]

The President was as put out as was de Gaulle. A seminal political encounter of the war had taken place, pitting American progressive political ideas against recalcitrant French imperialist ideology. There had certainly been no meeting of minds. What it showed was that the President's views on postwar world democracy, as enshrined in the Atlantic Charter, were going to be very, very difficult to apply.

Churchill then came back to the Villa Dar es Saada and, together with Harry Hopkins, Robert Murphy, and Harold Macmillan, they rehashed the evening's discussions and their implications.

Outwardly, the President seemed unconcerned. "Father seemed unperturbed by the mighty sulk to which de Gaulle treated him," Elliott recalled, as well as his father's philosophical attitude. "The past is past, and it's done," the President pronounced, attempting to be positive. "We've nearly solved this thing now. These two:" — meaning Generals Giraud and de Gaulle — "equal rank, equal responsibility in setting up the Provisional Assembly. When that's done, French democracy is reborn. When that Provisional Assembly starts to act, French democracy takes its first steps. Presently French democracy will be in a position to decide for itself what is to become of Giraud, or of de Gaulle. It will no longer be our affair."[12] A democratically elected French government would decide.

In his own mind, however, Roosevelt was far from happy. He was already worried whether his notion of global postwar democracy, based on the Atlantic Charter, would be honored in Europe, once the Russians began pushing back the Germans on the Eastern Front.

The Soviets were a major concern. His brief interview with de Gaulle had indicated all too clearly, though, just how obstinately the old imperial powers would seek to reestablish and then hang on to their colonial possessions — the "unity of her vast Empire," as de Gaulle proudly called it[13] — rather than pursue the ideal of postwar, postimperial commonwealths of sovereign countries bound by history and culture, not the gunboat. And in this respect, Churchill was little different from de Gaulle.

How, though, persuade those dying empires to embrace the *future* rather than the past? How encourage them to join in creating a new world order, not reestablish the tottering colonial empires that had doomed Europe and the Far East after World War I?

When Churchill finally left the House of Happiness at half past midnight, the President went to bed but asked Elliott to sit with him, and in the quiet of his Casablanca villa, he unburdened his soul.

Though he'd said to Churchill they must move on with the prosecution of the war and not permit themselves to be sidetracked by French factionalism, the President was in truth deeply affected by his contretemps with de Gaulle.

"We've talked, the last few days," the President told his son, "about gradually turning the civil control of France over to a joint Giraud–de Gaulle government, to administer as it is liberated. An interim control, to last only until free elections can again be held . . . but how de Gaulle will fight it!" he snorted. Not only did de Gaulle speak of himself as a sort of Joan of Arc, but his dream was the restoration of France on the back of its colonies. "He made it quite clear that he expects the Allies to return all French colonies to French control immediately upon their liberation. You know," Roosevelt confided to his son, "quite apart from the fact that the Allies will have to maintain military control of French colonies here in North Africa for months, maybe years, I'm by no means sure in my own mind that we'd be right to return France to her colonies at all, ever, without first obtaining in the case of each individual colony some sort of pledge, some sort of statement of just exactly what was planned, in terms of each colony's administration"[14] — much as Congress had done with regard to the Philippines in 1932.

Elliott was amazed. "Hey, listen, Pop. I don't quite see this. I know the colonies are important — but after all, they *do* belong to France . . . how come we can talk about not returning them?"[15]

Roosevelt's retort was instant. "*How* do they belong to France?" he countered. "Why does Morocco, inhabited by Moroccans, belong to France? Or take Indo-China. The Japanese control that colony now. Why was it a cinch for the Japanese to conquer that land? The native Indo-Chinese have been so flagrantly downtrodden that they thought to themselves: Anything must be better, than to live under French colonial rule! Should a land belong to France?" he demanded. "By what logic and by what custom and by what historical rule?"[16]

"I'm talking about another war, Elliott," the President told his son, "his voice suddenly sharp," Elliott recalled. "I'm talking about what will happen to our world, if after *this* war we allow millions of people to slide back into the same semi-slavery."

He looked deadly serious. "Don't think for a moment, Elliott, that Americans would be dying in the Pacific tonight, if it hadn't been for the shortsighted greed of the French and the British and the Dutch. Shall we allow them to do it all, all over again?"[17]

It would be hard enough to revive the battered economies of the world and guard against the insidious, antidemocratic ideology of communism, but how much harder it promised to be if Britain, France, and the Netherlands committed themselves to huge military and financial outlays to perpetuate imperialism. They would then be, he predicted, sucked into vain efforts to stop calls for self-government and self-determination in their former colonies — a recipe for postwar disaffection, revolt, and wars.

"One sentence, Elliott. Then I'm going to kick you out of here. I'm tired. This is the sentence: When we've won the war, I will work with all my might and main to see to it that the United States is not wheedled into the position of accepting any plan that will further France's imperialist ambitions, or that will aid or abet the British Empire in *its* imperial ambitions."[18]

And with that the President pointed to the door — and the light switch.

• • •

Before he returned to his photoreconnaissance unit in Algiers, Elliott Roosevelt had one more talk with his father. It was clear de Gaulle's determination to reassert French imperialism still enervated the President. De Gaulle had at least been open about his aims, however — to the point of outright rudeness. Churchill was, by contrast, keeping his own counsel for later. The President therefore interrogated Elliott as to opinion among U.S. troops and airmen — what did they, who were risking their lives, think?

Before Elliott could respond, his father launched into another deeply felt articulation of his views. "You see, what the British have done, down the centuries, historically, is the same thing. They've chosen their allies wisely and well. They've always been able to come out on top, with the same reactionary grip on the peoples of the world and the markets of the world, through every war they've ever been in.

"*This* time," his father continued, "*we're* Britain's ally. And it's right we should be. But ... first at Argentia, later in Washington, now here at Casablanca," the President reminded Elliott, "I've tried to make it clear to Winston — and the others — that while we're their allies, and in it to victory by their side, they must never get the idea that we're in it just to help them hang on to the archaic, medieval Empire ideas."[19]

Elliott agreed, but his father wasn't done. "I hope they realize they're not senior partner." America was — and would be more and more so, as the war progressed and the postwar world took shape. The United States was "not going to sit by, after we've won, and watch their system stultify the growth of every country in Asia and half the countries in Europe to boot," he warned. Britain had "signed the Atlantic Charter" at Argentia, and "I hope they realize the United States government means to make them live up to it."[20]

These were perhaps the most impassioned words Elliott had ever heard his father say — spoken after inspecting thirty thousand young Americans preparing for imminent combat, and having visited the cemetery of those who had already fallen. They also helped explain his father's determination to insist upon unconditional surrender of the Axis powers, precluding any possibility of negotiated armistice with nations simply too dangerous to be allowed ever to rearm.

Operation Symbol had been the code name given to the Casablanca Conference. The biggest symbol of Roosevelt's intent to end German, Italian, and Japanese military empires and establish a completely new, postimperialist global order would be, the President had planned, his forthcoming announcement to the world, on the field of battle, of his implacable condition for ending the war.

Hour after hour the President had hoped that de Gaulle would make at least a tentative agreement to work with General Giraud — one that could be announced at the President's looming press conference.

De Gaulle refused, however, to make any accommodation with his French rival. In particular he turned down a draft communiqué drawn up by Robert Murphy and Harold Macmillan, Eisenhower's British political adviser — declaring he would not be party to any solution to French political matters "brought about by the intervention of a foreign power, no matter how high and how friendly."[21]

The President, with a kind of bemused amazement, breathed another sigh of vexation. "Finished the staff conferences — all agreed — De Gaulle a headache — said yesterday he was Jeanne d'Arc & today that he is Georges Clemenceau," he scribbled to Daisy — for de Gaulle now insisted on a compact with Giraud in which he, Major General de Gaulle, would be the French political leader in exile, while Giraud would be merely the French military commander in chief — whom de Gaulle could dismiss. Giraud, who had come to hate de Gaulle with Gallic venom over the past few days, refused. There would thus be no unification of the Free French and Algiers committees — and with that, de Gaulle prepared to leave Casablanca.

The President was disappointed, but tried not to be unduly concerned.

De Gaulle, for his part, believed he'd made his point: proving to the President of the United States and the world that he, on behalf of *La France,* was not going to toady to American wishes, or dollars. He certainly seemed to have no idea how rude he'd been, or how small he appeared, in the President's eyes, despite his six-foot-six-inch height. History had given him the chance to lead a great reconciliation of neutral, Vichy, and Free French nationals in the struggle to defeat the Axis powers and to usher in a new world. Instead, he'd pursued the politics of personal ambition and an implacable view of French honor. However laudable the latter, it was sheer obstructionism in terms of the war against the Third Reich — something de Gaulle seemed unable to comprehend. To his aide, Hettier de Boislambert, he confided, the night he'd met the President at the Villa Dar es Saada: "You see, I have met a great statesman today, I think we got along and understood each other well" — but the truth was the very opposite.

For his part, Churchill was dumbfounded. Learning that de Gaulle was refusing to sign the proposed communiqué, prior to the President's press conference, "he was beside himself with rage," the historian of the Churchill–de Gaulle relationship later chronicled. "General de Gaulle's farewell visit to the Prime Minister was therefore uncommonly animated, even by Churchillian standards; the latter chose to omit any reference to it in his memoirs. Not so General de Gaulle," François Kersaudy chronicled.

Kersaudy was not exaggerating. De Gaulle's account, recording how Churchill had threatened to "denounce" him "in the Commons and on the radio" unless he signed the communiqué, pulled no punches. The Prime Minister was "free to dishonor himself," de Gaulle had retorted. "In order to satisfy America at any cost, he was espousing a cause unacceptable to France, disquieting to Europe, and regrettable to England."²²

Churchill was apoplectic, but in one sense de Gaulle was right. The President was a true statesman, and even if he disliked de Gaulle for making difficulties, he understood him, for all his foibles, as a statesman in the making. Thus at the Villa Dar es Saada shortly before noon on January 24, Roosevelt accepted that de Gaulle would simply not sign an interim communiqué or agreement of a three-man Committee for the Liberation of France — and did not turn away from Charles d'Arc, so to speak. Instead, in his inimitable fashion, the President asked for at least a *symbol* of French purpose in fighting the Nazis. "In human affairs the public must be offered some drama," Roosevelt said to the general. "The news of your meeting with General Giraud in the midst of a conference in which both Churchill and I are taking part, if it were to be accompanied by a joint declaration of the French leaders — even only a theoretical agreement — would produce the dramatic effect required."²³

The President's almost Olympian approach and charm moved de Gaulle, as Churchill's did not. "'Let me handle it,'" de Gaulle later recalled his response. "'There will be a communiqué, even though it cannot be yours.' Thereupon I presented my [French] colleagues to the President and he introduced me to his."²⁴

The press conference was due to take place at midday, but Harry Hopkins, mistaking de Gaulle's sudden graciousness, rushed out and grabbed General Giraud, asking him and Churchill to enter, in the hope that, if he could get "the four of them into a room together," then "we could get an agreement."²⁵

This was silly, in view of de Gaulle's stalwart refusal to allow a "foreign power" to dictate French agreements. Moreover, Churchill's renewed "diatribe and his threats against me, with the obvious intention of flattering Roosevelt's disappointed vanity," as de Gaulle put it in his memoirs, only made matters worse. But Roosevelt would not have been Roosevelt, the leader of the United Nations and a man of almost heartbreaking humanity, if he had not attempted a different approach. He therefore made one last request of de Gaulle, "on which he had set his heart," as de Gaulle recalled.

"Would you agree to [at least] being photographed beside me and the British Prime Minister, along with General Giraud?" he asked, in "the kindest manner."

"By all means," de Gaulle responded, "for I have the highest regard for this great soldier."

"Would you go so far as to shake General Giraud's hand in our presence and in front of the camera?"

"My answer, in English, was, 'I shall do that for you.' Whereupon Mr. Roosevelt, delighted, had himself carried into the garden where four chairs had been prepared beforehand, with innumerable cameras trained on them and several rows of reporters lined up with their pens poised."[26]

16

The Unconditional Surrender Meeting

"CASABLANCA, FRENCH MOROCCO," the AP reporter (once his report was cleared for release) described, was "probably the most important gathering of leaders of two great nations in history." It was also, the reporter maintained, even more extraordinary for the setting — the results "disclosed in the most informal press conference ever held."[1]

The picture, in the midst of a global war, was certainly unique — the scene a "garden of a villa on the outskirts of Casablanca," where "the entire area for blocks around was full of troops, anti-aircraft equipment and barbed wire. The correspondents were told they would have a conference at noon. They assembled in the rear garden of the villa, which is a luxurious gleaming white home with many windows overlooking the Atlantic. In the garden were two white leather chairs. A microphone was in front of them for newsreel camera men. Red flowers were in profusion. Inside, reporters could see Harry A. Hopkins and his son, who is now a corporal, rushing around making arrangements. Then Lieut. Colonel Elliott Roosevelt appeared at the rear door carrying two more chairs. The President appeared. He wore a gray business suit and a black tie, and, as usual was smoking a cigarette in a long holder. A minute later Prime Minister Churchill walked out with a cigar in his mouth."[2]

The two giant, giraffe-like French generals in their kepis were also brought out. "Some photographers called out, 'Generals shake hands!'" Captain McCrea recounted — and, as agreed with de Gaulle, when the President said, "Why not? You two Frenchmen are loyal to your country and that warrants a handshake anytime," they did so — not only once but twice, since cameramen complained they'd failed, in their surprise, to get a good photo the first time.

"The four actors put on their smiles," de Gaulle later recorded — in a chapter of his memoirs that he titled "Comedy." "The agreed-upon gestures were made. Everything went off perfectly! America would be satisfied, on such evidence, that the French question had found its *deus ex machina* in the person of the President."[3]

Giraud was as sniffy of the proceedings as de Gaulle, but for the opposite reason: to wit, his profound hostility to de Gaulle, a mere major general who had only minimal support from Frenchmen in Northwest Africa, appearing on the same stage — especially after having been so rude to him ever since he'd arrived. The very suggestion the two Frenchmen might work amicably together seemed to him dishonest, however noble its intention. "Excellent photos that will be transmitted across the world, and be seen as documentary evidence of irrefutable veracity," he recalled sarcastically several years later. "That," he added, "is how public opinion is fashioned."[4]

It was — unabashedly, since Allied unity was as important a weapon in the war as military arms. Even the President's naval aide was amazed. "The pictures went all over the world and I would suppose contributed to French unity in all parts of the globe," McCrea reflected, for even he had not foreseen the power of such simple imagery. "The President literally cajoled the two proud and greatly different persons into making a gesture of friendship — and did it well, indeed. The generals bade farewell to the President and the Prime Minister and then withdrew — forthwith," leaving the President to explain to reporters from across the world the purpose of the summit that had just concluded.

In his business suit and tie, sitting with his long legs crossed, the President "invited the assembled newsmen to seat themselves on the lawn and make themselves comfortable for the discussion which was to follow," the AP reporter described. "It was a beautiful day — brilliant sunshine and with these two heads of state the correspondents heard a complete description of the purpose and the reasons of bringing the British and our own Chiefs of Staff together in North Africa for discussions necessary for further prosecution of the war."[5]

The President certainly looked the picture of confidence and good health. Referring to Torch, he began by reminding his audience how the current campaign in North Africa had begun. "This meeting," he explained, "goes back to the successful landing operations last November, which as you all know were initiated as far back as a year ago, and put into definite shape shortly after the Prime Minister's visit to Washington in June.

"After the operations of last November," the President went on, "it became perfectly clear, with the successes, that the time had come for another review of the situation, and a planning for the next steps, especially steps to be taken in 1943." It was for this reason he'd arranged for Churchill to come to Casablanca, "and our respective staffs came with us, to discuss the practical steps to be taken by the United Nations for prosecution of the war. We have been here about a week."[6]

For the journalists who had been kept in the dark since the President's State of the Union address on January 7 in Washington, D.C., two weeks before, this was something of a bombshell. The very fact that the two leaders of the Western democratic alliance could have spent *an entire week* on the recent field of battle without anyone knowing was a shock — the more so as no American president had ever previously traveled abroad in wartime, or even flown in an airplane while in office. Yet here he was, in bright Moroccan sunlight, addressing them — largely extempore and in person.

> I might add, too, that we began talking about this after the first of December [1942], and at that time we invited Mr. Stalin to join us at a convenient meeting place. Mr. Stalin very greatly desired to come, but he was precluded from leaving Russia because he was conducting the new Russian offensive against the Germans along the whole line. We must remember that he is Commander in Chief [of the Soviet armies], and that he is responsible for the very wonderful detailed plan which has been brought to such a successful conclusion since the beginning of the offensive.

Knowing the Russians had cornered the German Sixth Army at Stalingrad, the President had felt certain the surviving Germans would now be killed or forced to surrender — whatever Hitler might order to the contrary. It was a tremendous Soviet victory in the making, after months of the most lethal, often hand-to-hand, combat of the war, involving vast casualties. Soon the Western Allies would be achieving a similar, momentous victory, however, the President implied. "In spite of the fact that Mr. Stalin was unable to come, the results of the staff meeting have been communicated to him, so that we will continue to keep in very close touch," Roosevelt assured the reporters. Meantime, with regard to the many meetings and discussions between the U.S., British, and French generals, the President expressed his great satisfaction as U.S. commander in chief. What had taken place was different, he said, from, say, Lincoln's visits to his generals in the field, or those of Allied leaders in World War I. This was now *coalition* warfare, on a global scale, but with the leaders and their military staffs working in the closest cooperation and harmony:

> I think it can be said that the studies during the past week or ten days are unprecedented in history. Both the Prime Minister and I think back to the days of the first World War when conferences between the French and British and ourselves very rarely lasted more than a few hours or a couple of days. The [U.S. and British] Chiefs of Staffs have been in intimate touch; they have lived in the same hotel. Each man has become a definite personal friend of his opposite number on the other side.
>
> Furthermore, these conferences have discussed, I think for the first time in history, the whole global picture. It isn't just one front, just one ocean, or one continent — it is literally the whole world; and that is why the Prime Minister and I feel that the conference is unique in the fact that it has this global aspect.
>
> The Combined Staffs, in these conferences and studies during the past week or ten days, have proceeded on the principle of pooling all of the resources of the United Nations. And I think the second point is that they have reaffirmed the determination to maintain the initiative against the Axis powers in every part of the world.

Over the past ten days, the President explained, the talks had examined how the Western Allies were to keep "the initiative during 1943," moreover to keep sending "all possible material aid to the Russian offensive, with the double object of cutting down the manpower of Germany and her satellites, and continuing the very great attrition of German munitions and materials of all kinds which are being destroyed every day in such large quantities by the Russian armies. And, at the same time, the Staffs have agreed on giving all possible aid to the heroic struggle of China — remembering that China is in her sixth year of the war — with the objective, not only in China but in the whole of the Pacific area, of ending any Japanese attempt in the future to dominate the Far East."

It was at this point that the President, looking down at his notes, came to the crux of his outdoor statement — its historic import belied by the lush surroundings. "Another point," he began:

> I think we have all had it in our hearts and our heads before, but I don't think that it has ever been put down on paper by the Prime Minister and

myself, and that is the determination that peace can come to the world only by the total elimination of German and Japanese war power.

Some of you Britishers know the old story — we had a General called U.S. Grant. His name was Ulysses Simpson Grant, but in my, and the Prime Minister's, early days he was called "Unconditional Surrender" Grant.

The elimination of German, Japanese, and Italian war power means *the unconditional surrender* by Germany, Italy, and Japan. That means a reasonable assurance of future world peace. It does not mean the destruction of the population of Germany, Italy, or Japan, but it does mean the destruction of the philosophies in those countries which are based on conquest and the subjugation of other people.

In order to give extra emphasis to the announcement, the President now declared: "This meeting is called the 'unconditional surrender meeting.'"

Unconditional surrender. No negotiation or acceptance of a compromise peace or armistice. And an implacable aim that would be pursued West and East.

While we have not had a meeting of all of the United Nations, I think that there is no question — in fact we both have great confidence that the same purposes and objectives are in the minds of all of the other United Nations — Russia, China, and all the others.

And so the actual meeting — the main work of the Conference — has been ended. Except for a certain amount of resultant paper work, it has come to a successful conclusion. I call it a meeting of the minds in regard to all military operations, and, thereafter, that the war is going to proceed against the Axis powers according to schedule, with every indication that 1943 is going to be an even better year for the United Nations than 1942.[7]

The fifty journalists in the garden of the Villa Dar es Saada were stunned. So, too, was Churchill.

True, the Prime Minister had agreed to the unconditional-surrender policy and even recommended it be part of the President's final pronunciamento, at the conclusion of the conference. Yet he seemed visibly surprised at the emphasis the President had placed upon it, as Captain McCrea vividly recalled. "I was standing nearby and when the President made that remark the P.M. snapped his head toward the Pres., giving the impression, to me at least, that the phrase came as a surprise to him."[8]

Pondering this in later years, McCrea could not quite explain the Prime Minister's body language — "I shall never forget," he wrote, "the quick turn of the head by the P.M. when the Unconditional Surrender of the Axis Forces was announced as to how the war would end."[9]

The fifty journalists, for their part, sat mesmerized. If they found themselves disappointed that the President was not willing to be more specific in terms of actual, forthcoming military operations, the Prime Minister followed up the President's statement by asking them to understand why the enemy should not be told in advance what the Allies would undertake that year — and why the Allies could be grateful for what had already happened, now that the United States was in command. "Tremendous events have happened. This enterprise which the President has organized — and he knows I have been his active Lieutenant since the start — has altered the whole strategic aspect of the war . . . We are in full battle, and heavy action will impend." He asked reporters therefore to convey to the world at home "the picture of unity, of thoroughness, and integrity of the political chiefs." The Allies were going to win the war. "Even when there is some delay there is design and purposes," he insisted, "and as the President has said, the unconquerable will to pursue this quality," he sought to find a quotable phrase, "until we have procured the unconditional surrender of the criminal forces who plunged the world into storm and ruin."[10]

Unconditional surrender, then, it was — the news soon flashing across the world, once the two leaders were out of harm's way.

Reports and images of the "unconditional surrender meeting" and the President's trip sent shockwaves across the Third Reich.

The President and Commander in Chief of the Armed Forces of the United States: Inspecting his troops on the battlefield. Ten days of U.S.-British military discussions — and with the French, too. Every battlefront of the globe examined, and its needs factored into the Allies' strategy for the prosecution of a global, offensive war — a war not only to win against the Axis powers, but to permit no compromise, no negotiated armistice, no agreement save unconditional surrender. And the President seated in the sun on a Moroccan lawn, speaking with such naturalness and confidence regarding the inevitable defeat of the Third Reich that those who'd experienced the German victories of the previous summer — the fall of

Tobruk, the second massive German offensive toward the Volga and the Caucasus — could only rub their eyes in wonder. "F.D.R.'s 'unconditional surrender' pronouncement" had swept "practically all other news from today's newspapers ... It will, no doubt, prove to be," predicted King George VI's private secretary, "one of the most momentous of all such conferences since that of Lucca" — when in 56 B.C. Caesar, Pompey, and Crassus had renewed their triumvirate.[11]

In the wake of Torch the tide had truly turned. In Berlin, Reichsminister Goebbels — who had been busy preparing the final touches for a forthcoming address of his own — was literally speechless.

At first Goebbels could scarcely believe what he read and saw in newsreel film being distributed throughout the neutral countries. In his diary Goebbels expressed utter consternation — especially at the failure of the German intelligence services to learn the whereabouts of a ten-day, top-level enemy conference involving the political leaders of the Western world, together with the chiefs of staff of their air, ground, and naval forces. Even on January 26, 1943, two days after the conclusion of the actual press conference and departure of the principals, Goebbels had been idly noting — alongside secret reports that the terrible battle of attrition at Stalingrad was "reaching its end"[12] — that it seemed "pretty certain that Churchill is in Washington."[13]

The next day Goebbels noted that the rumors of a parley between Roosevelt and Churchill were gaining strength, "only we still don't know where these gangster bosses are meeting."[14]

Goebbels, ever skeptical, had made nothing of the speculation. His own attention was locked on the approaching tenth anniversary of the Nazis' assumption of power, when he would make his own grand announcement at a huge, mass rally of Nazi Party stalwarts in the Sportpalast — urging them with all the declamatory zeal he could summon to devote themselves to their fresh task: to make available to the Führer the men, materiel, and conviction necessary for Germany to embark on a third, this time successful, great offensive on the Eastern Front ... *totaler Krieg*: total war.

Goebbels was thus floored by the seemingly authentic reports that finally reached Berlin on January 28, 1943. "The sensational event of the day, is the news that Churchill and Roosevelt have met in Casablanca," the Reichsminister dictated in his diary. He made no effort to conceal his amazement. "So the discussions have not, as we assumed, been taking place in Washington but on the hot coals of Africa. Once again our intelligence services have completely failed — unable even to identify the place where the talks were taking place," he fulminated. "They've been held now for almost a fortnight, and they're being heralded by the enemy press as the gateway to victory."[15]

Ever anxious to see signs of Allied dissension, Goebbels had assumed Churchill and Roosevelt, if they were meeting in Washington, might well be sparring over which man should take the reins of the Allied offensive war effort.[16] Reading the transcript of the Roosevelt-Churchill press conference in Casablanca, the Reichsminister became aware, however, that the earth had shifted. "It's worth noting," he reflected in his diary, "that Churchill officially designates himself now as Roosevelt's adjutant; no such humiliation has probably been seen in British history."[17]

Humiliation or not, the threat was becoming daily more real. Not only were the anti-Axis armies targeting Nazi Germany, Goebbels was aware, but so were their political leaders, Roosevelt, Churchill, and Stalin — leaders who, like Hitler, had taken command of their country's armed forces, and were now coordinating those forces against the Third Reich — in complete contrast to the motley democratic forces of the late 1930s.

Barely a year since Pearl Harbor and the Führer's ill-considered declaration of war on the United States, the President's appearance in Casablanca was a startling turnaround — his "unconditional surrender meeting" all the more disturbing to Goebbels, since it made clear there would be no peace feelers or possibility of a negotiated settlement with the leaders of the Third Reich. Along with the imminent extinction of von Paulus's Sixth Army at Stalingrad, Goebbels knew, Hitler's dreams of conquest and declaration of war on the United States now looked not only an unwise gamble, but raised the specter of the Thousand Year Reich — so gloriously proclaimed in the 1930s — being crushed in the nearest future, unless the Nazi Party, under their once victorious Führer, found some way to turn the tables.

Since the Führer still refused to appear in public at such a fateful time — he had not been seen in Berlin since the previous September[18] — his propaganda minister recognized that he, Joseph Goebbels, would have to work the harder to rally the German nation at home.

Accepting that the battle of Stalingrad would now end in utter defeat — the Führer confiding to Goebbels he'd had to sacrifice General Paulus's army lest the whole extended German frontline in Russia be broken — the Reich minister had intended to use the approaching German catastrophe in Russia to new advantage: namely as a wake-up call to the German Volk, once the battle of Stalingrad ended. The fate of so many hundreds of thousands of German soldiers would illustrate, as nothing else could, the mortal threat of Bolshevism — and the need for supreme, self-sacrificing heroism on the part of the loyal German soldier if they were to survive the struggle against Soviet communism.

The news from the Western (in fact, Southern) Front, however, eclipsed even Stalingrad. Coming after what the President had revealed in his State of the Union address on January 7, that the United States was on course to outmanufacture the collective output of the Axis powers several times over, the Casablanca declaration by the leaders of the world's foremost capitalist democracies — democracies working with the Soviet Union — now deprived Goebbels of his "anti-Bolshevist" German master card.

Every day there was more news in neutral countries about Casablanca. Film, photographs, newspaper stories — and discussion of what the conference would now presage for Nazi Germany. It completely turned the world's attention to the *Western,* not Eastern, Front, Goebbels lamented — removing the primary fear of Bolshevism. Overnight, in short, the communist threat had been replaced, thanks to Casablanca, by a dramatically announced determination of the Western democratic powers to destroy all vestige of Nazism as a danger to, and scourge of, mankind — far worse, in effect, than the dangers of communism.

The very words *unconditional surrender* — following the President's use of *total war* in his State of the Union address to Congress — infuriated Goebbels as a master of propaganda. Curt and harsh, they gave no hint of dissension or disunity among the United Nations now lined up against the Third Reich — unsettling Goebbels's ever-maneuvering assumptions, since it showed just "how confident the enemy now feels, or claims to feel, and how much we'll have to do," he noted, "to counter their machinations."[19]

For the second time that month, then, the President of the United States had beaten Goebbels to the punch. Instead of the Reich minister's still-undelivered declaration of total war surprising the world and striking fear in the hearts of Germany's enemies, his *totaler Krieg* speech, if Hitler authorized it, would now be viewed outside Nazi circles as a desperate effort, at best, of an unashamedly totalitarian regime to meet the prospect of defeat; at worst a sort of glorified willingness to countenance the complete destruction of the German nation rather than sparing it by surrender.

To make matters worse for Dr. Goebbels, however, the Führer had declined to make him the sole director of the *totaler Krieg* initiative, lest the Reich minister (and gauleiter of Berlin) become too powerful in Germany. Instead, Hitler had agreed only to a triumvirate of mediocrities to steer the extended mobilization program, enjoying circumscribed powers — with Goebbels granted a "watching brief." Isolated, ill, frustrated, depressed, and blaming others rather than himself for the Wehrmacht's failure on the Eastern Front, the Führer even rejected Goebbels's renewed appeals that Hitler return to the capital and rally the nation at such a time of crisis both on the Eastern and Southern Fronts.

For Goebbels as Reichsminister für Propaganda, this made Roosevelt's dramatic appearance in Morocco especially galling: the U.S. president seen by photographers, cameramen, and reporters so relaxed in the garden of a sunlit villa in Casablanca, while the Führer remained unseen by anybody: hiding out of sight at his freezing headquarters in East Prussia, moaning helplessly as he surveyed on his tabletop maps the sharp arrows of Russian advances, lancing into his besieged remaining forces at Stalingrad . . .

It was in this context that Goebbels had been heard to say — by Albert Speer, the Reich armaments minister, no less — that Germany did not have a leadership crisis, but a "Leader crisis."[20]

Goebbels was not alone in thinking this — though few if any dared say so aloud. Goebbels was especially disturbed by reports from the *Sicherheitsdienst* concerning new anti-Nazi graffiti appearing on the walls of German cities. Some of these openly accused the Führer of mass murder — not of Jews, but of German soldiers, in forcing the Sixth Army to fight to the death at Stalingrad rather than allowing the men to retreat.[21] There were even rumors circulating that Hitler was either dead or suffering mortal sickness in Prussia.

However hard Dr. Goebbels tried, then, it seemed impossible to "counter" the sensational international effect of the Casablanca Conference. In his diary the minister thus cursed the way he and the Führer had been outmaneuvered.

The very lack of military specifics in the President's Casablanca press conference — or even in the final official conference communiqué issued after *weeks* of military discussions held by the most senior Allied generals and admirals — aroused still further concern in Goebbels's suspicious, ever-calculating, yet in many ways brilliant mind. "They're trying to conceal the real decisions they've made at the conference," he dictated in his diary, "clearly to lull us into complacency. But there's no possible doubt in my mind the Anglo-Saxons are planning to invade the mainland of Europe when it suits them. We'll have to prepare for surprises," he noted on January 28. "From week to week," he added, "the war is moving into a bitter, ruthless stage."[22] And two days later, at the stated request of the absent Führer, Goebbels delivered before an audience of invited Nazis in the Berlin Sportpalast — and on German radio — Hitler's tenth-anniversary proclamation, celebrating the Nazis' seizure of power in 1933.

Compared with the President's Casablanca announcement, the proclamation was a dud.

Without new victories to boast of, indeed with the Russians erasing the last pockets of resistance in Stalingrad, Hitler had been reduced in the proclamation to a vague catalog of Nazi "achievements" over the past decade, as well as an assertion that National Socialism would "inspire everybody to fulfill his duty." If not, the Führer warned, woe betide the slacker. The Nazi Party "will destroy whoever attempts to shirk his duty," he'd written — having agreed with Goebbels on the phone that the most savage measures, including execution, were to be taken against any who dared contest the increased mobilization measures that would now be enacted.[23]

Thanks to the Führer and his accomplices, the war — Hitler's war — would indeed move now "into a bitter, ruthless stage."

Three weeks thereafter Dr. Goebbels would, finally, be permitted by the Führer to deliver, in person, his long-awaited *totaler Krieg* speech at the Berlin Sportpalast.

Goebbels was careful, in the days before, to pass word around that he'd be issuing more than a proclamation. One Goebbels biographer later described it as "the most important mass meeting" of Goebbels's egregious life.[24] Ignoring the President's recent reference to Germany's war of conquest and its subjugation of other peoples, Goebbels intended instead to portray Germany's struggle as a noble European battle, waged by the Third Reich and its allies against "international Jewry," and a fight to vanquish the forces of Jewish-sponsored chaos and aggression.

"Behind the Soviet divisions storming toward us we see the Jewish liquidation commandos, and behind them the specter of terror, mass hunger, and complete anarchy," Goebbels described. The goal of Bolshevism, he declared, "is Jewish world revolution. The Jews want to spread chaos across the Reich and Europe, so that in the resultant despair and hopelessness they can establish their international, Bolshevist, concealed-capitalist tyranny." International Jewry, he sneered, was an "evil fermentation of decomposition" — a threat that "finds its cynical pleasure in plunging the world into chaos, and thereby bringing about the fall of thousand-year-old cultures to which it has contributed nothing."[25]

Considering Jews had made German culture and science world famous, and that the Jewish percentage of Germany's population in 1933 had been less than 1 percent, Goebbels's claims were not only preposterous, but malevolent beyond belief — masking, sadly, the real truth: the SS liquidation teams that Hitler and Heinrich Himmler had unleashed when attacking the Soviet Union, as well as the deliberate extermination of innocent Jewish civilians across Europe. Yet before an audience of fifteen thousand Nazi stalwarts, Goebbels's newsreel cameramen "captured extraordinary scenes of emotion," his biographer would describe. "Within minutes the audience was leaping to its feet, saluting, screaming, and chanting" — their cries of "Führer command! We obey!" foreshadowing the shrill madness of Orwell's *Animal Farm*.

"The orgiastic climax was reached by the question: 'Do you want total war? Do you want war more total, if need be, and more radical than we can even begin to conceive of today?' And then, almost casually, 'Do you agree that anybody who injures our war effort should be put to death?'"

"The bellow of assent each time was deafening," Goebbels's biographer would record[26] — the Reich minister's speech interrupted more than two hundred times by literally hysterical applause. Not least would be the climax, when Goebbels reached his frenzied, rhetorical "masterpiece," modeled on Hitler's earlier "masterpieces."

"Nun, Volk, steh auf, und Sturm, brich los!" — "Now, people of Germany, rise up — and storm: *break loose!*"[27]

PART FIVE

Kasserine

17

Kasserine

SHORTLY AFTER THE President's return to Washington, the last pocket of forty thousand starving soldiers of the German Sixth Army at Stalingrad raised the white flag — knowing their chances of survival as prisoners of war were dim.

The SS and Wehrmacht had ruthlessly conquered, murdered, executed, pillaged, and despoiled too much, too mercilessly, since the launch of Operation Barbarossa to expect much mercy. Of the 113,000 German soldiers taken prisoner in the battle for the Russian city of Stalingrad, few would ever return to their Vaterland.[1] "I'm not cowardly, just sad that I can give no greater proof of my bravery," one soldier had written in his last, despairing letter home, "than to die for such pointlessness, not to say crime."[2]

For the Soviet armies, Stalingrad, not Torch, was the turning point of the war. Russian forces had been fighting the Wehrmacht and its Romanian, Hungarian, Finnish, Italian, Dutch, and other Axis assault forces relentlessly since June 1941. In those seventeen months, the Soviets had taken phenomenal casualties before finally learning how to halt and defeat Germans in battle. Americans had been in battle barely a few weeks.

The campaign in Tunisia against predominantly German forces would now evidence the same learning process, if on a considerably smaller scale.

As Allied units began to meet German rather than Vichy French forces in combat, the situation suddenly resembled chaos in Russia at the start of Barbarossa. Even as Roosevelt presided over the conference at Casablanca, in fact, armored German forces struck at the Allied line in the Eastern Dorsal region of the Atlas Mountains, manned by poorly armed

French troops. Some thirty-five hundred troops immediately surrendered; the rest ran for their lives. "The French began showing signs of complete collapse along the front as early as the seventeenth," Eisenhower jotted in his diary on January 19, 1943. "Each day the tactical situation has gotten worse."[3]

The President, who seldom if ever interfered in tactical dispositions, had urged while at Casablanca that another well-armed U.S. division be sent up the line from northern Morocco, but Marshall and Stimson's obsession with a possible German counterinvasion via Spain and Spanish Morocco had tied Eisenhower's hands. Transportation was a further fetter. "We've had our railroad temporarily interrupted twice," Ike lamented. "I'm getting weary of it, but can't move the troops (even if I had enough) to protect the lines."[4] Wisely waiting for better weather and more troops, he wanted to hold fast until Montgomery's British Eighth Army drew closer from Libya, and a proper, integrated Allied offensive could be readied within the capabilities of largely green troops.

The Germans, however, would not oblige. On January 30, 1943, five days after the President's departure from Morocco, the Twenty-First Panzer Division "struck Faid Pass in a three-pronged attack as precise as a pitchfork," campaign historian Rick Atkinson aptly described — killing almost a thousand French defenders in a day.[5] Then, luring counterattacking U.S. armored forces into a trap, the Germans decimated both U.S. infantry and tanks — leaving Wehrmacht forces, backed by Stuka dive-bombers, in control of Faïd Pass and the Eastern Dorsal.

This, however, was just the beginning. On February 14 the Germans launched a Valentine's Day massacre. Warned that German armor was on the move, Eisenhower wanted to withdraw fifty-nine-year-old Lloyd Fredendall's II Corps to safer positions in the Grand Dorsal, but General Fredendall resisted, and Eisenhower felt too much of a tenderfoot to insist, especially since Fredendall was a protégé of General Marshall's. The result would soon be a bloodbath — this time American.

A German officer "could not help wondering whether the officers directing the American effort knew what they were doing."[6] They didn't. Their forces were dispersed and were mutually unsupporting, as well as lacking effective air cover. They were, in short, completely unprepared for the two German armored contingents about to hit them: General von Arnim's *Frühlingswind* assault through the Faïd Pass to Sidi Bou Zid, and Field Marshal Rommel's attack further south: *Morgenluft*. "We are going to go all out for the total destruction of the Americans," Field Marshal Kesselring, the German commander in chief South, declared.[7]

"You're taking too many trips to the front," General Marshall had criticized Eisenhower at Algiers, after flying there from Casablanca. "You ought to depend more on reports," he'd advised — obtusely. Patton had counseled the opposite.

Eisenhower's deference to Marshall's authority pretty much condemned the Allies to defeat — Eisenhower still too young to defy the U.S. Army chief of staff. "Absolute priority" alerts had been sent out, once Ultra intelligence decrypts of German signals recognized something big was up, but it was too late. As German forces smashed their way forward with the latest Tiger tanks, new Nebelwerfer multiple-nozzled mortars, and Stuka ground-attack dive-bombers dovetailing with the Wehrmacht advance, American officers began openly yelling at their men to flee for their lives. In less than twelve hours von Arnim and Rommel's pincers had closed, having seized the high spine of the central Dorsal and threatening to end run the entire Allied line in Tunisia.

Absolute pandemonium characterized the initial U.S. response — followed once again by brave American tankers, ordered to counterattack, being lured into German 88mm mobile-artillery traps: almost a hundred American tanks destroyed with their crews, twenty-nine artillery guns, seven half-tracks, and sixteen hundred casualties suffered at Sidi Bou Zid alone. And this was just the start. Open Allied radio communications allowed the Germans to know American whereabouts and moves without difficulty. Huge Allied gasoline and ammunition dumps were blown up or surrendered, as were three U.S. airfields. The German 88s and Tiger tanks had a field day. The battle became a rout as American troops retreated, pell-mell. Fredendall abandoned his laboriously carved subterranean hideout, far behind the frontlines. By February 17 his corps had been thrown back fifty miles — in three days. On February 19 Rommel then attacked at Kasserine. Panic ensued, with the British First Army commander of the overall Tunisian front ordering "no further withdrawal," and to "fight to the last man." Or last American, wags sneered.

Fredendall even began moving his headquarters back to Constantine — more or less where Torch had begun, in November.

Concerned that he had not sufficient supplies or reserves to fight much beyond Kasserine, Rommel was satisfied with what he'd achieved; he obtained grudging consent to withdraw, sowing forty-three thousand mines as he did, and blowing up all bridges. He had given the Allies a "bloody nose" — inflicting six thousand casualties, destroying almost 220 tanks and over 200 artillery guns, for less than a thousand German casualties, and had set back the Allied timetable for advance by months.

Joseph Goebbels, ecstatic at the reception given to his *totaler Krieg* speech, was further delighted by the news of German victory in Tunisia, which went some way to overcome public despondency when word of the surrender of Stalingrad was finally released.

Once again German troops had proven they were the best soldiers in the world and could not be beaten, even by numerically larger forces. "The Americans have made a really terrible showing," Goebbels noted in his diary — "absolutely awful. Which is reassuring, in the event the Americans try to mount an invasion of continental Europe against German troops. They will probably be so smashed up," he commented, "they won't know what hit them."[8]

The next day, still savoring the news from Tunisia, he reflected: "This U.S. defeat gives us an excellent insight into American fighting ability in case of an American invasion of Europe. I think our soldiers would sooner rip their throats out than let them into Germany. At any rate, the spirit here among the German people is hard to beat."[9]

Hitler was *außerordentlich zufrieden* with Rommel — extraordinarily pleased, Goebbels added, after speaking with the Führer.[10]

18

Arch-Admirals and Arch-Generals

IN WASHINGTON, NEWS of the American defeat at Kasserine was met with disbelief.

The secretary of war and senior officers in the War Department who had urged the President to mount a cross-Channel invasion in the summer of 1943, as soon as Tunisia was cleared of enemy forces — even in tandem with an invasion of Sicily, should the President insist on Operation Husky, as it was code-named, to placate British anxiety to clear the Mediterranean sea route to Suez and India — were chastened. The prospects for a successful cross-Channel assault now looked pretty dire, even to Pentagon fantasists. For a moment, in fact, it looked as if Tunisia might be cleared not of Axis forces, but of American.

Stimson, sadly, took this as a sign the Allies should not have landed in Northwest Africa at all. The President demurred. The lesson, in his view, was the opposite: namely the need for more battle experience against German troops.

Combat, command, and campaign experience: these were crucial — not only at unit level, but in senior command and international-coalition cooperation. It was not only Fredendall who failed in battle. Colonel — later Brigadier General — Paul Robinett would afterward write, "One would have to search all history to find a more jumbled command structure than that of the Allies in this operation."[1] Until the onset of battlefield defeat, however, no one had seemed interested in command structures or battle techniques against a German enemy. In Tripoli, General Montgomery had organized a special "study week" or teach-in to "check up on our battle technique," launching it with a two-hour address that one British general thought "one of the best addresses I have ever heard and that is saying a lot." Thanks to Rommel's attack only a handful of U.S. officers were sent to attend, however, and among those who did go, General Patton was heard boasting, "I may be old, I may be slow, I may be stoopid, and I know I'm deaf, but it just don't mean a thing to me."[2]

On his return to Morocco, once the true extent of American debacle became clear, even Patton began to rethink his supercilious judgment. "The show was very bad — very bad indeed," he confided in a letter to his wife.[3] The matter of how to fight the Germans in battle had come to mean life or death to ninety thousand American soldiers in Tunisia. Even Stimson, in Washington, was shocked. "Heavy fighting is going on," he'd noted in his diary on February 15, "and we have yet to see whether the Americans can recover themselves and stand up to it."[4] That they hadn't, in the days thereafter, was galling.

Two days later Stimson was acknowledging that Rommel had mounted a veritable "coup" in southern Tunisia. "He has attacked our thin line of American troops in that region with a comparatively overwhelming force of tanks and has driven them back some thirty miles. Eisenhower has been expecting it and two or three days ago sent a full appraisal of the situation and of his expectation," Stimson recorded, "and he has withdrawn his force to a new line I hope without suffering irretrievable losses." The secretary worried, nevertheless, that the very distance that reinforcements would have to travel would count against the Allies. "We had such good luck in the beginning but these things were lost sight of" — thanks largely to his and Marshall's obsession with a German flank attack across Spain and the Mediterranean. "Now they will begin to count against us," he lamented. "Nevertheless we must not forget the tremendous and permanent gains which our adventure has brought us — the thus far safe occupation of northwest Africa; the acquisition of Dakar and west Africa; the diversion of Hitler's troops from the eastern front, and the irretrievable losses which he has suffered aided by that fact. All of these gains to us are, I hope, permanent and well worth any local setbacks."[5]

Elderly and obstinate to a fault when it came to the stark, bloody business of fighting real Germans in real battle, Stimson was still thinking of "gains" in strategic terms, however — not in combat and command experience: the blooding of those who had to do America's fighting, and who deserved better of their senior officers. Yet as the hours went by and reports came in of panic, desertions in the field, mass flight, surrenders, and demolitions, Stimson felt it was time to be honest. On February 18 he

Total War

On January 7, 1943, President Roosevelt announces "total war" to Congress, then secretly embarks for North Africa aboard a Boeing clipper. He will be the first U.S. president to fly while in office, and the first to visit the battlefield abroad in time of war.

Via Trinidad and Brazil, the President flies across the Atlantic to Gambia, where he tours the harbor in an American tender and spends the night on the USS *Memphis*. Then, using a special ramp for his wheelchair, Roosevelt (above right, with Captain Bryan) flies in a C-54 transport up the coast of northwest Africa to Casablanca, Morocco.

German intelligence mistakes "Casablanca" for "Casa Blanca," the White House, concluding that FDR and Churchill planned to meet in Washington. Meanwhile, in secret, FDR establishes his headquarters in a Moroccan villa (left, with his sons Elliott and Franklin Jr. and Harry Hopkins). His task: to set the Allies — and the U.S. chiefs of staff — on an implacable course for offensive victory in World War II.

At his villa headquarters, FDR assembles the Combined Chiefs of Staff. He must stop his own generals from committing U.S. forces to mass suicide before they have combat experience. He must also get the British to agree to a 1944 cross-Channel strategy. And get the fractious French to fight the Nazis, not each other.

Visiting Troops on the Battlefield

Generals Eisenhower, Clark, and Patton agree with FDR: U.S. forces need more combat experience before launching a cross-Channel invasion. The presence of the President on the North African battlefield is meanwhile inspiring.

Churchill has mixed feelings, but his British government applauds the policy Roosevelt announces to the press and to the world on behalf of the Allies: no negotiation with tyranny, and "unconditional surrender" of the Axis powers.

What should the Allies fight for? FDR and Churchill do not share the same vision, the President tells his son. They are at loggerheads over colonization: FDR is unwilling to sacrifice American lives just to restore British and French empires.

At Casablanca, FDR invites the Sultan of Morocco to dine, and admires the sunset with Churchill in Marrakesh. Before flying home, he insists on visiting Liberia, which became independent in 1847.

Totaler Krieg

At the Sportpalast in Berlin, Goebbels announces *totaler Krieg* (total war), not only as a battle of ideology, but of will.

Back in the States, the President tours the nation's military training camps where soldiers prepare for combat overseas. In secret, he orders P-38s from Guadalcanal to "get Yamamoto," the man (left) directing Japan's war in the Pacific.

finally gave a press conference that even Joseph Goebbels found "extraordinary in its frankness."[6]

"Today I had a sharp reverse to report to the press at the press conference," Stimson admitted frankly in his diary, having "decided to make no effort to whitewash it but to present it in its sharp outlines and simply in my own language to admit that it was a sharp setback and it would be folly to try to minimize it and it would be still greater folly to exaggerate it . . . I talked it over with Marshall afterwards. The only thing Marshall was worried about is that there are two extra divisions that apparently Rommel hasn't used of armored forces and is wondering where those are. Incidentally he told me that when they were in Casablanca the President wanted to divert another one of the divisions from George Patton's force at the gates of Gibraltar and ship them up into the attack in Tunisia. The Staff, however, had refused to agree to this."[7]

The true lesson — that Tunisia was America's military training ground — still eluded Stimson, though. Despite his own trip to Casablanca and then Algiers, General Marshall seemed similarly blinkered. At the Pentagon, Stimson shared with Marshall, on Marshall's return, his feeling they'd had extraordinary "luck so far and all the excitement of the success of the first attack, but now the length of communications is going to tell and we are going to be under constant pressure from the President, among others, to strip our force at the Gate [in Morocco] and send them out to Tunisia to meet the pressure that is going on there. He agreed with me that this would be disastrous."[8]

Disastrous?

That Marshall and Stimson should have continued to take counsel of such fears of a German invasion of Morocco through Spain and across the Straits of Gibraltar, even in mid-February 1943, was almost risible; certainly it made their continuing urging of a cross-Channel attack that coming summer, in tandem with the plan to invade Sicily, jejune beyond belief.

Fortunately, saner minds saw the situation differently. In the press, at least, the U.S. debacle in Tunisia did at least serve to dampen public ardor for a cross-Channel assault that year.

In Berlin, Dr. Goebbels was derisive. Reading British reports of the battle, expressing ill-concealed contempt for American fighting skills, Goebbels likened the situation to that of German forces having to fight with disappointing allies. "So the English now have their own Italians," he mocked. "We can grant them that. The British have always known how to get others to fight their battles; now they have to acknowledge Americans are even better at it,"[9] he sneered. As if this were not enough, he went on: "The Americans prefer to fight their battles in Hollywood rather than on the rough ground of Tunisia, where instead of facing paper tanks they're up against German panzers."[10] And given the awe of Rommel once again being expressed in London newspapers, his endlessly suspicious mind made him wonder if the British, in the aftermath of the battle, were using the American defeat to quieten calls for a Second Front, which the British wisely knew would fail—or at any rate "delay" the cross-Channel assault Stalin was calling for. "They're seriously doubting if they can really put together a successful Second Front."[11]

Kasserine, then, provided a wake-up call for the Allies. Obtaining authorization from Marshall to dismiss Fredendall and replace him with General George Patton, Eisenhower told Patton to fire the incompetent and "to be perfectly cold-blooded about it."[12]

Dimly—despite the lurid stories that General Wedemeyer and others had spread about how the British had "put one over" the American team at Casablanca, resulting in the outrageous delay of a Second Front—even the senior officers of the War Department began to come to their senses: accepting the President was right. A Second Front would never work until U.S. forces were battle-hardened and had had a chance to rehearse large-scale amphibious landings in Sicily.

Kasserine, moreover, put a temporary damper on the U.S. War and Navy Departments' ridiculous obsession with rank rather than experience.

No sooner had the Torch landings taken place than Admiral King had begun pressing his colleagues to back his bid to be promoted *above* four-star rank. "It seems to me that the time has come to take up the matter of more 'full' Admirals and more 'full' generals," he had written in a special memorandum to Admiral Leahy and General Marshall (though not to Lieutenant General Arnold) soon after the Torch invasion. Theater commanders in chief now needed to have four-star rank, to keep up with the British; this then meant that the Joint Chiefs, though not Arnold, should have even higher rank, he felt. "I therefore suggest that we consider the matter and make appropriate recommendations to the President," he'd urged.

Not satisfied with the idea of merely a fifth star for the chiefs, King wanted wholly new ranking nomenclature in the U.S. Armed Forces — indeed, he had his own pet proposal. "We need also to recognize that there is need to prepare for ranks higher than that of Admiral and General. As to such ranks, I suggest Arch-Admiral and Arch-General," he gave his considered view, "rather than Admiral of the Fleet and Field Marshal."[13]

Arch-Admiral King? Arch-General Marshall?

No one was impressed. King had continued to push, however. In the days leading up to Kasserine, Secretary Stimson had learned from Secretary Knox that Marshall was now slated to become a field marshal. He was appalled.

True, before Kasserine, on February 12, General Eisenhower had been promoted to temporary four-star rank in order to give him further authority as Allied commander in chief in Algiers. But for General Marshall to become an American "field marshal" when he had never actually held a field command as a general?

Stimson had asked Marshall what he thought of the idea. "Marshall was dead against any such promotion," Stimson noted with relief in his diary. "He said it would destroy all his influence both with the Congress and with the people, and he said that it really all came from the lower Admirals of the Navy Department forcing this upon King and Knox and upon the President." Stimson thus immediately wrote to the President, on February 16, in the midst of the battle in Tunisia, to try and scotch the idea — which the President did. Fiddling with more stars and "field marshal" titles — which would require Stimson and Knox putting the proposal in person before the Senate and House Armed Services Committees — seemed to Roosevelt a very poor way of defeating Field Marshal Rommel.

For his part, Dwight Eisenhower had not wanted a fourth star, even. He'd immediately cabled to thank the President for his temporary promotion to full general, in the field — but seven days later he wrote privately to his son John, at college. "It is possible that a necessity might arise for my relief and consequent demotion,"[14] he warned — glad to be able to say that his colonel's silver oak leaf in the regular army couldn't be taken away, whatever happened.

Eisenhower's untrumpeted humility did him proud. True, Ike had placed too much trust in Marshall's protégé, Fredendall. Only the cordite of *Blitzkrieg* combat could have exposed the dire weaknesses in American command and battlefield skills in the end, however. Along with many thousands of platoon, company, battalion, brigade, division, and corps commanding officers, Eisenhower himself would have to learn the "hard" way. As he wrote to his son, "You are quite mistaken in thinking that the work you are now doing is useless in the training of yourself for war." He was there, at college, to train his "mind to think. That is essential. No situation whether general or special, is ever the same in war as it was foreseen or anticipated. You must be able to think as the problem comes up."[15] And he instanced having to use Admiral Darlan to obtain swift surrender of Vichy forces in Morocco and Algeria to save American lives.

It was this very quality that President Roosevelt liked in Eisenhower. The President was certain Ike would mature in theater command. Far from demoting Eisenhower, the President was proud of the way he had handled himself and his relations with the British — authorizing General Alexander, his new field deputy, to take over day-to-day handling of the battlefront on February 19; his treatment of the press (Eisenhower accepting "full responsibility" for the debacle, off the record, with reporters); his quiet removal of General Fredendall; and his patient refusal to advance the launch date for Husky, the invasion of Sicily, by a month, as Winston Churchill pressed him to do, lest it prejudice the conditions for Husky's success.

No: in the President's view young General Eisenhower, at age fifty-two, was doing just fine — and U.S. troops, too. The President had seen them, in person, at Rabat, and was confident they'd learn the crucial lessons soon enough. Rommel was withdrawing from Kasserine, and would shortly be given his own drubbing by Montgomery at Medenine, on the Gulf of Gabès — probably the most perfect defensive one-day battle of the twentieth century.

It would all turn out for the best. It was Stalin who worried the President — for the ramification of the President's patient war strategy was this: that the United States would, by its step-by-step approach, win the global war, yet in delaying a Second Front, might well risk Russian domination of Europe in the war's aftermath.

Military prosecution of the war, in other words, was becoming every day more freighted with political consequences.

19

Between Two Forces of Evil

THE ENIGMA THAT was Russia — its communist purges in the late 1930s; its appeasement of Hitler in its infamous Molotov-Ribbentrop Pact in the summer of 1939; its subsequent occupation of eastern Poland, in the wake of Hitler's *Blitzkrieg* attack on western Poland; its similarly egregious invasion of Finland and the Winter War that had resulted in Russian annexation of 10 percent of Finnish territory, in Karelia; its fearsome NKVD police-state methods to maintain absolute communist control of the entire Soviet Union; its displacement and enforced migration of vast populations to Siberia; its veritable paranoia in terms of capitalistic, foreign influence or sway over its citizens — had not given most Americans much reason to support the Soviets, save as opponents of the even more egregious Germans.

The sheer refusal of Russian soldiers and citizens — often ill armed and ill trained — to cede their country to the German troops who had overrun all of Europe had aroused belated popular admiration in America, and growing confidence that Hitler — despite his control of Europe from Norway to Greece, and the whole of central Europe to the Crimea and Ukraine — could, in truth, be beaten. What would happen then, though? Would the Soviets, obedient on pain of death to absolute communist rule from the Kremlin, permit those countries of Europe liberated by the Soviets to become genuine, capitalist, functioning democracies? Or would they be "Sovietized" by Russia?

The President had been thinking of such matters with increasing concern in the fall of 1942, as he'd confided to the Canadian prime minister, Mackenzie King. The prospect, however, had become all the stronger once it became clear that Hitler had overplayed his hand at Stalingrad, and his Sixth Army was going to get a hammering on the Volga — indeed, that he might lose not only his Sixth Army at Stalingrad but his armies in the Caucasus, by the Black Sea, too. From being on the desperate defensive, the Russians would then begin to pose a mortal threat to the Third Reich — with or without a Second Front.

Certainly this was an eventuality that, in the privacy of his diary, Joseph Goebbels pondered. Far from causing him to question the Nazi ideology that he and Hitler had pursued over the past two decades, it only caused him to dedicate himself the more determinedly to the *Ausrottung* of the people he blamed for Europe's travails: the Jews, as he'd declared in his *totaler Krieg* speech. He now gave orders for the last Jews left in Berlin to be rounded up and sent to be liquidated in SS concentration camps — noting how much more psychologically free this made him feel. He also recorded his determination to stamp out any protest in Germany to his total-war policy in the most ruthless manner — in other words, via execution — as well as ruthless reprisals to be taken against any acts of disrespect or attempted assassination of Nazi officials in the occupied countries of Europe.

Between these two forces of pure evil, it was difficult to say which was the worst. The President had therefore, on November 19, 1942, asked his former ambassador to the Soviet Union, William C. Bullitt, to furnish him with a private report on how he saw the future of Europe, following the successful Torch landings. In particular, Roosevelt wanted to have the former ambassador's reading of Russian intentions.

Bill Bullitt had taken his time. He'd recently been used by the President as an ambassador at large, conducting a presidential mission to West Africa, Egypt, Libya, Palestine, Syria, Iraq, and Iran in the spring of 1942. Independently wealthy thanks to his second marriage, he had then become director of public relations to the secretary of the Navy, Frank Knox. It had taken him two months to comply with the President's new request — too late, unfortunately, for the Casablanca Conference — but when it was ready, it was dynamite.

"Dear Mr. President," Bullitt's covering letter ran, written on January 29, 1943, the day before the President's return to Washington. "The appended will take thirty minutes of your time. It is as serious a document as any I have ever sent you." He warned that "its conclusion is that you should talk with Stalin as soon as possible" — and wished Roosevelt good luck in the attempt.[1]

The President *did* read it — and swiftly invited Bullitt to lunch at the

White House to discuss its implications for Allied political and military strategy.

Bullitt's report pulled no punches. Having served as America's very first envoy to Moscow, he had, after all, an almost unrivaled perspective both on Stalin and the Russians. In addition, for an American he had a keen perspective on Europe, having been U.S. ambassador to France for four years, right up to the German conquest of France in 1940.

Bullitt's portrait of Stalin and his Soviet aims was uncompromising. His memorandum began by trashing former Republican president Herbert Hoover's notion that Stalin had changed his philosophy, wanted no annexations, and was only interested in Russian security. The dictator was reported, in the view of such innocents as Hoover, "to be determined to have the Soviet Union evolve in the direction of liberty and democracy, freedom of speech and freedom of religion. We ought to pray that this is so," Bullitt allowed; "for if it is so, the road to a world of liberty, democracy and peace will be relatively easy." If this was not so, however, "the road will be up-hill all the way." The free world would be tilting in one direction, the oppressive Soviet Union or empire in another.

In these circumstances, Bullitt felt, America must do everything to halt the Russian tilt before it was too late. It was, he wrote, "in our national interest to attempt to draw Stalin into cooperation with the United States and Great Britain, for the establishment of an Atlantic Charter peace," such as the President's teams in Washington were mapping out. "We ought to try to accomplish this feat, however improbable success may seem," for America would then be on the side of right, not merely might. But in dealing with Stalin, Bullitt was adamant, it was imperative to strip away any illusion.

"The reality is that the Soviet Union, up to the present time, has been a totalitarian dictatorship in which there has been no freedom of speech, no freedom of the press, and a travesty of freedom of religion; in which there has been universal fear of the OGPU [secret police] and Freedom from Want has been subordinated always to the policy of guns instead of butter." Stalin might well be persuaded to close down the nefarious Comintern, fomenting world communist revolution — but only because, in the end, Stalin actually *had* no real interest in world revolution by communists; his interest was only in communist-controlled nations serving as "5th column for the Soviet State" or empire. World communist revolution was but "a secondary objective."

As Bullitt pointed out from his intimate, personal knowledge of the dictator, Joseph Stalin had no illusions — or even belief in communism as a motivating faith. He "lets no ideological motives influence his actions," Bullitt warned. Whether the global future lay with the ideal of communism or the president's four freedoms, Stalin was indifferent. His only goal was to maintain and extend the power of the Soviet Union: greater Russia, in effect, as a police state ruled by fear. "He is highly intelligent. He weighs with suspicious realism all factors involved in advancing the interests or boundaries of the Soviet Union. He moves where opposition is weak. He stops where opposition is strong. He puts out pseudopodia" — amoeba-like tentacles — "rather than leaping like a tiger. If the pseudopodia meet no obstacle, the Soviet Union flows on."

The moral, then, was that the United States must do everything in its power to show genuine *desire* for cooperation, as well as to "prove to Stalin that, while we have intense admiration for the Russian people and will collaborate fully with a pacific Soviet State, we will resist a predatory Soviet State just as fiercely as we are now resisting a predatory Nazi State." If not, "we shall have fought a great war not for liberty but for Soviet dictatorship."

This was a sobering eventuality.

"How can we make sure that this will not happen," Bullitt asked rhetorically, "and achieve our own aim in a world of freedom and democracy?"

It would be a case of America Inc. versus Russia Red.

President Roosevelt nodded his head in agreement — for whatever was published in liberal-minded newspapers and journals in the United States, he himself had no illusions about Stalin, or the nature of the Soviet terror state, maintained entirely by patriotism and fear. Moreover, he was pleased to see Bullitt supporting his presidential policy of unconditional surrender of the Nazis and Japanese — whereas there were many, including Third Secretary George Kennan in Moscow, who favored making a deal with the German generals, or non-Nazis, to help fight the Soviet regime. To the President this would be tantamount to condoning German militarism, wars of conquest, and use of terror against its own citizens — whether Jews or gypsies, political prisoners or priests — just as it would be were Japan's example of inhumanity — its savage, genocidal war in China and its atrocity-ridden rampage across the Southwest Pacific — to be condoned. Unconditional surrender and disarmament of the Axis powers was a sine qua non of a permanent postwar peace in the world, beginning on a new page, the President felt strongly — and Bullitt, in his report, did not contest this.

One by one the President ticked Bullitt's points: that unless Russia was pressured into declaring war on Japan, for example, following German capitulation, the United States would be tied down, having to fight its way unaided, island by island, until it could finally bomb and invade the Japanese heartland, which might take years — while in the meantime Russia's amoeba would be left free to spread across Europe, infecting defenseless nations and hitching them to Stalin's Sovietizing wagon.

The answer to that, in Bullitt's view, was to press Stalin, while U.S. Lend-Lease assistance was still critical to Soviet military victory against the Wehrmacht, into agreeing not only to enter the war against Japan in due course, but to sign up to a formal agreement committing the Allies to establish a postwar democratic Europe — not, as was the alternative, a group of communist puppet states subservient to the Soviet Union.

This, as Bullitt articulately put it, could only be done by securing an early meeting with Stalin, since "our bargaining position will be hopeless after the defeat of Germany," when Russian troops would in all likelihood be in occupation of all central Europe up to the Elbe — perhaps even up to the Rhine. Churchill, too, must be harnessed to a European, rather than imperial British, cause, alongside the United States — with everything done, from this moment forth, to prepare the governments in exile and future European leaders to establish strong democratic structures that Stalin's fifth columnists could not successfully subvert.

World disarmament was, in Bullitt's realistic view, impossible — yet he doubted whether U.S. public opinion would willingly support yet another war in Europe to defend defenseless individual states. Ergo, rather than disarm those states, or press such states to disarm, they should be encouraged to arm themselves against Russian interference — forming a U.S.-and-British-supported coalition or alliance. They should be urged to become a European bloc of "Integrated Europe," which Stalin would not dare challenge. "Soviet invasion finds barriers in armed strength," Bullitt emphasized, "not in Soviet promises."

This prediction — an early 1943 version of what became, in 1948, the Western European Union and NATO — was very much the President's thinking. Using Lend-Lease as a lever, it would involve a carrot-and-stick approach to get Stalin, as soon as possible, to dissolve the Comintern as the instigator of world communist revolution; to agree to eventual entry into the war against Japan, once Germany was defeated; and to agree, in a formal document, to sign up to a United Nations world authority guaranteeing the independence and self-government of sovereign states — with the United States and Britain, as two of the world's Four Policemen, ready and willing to use air, naval, and, if necessary, ground forces to counter any attempt, by anyone, to invade such sovereign states.

Would Joseph Stalin, dictator of a police state supposedly wedded to Marxist-Leninist communist ideology, willingly sign up to a democratic concept like this, however — a charter that would be a permanent indictment of the Russian police state?

As Bullitt acknowledged, the Russians would have the "whip hand" at the end of the war. In all frankness, moreover, there seemed little evidence the Soviets, led and ruled by Stalin, were going to undergo a Pauline conversion and become guardians of democracy and freedom, together with the United States, Britain, and China, across the globe — at least not anytime soon. It was therefore imperative that the United States and Britain — since China, for all its millions of people, was in no position to police anyone, indeed would probably have to cede Manchuria to the Soviets — ensure that their own troops reached, as soon as possible, a demarcation line in Europe beyond which Stalin's troops could not march without going to war with the United States, the Soviet Union's great provider.

Where, exactly, as Bullitt surveyed the world in January 1943, would this line be, however — *and how could the Western allies hope to reach it before the Russians?*

This, indeed, was an interesting question.

A colleague of Bullitt's — Bullitt did not name him in his report — had recently posited the end-of-war Sovietization of Europe would include "at least Finland, the Baltic States, Poland, Rumania, Hungary, Czechoslovakia and the entire Balkan peninsula including probably European Turkey" — unless, Bullitt argued, the President beat Stalin to the punch. The United States should therefore "define as Europe the Europe of 1938," he suggested — "minus Bessarabia, which should go to the Soviet Union" — and seek to save that version of Europe from the predatory clutches of the Russian bear. In this respect there was, Bullitt reemphasized, "only one sure guarantee that the Red Army will not cross into Europe — the prior arrival of American and British Armies in the eastern frontiers of Europe."

The eastern frontiers of Europe — when U.S. forces still did not have a single soldier on the European continent?

Anticipating the President's frown, Bullitt had admitted in his report: "To state this is to state what appears to be an absurdity, if the assumption is made that we can reach the eastern frontiers of Europe only by marching through France, Italy and Germany" before the Russians. However Bullitt had a better alternative. "It may . . . be possible to reach this frontier before the Red Army," the former ambassador and now assistant to the U.S. Navy secretary wrote, "if we make our attack on the Axis not by way of France and Italy but by way of Salonika and Constantinople."[2]

Oh dear! the President sighed. Bullitt clearly had less idea of geography as it pertained to military matters than a schoolchild. Had he never heard of the disastrous "Salonika Front" in World War I, or Churchill's fatal Allied assault in the Dardanelles in 1915 — not to speak of the First and Second Balkan Wars of 1912 and 1913?

The President had recently heard similar Balkan proposals being trotted out by Prime Minister Churchill and the French high commissioner, General Giraud, at Casablanca. Given the disaster in the Dardanelles in 1915, it had been utterly amazing to hear Winston recommending such a military strategy. Yet General Giraud was just as unrealistic, the President had found. Both were men of great courage — but in the search for alternatives to "war by attrition," they were given to fantasies that were almost criminal in terms of the loss of human life to which their ill-considered ventures would lead — Churchill's Gallipoli fiasco having cost the Western Allies no fewer than a quarter million casualties.

Ignoring this, Churchill had at Casablanca favored pressing Turkey's president to declare war on Hitler, and revival of the idea of a Dardanelles campaign. He'd asked Giraud whether he agreed — at which the five-star French general had countered with his own equally amazing notion of Allied military strategy.

"*Tout simple*," Giraud had opined. "First, liberate Africa. Which is being done. This should be finished by spring this year. Then, without wasting a minute, occupy the three big Mediterranean islands: Sicily, Sardinia, and Corsica. Establish a base there, primarily air forces, to assault the mainland of Europe. As soon as the forces are ready, invade the coast of Italy, between Livorno and Genoa. Seize the Po valley. Clean up the rest of the Italian peninsula, and prepare to strike into the heart of Europe on the axis: Udine [northwest of Venice, between the Alps and the Adriatic] and Vienna, backed by air power serviced from bases across the whole of Italy. In one blow Germany can thus be invaded through the Danube valley: we will isolate the Balkans on the right, and have France on the left, and we will beat the Russians to Vienna, which is not to be sniffed at," he'd announced. "After that, following the fall of Germany, the business of Japan will be a piece of cake. QED."[3]

Clearly Giraud — who still pressed to be made Allied commander in chief in the Mediterranean instead of General Eisenhower, rather than have to deal with political matters he abhorred — saw himself as a modern Napoleon, though about a foot taller.

At Casablanca, Churchill had not discouraged this idea — though the President had refused to countenance such craziness. It was therefore nothing short of galling, at lunch at the White House, to have to listen to former ambassador Bullitt, the director of public relations in the Navy Department, now recommending, as an American, such military bêtises.

Bullitt claimed, to the President's concern, he was not alone in Washington in advancing such a war strategy. His discussions at the Navy Department and elsewhere had convinced him, Bullitt maintained, that "there is a large body of military opinion in Washington that favors — on purely military grounds — striking at the Axis by way of Greece, Turkey, Bulgaria and Rumania rather than by way of France and Italy."[4]

Dump the whole idea of a cross-Channel attack?

On paper the notion appeared bold and imaginative — if wars were conducted on paper. Like Giraud, Bullitt seemed convinced the Western Allies could make straight for central Europe, and secure its boundaries before the Russians got there, without problem — irrespective of the terrain. Or the Germans. "This is a question for you and Churchill, and your military advisors to decide," Bullitt allowed[5] — convinced that Churchill, who was nothing if not imaginative, would be of like mind.

The conclusion to Bullitt's twenty-four-page report to the President had climaxed with a three-point politico-military recommendation. Roosevelt should persuade Churchill to subscribe to a "policy of an integrated, democratic Europe." "Conversations between you and Stalin" should then be arranged. But behind the scenes, while negotiating on paper with Stalin, an "immediate study of an attack on the Axis by way of Greece, Turkey, Bulgaria and Rumania" should be ordered by the President.[6]

There was even a fourth recommendation: namely that Bullitt's archrival at the State Department, Sumner Welles, be fired — thus empowering the deeply anti-Soviet secretary, Cordell Hull, to take Bill Bullitt as his deputy, as the Allies raced through the Balkans into central Europe.

QED.

Bullitt's report — which would later be quoted as a kind of Lost Ark that could have changed the course of history, had it been followed — was, in its military naiveté, as senseless as it was callous in respect to the lives that would have been lost in pursuing such a course. Lunching with Bullitt, the President could only shake his head at a man so right about the Soviets and so wrong about military matters.

Winston Churchill, for his part, did not feel the same way. While the President had returned straightaway from North Africa to Washington via Liberia, Bathurst, Natal, and Jamaica (where a recuperated Admiral Leahy was picked up), the Prime Minister had nevertheless flown, against the advice even of his own cabinet, to Turkey, in a vain attempt to get President Ismet Inonu to join the Western Allies — and thus open the way to an invasion of southern Europe via the Balkans and Constantinople: the dream that had consumed him in 1915 and had led to his resignation as First Lord of the Admiralty when it failed.

Roosevelt had been skeptical whether President Inonu would comply with Churchill's request, any more than Portugal or Spain or Sweden could be expected to give up their neutrality in the war. He had, however, authorized Churchill to share with Inonu the President's notions of unconditional surrender and a postwar United Nations authority — not only as a bulwark against future wars of aggression, but as a counter to future Russian expansionism.

The President had cautioned Churchill, however, neither to promise too much military aid, if Inonu did decide to join the war, nor to suggest that the Allies were planning a new invasion of Salonika, as in 1915. The Germans, he warned, would be tougher even than Atatürk's army at Gallipoli — and the mountains beyond Salonika would make an Allied campaign a dead end. His remit, in terms of the U.S.-British coalition, was merely to explore the possibility of airfields and military staging bases being established in Turkey, and if not, to encourage Turkey in its neutrality: dissuading it from any thought of alliance or cooperation with the Third Reich, and encouraging it as a bulwark against communism. This, to his great credit, Churchill had attempted to do as part emissary, part negotiator, flying to Adana and meeting with Inonu onboard their two trains. To the relief of Sir Alexander Cadogan and General Brooke, the Prime Minister had been surprisingly circumspect — relying on his gifts of ratiocination and literary composition. No sooner had he arrived, therefore, than he handed President Inonu a paper he'd written en route to Turkey called "Morning Thoughts: Note on Postwar Security" — a copy of which he was careful to cable to the President in Washington.

Like Bullitt's report, Churchill's Turkish memorandum was to become an important historical document.

In Churchillian prose (Cadogan noting in his diary, "He was awfully proud of it"), the Prime Minister's paper summarized the outcome of the Casablanca Conference and the outlook for the world at the end of the war. As soon as the "unconditional surrender of Germany and Italy" was achieved, the "unconditional surrender" of Japan, too, would be procured — with subsequent "disarmament of the guilty nations" enforced by the victors. ("On the other hand no attempt will be made to destroy their peoples or to prevent them gaining a living and leading a decent life in spite of all the crimes they have committed," Churchill added the rider.) Reparations would not be demanded by the Western countries "as was tried last time," though Russia would have to be helped "in every possible way in her work of restoring the economic life of her people" after suffering "such a horrible devastation" as Hitler had inflicted. This, then, led to the President's plans for a United Nations authority.

The authority was to be "a world organization for the preservation of peace based upon the conceptions of freedom of justice and the revival of prosperity" — one that would not be "subject to the weakness of former League of Nations." It would be held together under the military protection of the victors, who would "continue fully armed, especially in the air." "None can predict with certainty that the victors will never quarrel amongst themselves, or that the United States may not once again retire from Europe, but after the experiences which all have gone through, and their sufferings and the certainty that a third struggle will destroy all that is left of culture, wealth and civilization of mankind and reduce us to the level almost of wild beasts, the most intense effort will be made by the leading Powers," Churchill summarized, "to prolong their honorable association and by sacrifice and self-restraint to win for themselves a glorious name in human annals." Great Britain would "do her utmost to organize a coalition of resistance to any act of aggression committed by any power;" moreover, "it is believed that the United States will cooperate with her and even possibly take the lead of the world, on account of her numbers and strength, in the good work of preventing such tendencies to aggression before they break into open war."[7]

Though it might not be as magically phrased as some of his prose masterpieces and speeches, Churchill's memorandum reflected the extent to which he now understood and agreed with the President's vision of the United Nations and postwar world security at this moment in the war. Given such a future, then, would not Turkey wish to guarantee its own security "by taking her place as a victorious belligerent and ally at the side of Great Britain, the United States and Russia," Churchill had asked President Inonu?

It was a beguiling prospect, but President Inonu, understandably, had declined. The Prime Minister's paper certainly exuded confidence in the inevitable eventual victory of the Allies — but it seemed oblivious to Hitler's likely actions in the meantime. The document made no mention of this, or of the military problems inherent in mounting an invasion of southern and central Europe through northern Italy and/or the Balkans. Or even of Stalin's possible reaction to such a change in Allied military strategy — a change that, if it stalled in the Mediterranean without a Second Front, would give Stalin every reason to scorn the President's plans for unconditional surrender and the establishment of a postwar United Nations authority as idle nonsense.

Both Bullitt's report and Churchill's memorandum were, to be sure, written before the reality of war against the Wehrmacht finally set in. In this respect the American defeat at Kasserine, two weeks after Bullitt's report, had quickly poured cold water on any idea in Washington or London that the Allies could race anywhere, let alone through the Balkans. At his private luncheon at the White House with the President, Bullitt had thus backed off his Balkan idea — for the moment. It was too early to be contemplating ambitious American campaigns in the Mediterranean when for a moment it looked as if U.S. forces would be driven out of Tunisia. Besides, the public would have to be encouraged to support a more interventionist role in American foreign policy if the President was to have any genuine credence in exploiting its current creditor-status with Stalin.

In this respect, at least, the President's vision of the postwar peace seemed to be gaining traction, unaffected by the reverse at Kasserine — in fact it began to become clear, as the weeks went by, that the President's State of the Union address was bearing amazing, anti-isolationist fruit.

Roosevelt had assumed his State of the Union address, with its description of "total war," its call for the disarmament of America's enemies, and his outline of postwar social programs and international security, would be strongly contested in Congress and outside. Far from it. His speech — and press coverage of the Casablanca "unconditional surrender meeting" — seemed to trigger, the President found, a sort of national American awakening to world responsibility that had never really existed before.

Burgeoning pride at the success of the Torch invasion and MacArthur's advances in the Pacific — where, in the battle of the Bismarck Sea, American B-25s carrying five-second five-hundred-pound bombs, carried out "the most devastating air attack on ships in the entire war," in the words of naval historian S. E. Morison[8] (sinking seven of the eight Japanese transports seeking to reinforce Lae following the evacuation of Guadalcanal) — left the noninterventionist voices of Charles Lindbergh, Joseph P. Kennedy, and Senators William Borah, Robert LaFollette, Hiram Johnson, Arthur Vandenberg, and Burton K. Wheeler looking like defeatists. The Casablanca summit — trumpeted in newspaper reports and pictures, as well as in movie-house newsreels shown across the country — lent a moral grandeur to the turnaround in the fortunes of war: photographs of brave, cigar-wielding Winston Churchill sitting beside the President, declaring himself to be his "active lieutenant," French generals shaking hands, the President inspecting and eating with U.S. forces in the field . . . Even Lord Halifax, the British ambassador, was full of congratulations when writing to the Prime Minister, extolling the results of the Casablanca Conference and noting in his diary how, in America, Republicans and Democrats were beginning to talk of the future in a new and wholly different way.

Lord Halifax was learning, himself, to see the world in a different way. Since his appointment to the embassy and America's entry into the war, he had had to meet with people of every stripe and to learn the complexities and nuances of the American political system, with its checks and balances — and vituperative press. As a result Halifax had become a more astute observer of trends in the United States than in his home country, where his aristocratic airs and way of life (hunting, shooting) had inured him, as a notorious appeaser, to the fact that the younger, post–World War I generation would, in fact, fight Hitler — but not for a colonialist, class-riven British Empire they no longer believed in. The President's latest postwar vision, which Roosevelt had shared with him in private talks at the White House, struck Ambassador Halifax not only as positive, but one that even former isolationist Americans seemed more and more willing to embrace. Even the former U.S. president, Herbert Hoover, who lunched with Lord Halifax on January 8, 1943, after the President's address to Congress, had expressed a more "friendly" view of America's association with Britain than before, the ambassador had found. "We discussed a great many post war things," Halifax recorded in his diary — relieved to hear the former president was "absolutely convinced of the necessity of our working together" as nations. "On the whole I was cheered by my talk with him and by his estimate of what American public opinion will accept in the way of international cooperation." Hitherto, public opinion had opposed any American treaty or involvement with other countries that could be "represented as infringement of [American] national sovereignty. This was the rock on which [President] Wilson broke — the idea that some League or conference should dictate United States action." But now — at least in Hoover's opinion — public opinion was changing, as were former president Hoover's own attitudes. "These difficulties would not in his view arise if you had some international organisation that would content itself with expressing moral opinions and leave it to the joint policemen, whom he sees as the United States, ourselves, and, if she will play, Russia, to take action on their own," Halifax noted. The United Nations — or "whatever the international body was" that would be set up at the war's end — would "make a report and recommendation to the policemen," which the policemen could either carry out or not.[9]

This exploratory notion of a United Nations Security Council was a momentous reversal — and when in Washington Lord Halifax addressed assembled British consuls from main U.S. cities, several days later, the ambassador advised them to push the notion of the "British Commonwealth," rather than "Empire," as having "a biggish part to play" in the coming times — yet to exercise "self-restraint, when Americans threw their weight around."

America, henceforth, would be top dog, Halifax made clear. From that meeting the ambassador had then gone to the State Department "to discuss the draft of a scheme for what the Americans call the rehabilitation of the world."[10]

Rehabilitation it certainly would be. The Russian ambassador, Maxim Litvinov, was present at the State Department meeting, too. "We got along fairly well and all did our best to be accommodating to one another. Some difference of opinion as to whether the inner management committee of the thing should be composed of the four Powers," as a security council, "or, as we [British] had suggested, seven" — which would "permit Canada as a great supplier to be on [it], probably a South American, and one of the smaller European allies. Litvinoff made a strong argument about this thing being used as a pattern for the future, and consequently the importance of keeping the four big powers undiluted. I thought there was a good deal in his argument," Halifax noted, approving the Russian's view.[11]

Ten days later, on January 18, 1943, barely a week after the President's State of the Union address, Halifax was noting that Dr. Alan Valentine, president of the University of Rochester — a Democrat who had campaigned for the Republican Wendell Willkie in the 1940 presidential election, organizing "Democrats for Willkie" in opposition to a third term for FDR — "did not think there was much danger of isolation." In fact, Valentine now found Willkie "too emotional and immature."[12] A new "American State [Department] book about American policy in the last ten years" had shown "how paralyzed their Executive was," after World War I, "owing to the prevalence of isolationist thought."[13] Even Willkie himself, when Halifax dined with him on January 27, emphasized the change of Republican mind — now claiming "that historically the Republican party had not been isolationist and had only accidentally been thrown into isolationism after the last war by Wilson's attempt to monopolise the international ticket. He was apprehensive lest something of the kind should happen again, and spoke very earnestly about the necessity of nothing being said in British quarters" of Republicans backing away from an internationalist stance, lest this actually revive isolationist sentiment. "He spoke with great certainty, as did Claire Luce" — a Republican congresswoman from Connecticut and wife of the publisher of *Life* magazine — "about the Republican party in 1944 being victorious."[14]

By the time the President returned from North Africa, therefore, it had been to find his utopian hen had laid its eggs — indeed, the next day Halifax noted a long talk with Henry Luce "about the prospects of the Republican Party being isolationist after the war." Luce dismissed the very idea, just as Willkie had — in fact claimed, like Willkie, that isolationism had been an aberration — the United States having "only accidentally got into that line in 1920," according to Luce. Halifax was then stunned as Luce proceeded to advance Roosevelt's internationalist agenda. "On the postwar business Luce said that he wanted to make a careful examination of just what an international police force might mean," but was not averse to it. "He said that there had been a curious revolution in American feeling in the last few years" — in fact, in the last few weeks. "A short time ago, if you had listened to any argument between the isolationists and internationalists, the isolationists would at once have clinched the argument by saying: 'You want to police the world, do you?' which was generally held to be conclusive against it. Now, he said, American public opinion was completely convinced that an international police force was desirable."[15]

When Halifax went to see the President in person at the White House on February 15, he was told that columnist Walter Lippmann, no less, was talking of "the United States being established in some European base after the war," so that "any infraction of European peace" should at once be addressed: the forerunner of NATO.[16]

20

Health Issues

THOUGH IT WAS too early to crow, the President thus seemed decidedly proud, Halifax found. His step-by-step military strategy for prosecuting the war had been set in stone at the Casablanca Conference — with the target, in writing, of almost a million U.S. troops and their weapons to be conveyed to Britain by December 31, 1943, ready to launch a full-scale invasion across the English Channel in April or May 1944. As Averell Harriman noted, based on his conference notes, a "new joint command (COSSAC, acronym for Chief of Staff to the Supreme Allied Commander) was created to begin immediate planning for this climactic operation known later as Overlord."[1]

The postwar world, too, with luck, might well turn out the way the President envisioned, with the growing support of the American public, the Republican Party, and America's British partners — though the latter would have a difficult row to hoe if they chose to reestablish their colonial empire as Churchill wished.

It was in this context that FDR's health raised some concern, however. Although in the immediate aftermath of his trip to Africa Roosevelt had seemed energized and rejuvenated, in the weeks following the Casablanca Conference it was evident that the journey had taken a physical toll on the President. At least to those in close contact with him. His cousin Daisy, especially.

Daisy Suckley had been relieved to see the President looking so well on his return — yet she remained disappointed by the meager medical attention her hero appeared to be receiving as president of the United States. After ten years in the Oval Office, Mr. Roosevelt still relied on a simple

U.S. Navy doctor as his personal White House physician: Dr. Ross McIntire, who'd been on his staff since 1933 and could be relied upon "to keep a close mouth" about the President's medical condition.

McIntire was an eye, ear, nose, and throat specialist by early training as an intern. He'd had an undistinguished record thereafter, becoming a simple naval dispensary physician, onboard and onshore. Nevertheless, he'd been recommended to the new president by former president Woodrow Wilson's floundering doctor, Cary Grayson — one incompetent recommending another, it would be claimed.[2] Beyond daily treatment of Roosevelt's notorious sinus problems, McIntire appeared to do little for his patient other than keep at bay those doctors who might offer the President more expert medical attention, in view of his fragile health: practitioners who might equally, however, blab inadvertently to reporters employed by Colonel McCormick, owner of the *Chicago Times-Herald,* or Cissy Patterson, owner of the *Washington Times-Herald* — both of them sworn enemies of the Democratic president and determined to oppose his reelection if he stood for a fourth term.

Despite McIntire's mediocre medical talents, the President, then, had been content to continue with a single doctor — in fact, in 1938 Roosevelt had appointed McIntire surgeon general of the U.S. Navy, in addition to his White House duties, and soon had him promoted to the rank of rear admiral — with responsibility for what became a vast naval medical system, involving 175,000 doctors, nurses, and professional medical staff. Such enlarged duties, however, were plainly incompatible with continuing daily care of the paralyzed chief executive.

Such was Roosevelt's authority, however, that by 1943 no one dared question McIntire's solitary supervision of the President, in spite of worrying signs of deterioration in FDR's health, even in the run-up to his historic flight to Africa.

Staying with the President on December 4, 1942, for example, the Canadian prime minister, Mackenzie King, had been alarmed by the President's physical condition. When he'd first gone in to see him, King reflected, "the President was smoking a cigarette in bed while reading the papers. I felt that even at that hour of the morning, he seemed a little tired and breath still a bit short."[3]

Given the President's vast responsibilities and the fact that his mental acuity seemed in no way impaired, King had given no further thought to the matter. The trip to North Africa, meanwhile, had seemingly done wonders for his state of mind and body, the President's staff felt on the

President's return, as did visitors to the White House. "The President was in fine form," the secretary of war recorded in his diary on February 3 — "one of the best and most friendly talks I have ever had. He was full of his trip, naturally, and interspersed our whole talk with stories and anecdotes." Though he found them amusing, Stimson was nevertheless discouraged "to see how he clung to the ideal of doing all this sort of work himself."[4]

The war secretary was seventy-four and in excellent health; the President, sixty-two. Stimson noticed nothing amiss in Roosevelt's form other than his messy approach to administration, which Stimson deplored. "He was very friendly but, as I expected, takes a different and thoroughly Rooseveltian view of what historic good administrative procedure has required in such a case as we have in North Africa," the secretary noted. "He wants to do it all himself. He says he did settle all the matters that were troubling Eisenhower when he was over there" — and even claimed Robert Murphy was in North Africa not "as a diplomat to report to Hull but as a special appointee of his own to handle special matters on which he reported to Roosevelt direct. This was a truly Rooseveltian position. I told him frankly over the telephone that it was bad administration and asked him what a Cabinet was for and what Departments were for," he recorded, "but I have small hopes of reforming him. The fault is Rooseveltian and deeply ingrained. Theodore Roosevelt had it to a certain extent but never anywhere nearly as much as this one."[5]

Stimson's criticism of the President was well founded, though his recommendation, namely that the United States should simply administer French North Africa in the same way as the War Department had ruled Cuba, the Philippines, and Puerto Rico, belied the secretary of war's ongoing turf battle with Cordell Hull rather than the tricky realities of the situation. With regard to the President's health, however, neither Stimson nor the majority of the President's visitors seemed alert to any problems.

Only Daisy Suckley paid attention to what was happening — or not happening. After she met with the President, at Hyde Park, she confided her concern to her diary — noting disorienting symptoms of transcontinental air travel that would later be called jet lag. "All his party have been feeling miserable since they got back," she recorded on February 7. "He just hasn't let himself give in until he got here — Then he 'let go' & feels exhausted — the President finding it hard, he said, to rise in the mornings, and sleeping late."[6]

• • •

Was it merely desynchronosis — disruption of circadian sleep rhythms — though, Daisy wondered? After Pearl Harbor the President had stopped swimming daily in the White House pool. He was still smoking several packs of cigarettes a day, but his doctor seemed to pay little or no attention to the President's elevated blood pressure, or to his cardiac condition — despite the fact that there had been worries on that account even before the 1940 election, when he'd been beset by heart problems he couldn't keep from those around him.

"His color was bad; his face was lined and he appeared to be worn out. His jaw was swollen as a result of a tooth infection . . . And I learned there was worry over strain on Roosevelt's heart," the chairman of the Democratic National Committee, James Farley, recalled later.[7] Bill Bullitt was more specific; he would claim that he'd been present at a White House dinner in early 1940 when the President had suffered "a very slight heart attack" and had collapsed.[8]

A *heart attack?* It was little wonder McIntire had been concerned at the height the airplane would have to fly on its journey to Casablanca and then home. On the positive side, however, the President had shown the world he was on the top of his form at Casablanca. Even the dark areas beneath his eyes had vanished, people noticed. "He looks well," Daisy acknowledged in her diary — her anxiety being more over the risk of a flying accident than his health at this stage. The plane carrying Averell Harriman and Brigadier Vivian Dykes — senior British aide to Field Marshal Dill in Washington — back to England had in fact crashed on landing in Wales. Though Harriman survived, Dykes had perished. As Daisy implored the President: "I told him we all thought he *should not* take the risks of such a trip."[9]

"Well — not for some time anyway," the President had responded at Hyde Park, where he reclaimed Fala, his Scottie — hugging the woolly black dog to his breast. When Daisy left to go back to her job at the president's library, which had been created in 1939 and for which she had been working since 1941, "Fala looked at me," she wrote, "but trotted after the P."[10]

Daisy was not convinced, however — and became less so when the President then fell ill again and again in February. The President's physician showed little concern. "Allied successes lessened the nervous strain," was all Dr. McIntire would later comment in a memoir he wrote, "and the President not only picked up weight but lost some of his care lines."[11]

• • •

Was the President really all right, though? Or were underlying, potentially serious health issues not being sufficiently addressed?

To Daisy, his confidante, the President had once remarked that "he caught everything in sight," as he put it. There was nothing new in this, he'd added — "all his life had been that way."[12] His near-fatal bout with virulent flu in 1918; his contracting of poliomyelitis in 1921; his repeated sinusitis; his collapses from possible heart or vascular failure — these were but the more dramatic examples of his proneness to infection and other ailments, he accepted.

Illness was not something Roosevelt dwelt upon or paid much attention to — an attitude Eleanor, his wife, did not discourage, since it absolved her of marital anxieties at a moment when she herself was undertaking such a demanding schedule as First Lady at the White House, spokesperson for the underprivileged, and mother to six children, not to speak of grandchildren.

This left Cousin Daisy, though, to worry all the more on behalf of the President. "The P. looked very tired, but did his usual part of 'Exhibit A,' as he calls it" — entertaining, for example, a party he was hosting at the White House on Valentine's Day, February 14, without Eleanor, who'd flown to Indiana. "At nine, he said he had to go to work & left the guests, calling to me to go with him. He got on the sofa in his study and said he was exhausted — He looked it. He said: 'I'm either Exhibit A, or left completely alone.'"[13]

Daisy was flabbergasted. "It made me feel terrible — I've never heard a word of complaint from him, but it seemed to slip out, unintentionally, & spoke volumes," she had penned in her diary that night. The wife of the President's military aide and appointments secretary, Mrs. Watson, had "said at lunch, on Friday, that 'he is the loneliest man in the world.' I know what she means. He has no real 'home life' in which to relax, & 'recoup' his strength & his peace of mind. If he wasn't such a wonderful character, he would sink under it."[14]

Toward the end of February, 1943, he did, in fact, sink, laid low yet again, this time by what he afterward called "sleeping sickness or Gambia fever or some kindred bug in that hell-hole of yours," as the President complained in a letter to the Prime Minister in London, that "left me feeling like a wet rag. I was no good after 2 p.m. and, after standing it for a week or so, I went to Hyde Park for five days."[15] Daisy looked after him there, recording in her diary on February 27 that it was "the P.'s. 4th day in bed, & he still feels somewhat miserable though his fever has gone. Last Tuesday, without any warning, he felt ill about noon. He lay on his study sofa & slept 'til 4.30, when he found he had a temp. of 102. The Dr. found it was toxic poisoning, but they can't ascribe it to anything they know of . . . The P. doesn't look well but is improving." After having supper with him, eating from trays, she gave him the aspirin Dr. McIntire had prescribed — and almost wept when he said: "Do you know that I have never had anyone just sit around and take care of me like this before." Apart from nurses when he was very unwell, "he is just given his medicine or takes it himself. Everyone else has been too busy to sit with him, doing nothing."[16]

If the President's condition — his tiredness, his fevers, and his everlasting sinus infections — caused him now to draw back a little from the more commanding role he'd taken in directing the U.S. military, this was understandable — in fact, to many in the War Department it was a relief, as planning for the Husky invasion, slated for July that year, went ahead. Even the U.S. setback at Kasserine had not worried him unduly or diminished his confidence in young General Eisenhower; it was, after all, proof of his wisdom in insisting American forces learn the skills of modern combat in a "safe" region of the Mediterranean, where they could swiftly recover.

When Eisenhower's naval aide, Lieutenant Commander Butcher, was brought to the Oval Office to report to the Commander in Chief on March 26, 1943, one of the first questions the President asked him was to give an account of the Kasserine debacle — from Eisenhower's perspective. "He wanted to know how things were going" in North Africa, Butcher recorded. Naturally, he knew them from "official reports," but he wanted to have the story from the horse's mouth. He was "inquisitive about Fredendall and other commanders at the front, the retreat of the Americans naturally being in his mind. I explained to him the reluctance Ike had in relieving Fredendall, and his hope that the change to Patton could be handled in such a way that Fredendall's fine qualities, particularly for training, would not be lost to the army."

To Butcher's surprise the President — who himself hated to have to fire people — seemed more interested in U.S. intelligence. He "wanted to know the circumstances that caused our G-2 [head of military intelligence] to predict that the main thrust of the Germans would come through the Ousseltia Pass rather than at Sidi Bou Zid. I explained to him

[British Brigadier] Mockler-Ferryman's reliance on one source of information, namely the interception of radio communications [Ultra] and that since this source theretofore had proven reliable, not only Mockler-Ferryman but [British General] Anderson, had relied on the 'Mock's' advice in this instance. This reliance had caused General Anderson to hold his reserve in the North when it may have been used to extra advantage to help Americans farther South."[17] It was unfortunate, but a lesson learned in the use and misuse of — or overreliance upon — Ultra.

Certainly the President's faith in Eisenhower was rewarded in March when Rommel, in ill health, was withdrawn to Germany to recuperate. The day of the Desert Fox was over; that of the President's protégé, Dwight D. Eisenhower, had come. He might not have the battlefield prowess of Rommel, Patton, or Montgomery, but he had something far more valuable to the Allies: the ability to get the soldiers, airmen, and sailors of an international coalition to fight together under his leadership. The result was often messy, sometimes contentious, and media-sensitive. As the President told Eisenhower's naval aide, however, such was the price of democracy. The virtue of the Casablanca Conference had been that it enabled the President, as de facto commander in chief of the Western Allies, to make his historic decisions on a 1944 Second Front as well as on unconditional surrender, without the press (let alone the enemy) even knowing he was in Casablanca. "He said for the first time all participants were enabled to explore each others' minds, get all the cards on the table, and reach decisions without distractions. These distractions, he said, are caused by newspaper men gaining small segments of the complete story and printing them under headlines that frequently mislead the public and failed to portray the complete story. 'In most conference[s], particularly where newspaper men have access to the conferees,' the President said, 'almost every participant has a pet newspaper man. By button-holing such friends, newspaper men can get a part of the story and the whole issue becomes tried in the press on the basis of only a small part of all the facts. The result is distortion to the public and disruption to the conferences.'"

No truer words were spoken by an American president — yet this had been the reality of American democracy since George Washington, and would never change. All one could do was, at certain times, employ a certain guile in order that the job got done. At this, the President, by his third term in office, was a past master — in war as well as in peace. "At Casablanca," he told Eisenhower's aide, "we had a secluded spot, well guarded and free from the press. Thus we were able to talk freely without feeling someone would start promoting his point of view in the press by means of contact with his favorite reporter."[18] So pleased was he with the "result of Casablanca" that he had arranged for the administration's looming "food conference," addressing the needs of allies and liberated countries, to take place in Virginia, "guarded by military police," and with "no press permitted . . . I think the press will cry out against this arrangement," but the "public good" was sometimes more important than "public discussion." Moreover, once the decisions were announced, there was freedom enough to debate the matters. "I am planning to make another swing around the country," he told Butcher, taking a group of White House correspondents who would only be allowed to file reports once the tour was over. "The press will yowl again I imagine, but the public seemed to appreciate that trip. In any event," he made clear, "I am going to do it again," yowls or no yowls.

Subtly, the President had been passing on to Eisenhower his advice on how best to deal with "distortions" and "distractions" of a free press — something Butcher was able to convey to Eisenhower as soon as he returned. Along with the President's parting words. "The principal message the President asked me to convey — and he spoke repeatedly of the General as 'Ike' — was: "Tell Ike that not only I but the whole country is proud of the job he has done. We have every confidence in his success."[19]

As the President prepared for his second "swing around the country" aboard the *Ferdinand Magellan,* Eisenhower duly readied his two Allied armies in Tunisia — gathering his twenty divisions like bloodhounds for the final act of the President's North African invasion: a battle the Germans themselves began to call "Tunisgrad."[20] More than a quarter million Axis troops were now hemmed in on the Cape Bon Peninsula, fighting for their lives. Two thousand German troops were being flown into the arena each day from southern Europe; Mussolini was begging the Führer to make peace with Stalin in order to save the Italian Empire; and three hundred thousand Allied troops were massing for the kill.

PART SIX

Get Yamamoto!

21

Inspection Tour Two

BEGINNING ON APRIL 13, 1943, the President set off by train for his latest two-week, seventy-six-hundred-mile inspection tour of U.S. military training bases: from South Carolina to Alabama, Georgia to Arkansas, Oklahoma to Colorado, Missouri to Kentucky. Following his repeated bouts of ill health in February, these inspections would allow the Commander in Chief to see — and be seen by — tens of thousands of young aviators, Marines, tank crews, infantrymen, Women's Army Auxiliary Corps trainees, and Navy crewmen.

Once again the President took Daisy Suckley with him — since Eleanor had her own agenda to fulfill — as well as his other cousin, Polly Delano, who was considered a "law unto herself," but who amused the President: the two women giving him the sense of being looked after. (Eleanor did agree to join the train, in Texas, for a brief three-day detour to Monterrey, to meet the Mexican president, Ávila Camacho.)

The President wanted to judge for himself whether young American servicemen, currently training at home, would fight abroad. Hundreds of young pilots taking off and landing, parades of ten to fifteen thousand men, tanks firing live shells in mock battle, soldiers in hand-to-hand fighting ("the sort of thing they have in the Pacific jungles, with the Japs — It's all horrible when you stop to analyze it, but it's a fight for survival," Daisy noted, amazed[1]).

The tour, the President was pleased to find, belied any German and Japanese assumptions that U.S. troops were too "soft" for the ruthlessness of modern warfare. Above all, however, it was the sheer magnitude of American mobilization for war — in manpower, munitions, organization — that awed the President's party aboard the *Ferdinand Magellan*.

"The impression I have is of vastness, and a miracle of quick construction," Daisy noted in Denver, where they inspected the Remington Rand Ordnance Plant. Propelled by Japan's sneak attack, America had become a new "melting pot," with "50% men and women at Remington, cheerful, well-fed human beings, who, with all their lack of culture, are the backbone of the country, & probably the finest 'mass' of population in the world," she noted proudly. "The women were dressed in pale blue 1-piece overalls (much like Mr. Churchill's air raid zipper suit) and red bandannas tied tightly about their heads . . . People were collected all along the route full of spontaneous enthusiasm. Women & girls jumping, waving, laughing & cheering. The men grinning broadly & waving."[2]

At the President's polio-rehabilitation center at Warm Springs in Georgia, Roosevelt stood tall, kept upright by his heavy steel leg braces, "holding on to his chair," and "made a serious, soft voiced little speech" to the hundred patients assembled in Georgia Hall, then was "wheeled to the door of the dining room where he stayed to shake hands with each patient that filed through."[3] Using "the little car he has had *for years* down here" — a 1938 Ford Roadster with brakes and accelerator he could operate by hand, as well as a license plate reading "F.D.R.-1 — The President" — Roosevelt himself drove his guests around the area.[4]

Daisy — visiting the Warm Springs center for the first time — was deeply moved. "It is certainly a monument to him, his imagination and his faith & his love for his fellow sufferers, and it is very lovely. Peaceful and beautiful. The houses homelike and attractive, mainly white, among trees." For the first time in months the President swam — and insisted Daisy and Polly swim too. He had seemed desperately tired when they left Washington. Now he was "visibly expanding and blossoming."

One night — after a simple, homely dinner which he loved, in contrast to the "pallid" White House food that Eleanor's cook, Mrs. Nesbitt, made and which Roosevelt "detested"[5] — Roosevelt took out "his stamps; the rest of us read. F. complained of a headache" and the women took his temperature — which was fortunately normal.[6] He'd seemed actually happy, though.

With the physical support of his new naval aide, Rear Admiral Wilson Brown — Captain McCrea having been assigned to command of the new U.S. cruiser, *Iowa* — the President was still able to stand and, by swinging his muscular torso, even walk. Visiting Fort Riley, in Kansas, he actually proceeded on foot to the exit of the amphitheater, where fifteen thousand troops had gathered for an Easter service. At the railway station, as the *Ferdinand Magellan* slowly pulled out, officers and men saluted the Commander in Chief. "It was a beautiful sight and the kind of thing that brings a lump in your throat, specially when the commander in chief is a man like F. & crippled besides — Our driver told us he had not the slightest idea that F. couldn't walk, that his brother officers also had never thought of it," Daisy noted. "F. is all the more an inspiration to them —."[7]

At dinner on the train on April 19, they were joined by Sumner Welles, and the Mexican ambassador, Francisco Castilia Nájero. "We stayed up until 10 listening to them talk about the future peace — Very interesting," Daisy recorded in her diary. There was, she recognized, a steeliness in her champion that was never going to allow him to let up until he'd achieved his dream — with little trace of magnanimity toward those responsible for the global holocaust the Nazis and Japanese were so adamantly pursuing. The "perpetrators of the war, like Hitler, Himmler, etc. shall be court-martialed in their own country" and hanged or "liquidated," as Daisy noted, quoting Hitler's sickening word — "not sent to some distant island to turn into heroes and martyrs, with the danger of their trying to come back."[8]

The President might show deep and natural empathy for his fellow polio sufferers, she recognized, and great charm toward visitors of every stripe — but his forgiveness did not extend to the Nazi "Aryans" who were exterminating not only the handicapped but, it was becoming increasingly evident, millions of Jews, homosexuals, gypsies, and political prisoners; sickening atrocities, moreover, that the Japanese were also reportedly committing, not only in the treatment of the populations of the countries Japanese troops had overrun, from China to the Philippines, but American POWs.

In his diary, Secretary Stimson made note of what the Operations Division of the War Department had learned. Colonel Ritchie "gave me a dreadful picture of what is happening to our prisoners of war at the hands of the Japanese in the Philippines. I have been thoroughly churned up over it ever since. They are being killed off and are dying off under mistreatment. The situation is frightful. Yet it is very dangerous for us to make it public because of the reprisals which would be undoubtedly visited upon these," he wrote — aware American prisoners would be tortured and executed for smuggling out news of their mistreatment. Nor could the United States threaten retaliation, "because we have only a few hundred prisoners" thanks to the Japanese code of Bushido, "while they have a good many thousands of our men . . . MacArthur is vowing vengeance and is keeping the score of injuries to our men which he has heard of which some day he hopes to live to avenge."[9]

News of the execution of captured crewmembers from Doolittle's air raid on Tokyo the previous year had aroused similar outrage — Stimson wanting Secretary Hull to issue a warning there would be American "reprisals" for such "an act of barbarism" if it went on.[10]

For such barbarians the President possessed, Daisy recognized, no sympathy. He would not permit MacArthur to carry out reprisals in the Pacific. But when, during his tour of U.S. training camps and manufacturing plants, a decrypt arrived via the communications car of the President's train of a Japanese signal giving the forthcoming flying itinerary of the Japanese commander in chief — the man who had launched the sneak attack on Pearl Harbor in peacetime, killing twenty-four hundred Americans in a single morning — the President, aboard the *Ferdinand Magellan,* had had no hesitation whatever.

22

Get Yamamoto!

SEVERAL WEEKS BEFORE leaving on his inspection tour the President had invited MacArthur's air commander, General George Kenney, to give him a literal bird's-eye view of the campaign in the Southwest Pacific, when Kenney accompanied MacArthur's chief of staff to Washington to ask for more reinforcements.

In Kenney—a World War I pilot almost as highly decorated (Silver Star and Distinguished Flying Cross) as MacArthur himself—MacArthur had recognized the right man to revolutionize the U.S. Army Air Forces in war: not only in combatting Japanese fliers and in bombing ground installations, but in decimating Japanese supply vessels. The result had proved transformative—and the President wanted to know how Kenney had done it.

Whereas carrier-plane pilots of the U.S. Navy had become expert at low-level attacks on Japanese shipping, the U.S. Army Air Forces' pilots had not, Kenney explained. He had therefore hurled himself into the challenge—developing new skip-bombing techniques and modified B-25 mast-height gunship tactics, which he'd ordered to be rehearsed against a partially sunken vessel off Port Moresby. Under his leadership the vessel-attack planes had adopted a new technique: to fly in at 150 feet—with P-38s and 40s providing higher air cover, and B-17s higher still.

At the White House the President had thus been enthralled as Kenney described his new approach. "I talked for some time with President Roosevelt, who wanted to hear the whole story of the war in our theater in detail," Kenney later recalled his first visit to the Oval Office, "as well as a blow-by-blow description of the Bismarck Sea Battle."[1]

Kenney's description of the battle had been especially telling, for the flier had explained how the Ultra secret decrypts of Japanese communications that the President was seeing in his Map Room in Washington had enabled Kenney to put into effect his deadly new aerial war tactics in the field.

"In the nose of a light fast bomber," as Kenney also explained to Eisenhower's naval aide — for transmission to Ike in Algiers — the general had installed "eight 50-caliber machine guns. Two planes thus equipped would approach a merchant vessel at low level, one from stern to bow, the other from the side. The one approaching lengthwise the ship would open fire with the eight guns at 1500 yards. No pilot was permitted to go on a mission until he could shoot so accurately that with the first burst at 1500 yards, he could sweep the ship from bow to stern or vice versa. The purpose was to keep the anti-aircraft fire from the ship so the accompanying member of the team could approach the side of the vessel just above the wave tops and drop a bomb that would skip on the water and hit the ship on the side just above or below the water line."[2]

The President had been intrigued to learn not only of such American air force ingenuity and specialized training, but the integration of air and naval tactics.

Code breaking had been the key, though. In the battle of the Bismarck Sea, between March 2 and 4, Admiral Yamamoto's order for Japan's vital troopship-reinforcement convoy, bringing fresh troops up to Rabaul and from there to New Guinea, had been deciphered.[3]

The first Japanese division to arrive in Rabaul, the Fifty-First Division, had hugged the coast of New Britain and then set off by convoy across the Solomon Sea — unaware the Americans knew its route and composition. Flying at high altitude, Kenney's B-17 bombers had sunk two of its transport ships, but the remaining six, escorted by eight destroyers and a hundred planes, had ploughed on. Expecting B-17s at high altitude again over the Dampier Strait, the Japanese fighters giving air cover to the convoy had failed to spot Kenney's one hundred retrained American and Australian B-25s, A-20s, and Beaufighter pilots skimming low across the water — the aircraft so low the Japanese sailors thought they were torpedo planes. In short order all surviving Japanese transports had been sunk, the infantry drowned, and four of the eight destroyers destroyed — the core of the Japanese Fifty-First Division extinguished in a single day.

The President was clearly delighted. His grasp of the intricate mosaic of islands in the Southwest Pacific amazed Kenney, given the President's other responsibilities. "I found the President surprisingly familiar with the geography of the Pacific, which made it quite easy to talk with him about the war out there," the general recalled with admiration and affection after the war. "He wanted to know how I was making out on getting airplanes. I told him that so far my chances didn't look very good. When he asked why, I said that among reasons given me was that he had made so many commitments elsewhere that there were no planes left to give me."

The President had taken this in good spirit; he had "laughed and said he guessed he'd have to look into the matter and see if a few couldn't be found somewhere that might be sent me. He said that if anybody was a winner, he should be given a chance to keep on winning."[4]

Backing winners was important in war, the President recognized — and was a key to Roosevelt's growing style of military command: assessing, encouraging, and supporting those whom he saw as inspirational and effective.

The President did manage to find Kenney more planes, to Kenney's relief. However, if the President was keen to back a winner in Kenney's air force leadership in the Pacific, he was similarly open to depriving the Japanese of *their* outstanding military leadership, if he could.

General Kenney's visit to the White House — a visit repeated on March 25, 1943, when Kenney had attended a Congressional Medal of Honor ceremony — had convinced the President that American fliers were finally proving better than their opponents in the Pacific. Especially when given the advantage of Ultra intelligence.

As the *Ferdinand Magellan* made its way across the American Midwest and South, stopping at military training camp after training camp, the President found himself, as Daisy noted, more and more confident in American professionalism. And though the matter was too secret to share with Daisy or her companion, Polly Delano — moreover, too secret ever to be revealed in his lifetime — he now had an opportunity to show his faith in his American airmen.

Over several days, starting on April 14, an extraordinary series of further decrypts had been brought to the President aboard the *Magellan* by Ship's Clerk William Rigdon, an assistant working for Admiral Brown, the President's naval aide, whose job it was to bring the latest fruits of Ultra to the President's attention twice a day.[5]

"The communications car housed a diesel-powered radio transmitting and receiving station," Rigdon recounted later, "that kept the President in constant touch with the Map Room at the White House. Special codes, held only by the Map Room and the car, were used. This car was just behind the engine. The Magellan was at the rear. Between the two I walked many miles taking messages to the President and picking up those he wished to send."[6]

Some were trivial. Others were more serious. One of them, in particular, related not to security for the President's train schedule — the twenty-six members of the Secret Service traveling with him, as well as military details protecting him at every stage of his 7,668-mile trip — but to the travel plans of another dominant figure in the war, with perhaps even more control over the struggle in the Pacific than the President: Admiral Isoroku Yamamoto.

"From Solomons Defense Force to Air Group #204, Air Flotilla #26," it began. "On 18 April C in C Combined Fleet will visit RXZ [Ballale Island, off Bougainville], R_ [Shortland] and RXP [Buin] in accordance following schedule: 1. Depart RR [Rabaul] at 0600 in a medium attack plane escorted by 6 fighters. Arrive RXZ at 0800. Proceed by minesweeper . . . At each of the above places the Commander-in-Chief will make a short tour of inspection and at _ he will visit the sick and wounded, but current operations should continue."

In case of "bad weather" the preliminary message had ended, "the trip will be postponed."[7]

A trip by the commander in chief of Japan's Combined Fleet, Admiral Yamamoto, to Ballale, Bougainville? An inspection tour by air and sea to a forward area of the Solomon Islands within reach of U.S. Air Force planes? Times and details of his itinerary?

The decrypted signal seemed almost impossible to believe. Admiral Yamamoto usually stayed on his grand battleship, the *Musashi*, at Truk, in the Caroline Islands, eight hundred miles to the north of Rabaul. Moving to a temporary forward command post at Rabaul, however, his strategy after the loss of Guadalcanal had been to pummel the Americans with massive air attacks before they could bring up enough forces to exploit their victory: Operation I-Go. By assigning not only Japanese ground-force pilots operating from airfields in the Solomons but hundreds of well-trained carrier pilots to assist them, Yamamoto had been able to apply massive Japanese air power to the initiative, involving more than 350 planes — the largest Japanese air assault since Pearl Harbor.

Mercifully, the Japanese air armada had been thwarted by Ultra intelligence — allowing Allied naval ships to disperse in good time, and U.S. Army and Naval Air Force units to be ready, off the ground, to meet the approaching aerial fleet each time it flew. A single Allied destroyer, a corvette, several Dutch merchant vessels, and an oiler had been sunk, and twelve Allied aircraft lost, but these were small pickings for such a concentrated and expensive air offensive — a fact that Japanese pilots, despite acknowledging the loss of forty-nine Japanese planes, had misconstrued in their after-action reports. Admiral Yamamoto had, instead, been told the fliers of his Third Fleet and Eleventh Fleet had sunk one American cruiser, two destroyers, and twenty-five transport ships, moreover had shot down 134 U.S. planes, as well as destroying 20 on the ground.[8]

The admiral had been well satisfied — in fact had sent Emperor Hirohito in Tokyo his own version of the triumph, which could be seen as avenging, in part, the recent losses of Guadalcanal and Buna. The Emperor had immediately responded with a congratulatory signal: "Please convey my satisfaction to the Commander in Chief, Combined Fleet, and tell him to enlarge the war result more than ever."[9]

The radio messages giving the itinerary of Admiral Yamamoto's inspection tour raised a number of questions. Was Yamamoto planning an extension of I-Go attacks? Was it a morale booster by the Japanese commander in chief, in person?

The message did not say — but its import was clear to all, from the South Pacific to the *Ferdinand Magellan*. Just as Yamamoto's planes had been able to hit Guadalcanal as part of I-Go, so could U.S. fliers hit Bougainville, on the admiral's itinerary — either attacking the admiral on the minesweeper to which he was slated to transfer, or in the air.

Why, though, had Yamamoto chosen to send such a message by radio?

As it later transpired, the admiral's administrative staff officer had wanted the warning order to be couriered by air, and then hand-delivered to its recipients. He'd been told by the communications officer at Rabaul not to worry, however; the Japanese naval code JN25 had recently been changed and was unbreakable.[10] The signal that first went out was dated April 13, 1943.

"We've hit the jackpot," the U.S. watch officer of Station Hypo, the two-thousand-man decoding unit in Hawaii, declared when the decrypt was handed to him. "This is our chance to get Yamamoto."[11]

If, that was, Admiral Nimitz, the commander in chief in the Central

Pacific, agreed. And if the U.S. commander in chief in Washington signed off on the attempt.

There were important repercussions to be considered. An aerial interception of Japan's most famous — or infamous — admiral might well squander, whether successful or not, America's prize weapon in the struggle against Japan: Ultra. Was it worth such a gamble? And what if it did not, in fact, succeed? Not only would Yamamoto be left in command of all Japanese forces in the Pacific, but the war-winning contribution of Ultra would have been given away, for nothing.

Ironically, Admiral Nimitz worried about something else when first shown the decrypt. Would a successor to Admiral Yamamoto prove a better Japanese commander in chief?

In view of the fact that Yamamoto enjoyed almost godlike status,[12] not only among Japanese forces in the Pacific but at home in Japan, killing him would, without doubt, make a huge dent in Japanese war morale, just as Japanese forces dug in for a do-or-die struggle in the countries they had conquered.

There were other questions, too. In the time-honored ethics of American warmaking, was it even acceptable to assassinate an enemy commander — since assassination was what such an interception, if successful, would be? As at Midway, Nimitz felt it would be a mistake *not* to use such a priceless intelligence breakthrough — but deferred, as before Midway, to Washington's decision.

The matter was thus passed for authorization to Admiral King — who passed it to Navy Secretary Frank Knox.

Knox — who had himself recently carried out an inspection tour of U.S. naval forces in the Pacific — passed the information via the White House Map Room to the *Ferdinand Magellan*.

The President's response was immediate and uncompromising: "Get Yamamoto."[13]

Secretary Knox, at the Navy Department, needed no further prompting. He instructed Admiral Nimitz to go ahead. In turn Nimitz gave the final green light on April 17, 1943, to Admiral Halsey — commanding Allied forces in the Solomons area.

There was now only one day to go. F4F Wildcats and F4U Corsairs had insufficient range for such a mission, but new U.S. Army Air Forces P-38s, flown by Army Air Forces, Marine, and Navy pilots, could do it. Vice Admiral Pete Mitscher, commander air, Solomon Islands, had already begun to explore different proposals with his subordinates. His U.S. Navy fliers recommended they attack the Japanese vessel that Yamamoto was to board at Ballale, but the U.S. Army Air Forces ace, Major John Mitchell, commanding the 339th Fighter Squadron, assigned to carry out the attack, felt it would be easier to spot the admiral's plane — a heavily armed but slow (265 mph) Mitsubishi G4M "Betty" bomber — than it would be to identify an indeterminate Japanese minesweeper. Such a ship would undoubtedly be escorted by other vessels, as well as shielded by extensive Japanese air cover, to judge by the U.S. planes sent up to protect Secretary Knox on his recent visit.

Mitscher wisely yielded the decision on April 17 to the man who would have to carry out the mission. Assembling a fighter group of eighteen Lockheed P-38G Lightnings, Mitchell — who planned a five-leg, low-level end run way out to sea before reaching Bougainville, so as to have the advantage of surprise — asked for special auxiliary-fuel drop tanks flown up from MacArthur's men on New Guinea. He also decided that the best point to intercept Yamamoto's flight would be just as the admiral's Betty bomber — similar to the Betty bombers that had sunk HMS *Prince of Wales,* the battleship on which the President had attended divine service with Churchill off Argentia, in August 1941 — reduced speed to land.

Tension was high. Mitchell was certainly aware just how much hinged on his mission, for Secretary Knox had sent a further signal to Nimitz on April 17, which Admiral Nimitz immediately forwarded to Admiral Halsey. Halsey sent it with a covering note to Admiral Mitscher — who placed it before Mitchell. It read, as the fliers later recalled: "SQUADRON 339. P-38 MUST AT ALL COSTS REACH AND DESTROY. PRESIDENT ATTACHES EXTREME IMPORTANCE TO MISSION."[14]

Almost seventy years later a similar targeted killing of an enemy commander in war — Osama bin Laden — would be revealed to an astonished world within hours. Because of the need to preserve the secret of Ultra in 1943, however, the President had accepted that the mission to assassinate Admiral Yamamoto, code-named Operation Vengeance, would not — perhaps ever — be made public. Other than acknowledging Japanese media reports, if the operation was successful, nothing would be said.

Early on the first anniversary of the Doolittle Raid the U.S. Squadron

339 fighter group — reduced to sixteen planes owing to two aborts — thus set off from Fighter Strip Number Two, Henderson Field, Guadalcanal, on its thousand-mile mission for the President.

Resembling huge flying catamarans — their single-pilot cockpits strung between two pontoon-like fuselages, each mounting a massive 1,325-horse-power engine and capable of speeds up to 400 miles per hour — the Lightnings wave-hopped in complete radio-silence for some six hundred miles to the west of the Solomon island chain and across the open Solomon Sea, in order to avoid radar and visual detection. Using a special naval compass, Mitchell then swung to the east, aiming to circle in from the ocean — four of his best pilots designated as killer sharks, while the remainder dealt with the six Japanese Zeros protecting their commander in chief.

The attack — the longest-distance fighter-intercept mission of World War II — went like clockwork. A stickler for punctuality, Admiral Yamamoto had rejected his staff's protests that his inspection tour would be too risky. Precisely on time, his bomber slowed to land at Ballale, Bougainville, at 9:35 a.m. on April 18, 1943.[15]

Mitchell's men were already there, sixty seconds early: surprised only that there were two Bettys, not one. Both would have to be shot down.

The ensuing melee took but a few minutes — the "killer" fighters attacking from below the Japanese bombers and their escort, the rest climbing above the encounter to fend off Zeros that would inevitably begin to take off from Buin airfield. As the lumbering Betty bombers dived to escape, the two lead P-38 pilots closed up on them, using the 20mm cannons and machine guns mounted in the planes' noses. Inside his bomber, Yamamoto, dressed in his green field-combat uniform but wearing white gloves, was killed instantly in his seat — the plane soon plummeting to earth in the jungle, amid smoke and flames. The other bomber was also shot down, crashing into the ocean. One American P-38 was lost, but the rest then turned for home, taking the direct route and encountering no opposition.

Ignoring all prohibition against radio transmissions that might give away the specific target of the operation, one of the P-38 pilots, with one engine already feathering for lack of fuel after a thousand miles of flying, radioed to fighter control at Henderson Field as he came in to land: "That son of a bitch will not be dictating any peace terms in the White House."[16]

23

"He's Dead?"

So secret was the Yamamoto operation — and so worried did Admiral King become, when leaks of the mission to journalists were only censored at the last minute — that the men of 339 Squadron, unlike Doolittle's Tokyo team, could not be decorated for their extraordinary bravery and professionalism. So shocking, however, was the death of Admiral Yamamoto to the Japanese government, that news of his passing was kept from the Japanese public for more than a month[1] — and only confirmed to American code breakers, in the meantime, by the absence of Yamamoto's name or rank in Japanese naval signals decoded in Hawaii and Washington.

Aboard the *Ferdinand Magellan* on April 18, after visiting Camp Gruber, Oklahoma, and messing with the troops training there, the President was informed that the mission had been successful. Pearl Harbor had finally been avenged — the author of the sneak attack dead in the jungle his men had so ruthlessly conquered, and where so many Japanese atrocities had been committed.[2]

Keeping the success of Operation Vengeance a secret among American forces, ironically, proved harder than keeping the Ultra secret from the Japanese. In the days after the mission, more sorties were flown up the Solomons "Slot" to Bougainville, in full view of Japanese radar and spotters, to make the fatal interception seem less extraordinary; reporters, meanwhile, were forbidden to file stories directly linking Guadalcanal's U.S. air aces to the great admiral's death.

In the context of a titanic battle of wills, courage, and morale in the Pacific, it was almost impossible to maintain the fiction of an accidental death of an enemy commander as iconic as Yamamoto, however, either in

American signals or media reports. Admiral Mitscher had immediately reported to Admiral Halsey by telegram, for example, informing him Mitchell's P-38s had "shot down two bombers escorted by 6 Zeros flying close formation . . . April 18 seems to be our day" — a reference to Colonel Doolittle's raid the year before.[3] This had not necessarily given the game away, but Bull Halsey — known for his ebullient, take-no-prisoners personality — had signaled straight back, "Congratulations to you and Major Mitchell and his hunters. Sounds as if one of the ducks in their bag was a peacock."[4]

Inevitably, as the weeks went by, an AP reporter dutifully tracking a story that was common knowledge on Guadalcanal, blew it in Australia in May 1943 — despite being warned it should not be used. Admiral King was incensed — just as he had been the year before, when a similar report had been published ascribing the great victory at Midway to naval code-breaking. Nimitz ordered a full-scale investigation and disciplinary action, with orders that every pilot on Guadalcanal, as well as staff officers and flight mechanics, be questioned. Four citations for Medal of Honor awards were withdrawn, and Halsey, blaming the pilots, declared they should be court-martialed, stripped of their rank, and jailed.[5]

By a miracle, the Japanese, however, proved unable or unwilling to investigate too closely their suspicions. The sheer shock and shame of the admiral's death — the six Zero pilots wishing to commit ritual suicide for their utter failure to protect him — caused a wave of gloom to spread from Bougainville to the Emperor's palace in Japan. Yamamoto's ashes were taken back to Japan aboard his battleship, the *Musashi,* and after lying in state in Tokyo, were interred in a state funeral.[6]

In later years there would be claims that Admiral Yamamoto's death had been a dangerous gamble and counterproductive, given that his earlier objections to war with the United States would have made him, if brought back into the Japanese government, more willing than his successor (who was killed in 1944) or other Japanese admirals to negotiate an armistice.[7]

President Roosevelt certainly had no truck with such hypotheticals. He had laid down a policy of unconditional surrender on the basis that neither the Germans nor the Japanese could ever again be trusted to keep the peace unless forced into complete surrender — and the way Japanese troops were fighting, from the Aleutians to the Solomon islands they had conquered, and the atrocities they were committing, bore out his contention. In Yamamoto's cabin aboard the *Musashi* the admiral had left a poem he'd recently written, lamenting his "dead comrades" in the war — but declaring "with an iron will I will drive deep / Into the camp of the enemy / And will show the true blood of a Japanese man."[8]

Japan's retreat into medievalism, like Germany's, was something America could only end by force of arms — not negotiation. In depriving the Japanese of their greatest admiral in the war, Roosevelt had struck an incalculable blow to the Japanese military machine and national morale at a critical moment in the war.

Certainly, as the President continued his national inspection tour, he was seen to be in great form. The training establishments he'd visited had given him a potent sense of American willingness to fight — and to win. At a press conference he convened onboard the *Ferdinand Magellan* on April 19, he spoke of the "great improvement I have seen since last September in the training of troops of all kinds," and referred to the "cutting down of the age of the higher officers than in the last war." There was, too, higher "morale" to be seen among the troops as they learned the deadlier skills of modern combat — "there is a great eagerness on their part to get into the 'show' and get it over with."[9] Moreover, the strategy he'd settled at Casablanca seemed to be working out. In North Africa, putting Kasserine behind them, American troops were moving in for the kill in Tunisia, close to the time frame Eisenhower had given him at the Villa Dar es Saada. And in the Atlantic — following the President's order to Admiral King to resolve the interservice argument regarding air coverage of the mid-Atlantic and the alarming success of U-boat wolfpacks or face dismissal[10] — King had buckled.

Finally setting aside his childlike struggle with the U.S. Army Air Forces over which service should be responsible for antisubmarine air patrolling, King — in fear of losing his job — had convened a conference of all parties in Washington at the beginning of March. Chastened, he'd belatedly established a special headquarters in the Navy Department, the so-called U.S. Tenth Fleet, to direct the anti-U-boat campaign: a campaign that would use new ASDIC 271M centimetric radar capable of detecting a submerged submarine four miles away; high-frequency radio direction finding (HFRDF) to pinpoint where U-boats were signaling from; "baby flattops" the President had earlier ordered to be constructed from merchant ship hulls as convoy escort carriers; incoming new Bogue-class aircraft carriers; and most important of all: American Liberator long-distance bomber planes.

Based on the Boeing B-24 USAAF bomber, but equipped with torpedo-like depth charges, radar, and Leigh lights to illuminate U-boats surfacing for night attacks on shipping, the Liberators would now almost instantly turn the tide of war in the Atlantic — completely disproving King's assumption that convoying was the only answer. Within weeks the new combination had worked — the results beginning to show already in April 1943. Sinkings of German U-boats increased — dramatically.

The President was relieved — and Admiral King relieved not to be relieved of his command. By May the demise of the wolfpack menace would become a rout, forcing the commander of the German navy, Admiral Dönitz, to admit defeat that month and recall his entire submarine fleet to safety in Europe, pending the construction of more modern submarines with "snorkels" that could hopefully evade air detection.

And with regard to the death of Admiral Yamamoto? The President was careful to say nothing to anyone until May 21, 1943, when giving his 898th press conference.

"Mr. President," one reporter asked innocently, "would you care to comment on the death of the Japanese admiral (Isoroku Yamamoto), who forecast he would write the peace in the White House?"

"He's dead?" the President asked, as if stunned.

"Q[uestioner]: The Japanese radio announced it. Yamamoto. Killed in action while directing operations in an airplane."

"The President: Gosh! (loud laughter)"

"Q: Can we quote that, sir?"

"The President: Yes. (more laughter)."[11]

To his own staff the President was less deceptive. In truth he could never forgive Yamamoto for his role in attacking Pearl Harbor, causing the deaths of so many thousands of Americans there and in the aftermath, after the many years of hospitality and education Yamamoto had enjoyed in the United States. Two days after the press conference, the President thus had his secretary, Grace Tully, type a letter, headed The White House, dated May 23, 1943, and which he signed.

"Dear Bill," the President scrawled across the top of the letter in his own hand as a memo to Admiral Leahy, "Please see that the Old Girl gets the following:

'Dear Widow Yamamoto,

Time is a great leveler and somehow I never expected to see the old boy at the White House anyway. Sorry I can't attend the funeral because I approve it. Hoping he is where we know he ain't.

Very sincerely yours,

Franklin D. Roosevelt'

"And ask her to visit you at the Wilson House this summer," Roosevelt added in a postscript to Leahy.

It wasn't kind, or gracious; indeed the President never sent the letter.[12] But it reflected something of what, in his heart of hearts, he really felt about Japanese perfidy. And his profound satisfaction that he'd been able to see Admiral Yamamoto get his just deserts.

Ending his long inspection tour at Washington's Union Station on April 29, the President certainly had good reason to be in high spirits.

April had been a bountiful month for the Allies. Admiral Mineichi Koga would be a very poor replacement for Yamamoto — indeed, I-Go was called off, and on Guadalcanal the 339th Squadron's seventy-six pilots did not encounter a single Japanese plane in combat for the rest of April and the whole of May.[13] Staging out of the Ellice Islands — which Marines had captured the previous October — Admiral Nimitz's long-range bombers had been able on April 20 to hit Tarawa, the atoll that was impeding future invasion of the Marshall Islands — some twenty-four hundred miles from Hawaii.[14] General MacArthur had begun to revise his strategy in order to do more with less — persuaded by Washington, in fact, to drop his costly notion of step-by-step advance and merely bypass Japanese "fortresses" in the Pacific, such as Rabaul, if possible. Such strongpoints would thus be allowed to wither on the vine as MacArthur's air forces, ground forces, and naval vessels pursued a leapfrogging, or island-hopping, campaign instead.

All in all, then, the Allies stood fair to succeed in a two-ocean war — if they made no more mistakes, and capitalized on their growing productive and fighting strengths. By the end of the current year, the President had been told by Secretary Stimson, the U.S. Army would have some 8.2 million well-trained men and women in uniform — including more than 2.5 million U.S. Air Forces personnel. With a target of a million U.S. combat troops to be ferried in the coming months to bases in Britain, the President felt the Allies had every prospect of mounting a successful

1944 Second Front, and be on course to win the war that year, or early in 1945 — after which the unconditional surrender of the Japanese could be obtained, he was confident, within months.

Such heady confidence, though, rested on a fundamental assumption: that Winston Churchill and the British would stand by the agreements made at Casablanca.

That, however, as Admiral Leahy and General Marshall informed the President at the White House on April 30, was probably misguided. Instead, the Prime Minister, they'd learned, was intent upon coming to Washington with a huge new posse of military advisers and clerks — determined to convince the President his whole strategy was wrong.

PART SEVEN

Beware Greeks Bearing Gifts

24

Saga of the Nibelungs

WITH EVERY NEW day, the news from North Africa had been getting better, the President had felt — under American leadership and arms.

By the end of April, American forces in North Africa outnumbered British, French, and other national contingents 60 percent to 40. From a frontline west of Bizerte that ran first south, then east to Enfidaville on the Tunisian coast, more than three hundred thousand Allied troops were preparing to launch Operation Strike: the final Allied offensive in North Africa to drive the Axis forces into the sea. Italian troops were beginning to desert in increasing numbers, but German troops were paradoxically selling their lives ever more dearly in battles to hold onto djebels and hill-tops many thousands of miles from their homes — infused with a blind, arrogant loyalty to their comrades, scorn for their opponents, and a sui-cidal unwillingness to question either what they were doing in North Af-rica or why they maintained such slavish faith in their führer.

Certainly the Führer was indifferent to their fate. At his meeting with Mussolini near Salzburg on April 8, he'd dismissed out of hand the notion of a negotiated armistice with Stalin, or revival of the Ribbentrop Pact. As at Stalingrad, he was banking upon his understanding of the unique Ger-man psyche: that the members of his chosen Volk would stay loyal to each other, whatever happened; and that, in the manner of the Nibelungen myths, they would only gain greater nourishment for their national pride from stories of heroic valor and self-sacrifice, even death in distant fields. *Nibelungentreue* — whether on the Volga or in the mountains of Tunisia. Not dishonorable retreat or evacuation.

The tenacity and blind courage shown by soldiers of the Wehrmacht to their comrades in battle in North Africa certainly suggested Hitler was right. German casualties had escalated as the end approached, yet in contrast to Italian troops, far from dispiriting the German survivors, the likely outcome appeared to make no discernible dent on their morale in the field. Nor would the Führer countenance plans for Axis flight. Just as he had ordered von Paulus to die rather than surrender his last remaining forces at Stalingrad, so now Allied code breakers read with amazement the decrypted signals in which, from his East Prussian headquarters at the Wolfschanze, or Wolf's Lair, the Führer not only ordered more infantry reinforcements to be flown into the last Axis redoubt — which was now down to only sixty-seven panzers — but declined to permit the word *evacuation* to be spoken.

The Saga of the Nibelungs was thus being enacted — in real life. Allied planners had assumed in early April that Hitler could, if he chose, save as many as thirty-seven thousand men of the Wehrmacht per day by evacuation — the better to defend the shores of mainland Europe. There came, however, no such order. Instead, on April 13, the Führer had dispatched his historic cable to General von Arnim, in command of the quarter million Axis troops in Tunisia. Except for a few "useless mouths" to be airlifted or shipped out of Tunisia, the Axis forces were ordered to fight to the death[1] — killing as many of the Allies as possible before they were themselves felled.

It was a bloody, tragic prospect. Yet thanks to his insistence on Torch as the means by which American forces could first learn how to defeat the vaunted Wehrmacht in battle before embarking on a Second Front, it was also a tribute to the President's patience and determination not to undertake military operations beyond the capabilities of his forces. General Patton — "our greatest fighting general," he called him[2] — had restored morale in II Corps after Kasserine, and was now slated to command all American troops in Husky, the invasion of Sicily, in July — which would allow the Allies to rehearse a major assault landing, this time against Axis defenders, not Vichy French. Meantime, U.S. air forces were beginning to take a huge toll of Axis shipping as well as of the Luftwaffe. Above all, despite the mischief being sewn by the American and English press — delighting in the rivalry between U.S. and British exploits in the field — General Eisenhower was doing a magnificent job in holding together the Allied military coalition in North Africa.

This, more than anything, was what reinforced the President's faith in the outcome of his grand strategy. Hitler and Hirohito might well wish to see their populations obliterated rather than save them, but as long as the Allies held together and continued to build upon their combined strength, they would prevail, he was certain. The timetable General Eisenhower had given him at Casablanca for clearing North Africa of Axis forces, as the final Allied offensive kicked off on May 6, 1943, looked remarkably prescient — indeed, in a brilliant armored coup, British tanks from Montgomery's Eighth Army, stalled beneath the high ground at Enfidaville, performed a magnificent end run, or left hook, which took them into the city of Tunis itself within twenty-four hours, on May 7 — where they took the unconditional surrender of all Axis troops there. Infantry and tanks of General Bradley's U.S. II Corps force simultaneously smashed their way down from the mountains in the northwest — including famously bloody combat around Hill 232 — into the port city of Bizerte.

General von Arnim's days, perhaps hours, seemed numbered — U.S. and RAF planes swooping on any German or Italian vessel attempting to leave North African shores, while Luftwaffe attempts to fly in final supplies were shot down.

By contrast, the *Queen Mary* — the vessel bearing the British prime minister — was making a mercifully safe passage across the Atlantic — indeed was approaching the East Coast of the United States surrounded by U.S. destroyers and escort vessels, the sky above thick with U.S. planes watching for U-boats as it made its way toward the Statue of Liberty without mishap. Ensconced in the grand staterooms he'd ordered to be reconstructed for his voyage (the transatlantic liner having earlier been converted into an Allied troopship), Mr. Churchill was toasting every new report from London and Algiers: drunk not so much from champagne as sheer excitement over the imminent Allied victory in Tunisia — one that would soon exceed the German Sixth Army surrender at Stalingrad.

After his long years of military failure, the Prime Minister felt wonderfully, arrogantly alive, his staff later recalled: seemingly certain he could, by the force of his ebullient personality and the scores of staff officers and advisers he was bringing with him, reverse the agreements he'd made on behalf of his country at Casablanca.

25

A Scene from *The Arabian Nights*

AT THE WHITE HOUSE, the President, having discussed with Admiral Leahy and General Marshall what the British might be plotting, still found it hard to believe.

The President had hitherto been under the impression that his partnership with his "active and ardent lieutenant" was a firm and happy one. Had the two leaders not motored together, after the Casablanca Conference, to Marrakesh — the fabled Berber city at the foot of the Atlas Mountains? Had they not spent the night there, in the house occupied by the American vice consul, Kenneth Pendar? Had they not settled together into "one of the showplaces of the world," as Pendar afterward described it, a "stylized, modernized version of a south Moroccan *kasbah*"?[1] Had not Churchill asked to be shown up the famous tower, and had he not counted the sixty steps before asking whether Pendar thought it possible "for the President to be brought up here? I am so fond of this superb view that it has been my dream to see it with him"?[2] And had it not so been arranged — the six-foot-three-inch paralyzed president of the United States borne up the sixty-foot tower by his attendants "with his arms around their shoulders, while another went ahead to open doors, and the rest of the entire party followed"? With Churchill humming "Oh, there ain't no war, there ain't no war," had not the President "amidst much laughing on his part and sympathizing with his carriers" been brought up to the open terrace of the tower, and had not a wicker chair been "fetched for him and the Prime Minister," allowing the two leaders to sit and survey the vast Atlas range? "Never have I seen the sun set on those snow-capped peaks with such magnificence," Pendar — who ordered highballs to be fetched and served — certainly recalled. "There had evidently been snow storms recently in the mountains, for they were white almost to their base, and looked more wild and rugged than ever, their sheer walls rising some 12,000 feet before us."[3]

Had not Pendar explained the history of the great twelfth-century Koutoubia Mosque tower that they could see some distance away, dominating the city? As the sun finally disappeared, had not electric lights come on at the top of every mosque, calling the faithful to prayer? "From where we were, we could see the going and coming of the innumerable Arabs on camel- and mule-back, as they made their way in and out of the city gate. Both Mr. Roosevelt and Mr. Churchill were spellbound by the view," Pendar recalled.[4] It had been a far, far cry from Washington, D.C. — followed later by more cocktails in the salon.

Had not the President — after slicing off the top of a huge profiterole representing the Koutoubia tower, in the manner of Alexander the Great — then raised a toast to the English king? Had not Churchill responded by raising a toast to the head of state before them: the President? For his part Pendar, sitting between such exalted modern rulers, had found himself "surprised," he later recorded. Traveling in England, he'd seen Mr. Churchill often in the prewar days, and had felt "sure that no one could eclipse his personality." Now, however, he was "struck by the fact that, though Mr. Churchill spoke much more amusingly than the President" — mesmerizing listeners with his antiquated yet masterly use of language, and his descriptive, imaginative storytelling ability — it was Mr. Roosevelt who "dominated any room they were in." Reflecting on this, Pendar attributed it not to Roosevelt's larger physique when compared to the diminutive prime minister, nor to his rank "merely because he was President of the United States;" no, Pendar had afterward mused, it had resided much more in the radiance of the President's "being": his lionine head and Caesar-like *presence.* Also an intense curiosity about others — others as real people, not simply an audience to entertain or impress. In this respect, despite the Prime Minister's extraordinary mind, the President exhibited, Pendar thought, "a more spiritual quality than Mr. Churchill, and, I could not help but feel, a more profound understanding of human beings," rather than just the course of history.[5] Most surprising to Pendar, perhaps, had been the President's seeming indifference to his own disability — as if employing his abundant interest in people not only to engage those he met in conversation, but to deflect attention from his own paralyzed lower limbs. Nor did he seem to mind being contradicted or corrected, as Churchill did — Pendar recalling how he'd talked "at length about the Morocco and the Arab problem" with the

President at dinner — who was not only well informed, but *listened.* "To my amazement and delight, I found that the President had an extraordinary and profound grasp of Arab problems, of the conflict of Koranic law with our type of modern life and its influence on Mohammedans, and of the Arab character with its combination of materialism and highly developed intuition." In the presence of a diplomat steeped in the history and culture of Morocco, the President had seemed fascinated to hear Pendar's views — Pendar subsequently recalling how, "some six months later, when I was in London talking with Averell Harriman," who had attended the dinner, Harriman "began to laugh and said: 'I will never forget your conversation with the President. I enjoyed hearing you explain to him, in no uncertain terms, that the New Deal simply wouldn't work in Morocco.'"[6]

Had not the two potentates then "set to work," after dinner, writing cables to Stalin and Chiang Kai-shek to tell them, cautiously, of the Casablanca meeting — cables that Churchill's ubiquitous secretaries typed, then retyped to incorporate further corrections and revisions? The President, at one point, had been "wheeled into his room so he could work alone at his dressing table which he used as his desk" — anxious not to dismay Stalin by revealing the Western Allies would not launch a Second Front before 1944, by which time their forces would have sufficient combat and command experience to make such landings in northern France decisive for the outcome of the war . . .

Why, then, three months later, was Winston Spencer Churchill on his way to Washington with an army of staff officers and advisers to argue against a cross-Channel invasion even in 1944? What alternative plan did Mr. Churchill have for continuing the war?

26

The God Neptune

THE PRESIDENT WAS as much in the dark about Churchill's plans as were his Joint Chiefs of Staff. In fact the more so, since he had fondly imagined that he and the Prime Minister were very much in unison with regard to the Allied prosecution and timetable of the war.

Instead, according to the President's best information, Churchill's ever-fertile mind was changing from day to day. According to sources known to the British representative on the Combined Chiefs of Staff Committee in Washington, Field Marshal Dill, the Prime Minister was said to be settling more and more on ditching the notion of a cross-Channel attack, and instead exploiting the Allies' impending victory in North Africa in the Mediterranean.

Churchill's preference, it was reported, was to pursue, instead, an opportunistic strategy of multipronged Allied attacks following the invasion of Sicily: not only on the Italian mainland but in the Aegean and the Balkans in late 1943 and 1944, especially if — President Inonu's unwillingness nothwithstanding — Turkey could be persuaded to enter the war on the Allied side. By this scattershot, indirect method Churchill apparently hoped the Allies would not only draw away from the Eastern Front crucial German forces that Hitler might otherwise employ to hold back the Russian armies, but would provide the Western Allies with the launch pad for a drive into central Europe via the "soft underbelly" of southern Europe: an Allied advance such as the one General Giraud had outlined to him at Casablanca. Or through the Balkans — an avenue of advance that harked back to Churchill's abiding Dardanelles obsession. Either way, such a peripheral strategy would serve to avoid a Second Front bloodbath across the English Channel, which the Prime Minister had always feared.

More disturbingly — again, according to Field Marshal Dill — the British chiefs of staff were now deferring to their prime minister's ideas. The result would be to delay, if not rule out, the agreed Second Front assault across the English Channel to 1945 — two years away — at the earliest.

How the Russians would respond to such delay was predictable. So too would be the response of the American press and public, if they learned of it.

It was small wonder, then, that the U.S. chiefs of staff had grown each day more worried as the *Queen Mary,* which had left port on May 5, drew closer — even as Allied forces moved in for the kill in Tunisia.

"Some of our officers have a fear that Great Britain is desirous of confining allied military effort in Europe to the Mediterranean Area in order that England may exercise control thereof regardless of what the terms of peace may be," Admiral Leahy had noted in his diary on May 2 — his contacts in the State Department fueling his fear that the British were "principally concerned with a post war control of the Mediterranean."[1] Moreover, in view of rumors the Russians were already exploring peace feelers with German representatives, Leahy was doubly concerned lest the Soviets would fight only to liberate Soviet republics, not to defeat the Third Reich. In this potential scenario, Hitler would remain master of western and central Europe, making nonsense of the President's "Germany First" strategy since Pearl Harbor.

For his part, Secretary of War Henry Stimson worried about Churchill's eloquence — and what he saw as the President's unwillingness to put Churchill in his place.

Stimson had not attended the Casablanca Conference, but what he had gleaned of it had been alarming — an account obtained in large part from officers such as Major General Wedemeyer. The British team had run rings around their American "opponents," he'd been told, not only because the U.S. team had been too small, but because the President himself was too accommodating to the British.

By May 7, with U.S. troops entering Bizerte and British troops entering Tunis, Stimson was cock-a-hoop at the "great victory" at hand — one that would "hearten the Russians and discourage the Germans." The Western Allies should therefore be thinking big, not small, in his view: of direct assault, not peripheral piddling.

In Britain and America, where "we are now deliberating over the future conduct of the campaign," the impending triumph in Tunisia "will I hope stiffen the resolution of our British allies for a northern [European] offensive," Stimson wrote in his diary[2] — and he became especially nervous when Marshall told him, the next day, that the President had only agreed "in principle" to what the U.S. chiefs were going to say to the British chiefs when they finally arrived.

Would the President be swayed by Churchill's anti–Second Front rhetoric, once the Prime Minister arrived at the White House for the new conference — code named, ominously, Trident? Was Churchill a new version of the great god Neptune, rising out of the sea to defeat American strategy for winning the war?

As the British arrival-day neared, General Marshall, for his part, "expressed his reservation as to how firmly the President would hold to his acquiescence" to the U.S. chiefs' position. "I fear it will be the same story over again," Stimson despondently recorded in his diary. Repudiation redux: "The man from London will arrive with a program of further expansion in the Mediterranean and will have his way with our Chief, and the careful and deliberate plans of our Staff will be overridden. I feel very troubled by it," Stimson lamented[3] — the British contingent expected to arrive in Washington the next evening, May 11, 1943.

27

A Battle Royal

WHEN HEARING THE sheer size and composition of the approaching British contingent — 160 officers, with their assistants and chief clerks — the Canadian prime minister thought it a crazy gamble. "I was astonished when I saw the list of names," Mackenzie King noted in his diary, the day of their scheduled arrival in New York. "It is a tremendous risk to have so complete a representation of the military heads, chiefs and their experts and advisers cross the ocean at one and the same time."[1]

Why, though, had they come at all? Had not the overall strategy and timetable for the war in 1943 and 1944 been agreed at Casablanca?

The President had summoned all his chiefs of staff once again to the White House on May 9. There, in the Oval Office at 2:30 p.m., he'd rehearsed with Leahy, Marshall, King, and Arnold "the attitude that should be taken by the U.S. Chiefs of Staff at the conference with the British war officials who will arrive in Washington Tuesday," as the President's chief of staff noted dryly in his diary.[2]

All had been agreed. "The principal contention of the American government will be a cross Channel invasion of Europe at the earliest practicable date and full preparation for such an invasion by the Spring of 1944," Leahy had recorded that night — adding sniffily: "It is expected that the British Chiefs of Staff will not agree to a cross channel invasion until Germany has collapsed under pressure from Russia and from allied air attack."[3]

No cross-Channel Second Front before the Germans *collapsed*?

The likely British proposal seemed to Leahy a pretty awful way to run a war — one that would either leave Hitler in control of mainland Europe, or if not, give the Russians a head start in the overrunning of western

Europe. Though thanks to his fever he had not attended the Casablanca Conference, Leahy had read all the minutes and final agreements, as well as hearing firsthand from the President, Marshall, Arnold, and King the accords the British had made. What on earth were the British up to now, he wondered?

Early on the evening of Tuesday, May 11, the U.S. chiefs of staff congregated for the third time in a week at the White House. The arrival of the *Queen Mary* in New York Harbor had been reported, and the Prime Minister's huge retinue had apparently entrained for the capital. Then at "six forty-five p.m. the American Chiefs of Staff accompanied the President," Leahy recorded in his diary, "to meet a special train bringing to Washington the British Prime Minister and his War Staff."[4]

"Reached Washington at 6:30 pm where we were met by Roosevelt, Marshall, Dill, etc," a tired General Alan Brooke recorded in his own diary that night.

Ambassador Halifax was there to greet them, too. Churchill and his secretaries were immediately whisked off by the President to the White House; Brooke was invited to stay with Field Marshal Dill, his former boss.

It was a "hot and sticky night," Brooke noted before he went to bed at Dill's rented house in Virginia.[5]

He was nervous — embarrassed at the friendliness being shown by his American hosts, given that he was carrying a veritable bombshell. He'd been required first to go to the recently opened Statler, where the rest of the British party would be accommodated, to attend "a cocktail party given in our honour" by his hosts, the American chiefs. "From there," he recorded in his diary, "we did not escape till 8.15 pm." "I must now prepare my opening remarks for tomorrow's Combined Chiefs of Staff conference and muster up all our arguments," he added to his entry. "We have a very heavy week's work in front of us!"[6]

At the White House, the Prime Minister and his closest personal staff were meantime shown to the rooms where they would stay. The First Lady, however, was nowhere to be found. Irritated that the President had seen fit to receive Churchill for an unspecified length of time in the White House, and knowing her husband was having to steel himself for the confrontation he was rather dreading, she had simply decamped — going in the opposite direction, to their house in New York.

For his part, Churchill had begun to show signs of anxiety over his mission — in fact he'd suggested he might stay at the British Embassy on Massachusetts Avenue. Roosevelt had refused to hear of it — figuring it might be better to suborn the recalcitrant prime minister under lock and key, so to speak, in the White House mansion, where he'd have a better chance of countering whatever it was that Winston was harboring or plotting in his brilliant but sometimes dangerously inventive mind.

Instead of cocktails, then, the President wined and dined Churchill on Pennsylvania Avenue, with just his daughter, Anna Boettiger, and Harry and Louise Hopkins, present. Though the Prime Minister's office assistant, Leslie Rowan, and Churchill's aide-de-camp, Commander Tommy Thompson, were asked to eat with them, no invitation was extended to Churchill's military advisers. The dinner ended shortly after 9:00, after which the President invited Churchill to his Oval Study on the second floor. There the two men talked until after midnight.

Secretary Stimson, at his own house across the Potomac, remained on tenterhooks. As he noted anxiously in his diary the following day: "Churchill arrived last night with a huge military party, evidently equipped for war on us."[7]

"I fear it will be the same story over again," the secretary lamented — furious that Churchill had come with such a huge contingent. He was all the more concerned since General Arnold had suffered "a severe heart attack" immediately after the May 9 Joint Chiefs meeting at the White House. The U.S. chiefs would thus be fielding a man short at the top, and might, Stimson feared, now be overwhelmed by their British colleagues in the talks — talks he had not been asked to attend.

Though the air in Washington remained warm and sticky on the morning of May 12, the atmosphere in the White House seemed somewhat frosty — a far cry from the happy spirit that had invested the Casablanca Conference. The President only went to his office at 11:10 a.m., where he had a succession of appointments — the American Legion, the mayor of Chicago, American labor leaders (regarding the national coal strike — the largest single strike ever called in the United States, involving more than half a million miners demanding more pay). And then lunch in his Oval Study with Hopkins, Churchill, and Lord Beaverbrook — former British minister of munitions, who had come without portfolio, as he was no longer in the British cabinet or government.

If there was open debate at the White House lunch, none recorded it. Indeed, no one recorded the luncheon — reflecting, perhaps, the awkwardness. Given that Beaverbrook was an outspoken advocate of a Second Front to be mounted as soon as possible — at the very latest, he pleaded, in the spring of 1944 — and since Harry Hopkins remained an unrepentant advocate of priority being given to such a direct, cross-Channel strategy, even by inexperienced troops, the Prime Minister was on his own at table. At all events, Churchill's narrative of the trip, written seven years later, jumped straight from joyful arrival in Washington, the night before, to a fictitious account of the discussion that took place that afternoon with the Combined Chiefs of Staff — pretending in his memoirs that he, too, was in favor of a spring 1944 Second Front.

This was, in truth, mendacious — for minutes of the meeting, held in the Oval Office immediately after lunch, were kept by General Deane, secretary of the Combined Chiefs of Staff: minutes that documented, in writing, the rift between the President's and the Prime Minister's views on global strategy.

Anxious to maintain at least a semblance of Allied unity, the President opened the meeting at 2:30 p.m. with a look back across the past year — reminding the generals how far the United Nations had come since their last get-together in Washington. It was, he said, "less than a year ago when they had all met in the White House, and had set on foot the moves leading up to TORCH. It was very appropriate that they should meet again just as that operation was coming to a satisfactory conclusion" — for Allied troops had already "seized Bizerte and British troops had fought their way into Tunis," General Deane noted the President's words. Given complete Allied air and naval control of the southern Mediterranean now exercised by the Allies under General Eisenhower, no Dunkirk-like evacuation of German or Italian forces was possible. It had taken time, but Torch had led, methodically, to a great Allied victory.

What a turnaround the campaign in Tunisia had brought, he remarked. The final surrender of German and Italian troops was expected momentarily, and might possibly number over 150,000 men — perhaps even a quarter million.[8] The invasion and subsequent combat had thus provided the Allies with the safe learning experience they needed. Its sequel had been decided upon at the recent Casablanca Conference, the President recapitulated: namely "operation HUSKY," the invasion of Sicily, which he hoped "would meet with similar good fortune," as the Allies made ready to throw "every resource of men and munitions against the enemy" under July's full moon.[9] The chiefs were assembled now, however, in Washington, to review what should happen after the fall of Sicily: "What next?"

With that, the President asked Mr. Churchill to give his own introductory remarks.

It was a delicate moment.

Churchill's lengthy *tour d'horizon* in the President's study, delivered with his characteristic rhetorical flair, bons mots, cadences, and flattering flourishes, certainly impressed his listeners for its brilliance ("very good opening address," General Brooke noted in his diary).[10] However, it completely failed to dispel the U.S. chiefs' fears of what the British were plotting. With every word, in fact, it became clearer that, whereas the President had seen Torch operations in the Mediterranean in 1943 as a means to gain the vital battle and command experience necessary for a cross-Channel Second Front in 1944, the British were not so confident — indeed, were not seriously interested in crossing the Channel anytime soon, unless the Germans collapsed. Thus the U.S. chiefs were compelled to listen as the Prime Minister lyrically described the triumph of Torch and the imminent conquest of Sicily as the means to a much richer, more byzantine, strategic end: not the defeat of Germany but merely the further clearing of Britain's vital seaway to India, and a staging post for expeditions into the "soft underbelly of Europe," beginning with the knocking of Italy out of the Axis coalition.

Before the assembled generals and admirals, Winston Churchill proceeded to outline how, surely, it ought to be the objective of the Allies, after securing Sicily, to invade Italy, obtain its surrender, then exploit the huge gap this would leave in the Adriatic and the Balkans, where twenty-five Italian divisions were currently helping the Germans in Yugoslavia. Once Italy fell out of the Axis alliance, those Italian forces would be hors de combat — offering an even softer European "underbelly." If, in turn, the Turks saw such a door into southern, mainland Europe opening, they might be persuaded to join the Allies or at least be encouraged to permit the Allies to use Turkish positions and airfields in order to attack the Third Reich from the south and southeast — thus disposing of the need for a cross-Channel operation at all, unless it were to be conducted as a pro forma operation, following the "collapse" of the Germans, similar to 1918, after the "defection" of Bulgaria.

1918?

Bulgaria?

There was a deathly hush in the Oval Office. Admiral Leahy, as chairman of the Combined Chiefs of Staff, was caustic in the entry he made in his office diary that evening. "The prime Minister spoke at length on the advantages that would accrue to the allied cause by a collapse or a surrender of Italy through its effect on the invaded countries of the near East and Turkey. In regard to a cross channel [Second Front] invasion in the near future," the admiral added with ill-concealed disgust, "it is apparently his opinion that adequate preparations cannot be made for such an effort in the Spring of 1944." Such an invasion, Churchill had allowed, "must be made at sometime in the future."[11] Sometime — but not 1944.

Even though Admiral Leahy, Admiral King, General Marshall, and General McNarney (deputizing for the literally heart-stricken General Arnold) had all been told by Field Marshal Dill to expect something on these lines, they still found themselves speechless. That Churchill would openly contradict and defy the strategy laid down by the President of the United States and agreed to at Casablanca, in front of the President and to his face, before his top military advisers, seemed incredible. "There was no indication in his talk of a British intention to undertake a cross channel invasion of Europe either in 1943 or 1944," Leahy repeated in frustration. In order to be quite clear as to the Prime Minister's precise argument, he added that the Prime Minister was recommending that no such invasion take place "unless Germany should collapse as a result of the Russian campaign and our intensified bombing attack."[12]

No cross-Channel invasion, then, even in 1944, unless there was a German collapse.

All eyes thus turned to the President.

To General Brooke's irritation, the President contradicted the Prime Minister. In the nicest yet firmest way possible the President made abundantly clear he did *not* agree with Churchill's new alternative strategy. "The President in a brief following talk," Leahy noted, "advocated a cross channel invasion at the earliest practicable date and not later than 1944."

To the relief of the U.S. chiefs of staff, the President explained that, in order to make certain of success in mounting a spring 1944 cross-Channel assault, U.S. operations in the Mediterranean *must* be curtailed as soon as possible after the fall of Sicily. The Allies would by then have all the command and battle experience they needed from the Mediterranean — in the air, on land, and at sea — for a Second Front invasion from Britain. In combat skills, in field command, in coalition planning and fighting, and in logistics. Mr. Roosevelt therefore categorically "expressed disagreement with any Italian adventure beyond the seizure of Sicily and Sardinia."

The President's tone had now turned from warm politeness to firmness. With regard to the Far East, he made clear he was disappointed by the latest British refusal to carry out the Anakim offensive that had been agreed upon at Casablanca, and stated "that the air transport line to China" — which Chiang Kai-shek was pleading be intensified — must "be placed in full operating condition without any delay, and that China must be kept in the war."[13]

With that, the strange meeting in the President's study came to a close.

Brooke, in his diary, was alarmed, noting the President "showed less grasp of strategy" than the Prime Minister.

The two top military teams then filed out. As the chief of staff to the Prime Minister, General Ismay, later recounted, "there was an unmistakable atmosphere of tension" and "it was clear there was going to be a battle royal."[14]

28

No Major Operations Until 1945 or 1946

EVEN CHURCHILL'S OWN wife, Clementine, worried lest the United States abandon its "Germany First" policy. In fact, Clemmie sent Winston cable after cable, while he was staying at the White House, expressing her abiding fear that, in the aftermath of the massive German surrender in Tunisia — with the numbers of German and Italian prisoners reportedly mounting by the hour — the United States might consider the campaign at an end, and choose to redirect its primary efforts to the Pacific. "I'm so afraid the Americans will think that a Pacific slant is to be given to the next phase of the war," she wrote him on May 13. "*Surely* the liberation of Europe *must* come first," she confided. And in a PS she added that she'd just heard of the "terrific" RAF bomber raid on Duisburg, in the Ruhr. "Do re-assure me that the European front will take 1st place all the time," she begged.[1]

Winston, however, was Winston: endowed with inspirational intellectual energy and romantic imagination yet burdened, too, by an often fatal penchant for peripheral rather than direct, frontal attack. It was a tendency that went back to his justifiable indignation as an infantry battalion commander in the trenches of the Western Front in World War I before the Battle of the Somme, and the bloodbath he witnessed on the plains of France.

Churchill's alternative — his Dardanelles landings — had proven just as futile as Allied offensives on the Western Front in World War I, however. There had simply been no easy military alternative to frontal attacks in World War I in the West — attacks that did, when no diplomatic solution could be found, ultimately decide the outcome once U.S. troops were committed to battle in France in 1918. Certainly the Prime Minister was

fully entitled to ask his own chiefs of staff and then the Combined Chiefs
to explore other scenarios before confirming the Casablanca decision to
pursue a cross-Channel invasion — but that was not how Churchill presented his case at the White House.

Nor was it the case the next morning, when the first so-called Trident
meeting of the Combined Chiefs of Staff opened in the Board of Gov-
ernors Room of the Federal Reserve Building on Constitution Avenue.
There, to Admiral Leahy's disgust, it became clear that an extension of the
war in the Mediterranean and the Balkans rather than the agreed assault
of northern Europe was no mere Churchillian fantasy. General Brooke,
the bespectacled, owlish-looking "strongman" on the British team, announced he was even *more* opposed to a cross-Channel Second Front in
1944 than Prime Minister Churchill.

Brooke's apostasy in seeking to overturn the Casablanca agreement on a
1944 Second Front was potentially crippling to the Allied military alliance.

A solitary, self-contained man of incisive mind, Brooke had done
his best since succeeding Sir John Dill as British Chief of the Imperial
General Staff in 1941 to curb the Prime Minister's penchant for madcap
schemes — especially red herrings that detracted from the Allies' primary strategic effort. Now, however, as CIGS, Brooke was supporting
Churchill's alternative strategy.

How, though, the U.S. chiefs countered, would an as-yet-unplanned
invasion of the mainland of Italy, the Balkans, and Greek islands miraculously lead to the collapse or defeat of the Third Reich?

In hindsight — given German determination to pursue the war to the
bitter end — it couldn't. But in truth that was not Brooke's real reason, in
May 1943, for backing rather than dissuading the Prime Minister. The fact
was, despite the success of the Western Allies in North Africa, he too had
lost faith in the essential feasibility of a Second Front in 1944.

Brooke had commanded heavy British artillery in World War I and large
numbers of troops in France early in World War II — command that
had ended in tearful defeat. The humiliation of British evacuation first
at Dunkirk and then Brest, Cherbourg, and Saint-Nazaire in 1940, on
top of the complete collapse of the French armies, had cut to his heart.
Half-French himself, he simply lacked belief that an Allied cross-Channel
invasion could ever succeed. The Wehrmacht drubbing given to Opera-

tion Jubilee, Mountbatten's August 1942 mini-rehearsal at Dieppe for an eventual cross-Channel assault landing, had in Brooke's view proved the point. The German massacre of an entire Canadian brigade on the beaches of the little French seaport was clearly a beach too far, given the literally dozens of tough Wehrmacht divisions stationed across northern Europe to repel such an attempted invasion — including panzer divisions.

The result was that in Washington, General Brooke exuded not energy — which at least his Prime Minister did — but a kind of dour, Northern Irish Protestant skepticism amounting to obstructionism. Not only about plans, moreover, but about people.

At Casablanca he had gotten a very poor impression of General Eisenhower as a fighting commander — blind to the way the young Allied commander in chief was not only learning on the job, but inventing a new kind of coalition command that might be messy and might result in many an upset or failure, but which brought together the collective *power* of Western arms — naval, air, and army — in a way that even the most disciplined of German troops could not stand up to, in the end. Even news of the surrender of General von Arnim together with many hundreds of thousands of Axis troops at Cape Bon, when he received it immediately after the meeting in the President's study, failed to change Brooke's mind, or convince him the Allies would ever be ready to fight whole German armies in northern France, unless the German government collapsed, as in 1918.

Wearing his trademark round black spectacles, Brooke sat in his chair at the Combined Chiefs of Staff meeting the next day, May 13, 1943 — his thick black mustache and slightly hooked nose giving him a fierce, intimidating countenance. He listened silently as Admiral Leahy was first acknowledged as the chairman of the proceedings and then read aloud to the meeting the U.S. chiefs' opening paper. This was titled "A Global Strategy, A Memorandum by the United States Chiefs of Staff." Copies of the document, moreover, had been handed to all the chiefs around the table. Looking through the document as Leahy spoke, Brooke hated it.

Word for word the document set down in typed script the strategy the President had outlined the day before at the White House. The "concept of defeating Germany first involves making a determined attack against Germany on the Continent at the earliest practicable date," the U.S. chiefs' document stated, "and we consider that all proposed operations in Europe should be based primarily on the basis of contributions to that end."

Lest there be any misunderstanding on this score, Admiral Leahy spelled it out in the simplest of sentences: "It is the opinion of the United States Chiefs of Staff that a cross-Channel invasion of Europe is necessary to an early conclusion of the war with Germany."[2]

Not to be outdone, General Brooke responded by handing across the table copies of the British chiefs of staff counterpaper — a paper that Brooke then read aloud to the meeting.

Entitled "Conduct of the War in 1943–44," the document was three times as long as Leahy's. In it the British chiefs argued that Italy might *not* surrender after the fall of Sicily, or by the threat of Allied bombing.

In order to achieve Italy's capitulation, the British paper contended, there would probably be need for "amphibious operations against either the Italian islands or the mainland." This "continuance of Mediterranean operations" would, "of course have repercussions elsewhere and will affect BOLERO," the cross-Channel assault, as well as operations in the Pacific, the document allowed. However, the fruits of Italian collapse would, the British chiefs argued, be worth the cost of delaying the cross-Channel invasion for several years, for it would make possible "increasing supplies to the Balkan resistance groups, and by speeding up our aid to Turkey."[3]

Silence again ensued — the two Allies at a strategic stalemate.

After a pause, General Marshall, the chief of staff of the U.S. Army, pointed out that, as the President had said the day before, there was no reason to venture into southern Europe at all. The Ploesti refineries, in Romania, which provided Germany's all-important oil supplies, should certainly be bombed by long-distance B-25 and B-17 bombers, operating from the Mediterranean. In fact, Marshall continued, the use of vastly superior and constantly increasing Allied air power "might enable us to economize in the use of ground forces in the Mediterranean Area," since footling amphibious and ground operations would not achieve more than local advantage — while merely delaying the Allies' main offensive capability. The Allies would then "deeply regret not being ready to make the final blow against Germany, if the opportunity presented itself, by reason of having dissipated ground forces in the Mediterranean Area."[4]

Again, there was silence.

Brooke countered that Allied air power was all very well, as in bombing the Ploesti oil refineries, "but this must be examined in relation to the whole picture of knocking Italy out of the war."

To this Marshall delivered the stunning rejoinder: namely that the aim of the "Europe First" strategy had never been to focus on *Italy*—Germany's junior partner in crime. The objective was to defeat *Nazi Germany,* their real adversary. Thus, rather than dispersing their forces in subsidiary ventures, he rebuked Brooke, "we should direct our attention to knocking Germany out of the war."[5]

The first formal Combined Chiefs of Staff (COS) meeting of the Trident Conference now turned into a free-for-all, as General Brooke, under attack, revealed more and more of his hand—this time claiming that by dumping the Casablanca agreement they would help Stalin—for if Italy fell, the Germans would be compelled to deny reinforcements to their Eastern Front and instead occupy and defend the Italian mainland, as well as defending the Balkans and Aegean Islands, just as they had done when compelled to send German reinforcements to Tunisia. Hitler would thus be able to provide "20 [percent] less on the Russian front," aiding the Soviets.

This aspect might well be so, Leahy, Marshall, and King accepted. But would not the mere *threat* of Allied invasion compel Hitler to station that number of divisions in Italy and the Balkans—much as he had stationed four hundred thousand German troops in Norway, and twenty-five divisions in France? Brooke's other claim, namely that successful Allied amphibious operations to seize yet more Mediterranean islands and occupy the Italian mainland would then provide a springboard from which to mount an attack on southern France, sounded equally irrelevant. Since when had *southern France* been deemed a way of "knocking Germany out of the war"?

Pushed against the ropes, General Brooke was thus driven to confess his deeper fear: that, unless fighting continued in the Mediterranean, "no possibility of an attack into [northern] France would arise"[6]—*for it would surely fail.* Even if Allied troops succeeded in achieving a beachhead across the English Channel, the subsequent battle or campaign in northern France, he believed, would be a disaster—for the Allies. Even after a bridgehead had been established, "we could get no further," he predicted. "The troops employed would be for the most part inexperienced."

With only fifteen to twenty U.S. and British divisions, the Bolero operation would be "too small and could not be regarded in the same category as the vast Continental armies which were counted in 50's and 100's of divisions" in the previous war.[7]

At this defeatist assertion, however, General Marshall really bridled. The discussion was "now getting to the heart of the matter," he acknowledged. The big lesson of Torch—and in planning for the forthcoming invasion of Sicily—was the way such a campaign, inevitably, "sucked in more and more troops." If "further Mediterranean operations were undertaken," Marshall pointed out, "then in 1943 and virtually all of 1944 we should be committed, except to a Mediterranean policy." Not only would this subsidiary campaign detract from the war in the Pacific, in terms of supplies, but it would mean "a prolongation of the war in Europe, and thus a delay in the ultimate defeat of Japan, which the people of the U.S. would not tolerate. We were now at the crossroads—if we were committed to the Mediterranean" rather than northern France in 1944, then "it meant a prolonged struggle and one which was not acceptable to the United States."[8]

Pinned against the ropes, poor Brooke now blamed a paucity of men. He explained that the "British manpower position was weak," and its forces were, in all candor, not up to the challenge of a cross-Channel invasion—neither that year, 1943, when a lodgment area in Brittany might possibly be attained (though one that would be easily cauterized by the Germans, he claimed), nor in 1944, either.

The U.S. chiefs were stunned by Brooke's open confession.

"No major operations," Brooke affirmed, adding insult to injury, "would be possible until 1945 or 1946."[9]

Again, the U.S. chiefs could hardly believe their ears, especially when Brooke explained "that in the previous war there had always been some 80 French Divisions available to our side." Now there would only be a handful, if that. Any advance from the Channel "towards the Ruhr would necessitate clearing up behind the advancing Army and would leave us with long lines of communication," subject to German air and land counterattack. Not only was British manpower "weak," but the RAF lacked mobility, having concentrated on bombing German cities, not supporting land armies; its planes and crews were therefore ill-equipped to support an invasion or subsequent campaign.[10]

Despite the current Allied victory in Tunisia, the picture that Brooke presented was, then, bleak in terms of the defeat of Hitler's Third Reich.

The two Western Allies were at loggerheads.

Without the British as allies, an American invasion of Europe was a nonstarter, and the President's "Germany First" strategy — as well as unconditional surrender of the Axis powers — would be in tatters.

No major cross-Channel operations until 1945, perhaps 1946?

When the President, at the White House, heard what Brooke had, at the Federal Reserve Building, openly declared — an assertion going further even than the Prime Minister had revealed at the meeting at the White House the previous day — he was amazed. So this was the "vast amount of work" the British chiefs had been doing — as Churchill had boasted in a telegram to the President from the *Queen Mary* as it neared New York![11]

The President was disappointed; in fact he was shocked. The British position seemed not only disingenuous but deceitful, in retrospect. Where the President had seen Torch and its Sicilian sequel as a crucial learning curve and rehearsal for a Second Front to be launched across the English Channel in 1944, the British had clearly backed Torch and the impending invasion of Sicily only to secure the Mediterranean as a shorter sea-lane to their occupation troops in India — while doing their best to *avoid* frontal combat with the Nazis in northern Europe.

The President shook his head. That very morning he had been discussing with the president of the Czechoslovak government in exile, Dr. Edvard Benes, the unconditional surrender of Germany, and what might be done to partition or police the country to ensure the Germans could never threaten world peace for a third time. Now, at lunchtime, he was hearing from Air Marshal Charles Portal that the British chiefs had no intention of launching a cross-Channel attack before 1945 or, possibly, 1946, three *years* away. How could this new stance be explained to the majority of Americans who saw Japan, not Germany, as the nation's primary enemy, yet had loyally backed the President's "Germany First" strategy?

The President had been told, in December 1942, that almost two million Jews had in all probability already been "liquidated" by Hitler's SS troops.[12] How many more Jews and others would Hitler exterminate by 1946? And all this so that Britain could sit out the war in Europe, at its periphery — not even willing to open the road to China, but hanging on to India and merely waiting for the United States to win back for Great Britain its lost colonial Empire in the Far East? It seemed a pretty poor performance.

Although disappointed, the President was not defeated. Great leadership demanded positive, not negative, thinking, and Portal, as an airman, did not sound quite as obstinate or defeatist as Brooke.

The British were visitors in a foreign land, and the best way to coax them out of their funk was, the President felt, to encourage them to overcome their understandable fears, not berate them; to help, not shame, their generals into recovering the confidence they would need to partner the U.S. military in mounting a cross-Channel invasion next spring.

The home team must therefore, the President decided, be firm in class, but as nice as possible outside. He'd already planned with Marshall that the Combined Chiefs were all to be taken to Williamsburg, in Virginia, at the weekend — any talk concerning conference matters strictly forbidden. For his own part, while the U.S. chiefs of staff hosted their opposite numbers at the site of the first British settlement in America (a source of cultural pride for the British visitors, but also a reminder of the successful American revolution to wrest independence from the British), the President now decided he wouldn't in fact take Churchill to Hyde Park, as he'd originally planned. Instead he would take him to his little mountaintop camp at Shangri-la. There he would work on him — insisting that Lord Beaverbrook, as an ardent supporter of an immediate Second Front, come too.[13] And Eleanor, who'd returned from New York, would be asked to at least drive with them to the cottage — thus prohibiting Churchill from any attempt to talk alternative Allied military strategy.

Extreme hospitality would thus be the order of the day. By burying the British with kindness, after working hours, the American hosts, in Williamsburg and at Shangri-la, would hopefully encourage their visitors to overcome their fears and confirm the Casablanca commitment to a fully fledged trial-by-combat cross-Channel invasion of northern France next spring: April or May 1944.

Such was the plan. Whether it would work was another matter.

At Shangri-la, once they settled in, the President took Churchill fishing. They settled by a local stream — the wheelchair-bound president "placed with great care by the side of a pool," Churchill recollected, where he "sought to entice the nimble and wily fish. I tried for some time myself at other spots."

It was in vain. "No fish were caught,"[14] Churchill recalled. Nor was Winston's mind changed about a doomed Second Front.

The three days in the Maryland mountains thus became something of a test of wills.

Shangri-la and the President's handling of Churchill on May 14, 15, and 16, 1943, mirrored Casablanca and the president's handling of de Gaulle — *prisonnier,* as de Gaulle had complained, in the President's Anfa camp. Now it was the Prime Minister's turn to feel that way.

Shangri-la was neither the White House nor Hyde Park. Instead it was, as Churchill later put it, "a log cabin, with all modern improvements." He watched "with interest and in silence" as General Pa Watson brought the President not war documents but colorful stamps: "several large albums and a number of envelopes full of specimens he had long desired," after which Roosevelt "stuck them in, each in its proper place, and so forgot the cares of State."[15]

For all the pretty mountain setting, the proximity to nature, and the restful quiet, the Prime Minister would not yield. The more the President and his supporting cast worked on him — both Hopkins and Beaverbrook attacking Churchill's obsessive argument for the invasion of Italy and the Balkans rather than northern France — the more determined Churchill became. So testy, in fact, that he even declined the President's request that he accept an invitation from Madame Chiang Kai-shek to go to New York, where she was staying while receiving medical treatment — risking, as Churchill candidly described his refusal, the "unity of the Grand Alliance," given the importance of the Generalissimo's struggle against the Japanese in China.[16]

Refusing to commit Britain to the 1944 cross-Channel invasion threatened, however, a far greater schism in the unity of the Grand Alliance than Madame Chiang Kai-shek's wrath. As obstinate as de Gaulle, the Prime Minister relentlessly clung to his Mediterranean preference, fearful of a cross-Channel debacle.

Pondering Churchill's behavior at the time, Sir Charles Wilson, the Prime Minister's doctor, wondered if the Prime Minister was suffering some sort of physiological problem. Churchill had, after all, hitherto pursued the "special relationship" with the United States with extraordinary patience, deference, and understanding. Now he was neither patient nor deferential, and certainly unwilling to conceive the strategic problem from an American perspective. His failure to grasp the import of what he was demanding — an extra year, perhaps two, of war in Europe without a Second Front, and a further year after that to defeat Japan — raised serious questions about the Prime Minister's state of mind. He'd come down with pneumonia in February (at the same time the President had fallen ill, after returning from Casablanca), which had been more serious than could be made public at the time — and in its aftermath, Dr. Wilson wondered whether it might have affected Churchill's judgment. Wilson himself had been stricken by fever on the voyage to America aboard the *Queen Mary,* and had had to be hospitalized in New York. When finally he caught up with his patient in Washington on May 17, he was frankly shocked. The Prime Minister had just returned from Shangri-la with the President — and what Wilson heard was amusing, but not encouraging.

The Prime Minister had, according to members of the President's entourage and Lord Beaverbrook, lost nothing of his extraordinary memory. On the return trip to Washington the presidential party had passed several Civil War battlefields, and Harry Hopkins regaled Dr. Wilson with an account of how Winston, hearing Hopkins could recite only two lines of John Greenleaf Whittier's famous Civil War poem, had recited the entire poem. "While we were still asking ourselves how he could do this when he hadn't read the darned thing for thirty years, his eye caught a sign pointing to Gettysburg. That really started him off," Hopkins recounted in awe — Churchill's summary of the battle, with character portraits of the rebel generals Jackson and Lee, being equally amazing. About the current war, however, "Hopkins was a good deal less flattering about the P.M.'s contribution to the discussions which had begun on May 12 in the oval study of the White House," Dr. Wilson recalled. "Indeed, he looked pretty glum as he assured me that I had not missed anything."[17]

The impasse appeared to be the same as the one the year before, when the Prime Minister had journeyed to the White House for the same reason: namely to explain why the British could not agree to a cross-Channel invasion that year. The British surrender at Tobruk, moreover, had made his point: the British were simply not ready for such a challenge in 1942, at a moment when they might even lose control of the Middle East to Rommel's advancing Panzerarmee Afrika.

Now, eleven months later, "damn it all," Churchill was back, with "the old story once more, shamelessly trotted out and brought up to date," Dr. Wilson recalled with concern, recording in his diary the sense of frustration felt by Hopkins: Churchill simply refusing to countenance the Casablanca strategy, unless Italy was swiftly defeated and the Third Reich miraculously fell apart.[18] Hopkins had even imitated Churchill, saying: "Bulgaria's defeatism in 1918 brought about the collapse of Germany; might not Italy's surrender now have similar consequences? It will surely cause a chill of loneliness to settle on the German people and might very well be the beginning of the end."[19]

Loneliness as the beginning of the end — without the Wehrmacht actually being defeated in battle, or even forced back onto German soil? To those who remembered the consequences of the "collapse of Germany" at the end of World War I, this was understandably alarming.

Dr. Wilson had asked Hopkins "what the President made of all this."[20]

"'Not much,'" Hopkins had answered. "'This [idea of] fighting in Italy does not make sense to him,'" he'd explained the President's view. United States naval, air, and ground forces had been sent to the Mediterranean — against the advice of Hopkins, Stimson, Marshall, and the U.S. chiefs of staff, it was true — to learn *how* to defeat German troops in close combat, the President had insisted. As soon as the Sicily invasion and campaign were won, those forces — commanders and troops — were to be switched to England for the invasion of northern France in the spring of 1944, in accordance with the President's strategy. "He wants the twenty divisions, which will be set free when Sicily has been won, to be used in building up the force that is to invade France in 1944," Hopkins made clear.[21]

At the Pentagon and Navy Department, the U.S. chiefs of staff were similarly frustrated.

Brooke's stonewalling, once the chiefs returned from Williamsburg, was especially irritating. "A very decided deadlock has come up," Secretary Stimson noted in his diary on May 17, after speaking with General Marshall. "The British are holding back dead from going on with Bolero. They have done the same thing in regard to Anakim [the campaign to retake Burma] and are trying to divert us off into some more Mediterranean adventure. Fortunately," he added, "the President seems to be holding out."[22] Stimson decided he must call the White House and make sure, though. "I called up the President, told him that I had prepared myself fully by reading all the minutes and was ready to talk with him at any time that he wanted to, although I did not want to intrude myself on him. He told me he was coming to the conclusion that he would have to read the Riot Act to the other side and would have to be stiff."[23]

Stimson, conscious of how the President liked to quote Lincoln, told him how President Lincoln had remarked of General Franz Sigel that, though he couldn't "skin the deer," he "could at least hold a leg." By his intransigence, however, the Prime Minister was in danger of causing the Western Allies — Americans and British — to be Sigels in the war against Hitler: only daring to hold the Nazi leg while the Russians did the skinning. "Stalin," he told the President, "won't have much of an opinion of people who have done that," he warned, "and we will not be able to share much of the post-war world with them."[24]

The President did not need reminding. Yet how *compel* an ally like Britain to conform to American strategy?

The most worrying thing was that Churchill was now threatening to disrupt the Western military alliance just at the moment when the President was becoming more and more anxious to pressure Stalin to sign up to a postwar United Nations authority while the United States — furnishing more than 10 percent of Russia's war needs — still had significant leverage. All in all it was too bad — with no breakthrough in sight.

Whatever Stimson, Hopkins, the U.S. chiefs of staff, and later critics might say about Churchill's sudden intransigence in May 1943, however, it is important to note that Churchill and his British contingent were not the only ones arguing in Washington against a Second Front. The prospect of heavy casualties in head-on combat with the Wehrmacht in northern France was sobering. Outside the War Department more and more people were objecting — especially people in the Navy Department who foresaw a long war with Japan if the "flower of our army and air force" was first expended "in combat with Germany," as Bill Bullitt, assistant to the secretary of the Navy, warned in a renewed memorandum he wrote for the President on May 12.

It was vital the President should, Bullitt argued, put more pressure on Stalin to declare war on Japan at the conclusion of the war against Hitler, lest the United States should have wasted its manpower and resources in a cross-Channel campaign that could get bogged down, as in World War I — thus leaving itself, even after assumed victory, having to fight against Japan "while the Soviet Union is at peace," and Britain contributing only insignificantly to the defeat of the Japanese. In that situation, "we shall have no decisive voice in the settlement in Europe," Bullitt warned. "Europe will be divided into Soviet and British spheres of influence — according to present Soviet and British plans — and further wars in the near future will be rendered inevitable."[25]

Bullitt's recommendation, once again, was the same as Churchill's — to drive swiftly into central Europe through the Dardanelles.

After Roosevelt's death, Bill Bullitt would spend the rest of his own life lancing the memory of the President for having failed to take his recommendation. Only American "boots on the ground" in central Europe would stop Stalin's "Sovietization," Bullitt pointed out again in his memorandum — and the Balkans was the place to plant those boots.

The President could only groan at this extra pressure from his own American side, given the latest British intransigence. Bullitt might have an excellent understanding of Russian communism; his Balkans strategy, however, remained militarily illiterate. Moreover, his latest political recommendation, namely that the President should threaten Stalin with a switch of American forces to the Pacific unless he agreed in writing not to Sovietize central Europe, was, at a time when the Western Allies did not have a single boot on the ground in Europe, less than realistic.

No, the fact was, the President had little option but to stick to his own program: refusing to countenance a quagmire in the Balkans or the northern Italian mountains, and instead holding to the timetable for a U.S.-British Second Front that had been agreed at Casablanca: spring 1944. This strategy, if followed, would at least take U.S. and British forces to Berlin, ending the Third Reich and saving the western part of Europe from Sovietization. He would meantime continue to press Stalin, in order to see if he could get the Soviets to sign up to his postwar plan and to declare war on Japan as soon as Germany was defeated. Without a genuine plan to launch a Second Front by 1944, however, it was unlikely to get very far, as Secretary Stimson had commented.

To produce such a genuine plan, he would have somehow to bring the British back into the fold, or the Second World War might well end in failure.

PART EIGHT

The Riot Act

29

The Davies Mission

ON THE SURFACE, the great victories at Stalingrad and then Tunisgrad boded well for Allied cooperation in eventually defeating the Third Reich.

In truth, however, relations with the Soviet Union were not good — indeed were getting worse. Stalin's rejection of the President's invitation to the summit at Casablanca (or alternative venues the President had offered) had resulted in the sheer scale of the Russian war effort being underappreciated in the West. Even Stalin's own ambassador to Washington, Maxim Litvinov, had warned the Russian Foreign Ministry that such standoffish behavior was counterproductive, indeed would make it harder, not easier, to get the Western Allies to commit to a timely Second Front.

Stalin had paid no heed. This was hard for even the most sympathetic of American observers and reporters to understand. In terms of Allied military cooperation, Russia was, sadly, a write-off — Stalin constantly demanding more U.S.-British convoyed deliveries of war materials to Murmansk, yet refusing to order Russian aircrews to fly out of northern Russia to protect them, lest they leave the borders of the Soviet Union and not come back. This had led to, and continued to result in, terrible British and American shipping losses, not only in Lend-Lease war materials and food but Allied lives as well. Nor would the paranoid dictator allow Allied officers, or representatives, to monitor whether the contents of the convoys were being efficiently unloaded at Murmansk, or were appropriate to actual Russian war needs. The Russians had also refused for months to respond to whether U.S. bomber crews could land in the Soviet Union if they bombed the Ploesti oil fields in Romania — and when they finally did respond, they refused to allow Ploesti raids to be launched from Russian airfields, despite being at war with the Third Reich and its eastern European partners, Romania and Hungary. Whether it was paranoid fear that Russians might become infected by rich capitalist partners, or that Russia's capitalist allies might obtain genuine, accurate, and detailed information — military, political, economic, social — about the Soviet Union, no one really knew. Nor had this changed as the tide of war against Hitler turned. As Western diplomats and journalists — who were forbidden to venture outside Moscow without close supervision — complained, there was virtually not a single Russian who dared question, counter, or ignore Stalin's oppressive policies for fear of arrest, imprisonment, or even execution.

More troubling still had been the sickening revelation, in April 1943, that more than twenty thousand Polish officers, police officers, and members of the intelligentsia had, on Stalin's orders, been murdered in cold blood by Soviet occupation forces in 1940, during the time of the German-Soviet Nonaggression Pact.

That disclosure — the decomposing Polish bodies unearthed by the Germans in the Katyn forest near the Russian city of Smolensk, but the Soviets denying culpability — had given cause for grave trepidation in the West, especially among Polish forces in exile.

Nothing, but nothing, could excuse such mass murder. News of the massacre, at a moment when the tide of war had turned and the forces of the Third Reich seemed to be everywhere on the defensive, had offered the embattled Dr. Goebbels a heaven-sent opportunity to demonstrate to the German Volk,[1] as well as people abroad, just how merciless a Russian victory in the war, and a subsequent Russian-imposed "peace," would be.

Stalin naturally protested it was a Nazi ruse. He denounced the leader of the Polish government in exile for suggesting Russian complicity, loudly claiming the Nazis, not the Soviets, had been responsible for the massacre. Both Roosevelt and Churchill had on good authority been told the bitter truth, however: that it was Stalin himself who had given the orders for the mass execution in 1940.

With Stalin's Soviet Union such an uncooperative, undemocratic, often downright evil partner of the Western democracies — though one that was still taking the brunt of casualties in the war against Hitler — both Roosevelt and Churchill were put in the iniquitous position of publicly accepting, or declining to comment on, Russian lies over the Katyn massacre. Besides, in the balance of atrocities, the Germans were still way ahead of the Soviets, both in SS mass-murder concentration camps and in the treatment of Russian POWs.[2] Continued do-or-die Russian resistance to Hitler on the Eastern Front was crucial — no matter how ungrateful, paranoid, deceitful, and barbarous the Russians, and however chilling the prospect of postwar Sovietization.

How maintain that morally dubious anti-Nazi coalition, though — let alone seek to move the Russian communists from their reign of terror into a more positive postwar world?

It was in this respect that the relationship, or partnership, between the President and the Prime Minister was of the highest importance for the history of humanity. And in Washington, in May 1943, Prime Minister Churchill was coming very close to breaking it.

Hitherto, Churchill had taken the same view as the President — that the enemy of my enemy is my friend, however odious in certain respects. But with Churchill threatening to pull out of the Casablanca accords and refusing to mount a Second Front in 1944, the question arose: would Stalin remain a friend? As Secretary Stimson warned, without a cross-Channel invasion — one that would force Hitler to fight on two fronts — would not the Russians lose military respect or faith in the Western Allies, and be minded to seek an armistice with the Third Reich, even a new Ribbentrop Pact that would leave Hitler master still of all western and central Europe?

Roosevelt didn't think Stalin would stoop to that, after the millions of casualties the German onslaught had already cost the Russians. But it could certainly undermine the President's attempts to get Russian agreement to make air bases available and declare war on Japan, if and when the war with Hitler was successfully concluded, as well as getting Soviet participation in the postwar security system the President had in mind. The Second Front, in other words, was a sine qua non: a test that the Western, democratic Allies *must* meet if they were serious not only about the war but the postwar. Not footling around in the Mediterranean, but a willingness to face up to the war's greatest challenge: D-day, as it would become known.

The President thus changed his mind about a summit with Stalin — feeling it would be better to keep Churchill *out of* any meeting for the moment, if one could be obtained, lest the Prime Minister's opposition to a cross-Channel operation give away their weak hand: namely the fundamental unwillingness of the British to countenance the heavy casualties involved in a Second Front. Somehow, Roosevelt was aware, to defeat the Nazis he must keep the Russians fighting in the East — and get the British to *fight* in the West, not footle about in the South!

This was easier said than done. His cables to Stalin after Casablanca had deliberately, perhaps disingenuously, held out the possibility of a Second Front being mounted in the summer of 1943, after Husky; how then was he to explain to Stalin the Western Allies were not only abandoning any plans to launch a Second Front in 1943, but that the purpose of Churchill's current visit to Washington, together with a military staff of 160 advisers, was to argue against a Second Front *even in 1944*? In fact, according to Churchill's Chief of the Imperial General Staff, that no Second Front should be planned before 1945 or even 1946?

"The Soviet troops have fought strenuously all winter and are continuing to do so," Stalin had assured the President in March. The Führer had lost more than a whole army at Stalingrad, but he had many more at hand—perhaps as many as two hundred divisions, including whole panzer armies. The Germans were preparing for "spring and summer operations against the USSR," Stalin wrote; "it is therefore particularly essential for us that the blow from the West be no longer delayed, that it be delivered this spring or in early summer"—i.e., 1943.[3]

It was in this context that the President had summoned another former ambassador to Moscow, Joseph Davies, to the White House the day after Churchill set sail for Washington. As the President explained to Davies, he'd decided to send Stalin a new letter by hand, to be delivered in such a way that Stalin would be forced to respond to the President's renewed request for a private meeting.

Davies was elderly and had been particularly naive in his acceptance of Russian propaganda regarding their communist show trials, arrests, and deportations in the 1930s. He was sincere in his judgment of Hitler and the barbarity of Nazism, however, and his evaluation of the Soviet will to defend Russia had proven more sophisticated than that of the U.S. military attaché in Moscow—in fact, he'd been the man who correctly reported to the President that Operation Barbarossa, Hitler's invasion of the USSR in June 1941, was going to fail. As an emissary to show goodwill and firmness of American purpose in prosecuting the war against Hitler, the President could not have chosen better. The new, private letter Davies would hand carry would be a direct, personal invitation from the President to meet somewhere that summer and resolve their differences over strategy and timing—one the Russian dictator could not now refuse without giving offense to the President of the one country in the world supplying the Soviet Union with a significant amount of its war needs.

The Prime Minister was not now to be invited to the proposed summit, the President made clear in the letter — though he could not give the true reason, even to Davies, who would doubtless be asked by the dictator, once he reached the Kremlin. Since the President could not reveal Churchill's impending visit to Washington and his reported unwillingness, supported by his chiefs of staff, to launch a timely Second Front, he had merely told Davies he wished to meet Stalin, informally, to discuss the long-term future with him. Not, in other words, to address the matter of impending operations, but rather the conclusion of the war: unconditional Axis surrender, winning the war against Japan, and the establishment of a postwar United Nations authority. It would be, the President explained to Davies, a preliminary discussion, man to man, without risking, Roosevelt told his emissary, any international arguments over British — or French — postwar colonial empires. "Churchill will understand," the President had assured Davies when giving him his instructions in the Oval Office on May 5. "I will take care of that."[4]

As Davies set off for Moscow via the Middle East, Churchill had arrived in Washington — and the Prime Minister's refusal to countenance a Second Front had only reinforced the President's determination to meet Stalin alone. Davies would hopefully convince the Russian dictator that the Western Allies were united and sincere in their commitment to launch a Second Front — the President's willingness to travel halfway across the world to meet in person with the Russian leader surely a gauge of that sincerity.

In the meantime, however, the President was determined to bring Winston Churchill to heel, lest he and his huge military team cause the Grand Alliance, rather than the Third Reich, to collapse.

This, in essence, was the challenge of Trident: suborning Neptune.

Adding to the behind-the-scenes war drama was the fact that the British chiefs of staff now parted company — physically and metaphorically — with their own Prime Minister.

The chiefs' weekend in Williamsburg, Virginia, went well — the officers glad to be out of Washington not only to be able to relax but to get to know their Allied counterparts as human beings. Talks had then resumed at the Federal Reserve Board building at 10:30 a.m. on Tuesday, May 18, 1943.

Admiral Leahy, General Marshall, and Admiral King had feared the worst in terms of British intransigence, once back in uniform, so to speak. So worried, in fact, were the U.S. Joint Chiefs that they came to the table with a compromise whereby they would ask only for a minimum "lodgment area" across the English Channel in 1944, if the British were still so afraid of failure, and would only seek to expand it the following year, 1945.

Once seated in the room, however, it was to find the "battle royal" was already won. To their astonishment, the President's tactic of extreme hospitality appeared to have worked — the weekend away in Williamsburg, with wholesome food and wine and civil conversation having seemingly done the trick. Aided also by Field Marshal Dill — who'd reasoned with his successor as CIGS, General Brooke, that he must give in or risk a breakdown in what was a historic military coalition between the United States and Great Britain. The American people, the field marshal had made clear to his British compatriot, would not stand for the war in the Pacific being deliberately starved of men and resources for years, simply so the British could fiddle around in the Mediterranean — leaving Hitler's legions in almost complete control of continental Europe. A firm date for a cross-Channel invasion *must* be tied down, and the necessary forces assembled to make it work.

A new paper on "The Defeat of Germany" — not Italy — had therefore been ordered from both planning staffs over the weekend, while the Prime Minister was away at Shangri-la, to define exactly how Hitler was to be brought to unconditional surrender — namely by defeating Germany, not simply Mussolini's Italy. By Monday night, May 17, the British version, approved by General Brooke, had been ready. When General Marshall read it through at the meeting on Tuesday, May 18, he was delighted. Though it talked a lot about further interim operations in the Mediterranean, it "appeared that [even] if Mediterranean operations were undertaken in the interval, a target date for April 1944 should be agreed on for cross-Channel operations." In writing.

General Marshall breathed a sigh of relief. Brooke then confirmed this was the case, the date formally recorded in the minutes of the meeting.[5]

April 1944.

Mirabile dictu, Marshall reflected. General Brooke had seemingly dropped his call for a postponement of a Second Front until 1945 or 1946, and was now definitely onboard — if, in the meantime, operations in the Mediterranean were allowed to continue that summer. "The rate of build-up of German forces in western Europe would greatly exceed our own on the Continent unless Mediterranean operations were first undertaken to divert or occupy German reinforcements," Brooke maintained. "If these operations were first undertaken," Brooke conceded, "April 1944 might well be right for a target date, though the actual operation would be more likely to be possible of achievement in May or June."[6]

Genuine, serious military preparations for a massive spring 1944 cross-Channel invasion by the Western Allies could now commence, the generals agreed — with only the thorny question left as to how far to limit interim 1943–44 operations in the Mediterranean so that they did not prejudice preparations for D-day.

Leahy, Marshall, and King were still skeptical. The matter of "interim" operations in the Mediterranean would, they predicted, prove tortuous — but at Marshall's insistence a formal commitment to D-day had been given by the British, in writing. Some seven battle-hardened U.S. and British divisions would be withdrawn that very fall from the Mediterranean theater to the United Kingdom. There they would begin training and rehearsals for the spring 1944 D-day assault. It seemed a reasonable compromise.

For Secretary Stimson, at the Pentagon, the British climbdown was as much a relief as it was to General Marshall.

The Prime Minister, meantime, had been kept well away from the daily Combined Chiefs meetings. Instead, he had been pressed by the President to go address a joint session of Congress again — "a very good speech, noteable for its good, downright eloquence," Stimson recorded, after attending the performance on Capitol Hill, "on the main lines of war history and strategy and also for the adroitness with which he avoided any allusions to the real points of issue which are now being fought over between the staffs of the two countries.[7]

"These points of difference have come out sharply in the two plans and it is taking all Marshall's tact and adroitness to steer the conference through to a result which will not be a surrender but which will not be an open clash. The President seemed to be helping us," Stimson added — Mr. Roosevelt adopting the same approach as his U.S. team, as "indicated by his telephone talk with me the other evening." The President, Marshall had reported to the Secretary, was not only "taking the same line" but "insisting that the planners decide what will be the cost in shipping and men for the 'big point' (as the President called it)": the cross-Channel invasion. Only when these requirements had been met would the planners be permitted, the President had said, to "determine from what is left over what can be done otherwise" in the Mediterranean.[8]

The Second Front, in other words, would now be First Priority for the Western Allies.

As to the sincerity of the British volte face not all were convinced, however. Admiral King, in particular, remained less than happy. Though the British seemed resigned to join the U.S. in launching a Second Front invasion in April or May 1944, they were insisting on so many landing craft, naval forces, air forces, ground forces, and logistics being assigned in the "interim" to the Mediterranean that — in King's eyes — this could well prejudice the success of the primary cross-Channel strategy. More significantly to King — a true believer in prosecuting the war in the Pacific more robustly, now that the Americans and Australians were on the successful offensive there — such an interim policy threatened to slow down Nimitz's and MacArthur's plans, thus allowing the Japanese to "dig in." The result would inevitably be grave American casualties — an aspect that seemed not to register with the British, whose main forces were being held in India as an army of colonial occupation, and were making every excuse not to take the offensive against the Japanese.

There was, moreover, public impatience in America to consider.

"I am very much afraid that, if the British succeed in getting us pulled out any further onto the limb in the Mediterranean," Stimson noted, "we shall face a widespread loss of support for the war among our people." This was serious. "Polls show that the public would be very much more interested in beating Japan than in beating the European Axis [powers]," he acknowledged, thanks to Pearl Harbor — something that could easily translate into "all kinds of personal and party politics" that could damage the bipartisan, "Germany First" war effort.[9] This danger extended, he knew, to his fellow Republicans across the country, who were once again demanding that General MacArthur be recalled from Australia to stand in the 1944 presidential election — a campaign in which MacArthur would doubtless call for a switch of U.S. priority to the Pacific to face not Hitler, but America's "true" enemy, Japan.

What Stimson and Marshall failed to realize, however, was that General Brooke had now parted company with his prime minister — and that Winston Churchill would be the problem, not the British chiefs of staff.

30

A Dozen Dieppes in a Day

SEATED AT THE Federal Reserve Board in the Combined Chiefs of Staff meetings, General Brooke had failed to noticed the Prime Minister's increasingly divergent trajectory. Even the President, living with the Prime Minister each day at the White House, had been unaware of what Churchill was saying behind his back.

Hearing from Admiral Leahy on May 18 that the British chiefs had backed off their opposition to a 1944 or 1945 invasion of France, the President had been delighted by news of his team's success. This would be of inestimable help when and if he met with Stalin, since he would now be able to reveal to the Russian leader, in person and in all honesty, a firm date for the Second Front. It would be a formal U.S.-British military commitment that, even though Stalin had fervently hoped it would take place in 1943, would nevertheless encourage the Soviets to hold out against Hitler's impending summer offensive on the Eastern Front.

The President was crowing too early, however.

The first intimation the Prime Minister was charting his own course in opposition even to his own British team had come on the evening of May 18, 1943 — reported to the President by none other than the Canadian prime minister, Mackenzie King, who had accepted the President's invitation to attend the latest meeting of the Pacific War Council and to stay at the White House.

From his train, Mackenzie King had gone to Pennsylvania Avenue to settle in and have a word with his fellow prime minister. It had been 6:00 p.m., but Churchill was in bed, in the Queen Elizabeth Room on the second floor. He had looked "very frail," and was wearing "a white nightgown of black and white silk," King described in his diary. "He has lost the florid coloring and his face was quite white. Looked soft and flabby. He had a glass of Scotch beside him near his bed," and "looked to be very tired" — as well he might. On a special writing tray Churchill was still, after some seven hours, working on the draft of the address the President had asked him to give to Congress the following day. He was keen for Mackenzie King to read the text — anxious not to say anything impolitic, given that people in Washington were already talking about the 1944 presidential election, still more than a year away. "He indicated that he had not completed his speech and would be taking a little sleep before dinner, which I took to mean that he would not wish the conversation to take up too long."[1]

The two prime ministers had first talked of the recent Allied victory in Tunisia, where General von Arnim had finally surrendered on May 12. It was "really shocking" Churchill claimed, "the way the Germans came in at the end" — "giving themselves up, falling and crawling; some of them waving plumes [white flags], and [he] said that an hour before, when they thought they could win, they were most savage and brutal. He imitated their different attitudes in his own face."[2]

This was vintage Churchill: his vivid imagination running free (since he had obviously not been present at the surrender), yet amazingly astute in his reading of German moral duplicity: able to switch from barbarous hubris toward other humans to shameless appeals for "humanitarian" clemency when they themselves were overpowered.

Once again Mackenzie King found himself entranced by the British prime minister's mind and his colorful use of language. They swiftly moved on to the reason for Churchill's presence in Washington, however. "Churchill began to tell me about the conferences here," King noted in his diary that night. "Said that they were discussing the plans. That he and the Americans were very good in accepting Roosevelt's decisions in the end" — as they had at Casablanca. "He thought that he and Roosevelt were very much of the same view," even if there were "differences of emphasis."[3]

Prime Minister King was baffled. This was not what he'd been told that very afternoon on his visit to the Canadian legation in Washington. There he'd been informed that "the Americans were pressing for a cross-Channel Second Front" — "invasion from the North" — whereas "the British plan was for invasion [of Europe] from the South, either through the Balkans or [southern] France. Views had not yet been reconciled."[4]

How, then, could Roosevelt and Churchill be on the same page? Was Churchill now accepting the President's Second Front strategy? Or was the President accepting Churchill's new strategy—and what was it, in fact? A second Dardanelles? Had he misunderstood? What was Churchill really saying—or not saying?

It was at this point that Churchill made clear "that as far as he was concerned, the plan was to follow on the decisions of the Casablanca conference," which had authorized landings in Sicily in July that year, in Operation Husky—*but had not explicitly gone further than that,* he now claimed. "The thing to do was to get Italy out of the war," Churchill explained. "Altogether he believed this could be done, and said he would not treat them [Italians] too badly if they were to give up and particularly if they were to yield up their fleet. If he could get the fleet, he would be prepared to use it to attack the Japanese." Meantime, however, there was the matter of Europe—and the defeat of Hitler. "The plan was to start the invasion of Europe through Sicily and Sardinia," Churchill now told Mackenzie King, confidentially, "either on through the Balkans or possibly through [southern] France depending on how matters developed." It would be easier than a cross-Channel attack.

"They would be getting footholds all along the way, and Russia might put on a very strong offensive and they [the Allies] would be working toward Russia"—via "southern Europe," the Prime Minister explained. "There was a chance, too, that Turkey might come in," King noted Churchill's words, "though not until she got plenty of equipment. He was not pressing her at present."

King—aware that the Pacific Council would have to wrestle with the implications of Churchill's alternative new strategy, so similar to his notorious failure in World War I—pressed Winston to explain in more detail.

Lest there be any misunderstanding, Churchill privately confided that he remained as implacably opposed to the notion of a cross-Channel Second Front as he had been the year before—indeed *more* so, now, after the catastrophe of Dieppe. "Speaking of invasion [of France] from the North," across the English Channel, "he said that he did not want to see the beaches of Europe covered with slain bodies of Canadians and Americans. That there might be many Dieppes [suffered] in a few days," were such an operation to be launched. "That he, himself, could provide 16 divisions which would include ours [i.e., Canadians] but there was only one American division in England. This was all they had against the numerous divisions Germany could muster; unless Americans were prepared to send a large number of divisions to cross at the same time, he did not see how they could attempt anything of the kind."[5] It would be, King again recalled Winston's actual words, "slaughter" — "a dozen Dieppes in a day." "I thought," King noted, "this was pretty strong language."[6]

Mackenzie King was now doubly dubious as to Churchill's claim that he and the President — let alone the U.S. chiefs of staff — were of the same mind. "I asked if the Americans were likely to make much difficulty over these particular plans," King noted. "He replied that the President and he were very close together; that they could not settle all these things at once. They had to run along for a time" — in order to dupe the U.S. Joint Chiefs. "The President was inclined more his way and he thought that his [U.S] chiefs of staff would accept loyally his decisions in the end."[7]

Mackenzie King said nothing. In truth he was gobsmacked, however.

Yes, the President had indeed insisted, at their last meeting, in December 1942, that further operations should first be carried out in the Mediterranean in 1943, in order to learn the hard, attritional lessons of modern war before attempting anything as hazardous as a cross-Channel invasion. But the President had never said anything to suggest he believed the Allies should attempt to defeat the Third Reich by attacking from the south. Was Churchill, with his "glass of Scotch" on the table beside his bed, making this all up? Was he living — as he tended to do, in the eyes of the abstemious Canadian who had vowed not to drink liquor for the duration of the war — in an alcohol-laced cocoon? Alcohol seemed certainly to fuel Churchill's fertile imagination and brilliant rhetorical skills — but did it equip him to *listen* to what President Roosevelt and the Combined Chiefs were telling him rather than to his own voice?

Dimly, though, Churchill seemed aware the President had been keeping him away from the Combined Chiefs of Staff over the weekend — indeed from anyone who might become alarmed over his Mediterranean ambitions. "He said that the President and he had been off together at Blue Ridge over the week-end," at Shangri-la. The following weekend, however, Churchill "wanted to see a few friends," and was going to insist he be allowed to stay at the British Embassy on Massachusetts Avenue, where he could meet with and telephone anyone he wanted. "Thus far, he had not seen hardly any."[8]

King was somewhat alarmed, but held his tongue, unwilling to disconcert Churchill on the eve of his important appearance before Congress — which, as prime minister of Canada, King had been invited to attend.

Mackenzie King's worst fears indeed materialized the next day when, at the Capitol at midday on May 19 — the very day Ambassador Davies arrived in Moscow bearing the President's private letter to Stalin — Churchill followed up his congressional address by talking frankly to senior members of Congress.

"After the luncheon, members of the Senate and representatives of the foreign committee came into the room, and Mr. Churchill was subjected to a quiz," Mackenzie King — who attended this meeting, too — recorded that night in his diary. "He faced squarely the question as to strategy. Told those present that he felt the great objective now was to knock Italy out of the war." This would, he said, "clear the Mediterranean which would mean a through route to India, China; make all the contacts with the Orient much easier. He believed the great offensive was coming against Germany on the part of Russia," and "in the Southern part by allied forces pressing up through the Balkans, and there would be a relief of the pressure on Russia. They might, too, get some of the satellite states of Germany to change their attitude. They would also get additional help from Yugoslavia where some 10 [Italian] divisions were tied up there which could be added to the allied numbers. Thought that all this would be helpful to Stalin. He thought the Germans could be driven entirely out of Italy and would probably leave Italy to look after herself."

King was puzzled. Driven entirely out of Italy? Churchill's forecast of Hitler's likely reaction to an Allied invasion of Italy and the Balkans — especially after the example of German tenacity in reinforcing Tunisia over the past six months — sounded disturbingly naive, even schoolboyish. His prediction, moreover, seemed at odds — very poor odds — with his defeatism concerning the prospects for a Second Front. To the postprandial group of senators and congressmen, Churchill "made it pretty plain," King noted, "he did not favor any immature attack on Europe from the North," across the English Channel. "He spoke of the few divisions they have in Britain — I think 18 altogether including our own, only 1 American division, and that Hitler was able to move many divisions from one part of the continent to the other in a very short time. Referred to the scarcity of ships, etc" — going "pretty far in making clear the plan is to attack across the Mediterranean into Europe either via [southern] France,

Sicily or further East [in the Balkans], without designating what locality would be first."[9]

Even more astonishing to the Canadian prime minister was Churchill's complete lack of shame or caution in opposing the President's strategy in front of U.S. lawmakers, behind the President's back — having "instructed them," Mackenzie King noted, that with regard to questions they were welcome "to try and knock him off his [strategic] perch."[10] He even outlined the idea of a "peace conference," similar to Versailles in 1919, that would take place, perhaps in England, at the end of hostilities — with both Republican as well as Democratic members of Congress "invited" to participate.[11]

Versailles, then, moved to Westminster . . .

That Churchill was playing a dangerous double game became clear later that afternoon when the President invited the Combined Chiefs of Staff to the White House, following their afternoon meeting at the Federal Reserve Building. The President had heard via Admiral Leahy that the chiefs had confirmed their agreement to an April or May 1944 cross-Channel Second Front — but that tempers in the morning's meeting, when addressing remaining "interim" operations in 1943, had become so frayed the secretaries had been asked to leave the room while the chiefs dueled it out.

General Marshall's contention that further operations in the Mediterranean that fall would inevitably suck in the forces needed for a successful cross-Channel attack had hit home — Brooke defending his own strategy by claiming a cross-Channel attack would never succeed unless the Wehrmacht was first forced to fight hard not only on the Russian front but in Italy. Heavy fighting in Italy was thus the prerequisite of a successful invasion in the spring of 1944. "After the capture of a bridgehead" in northern France, "a Cherbourg might be seized, but the provision of the necessary forces to cover this would be difficult unless the Germans were greatly weakened or unable to find reserves," Brooke had warned.[12] A serious military campaign in Italy, in other words, would be the weakening blow: essential in order to make the April or May 1944 operation work.

Marshall had countered that such a strategy might very well achieve the opposite. The British, he'd summarized, were exaggerating the ease of a campaign in Italy, while perilously underestimating the need to throw maximum logistical effort into the real priority: the cross-Channel invasion. It should, Marshall reminded Brooke and the other committee members, "be remembered that in North Africa a relatively small German force had produced a serious factor of delay to our operations," given the mountainous terrain. "A German decision to support [defend] Italy might make intended operations extremely difficult and time consuming."[13]

No truer warning to the British was ever given in World War II — though Brooke would never admit, either then or in retrospect, that Marshall was right. Marshall had, Brooke merely confided to his diary that night, "suggested that the meeting should be cleared for an 'off the record' meeting between Chiefs of Staff alone. We then had a heart to heart and as a result of it at last found a bridge across which we could meet! Not altogether a satisfactory one, but far better than a break up of the conference."[14]

The compromise was certainly vague and open-ended. Rather than halting major offensive operations in the Mediterranean after the successful seizure of Sicily, as the President and Marshall wished, Eisenhower would be authorized to capitalize on any signs of an Italian collapse to seize airfields in southern Italy — but only assigning experienced Allied forces for the remainder of the summer. Then — at the very latest on November 1, 1943 — the best battle-hardened U.S. and British divisions were to be withdrawn from combat and transferred to Britain to prepare for D-day. This, they all agreed, should be mounted either in April or in early May, 1944.

This compromise, confirmed by all, had duly been reported by the Combined Chiefs when summoned to meet with the President in the Oval Office at 6:00 p.m.

They were then joined by the Prime Minister, on his return from the Capitol.

Nine Allied divisions were to be ferried in the assault across the English Channel on D-day itself, with twenty more in the days that followed — a massive rolling offensive backed by Allied air power and naval support. Whatever was left in the Mediterranean could be used by Eisenhower to "eliminate Italy from the war and contain the maximum number of German divisions."

According to the minutes of the Oval Office meeting, "the PRIME MINISTER indicated his pleasure that the Conference was progressing as well as it was and also that a cross-Channel operation had finally been agreed upon. He had always been in favor of such an operation and had to submit to its delay in the past for reasons beyond control of the United Nations."[15]

Given what Churchill had told U.S. congressional representatives *that very afternoon* — namely, that he did not favor what he saw as a "dozen Dieppes in a day" on the beaches of northern France — and given that he favored, instead, an Allied offensive through Italy and the Balkans, this was tantamount to perjury, unless the Prime Minister had truly had a Pauline conversion.

Only time would tell.

31

The Future of the World at Stake

HALF AN HOUR after the Combined Chiefs departed the White House, the President dined upstairs with Mackenzie King, Churchill, and Crown Princess Martha of Norway.

In deference to Princess Martha, the three leaders put aside any discussion of military strategy, and after the meal the President arranged for a Sherlock Holmes film to be shown as light relief. Churchill then "begged off" and went to bed, as did Princess Martha, leaving the President to talk quietly with his Canadian guest.

Gingerly, Mackenzie King sought to find out the President's intentions, in terms of Allied military strategy. "Tonight when I was talking alone with the President and asking how he and Churchill had got on, he said he thought an agreement was practically in final shape by now; that he, himself, would probably want to recast it a little more in the way of bringing up to the beginning some matters that were near the end."

The British had said they couldn't carry out the Anakim offensive to which they'd committed themselves at Casablanca, and there had been initial, heated discussion of this; the primary decision, however, was the Second Front in 1944. The President wanted to ensure the British commitment was not only firm but set down in ink, on paper, and in official accords — which Admiral Leahy, the Combined Chiefs chairman, had assured him would be drawn up formally by the weekend. As the President explained to Mackenzie King, it was vital to tie down and chain the wily British to a solid commitment, not simply rely on the understanding he thought they had come to at Casablanca. "He wanted to emphasize the building up of the forces in Britain so as to be certain of an attack from the North in the spring of 1944. He said he felt that this was the top feature of it all. He did not use that expression but that was the inference. It meant the determining blow in the spring of next year."

Listening to this, King was somewhat perplexed. Given what Churchill had said openly at the Capitol, in King's hearing, it seemed the President and the British prime minister, though sleeping under the same roof, were poles apart. Mackenzie King therefore relayed to the President what Churchill had said at the Capitol — including the Prime Minister's remarks about a Versailles-type conference in London.

President Roosevelt "put his hands to his face and shook his head, a bit as much as to say he wished that part had been left well alone," King recorded the President's pained reaction. "He then said to me that he did not know that there would be any peace conference," given its connotation with Versailles 1919. "As far as he was concerned, there would be total surrender" of Germany and Japan. And certainly nothing "in the nature of a Versailles conference," which Congress would have to ratify.[1]

Hearing of Churchill's behavior at the Capitol, the President had reason to be anxious, however. He liked Winston, in fact he felt enormous affection, bordering on love, for him at times. But he had cause never to quite trust him — and for that reason he preferred to see Stalin alone, without the Prime Minister. Who knew if Churchill would start hedging over the Second Front, if they met *à trois?*

It was going to be difficult enough to explain to Stalin that the Western Allies were not going to launch a Second Front before spring 1944. If Churchill, in a tripartite meeting, were to begin talking in front of Stalin of dumping the invasion of France and concentrating Allied efforts instead in the Mediterranean and the Balkans, the Soviets — preparing at that very moment for the onslaught of *fifty-nine* concentrated German divisions aimed toward Kursk — would rightfully be incensed: vitiating any hope of the Third Reich being defeated any time soon, or of Russian assistance in the war against Japan, or of arriving at a common postwar security agreement. The notion of a United Nations assembly, with a security council of the Four Policemen acting in concert, would thus be out the window.

The President's postwar vision still filled King with awe — as did King's possible role in it. According to the President, the United Nations organization would have a "supreme council representing all the United

Nations," and would need at its head "someone who would fill the position of moderator — someone who would keep his eye on the different countries to see that they were complying with the agreements made in connection with the peace, for example, limitation of armaments, not rebuilding, munitions, etc — not be allowed to build airplanes or any of the paraphernalia of war. It would be the Moderator's duty possibly to warn in advance and, if necessary, to have the council meet to take such action as necessary" — a person who would "have the confidence of all the nations."[2] And, having abjured any idea he himself might take that role, after the presidency, Roosevelt intimated he thought Mackenzie King, at the end of the war, would make an excellent such secretary general.

King was understandably flattered — but in the meantime, like Roosevelt, he remained perplexed by the contradictions in Churchill's character. At the Pacific War Council, Winston had flatly denied in front of the Chinese representative that he'd ever made a formal undertaking to mount Operation Anakim, a British offensive from Indian territory to help China — even though Dr. T. V. Soong had documentary evidence of the commitment.

Like Mackenzie King, the President had shaken his head over such unnecessary falsehoods — "The President said that the trouble with Winston is that he cannot get over thinking of the Chinese as so many pigtails."[3] Similarly, over India, Churchill was as stubborn and indifferent to world opinion as he could get away with — having instructed the viceroy of India to make sure the American minister in Delhi not be permitted to interfere in any way with Mahatma Gandhi's 1943 hunger strike — and cabling Lord Halifax to tell all Americans in Washington that the British government "will not in any circumstances alter the course it is pursuing about Gandhi," even if this resulted in Gandhi's death.[4] He'd insisted, moreover, on speaking in public of "British forces" rather than "British Commonwealth forces"[5] — which was much resented in Canada, and would be even more resented once Canadian forces went into combat in Sicily. Churchill was, in short, a law unto himself — and yet the repository of such underlying humanity, understanding of history, and noble sentiment that it was impossible not to admire him.

The question, then, remained: Would Churchill stand by what he'd told the President and Combined Chiefs of Staff earlier that evening in the Oval Office — or by what he'd told members of Congress that afternoon at the Capitol?

246 | THE RIOT ACT

The matter was not academic; the future of the world was literally at stake—and Prime Minister Mackenzie King now watched Churchill's double game with growing concern.

When addressing the Pacific War Council the next day, May 20, at noon, Churchill refrained from discussing strategy in Europe in front of the President. Late in the afternoon, however, the Prime Minister addressed a special meeting of the chiefs of staff of Britain and Canada and representatives of other parts of the British Empire, held in the White House dining room, which the President had kindly made available to him.

Lord Halifax, who attended this "imperial" meeting, dismissed it in his diary. Churchill's "long speech of fifty minutes about the war" had been "very well done but with nothing very fresh in it except two or three things that could have been said in five minutes. I never saw anybody who loves the sound of words, and his own words more."[6] General Brooke, exhausted by the Combined Chiefs of Staff meetings (involving yet another "off the record" battle), dozed off, but Mackenzie King listened very, very carefully.

"After a moment's pause," King recorded that night, Churchill "started in saying he would sharpen and heighten somewhat the points he had made in his address before Congress." This the British prime minister proceeded to do, "following pretty much the sequence" King had heard on the Hill. In this there was "little else that was new." "The most interesting part," King noted that night, however, "was the account he gave as to why it would be advisable to proceed against Europe from Africa as a base." It was, Churchill stated, "advisable to get ahold of a few islands in the Mediterranean, use them as stepping-stones toward Europe. The great effort should be made to get Italy out of the war."

Few could argue with this—or with Churchill's magnanimity. Unconditional surrender was an agreed Allied policy, but one should not be "too particular about the terms on which peace could be made with Italy," Churchill suggested. "Her people had never had their hearts in the war. He was not anxious to see their country destroyed. If he could get the Italian fleet, that would be an immense gain. He would then have more ships to be employed against the Japanese . . ." With regard to the Second Front, whether in 1943 or 1944, he was strangely reticent, however—and King remained uncertain whether Churchill had really changed his view that it "would be slaughter."

Given the loss of so many Canadian lives in the Dieppe assault the previous August, Mackenzie King was understandably sensitive to this, having noted it was "pretty strong language and indicated a feeling that Dieppe had been a real sacrifice, perhaps an unnecessary one." At any rate, the "picture he presented was of the beaches being long and in stratas; in some places, water deeper than others. Very difficult to land troops. He was determined not to have men sacrificed anymore than could be helped."[7]

Whatever the U.S. and British chiefs might agree upon, then, it was still questionable whether Churchill was really willing to commit British and Canadian troops to a Second Front.[8] In fact he "spoke emphatically about not being in too great a hurry to invade Europe even from the South," Mackenzie King noted. "He said opinion was divided as to the best way to win against Germany. Some thought bombing would be sufficient. There was no harm, however, in trying other methods, as well, while trying to do the best they could with bombing."[9]

If bombing was Churchill's only plan to defeat Germany, it did not sound very convincing to King. Moreover, it was certainly not how the President and the Combined Chiefs of Staff, in their long and trying meetings, were approaching the question of how to vanquish the Third Reich and move on to defeat Japan. Churchill seemed unabashed, though. He was not, as King recognized, a strategist in the true sense of the word, but an *opportunist* — opposed down to his entrails to "giving commitments versus tactics," as King noted.[10] And with that the Commonwealth meeting had ended.

Mackenzie King was to spend the night aboard his train, since he would be returning to Canada, via New York, on May 21. Harry Hopkins had asked King to see the President before leaving the White House, however, and this the Canadian did after midday, on the twenty-first, in the Oval Office. Despite the heat the President "looked very fresh and cool. Was seated on his swing chair. I sat to his left looking out of the window toward the garden. A lovely feeling. An ideal office with a little court opening out of the room." The President seemed confident the Allies now had an agreed plan for winning the war — and one he could put to Stalin, confiding again to King his invitation to meet the Russian dictator in the Bering Strait.

What might be Churchill's reaction at being deliberately excluded, the President then asked King, given Churchill's erratic position over a

Second Front? To encourage the President, King assured him that Winston — who had, after all, had his own private meeting with Stalin the previous summer — would get over it. Besides, the main thing was not the Prime Minister's pride or dependability, but the President's hugely important global goal — moral, military, and political — that promised to shape the postwar world.

On that note the two leaders parted company — though King wanted also to say goodbye to Churchill. He therefore walked from the Oval Office through to the White House mansion and up to Churchill's guestroom, just after 1:00 p.m. There he found the Prime Minister still in his underwear, dressed "in his white linen under-garments; little shirt without sleeves and little shorts to his knees, otherwise feet quite bare excepting for a pair of slippers. He really was quite a picture but looked like a boy — cheeks quite pink and very fresh."[11]

King said he wanted "to be perfectly clear in my own mind what is to be done," in terms of military strategy — strategy that involved tens of thousands of Canadian lives — lest there be any misunderstanding.

To this, Churchill responded by saying "there will be no invasion of Europe this year from Britain. I tell you that" — but the Mediterranean was another matter. There, Canadian troops would shortly take part in the invasion of Sicily in July, to gain battle experience. Canadians would, in fact, "be in the forefront of the battle."[12] Moreover, instead of returning direct to London, Churchill himself was going "to Africa from here" — a "dead secret."[13]

What of Allied war strategy *beyond Sicily*, though?

Delicately, King "did say that I thought there was a certain possibility of divergence of view" between the senior Canadian forces' commander and "some of the plans he, Churchill, had in mind; also between some of the plans that our own chiefs of staff or the British chiefs might have." The Canadian War Cabinet was prepared to go along with what would "best serve" the need to win the war — but only a strategy that was feasible "in the opinion of the military advisers who had charge of the strategy of the war."[14] In other words, the Combined Chiefs of Staff.

Churchill, somewhat surprised, reassured King there was no divergence — indeed that King was at liberty to speak with General Brooke, the CIGS, before returning to Canada, if he was in any way unsure or confused.

Still the Canadian prime minister remained skeptical, however. He had another talk with the Canadian minister of national defense that afternoon — who said he had it direct from Brigadier Jacob, Churchill's military assistant, that the strategy agreed by the Combined Chiefs of Staff would now stand. "In the light of this," King noted, "I thought it was just as well not to attempt to see Sir Allen [*sic*] Brooke. It might have looked to the Defense Ministers that I was distrustful of them" — and of Churchill.[15]

That he had every right to be, however, would only become clear after Mackenzie King's departure.

32

The President Loses Patience

EVEN GENERAL BROOKE was disbelieving.

The President had spent the weekend at Shangri-la, while Winston Churchill moved for a few days to more comfortable quarters at the British Embassy on Massachusetts Avenue. Once the two leaders returned to the White House, however, the Combined Chiefs of Staff were asked to come to the Oval Office—and on the afternoon of Monday, May 24, they did: there to present the final terms of the Trident agreement. When they sat down before the President and Prime Minister, however, it was to find Neptune flatly refusing to accept the agreement they had reached.

Brooke had known his prime minister to be an occasionally maddening individual—obstinate, brilliant, sometimes tender, sometimes rude, and with a predilection for chasing red herrings. But to behave like a spoiled adolescent in front of the President of the United States of America—a president who was not only directing a global war but was furnishing the materials and fighting men to win it—seemed to Brooke the height of folly.

As Brooke understood it, the Combined Chiefs had been summoned to be thanked. Instead, Brooke found, "the PM entirely repudiated the paper we had passed, agreed to, and been congratulated on at our last meeting!!" as he recorded with exasperation that night. "He wished to alter all the Mediterranean decisions! He had no idea of the difficulties we had been through," the Ulsterman exploded in the privacy of his diary, "and just crashed in 'where angels fear to tread.' As a result he created [a] situation of suspicion in the American Chiefs that we had been [going] behind their backs, and had made matters far more difficult for us in the future!"[1]

Brooke was riven by shame and embarrassment. "There are times when he drives me to desperation! Now we are threatened by a redraft by him and more difficulties tomorrow!"[2]

General Marshall was equally furious. Admiral King boiled. Admiral Leahy, as chairman of the Combined Chiefs, was simply outraged. "From four-thirty to seven p.m. the British and American Chiefs of Staff presented to the President and the Prime Minister their report of agreements reached during the present conference," he noted in his own diary that night. "The Prime Minister refused to accept the Mediterranean agreement."

The Combined Chiefs' report had made no commitment by the Allies to invade mainland Italy, but instead only to "plan such operations in exploitation of Husky as are best calculated to eliminate Italy from the war, and to contain" — either by threat or by operations — "the maximum number of German divisions" while the cross-Channel invasion of northern France was readied for launching on May 1, 1944.

Mr. Churchill, Leahy noted in exasperation, had other ideas. He "spent an hour advocating an invasion of Italy with a possible extension to Yugoslavia and Greece."[3]

Leahy was as incredulous as Brooke. An "extension" of operations to Yugoslavia, Greece, and the Aegean that risked making a May 1944 cross-Channel Second Front impossible? Churchill was undeterred, however — and adamant.

Since Churchill was not only British prime minister but quasi–commander in chief of all British Commonwealth forces, this was a major stumbling block. "Final decision was by his request postponed until tomorrow," Leahy recorded.

As Brooke feared, this made the U.S. team almost apoplectic. Oh, perfidious Albion! "The Prime Minister's attitude is an exact agreement with the permanent British policy of controlling the Mediterranean Sea, regardless of what may be the result of the war," Leahy noted in disgust in his diary. "It has been consistently opposed by the American Chiefs of Staff," he added, "because of the probability that American troops will be used in the Mediterranean Area" — "at the expense of direct action against Germany." It was a Churchillian demand "which in our opinion [will] prolong the war."[4] If, that was, it did not lose it.

In shock and no little confusion, the British and American chiefs were ushered out of the White House and into their cars.

Churchill went straight to his room. After dinner and a movie there was a meeting in the President's Map Room, with Harry Hopkins and the Prime Minister's chief of staff, General Ismay.

In the narrow, windowless room, its walls hung with giant maps and thousands of the most secret reports, cables, and memoranda locked in filing cabinets in the center, the President pulled no punches. The date for the cross-Channel invasion was now set, he told Churchill, and the forces for it must be withdrawn from the Mediterranean by November 1, 1943 — period.

Churchill was furious. Returning finally to his room at 2:00 a.m., the Prime Minister summoned his doctor.

Sir Charles Wilson found "the P.M. pacing his room" — and blaming the President. "There was no welcoming smile. When I asked him how he had been he did not answer. He had other things to think about besides his health. He stopped and said abruptly, 'Have you noticed that the President is a very tired man? His mind seems closed; he seems to have lost his wonderful elasticity.'"[5]

Dr. Wilson — ignorant of the cause — watched as Churchill "went up and down his room, scowling at the floor." "The President is not willing to put pressure on Marshall," he explained. "He is not in favour of landing in Italy. It is most discouraging. I only crossed the Atlantic for this purpose. I cannot let the matter rest where it is."[6]

Dr. Wilson could prescribe sleeping medication, but he could do nothing to change the situation. Nor could Churchill. The President had said no — and there was little that could be done without seriously undermining, even wrecking, the Western alliance. The Prime Minister would have to accept defeat. The die, after all, was now cast. Even the Canadians were getting ready for a cross-Channel assault in 1944, with no interest in fighting in Italy — let alone Yugoslavia. Once back in Ottawa, Prime Minister Mackenzie King was preparing to tell his War Cabinet that it had been agreed in Washington that "the big battle will come early next year." Moreover, that "the Canadian army will be used along with the American army and the British army to make the final assault on Europe from the North" — not Italy or the Balkans. And "that we may expect the end of the war not before the end of this winter but before the end of another winter (1945).”[7]

Churchill continued to pace. He had not become prime minister of Great Britain and the one leader able to stand up to Hitler, however, by caving in to force majeure — particularly pressure from his own countrymen. Dr. Wilson’s medication would permit him to sleep, briefly — but not to alter his convictions.

Before the Combined Chiefs of Staff could reappear before their political and military masters at the White House on the morning of May 25, therefore, Churchill began a new attack on the Trident agreement.

That the Prime Minister meant well was not at issue. Long-term geopolitical British considerations had to be taken into account. But single-handedly to attempt to bend the president of the United States to follow a British agenda was foolhardy — especially in opposition to his own military team.

Dr. Wilson had already been worried lest the Prime Minister, by undertaking so many responsibilities, by refusing to delegate, by drinking so much, and by making so many wild trips abroad, might be approaching a mental breakdown, or “a gradual waning of his powers, brought on by his own improvidence, by his contempt for common sense and by the way he has been doing the work of three men. There is no hour of the night when I can be certain that he is in his bed and asleep. Of course, this cannot go on forever.”[8]

It couldn’t — and explained in part the Prime Minister’s amazing behavior, to the embarrassment of all, especially the President.

The Combined Chiefs assembled again in Roosevelt’s office at 11:35 a.m. Once again they were treated to Churchill at his most petulant. “We were therefore exactly as we had started so far as the paper we had submitted to the President and PM was concerned,” Brooke recounted in despair in his diary, adding, in his slashing hand, “the PM had done untold harm by rousing suspicions as regards ventures in the Balkans which we had been endeavouring to suppress.”[9]

Churchill, Secretary Stimson afterward learned from the President, “acted like a spoiled boy the last morning when he refused to give up on one of the points — Sardinia — that was in issue. He persisted and persisted until Roosevelt told him that he, Roosevelt, wasn’t interested in the matter and that he had better shut up.”[10]

For that, at least, General Brooke was grateful to the President.

With the President's final loss of patience and his stern word to Churchill, the meeting had mercifully come to an end.

Debate was over — and with that dramatic finale, the Trident Conference done. D-day, to be called Operation Overlord, would take place, come hell or high water, in the spring of 1944.

A grand, celebratory luncheon for the Prime Minister, Combined Chiefs of Staff, and all the senior staff officers involved in the conference was given by the President at the White House at 1:30 p.m. on May 25.

Early the next morning, Roosevelt drove down with Churchill to the special Clipper terminal on the Potomac River. The 160 members of the British military contingent would be sailing home from New York, but the Prime Minister and General Brooke were to board a huge Boeing seaplane that would fly them first to Newfoundland, and from there to North Africa.

The President had been skeptical regarding Churchill's new mission — as the Prime Minister was aware. It had not stopped Churchill, however, and the two leaders had come to a compromise. Churchill had assured the President he had no motive other than to review British and Allied HQ preparations in Algiers for the impending assault on Sicily, Operation Husky. Given the President's chariness, Churchill had felt compelled to suggest that General Marshall accompany him, as a gage of his fealty to the President and the war strategy finally and formally agreed between allies. The President had thought this an excellent idea — General Marshall flying, so to speak, as a U.S. marshal.

Poor Marshall had not been consulted.

At the Pentagon, Secretary Stimson had been furious — on Marshall's behalf. "Marshall told me of it," Stimson recorded in his diary, "and said he rather hated to be traded like a piece of baggage."[11]

The U.S. war secretary remained deeply suspicious, moreover. Churchill was "going to take Marshall along with him" for no other purpose, Stimson protested, than "to work on him to yield on some of the points that Marshall has held out on in regard to the Prime Minister's excursions in the eastern Mediterranean." This was too bad. General Marshall was worn out having to deal with Churchill's two-week visit, along with his vast retinue of military chiefs and advisers seeking to overturn the Casablanca agreement. Of all people, the general now surely deserved a break. In this respect, "to think of picking out the strongest man there is in America, and Marshall is surely that today, the one on whom the fate of the war depends, and then to deprive him in a gamble of a much needed opportunity to recoup his strength by about three days' rest and send him off on a difficult and rather dangerous trip across the Atlantic Ocean where he is not needed except for Churchill's purpose is I think going pretty far," Stimson frothed in his diary, outraged by the iniquity. "But nobody has any say"[12] — the President being the elected president, by far and away the most powerful man in America, and this his will.

For his part, the President found it ironic he was having to send Marshall to North Africa to keep the irrepressible Churchill on the rails. Roosevelt was not sorry, though. Seeing Eisenhower, Clark, Patton, perhaps, and the general lay of the land following General Eisenhower's great victory at Tunis would be no bad thing for his Army chief of staff. The number of Axis troops that had surrendered was now said to have exceeded even those at Stalingrad; the omens were good.

Word had also come from Moscow, moreover, that Stalin had finally agreed to a personal meeting. This would probably now take place in August. The President would pretend to be going to Canada to see Prime Minister King — and secretly fly north across Alaska to the projected rendezvous with the Russian dictator.[13] It was a relief, in these circumstances, that he, the President, would be able to convince Stalin that the Western Allies were united in their resolve to mount the Second Front in the spring of 1944 — and important that Marshall hold the Prime Minister tightly to this agreement. No more reneging, or alternative ventures, or pessimistic doomsaying behind his back!

The cross-Channel invasion would not take place in 1943, to Stalin's likely disappointment, but it would definitely be mounted in overpowering, U.S.-dominated force in May 1944 — and would, the President was confident, lead to the end of the war, either at the end of 1944, or early 1945. Only Churchill, in his unpredictable way, could possibly mess this plan up.

Admiral Leahy remained suspicious. As he noted with scarcely concealed distrust, the "agreements finally reached" were excellent, and would advance the American cause: to defeat Hitler. "This is, of course, based on an assumption that the agreements will be carried out by our allies."[14]

• • •

Ironically, General Brooke was just as skeptical as Leahy — at least with regard to his boss, the Prime Minister. Churchill's great qualities did not include consistency of military strategy. As Brooke had noted in exhaustion on May 24, summarizing his colleagues' contributions to the "Global Statement of Strategy" that the Combined Chiefs had drawn up, Admiral King was still besotted by war in the Pacific theater; General Marshall was too bold, willing to chance a cross-Channel invasion that would risk putting into the cauldron of battle "some 20 to 30 divisions, irrespective of what happens on the Russian front, with which he proposes to clear Europe and win the war"; Air Marshal Portal, by contrast, was imagining the war in Europe would be won by "bombing" alone; Admiral Pound was believing "anti-U-boat warfare" was the key; while Brooke himself favored all-out war in the Mediterranean, not to defeat Germany, per se, but to "force a dispersal of German forces, help Russia, and thus eventually produce a situation where cross-Channel operations are possible."

"And Winston???" Brooke had continued, rhetorically, in the privacy of his diary. "Thinks one thing at one moment and another at another moment. At times the war may be won by bombing and all must be sacrificed to it. At others it becomes essential for us to bleed ourselves dry on the Continent because Russia is doing the same. At others our main effort must be in the Mediterranean, directed against Italy or the Balkans alternatively, with sporadic desires to invade Norway and 'roll up the map in the opposite direction to Hitler'! But more often than all he wants to carry out ALL operations simultaneously irrespective of shortages of shipping!"[15]

To his credit, Churchill was not unaware of or even embarrassed by his own impetuous, pepper-spray, relentlessly demanding/urging nature — "I am arrogant, but not conceited," he told a companion in 1943[16] — but had no idea Brooke was keeping such a candid journal, especially one that might be used to indict him, later, as a volatile commander in chief of lamentably poor and inconsistent judgment. After all he, Winston Spencer Churchill, would ensure his own skills as a writer and historian would make certain he came out smelling of roses — as he openly confided in North Africa some days later. Veracity would not be his objective as an eventual memoirist/historian, he would tell General Eisenhower and a dozen top American and British generals invited to dinner at Eisenhower's headquarters in Algiers. Having imbibed several whiskeys, he announced that "it was foolish to keep a day-by-day diary because it would simply reflect the change of opinion or decision of the writer" — a diary "which, when and if published, makes one appear indecisive and foolish."[17]

To illustrate his dictum Churchill instanced the daily journal of British Field Marshal Sir Henry Wilson. Sir Henry had left copious diaries detailing his role before and during World War I. In one entry he had unwisely forecast: "There will be no war." This was unfortunate because "on the next day war was declared," Churchill told his enthralled listeners.

Since Eisenhower's naval aide was himself keeping a daily diary this was unwise, but Churchill had by then imbibed too much alcohol to care.

The English field marshal, Churchill went on happily, had subsequently been assassinated on his doorstep by Irish republicans, in 1922 — leaving the question of what to do with his precious war diaries. "The wife had insisted the diary be published post-humously," Eisenhower's aide recorded, "and, consequently, General Wilson was made to appear foolish. For his part, the Prime Minister said, he would much prefer to wait until the war is over and then to write his impressions so that, if necessary, he could correct or bury his mistakes."[18]

Bury his mistakes. It was a telling phrase.

Flying to North Africa with Winston, however, General Marshall would at least exert adult supervision, the President was satisfied. Marshall could be counted upon not to permit the Prime Minister to veer off into any wild ventures now that the cardinal issue of the Second Front and its timing had been formally resolved.

This still left open, however, the question of command.

Who should be the cross-Channel assault supreme commander — an appointment that, in order to help bolster the somewhat tentative British commitment, the President had at Casablanca suggested should go to a British officer?

In the wake of Trident, however, the President was not so sure. General Marshall's faith in Bolero, now renamed Operation Overlord, had been constant and unremitting. Might not General Marshall, an American, be a surer bet as supreme commander — not only in making certain the assault was actually carried out on time, but in dealing at close quarters with a British prime minister whose penchant for meddling in battles was now notorious?

By spending time not only with General Eisenhower but with English field and staff generals at Ike's headquarters in Algiers, Marshall would get to know potential British colleagues, generals, and subordinates better, the President felt. As well as the British prime minister.

By contrast, Churchill was concerned that, if the Second Front was indeed to be launched at American insistence, his candidate for supreme command, General Alan Brooke, should be on the best of terms with the President. There thus arose, on May 26, an added irony, as the two army chiefs of staff of their respective nations boarded the former British Overseas Airways Boeing 314A seaplane, registration number G-AGBZ, bobbing on the Potomac early that morning. Churchill had duly boarded the Clipper, having made his farewells. Aware that he'd promised Brooke command of Overlord, however, he had told the CIGS to go and sit for a few minutes with the President in his car, in case the President decided to raise the matter.

The President gave nothing away. "He was as usual most charming," Brooke noted in his diary that night, "and said that next time I came over I must come to Hyde Park to see where my father and Douglas [Brooke's brother] had looked for birds."[19]

Roosevelt's invitation was typical of the President — wanting the conference to end on a happy, personal note. Brooke was certainly touched, and the two men shook hands.

The ornithologist and his thorny opposite number, General Marshall, then took their seats inside the body of the huge Boeing seaplane as its engines roared to life, ready for takeoff — the President waiting to watch. Both Marshall and Brooke were now contenders to command the greatest amphibious invasion in human history — one that would undoubtedly, as Hitler himself remarked, "decide the war."[20]

PART NINE

The First Crack in the Axis

33

Sicily — and Kursk

AT THE WHITE HOUSE on the evening of July 9, President Roosevelt was giving a state dinner for General Giraud. He was also waiting patiently for word from General Eisenhower as to how the invasion of Sicily, timed to start soon after midnight in the Mediterranean, was going. Had Allied deception measures worked? Were the Germans waiting for the Allied armies to come ashore in the south? How would Italian forces fight on their home soil?

Finally Admiral Brown, his naval aide, brought him the news.

Taking General Giraud upstairs to his study, Roosevelt met Daisy Suckley, who was staying in the Blue Room, on the landing. The President had told her the dinner would go on until a quarter to eleven, so Daisy was happily sewing a seam on her new nightgown when "the elevator door suddenly opened — I heard the P's voice — I grabbed my diary, my pen, my workbox, & my nightgown — started to flee! The President stopped me, laughing, halfway down the hall already, & followed by the General. My thimble flew to the right, my spool to the left. The General laughed & we shook hands — the P. spoke over his shoulder as he was wheeled into his study: 'The General & I are going to have a heart to heart talk — We have landed in Sicily! The word has just come!'"[1]

For his part, Admiral Leahy noted in his own diary: "During the dinner the president announced that British-American-Canadian troops were in process of invading Sicily. Our best information indicates that the enemy force now on the island consists of 4 or 5 Italian divisions and two German divisions, which we should be able to defeat in time if the landing is successful."[2]

The President was pleased, but like Leahy, he was determined not to give way to overexpectations. Failure would delay but by no means wreck the agreed timetable for a cross-Channel assault the next year; victory, however, would give the Allied forces — including French troops fighting under Eisenhower's command — further confidence that they could mount a major amphibious invasion and defeat the Wehrmacht in combat: the prerequisite for a successful Overlord.

And with that quiet confidence the President set off the next day to spend the weekend in Shangri-la with his de facto domestic deputy president, former Justice James Byrnes — his head of the Office of War Mobilization — and Byrnes's wife, as well as Harry Hopkins and his wife, and Daisy Suckley. After watching a movie in the mess hall, "We sat around," Daisy Suckley, "to get news about the invasion of Sicily — During dinner, we had tried also, but static is very bad and reception not good up on this hill, even when the weather is clear . . ."[3]

The President had every reason to be hopeful.

Operation Husky was the largest amphibious invasion ever attempted in war: three thousand Allied vessels, troop planes, and hundreds of gliders setting 160,000 soldiers ashore in Sicily in a single day from across the Mediterranean, departing from ports and airfields in Algeria, Tunisia, Malta, Libya, and Egypt in appalling weather (which caused almost half the gliders from Tunisia to land in the sea) to their rendezvous at dawn on July 10.

General Eisenhower had overruled his own planners and had accepted General Montgomery's preference for a concentrated invasion of the southeastern corner of Sicily, stretching from Gela to the Gulf of Noto and Cassibile. This was just as well, since the German commander in chief, General Kesselring, sent the first of his two panzer divisions (with 160 tanks and 140 field guns) to the west of Sicily — leaving only a single panzer division in the east. However hard they fought, the men of the remaining Hermann Göring Panzer Division were unable to prevail against Allied troops debauching across twenty-six beaches there. Italian defenders, ill armed and ill motivated, for the most part crumpled under the weight and power of the Allied bombardment.

Despite the poor weather — with gale force 7 winds — the invasion thus proved brilliantly successful.

• • •

At the Pentagon in Washington there was an air of near jubilation, especially when the casualty rolls turned out to be less than a seventh of what had been estimated. Once again it was the President, in his capacity as U.S. commander in chief, who had made victory happen. Over the objections of his top generals and secretary of war in January, he'd insisted upon success in the Mediterranean in 1943, rather than sure defeat in France. How wise he'd been proven, all now agreed; only two German divisions in Sicily, instead of more than two dozen in France.

Many things went wrong in the landings, not simply owing to the high wind but also because of friendly fire: trigger-happy naval gunners shooting down dozens of Allied aircraft. Patton's Seventh Army landing at Gela was initially touch-and-go, requiring naval artillery to beat off determined Axis counterattacks — Kesselring having instructed the Hermann Göring tanks and troops to move "at once and with all forces attack and destroy whatever opposes the division. The Führer has ordered all forces to be brought into operation immediately in order to prevent the enemy from establishing itself."[4]

For the Germans, it proved a losing battle, as it had for Vichy defenders in Torch. For the Allies, however, the military lessons provided by Husky would not only be legion but gold — not least in terms of intelligence, deception measures, command experience, army air and naval cooperation, and cohesion. Launched in such overwhelming, concentrated Allied force, there was little the Germans could do to halt it. A U.S. general, Dwight D. Eisenhower, was the Allied supremo, with one American and one British army field commander serving under him. George Patton, who had commanded the invasion forces at Casablanca, now led the U.S. Seventh Army, with excellent U.S. corps and divisional commanders such as Omar Bradley, Geoffrey Keyes, Manton Eddy, and Terry Allen coming to the fore. Montgomery again commanded the British Eighth Army — this time with both veteran and untried troops, including a full Canadian corps determined to obliterate the "fiasco" of Dieppe. Inter-Allied coalition command was rehearsed in real time, as well as interservice cooperation — improving exponentially as the battle for Sicily progressed.

With the Allies achieving complete naval and air superiority over Axis forces in the Mediterranean, moreover, and Patton and Montgomery's ground forces threatening to strike out from the beaches of Sicily, there arose a real prospect that the Italians — who for the most part were refusing to fight to defend their homeland — might overthrow Mussolini and submit to unconditional surrender without the Allies needing to invade Italy.

Hitler's hand was forced, therefore. He would have to call off his latest offensive on the Eastern Front and deal with the Western Allies before they dealt with him.

34

The Führer Flies to Italy

On July 13, three days after the Western Allies landed in Sicily, the Führer summoned his army commanders to his headquarters in East Prussia.

He had changed his mind. Operation Citadel, his massive, long-awaited offensive on the Eastern Front, was doomed. Nervous lest the Western Allies stab him in the back just as the Wehrmacht attacked in Russia, he had already scaled back his objectives for the battle. Instead of seeking to push deeper into the Soviet Union, he had decided to destroy the Russian armies in situ, near the city of Kursk, where their forces formed a salient that could be pinched off by German armies thrusting north and south. In this way, the Soviet armies would be decimated — destroying any chance of a Russian offensive that year, and allowing Hitler to deal decisively with any Allied operation in the west or south.

To their consternation, Hitler now told his generals he was going to call off the Kursk offensive — the biggest tank onslaught yet of the war — in mid-battle. It had been raging for eight days and the Wehrmacht, according to Field Marshal Erich von Manstein, was now on the cusp of victory: ready to close its pincers and destroy Russian forces left in the salient. But as Hitler explained, "the Western Allies had landed in Sicily," and "the situation there had taken an extremely serious turn," Manstein recalled. "The Italians were not even attempting to fight, and the island was likely to be lost. Since the next step might well be a landing in the Balkans or Lower Italy [the heel], it was necessary to form new armies in Italy and the western Balkans. These forces must be found from the Eastern Front, so 'Citadel' would have to be discontinued."[1]

Manstein felt as if the wind had been knocked out of him. The Allied invasion of Sicily, in other words, would now save the Russians from the drubbing the Wehrmacht was poised to administer in the East — Manstein later cursing that "Hitler ruled that 'Citadel' was to be called off on account of the situation in the Mediterranean. And so," the field marshal went on, "the last offensive in the east ended in fiasco."[2]

Even more symbolic for the course of World War II, however, it caused Hitler to fly south, to Berchtesgaden, hopefully to meet with Mussolini in person there.

In the event, Mussolini refused to fly to Berchtesgaden. Ignoring the poor performance of the 230,000 Italian troops he'd stationed in Sicily to defend the island against Allied assault, the Duce blamed the Führer for the success of the U.S., Canadian, and British invasion. The Luftwaffe, he complained, had withheld the necessary planes and equipment with which to defend such a big island, and the responsibility, he claimed, was therefore Hitler's.

Returning to the White House from Shangri-la, by contrast, the President was intensely proud of the Allied performance in Operation Husky. "The news from Sicily is pretty good. Thank Heaven," the President's cousin Daisy noted in her diary on July 14[3] — the President confident Stalin would now see the merit of Allied strategy, which had clearly taken Hitler completely by surprise, and was threatening, overnight, to sever the German-Italian partnership in the Axis Pact.

From all he'd heard, Stalin was nothing if not astute. With Hitler now compelled to send major forces to southern Europe, rather than to the Eastern Front, indeed to move forces away from battle on the Russian front, Stalin would eventually recognize both the political and military ramifications, he was sure. On July 15 the President therefore cabled to congratulate Stalin on the stalwart Russian defense of Kursk — urging him, however, to respond "about that other matter which I *still* feel to be of great importance to *you* and *me*": namely their meeting together to discuss the end of the war — and the postwar.

"The P. is awaiting word from Stalin as to when they can meet — I hate to have the P. take the risk, but he feels it essential for the future," Daisy recorded in the privacy of her diary. "If it occurs now it will be in Alaska; if it occurs late in the Fall, it will be North Africa." Stalin might "not feel able to leave Russia now," she allowed; in fact she actually hoped so, as she considered "the risk of the trip" for the President, "is very great."[4]

There was no response from Stalin, however.

At Hyde Park the following Monday, July 19, Daisy noted the President "looked preoccupied & a little worried." He had "on his mind his possible meeting with Stalin in Alaska—Stalin has set no date & has [still] not committed himself." The President had, however, finally informed Churchill of his invitation to Stalin—but had not extended the invite to include the Prime Minister. "The P. said W.S.C. wanted to go to the meeting, but F.D.R. won't let him," Daisy noted, surprised, but accepting the President's logic. The stakes, in terms of postwar peace and international security, were too high to take the risk of Churchill embarrassing him by his opposition to a cross-Channel assault. "He wants to talk, man to man, with Stalin, & try to establish a constructive relationship. He says that the meeting may result in a complete stalemate, or that Stalin may refuse to work along with the United Nations, or, as he hopes, that Stalin will be willing to work with the U.N.," but it was, surely, worth trying. "How much F.D.R. has on his shoulders! It is always more & more, with the passing months, instead of less & less, as he deserves," she mused—and, she added sagely, as "he gets older."[5]

Hitler rushed two more German divisions to Sicily to stiffen the Axis line, as well as warning his panzer reserve group on the Eastern Front to prepare to head south to Italy. He knew, however, it was hopeless to imagine he could hold on to Sicily itself, given the weight of the Allied assault and the flight of his supposed Italian partners. With Patton racing forces northeast to Palermo, and Bradley and Montgomery pushing the German panzer, paratroop, and infantry defenders back toward Mount Etna, the war seemed to many observers, on all sides, to be, if not won, then winnable in the near future: Sicily the keystone to a possible collapse of the Axis Pact, and even German solicitations for peace . . .

For his part, Hitler agonized over what to do about Mussolini—knowing he would have to breathe fire into the Duce's soul if he was to stop an Italian surrender that would expose his entire southern European flank to Allied invasion. Yet to his chagrin, waiting at the Berghof—the holiday home in the Bavarian Alps he'd bought with the royalties earned from *Mein Kampf*—he simply could not persuade Mussolini to come meet him in Germany.

Every day the situation had become more menacing—for both men. Even Hitler's most loyal supporter, Dr. Goebbels, was forced to acknowledge that, thanks to the Western Allies, Operation Citadel in the East had failed. The Allied forces invading Sicily were simply too massive. "The English and the Americans are expanding their bridgehead on a scale that's really stunning," the Reich minister had already noted in his diary on July 17.[6] "The question keeps coming up, how on earth we will be able to deal with war on two fronts, which we're slipping into. It has always been Germany's misfortune, past and present," he mused.[7] In the circumstances, it would be "almost a miracle were we able to hang on to Sicily."[8]

All Goebbels could think of now was to drive a wedge between the Russians — who were still demanding a Second Front that very year — and the Western Allies. "We haven't really any other alternative than to try to ease the situation through political means," he reflected.[9] Ignoring the millions of Jews and others the Nazi SS had "liquidated" — with more being "exterminated" every day — he wondered how, in view of the evidence of the massacre of Poles at Katyn, the Western Allies could imagine they could seriously do business with Russian barbarians. Could Katyn be the wedge issue?[10]

Political possibilities aside, the Führer had meantime to hold together his military alliance, Goebbels recognized: the Third Reich, the Empire of Italy, and their satellites and puppet regimes, from Norway, Hungary, and Romania to Bulgaria. It was an Axis military coalition that suddenly appeared in grave jeopardy — the once-triumphant Axis forces rocked on their heels both in Russia and the Mediterranean. "What's undeniable is that we find ourselves in a really critical situation," Goebbels admitted in his diary. "In previous summers," he reflected — thinking of 1940, 1941, and 1942 — "that was never the case." Now, however, it was different. "For the first time since the beginning of the war we've not only nothing to show for our summer offensive but we're forced to fight tooth and nail to defend ourselves — something that is casting a dark shadow over world opinion in the neutral countries."[11]

If the mountain would not come to Mohammed, then Mohammed must to the mountain go, Hitler was forced to accept. "The Führer has flown to Italy," Goebbels thus noted on July 19, on hearing the news from his liaison officer. "It's good the Führer is going to have it out with the Duce," the Reich minister added, having learned the meeting would take place north of Venice, "for Mussolini is the heart and soul of Italian resistance, and it's always been noticeable that after he's only been a couple of hours with the Führer, Italian politics and its war effort get a whole new infusion of blood."[12]

. . .

Flown to Treviso airport, the Führer was then taken by train to Feltre, and from there by limousine to the chosen meeting spot: Villa Gaggia. There the two fascist leaders finally conferred.

Despite a two-hour monologue by the Führer there was no infusion of blood or confidence, however; midway through the meeting the Duce was told the Allies were bombing Rome.

The summit proved so disappointing the two dictators decided neither to issue a communiqué nor make the meeting public. Confiding to his diary the inevitable, bitter conclusion behind the false bonhomie, Goebbels recognized that "we will have to move into Italy."[13]

"We" meant the Wehrmacht. And with this decision the war took a new, yet more ruthless and destructive turn.

Mussolini's protestations of loyalty to the Axis Pact, Hitler knew, were sincere, but they were not backed by the Italian people — especially the aristocracy, royal family, and upper middle class. Flying back to his Wolf's Lair headquarters, the Führer ordered Field Marshal Rommel to prepare something akin to Operation Anton, the previous November, when German and Italian troops had secretly readied themselves to occupy the remaining Vichy-administered area of metropolitan France. German troops would now be ordered to occupy the country of their own war partner, Italy, *by force*; it would, cynically, be called Operation Axis.

It was not a moment too soon, from Hitler's perspective. Days later, on July 25, the Italian Grand Council of Fascism convened its first meeting to take place since the early days of the war, in the Palazzo Venezia, in Rome. By a vote of 19 to 7, the members affirmed asking the king to save Italy from destruction, in view of the critical situation in Sicily and the bombing of the Rome rail yards, which President Roosevelt had personally authorized on the very day Hitler met with Mussolini.

Goebbels had assumed the American bombing might stiffen Italian resolve to defend their mother country, as it had in Germany. Instead, however, it caused the Rome police to arrest Mussolini as he left the palace — bundling him into an ambulance and taking him to a destination unknown. Marshal Pietro Badoglio, former chief of the Italian General Staff who had resigned in 1940 after disagreeing with Mussolini's war strategy, was tasked with heading a new government — "our grimmest enemy," as Hitler referred to Badoglio[14]: knowing Badoglio would, inevitably, terminate the Axis Pact.

• • •

It was war in the Mediterranean, then, not in Russia, that had seized the world's headlines and seemed suddenly to bring the global struggle against predatory fascism to a climax. Hitler fired off instructions for the arrest, if possible, of the new Italian government and the members of the royal family, before they could pursue surrender to the United Nations. They were too wily, however, and German forces in Italy still too thin on the ground to effect such a move.

So anxious did the Führer become that he now decided the Mediterranean must take priority over the Eastern Front. He therefore gave final orders to transfer to Italy his top SS armored divisions from Russia — telling Field Marshal von Kluge, who protested at the removal of the Wehrmacht's vital striking reserve, "We are not master here of our own decisions."[15]

The Western Allies were — or seemed to be.

35

Countercrisis

As HITLER CONFRONTED the crisis caused by the overwhelming Allied invasion of Sicily and the imminent defection of Italy from the Axis Pact, there arose a countercrisis or dilemma for the Allies — their biggest, in many ways, since Pearl Harbor.

This would be one of the great ironies of history: that at a moment when victory seemed to many to be within reach that year, the prosecution of the war by the Allies lurched and wobbled — with recriminations, accusations, and blame that have continued among war historians and writers to this day.[1]

The President had pressed Stalin again and again for a one-on-one meeting — determined to assure him, in person, that the United States, as the dominant partner in the Western Alliance, was committed to opening a Second Front at the earliest possible time.

"Referring to the Second Front," former ambassador Davies had told Stalin as the President's personal emissary on May 20, "no-one, I told him, had been more disappointed when, after consideration of all the risks and logistics involved in a cross-channel operation, and also the hazards as affecting the world battleground — the Pacific as well as the Atlantic and the Mediterranean — that for the sake of an assured victory, he [the President] had to agree to postponement of the Second Front cross-channel operation. No one, I said, was more firm in the belief that the quickest and most direct way to defeat Hitler was by a cross-channel invasion, when it could be done after every available means had been exhausted to prevent disaster and assure success."[2]

Overcoming Stalin's leeriness of Churchill with regard to a Second Front had been a tough assignment, Davies had told the President on his return to Washington on June 3. "Stalin said to me expressly that he could accept neither the African invasion [Torch] nor the Air Attack on Germany as the Second Front . . . He was suspicious, not only of the British, but of us, as well," Davies had reported. "They are convinced that Churchill, if he can help it, will consent to a cross-channel crossing only when there is no risk to them" — the British. "They believed that Britain is stalling on a cross-channel operation," both to "save her manpower" and to "divert the attack through the Balkans and Italy" in order to "protect the classic British Foreign policy of walling Russia in, closing the Dardanelles, and building a countervailing balance of power against Russia."

This was a pretty astute reading of British policy — but one that completely ignored the problem of defeating Hitler and the Nazis. As Stalin had pointed out to Davies, Allied operations in the Mediterranean were simply not on the scale of war as on the Eastern Front — where the "Germans had not less than three million" troops "attacking another three million of the Red Army — a total of at least six million — ten times as many as engaged in the African campaign."[3]

Stalin had seemed to Davies to be disappointed in the Western Allies, yet mollified by Davies's sincerity — and the President's firm commitment to mounting a Second Front as soon as feasible.

For his part, the President nevertheless continued to worry lest his "active and ardent lieutenant" become too ardent in terms of Mediterranean operations in the wake of success in Sicily. He'd heard from General Marshall that the Prime Minister was once again seized by excitement, and was plotting a new course in London — one he'd coyly revealed to Secretary Stimson, who was visiting American forces in Britain.

The Prime Minister was still only paying lip service to the Trident agreement, Stimson reported to Washington, after meeting with Churchill — and might well go off on a Mediterranean tangent unless leashed by the President. So worried had Stimson become, in fact, that he'd made a transatlantic telephone call to the Pentagon on July 17, a week after the invasion of Sicily. "The scrambling noise over the wires produced a peculiar effect on Marshall's voice," Stimson noted in his diary that night, "rendering the tones quite unrecognizable," but the secretary found he could "recognize the peculiarities" of Marshall's speech. "I began telling him of my conferences with the P.M., particularly last Monday the 12th. I summed up what I thought was his position, namely, that he was honestly ready to keep the pledge as to 'Roundhammer' [Overlord] but was impulsively likely to branch out into commitments which would make it impossible" — tying up in the Mediterranean the very battle-hardened U.S. and British forces and landing craft needed for a successful cross-Channel invasion early in 1944. Churchill seemed to Stimson to be fixated on seizing the Italian capital — that "he was very set on a march to Rome." More worrying still in terms of the suction-pump effect of the Mediterranean, Anthony Eden, the British foreign secretary, "was dead set on the Balkans and Greece."

The President had winced at the news. Churchill had even claimed that General Eisenhower's "heart," too, was invested in a bold new stroke in the Mediterranean — such as an airborne drop near the Italian capital: Operation Giant. Stimson was concerned that a dangerous overconfidence seemed to be infecting not only Churchill's bunker in London, but possibly Algiers.

The acting commander of American forces in Britain, General Jacob Devers, had assured Stimson, however, that Eisenhower's three service commanders in the Mediterranean — all of whom were British — had poured as much cold water on Eisenhower's idea as did Devers. Not only was this because of "the danger of executing an operation beyond the reach of air cover," but because of the "drain on landing craft" — craft that would be needed for Overlord. Others, too, were putting an oar into the debate — Stimson even told Marshall of a telegram to Churchill from Field Marshal Smuts, supporting Anthony Eden's Balkan aspirations. Marshall responded that he had not seen this — and was worried by the news. "Marshall said that in the light of these circumstances he thought I ought to go as promptly as possible to see Eisenhower where I would be able to round out what I had gotten here in London with the views of the people in Africa."[4]

The U.S. secretary of war having to fly to North Africa to try and head off an abrogation of the Trident agreements?

The situation, from the point of view of clear Allied purpose, was alarming, but it only became worse in the days that followed. On July 19, the day Hitler flew to Italy, the Prime Minister had warned his chiefs of staff, Stimson learned, to prepare plans to dump the Second Front if operations in the Mediterranean prospered and the seven battle-hardened divisions were not sent back to the U.K. In which case, the Prime Minister had said, he favored Allied assault landings in Norway, mounted from

England with whatever forces remained in Britain or could be scraped together.

Norway?

Occupied by some four hundred thousand German troops, Norway was the mountainous country where Churchill's ill-fated Franco-British Expeditionary Force had been completely worsted by a German counter-invasion and its survivors evacuated in the spring of 1940.

It was a disturbing scenario. On Thursday, July 22, Stimson had had it out with Churchill — who was soliciting Stimson's help in getting U.S. restrictions on the sharing of atom-bomb research lifted between the two nations.

The latest reports of heavy fighting around Catania had only reinforced Churchill's continuing skepticism regarding Overlord. He "said that if he had 50,000 men ashore on the French channel coast, he would not have an easy moment because he felt that the Germans could rush up in sufficient force to drive them back. On my direct questioning he admitted that if he was C-in-C, he would not figure the Roundhammer [Overlord] operation [as feasible]; but being as it was, he having made his pledge, then he would go with it loyally. I said to him that was like hitting us in the eye and he said 'Oh, no, if we start anything we will go through with it with utmost effort.'"[5]

In the meantime, Churchill pointed out, there was Italy — a country begging to be invaded by the Allies. The Prime Minister was, as he told Stimson, surely "justified in supporting his faith in the Italian expedition," given the potential rewards. "He spoke of two possibilities; one, going to Rome with the advantages that would come from this, even without capitulation; and second, with an Italian capitulation, it would throw open the whole of Italy as far as the north boundary and would give us opportunities to go and attack southern France. He asserted that he was not in favor of attacking the Balkans with troops, but merely wished to supply them with munitions and supplies."[6]

This was, at least, a mercy. For an hour and a half the two men — one approaching sixty-nine, the other, seventy-six — battled over strategy and tactical operations: Stimson attempting to point out the inevitable suction effect of major operations in the Mediterranean that would "hinder" Overlord, Churchill denying this; Stimson claiming he had the support of the "entire General Staff" in the "Roundhammer [Overlord] proposition,"

Churchill claiming Eisenhower to be "strongly in favor of going as far as he could in Italy."[7]

Stimson had been understandably perturbed — unaware, even as he spoke and exchanged cables with Marshall, that it was not only Churchill who now favored immediate exploitation of seeming Allied success in the Mediterranean. For Churchill's excitement was being replicated among senior U.S. generals in the Pentagon, in Marshall's own War Department.

On July 17, as tanks of Patton's Seventh U.S. Army raced to Palermo in the west of Sicily, the War Department's chief of Operations Division, Lieutenant General John Hull, declared he'd had a change of heart.

Hull's defection from the Trident strategy aroused fierce debate in the Pentagon. From "the very beginning of this war," Hull — who had hitherto been General Marshall's most loyal subordinate — wrote, "I have felt that the logical plan for the defeat of Germany was to strike at her across the channel by the most direct route." He'd now changed his mind, he declared. In a document he drew up for his deputy, General Handy, and his War Department team, Hull pointed out the strategic harvest to be garnered in the Mediterranean. As he put it, "it is a case where you cannot have your cake and eat it."[8] With half a million U.S., British, and Canadian troops in the Mediterranean, and barely 180,000 U.S. troops in England, he'd come to "the belief that we should now reverse our decision and pour our resources into the exploitation of our Mediterranean operations." Summarizing his extraordinary change of mind, he concluded: "As to Germany, in my opinion, the decision should be an all-out effort in the Mediterranean."[9]

Not only did General Hull's renunciation set off furious disputation at the Pentagon, it played straight into the hands of senior admirals in the Navy Department: sailors who had refused to move their offices into the Pentagon and were now in favor of backing out of a cross-Channel "Germany First" strategy, too — a change of objectives that would permit Japan to become America's Enemy Number One. Reexamining the Trident agreement to send seven battle-hardened divisions from the Mediterranean to the United Kingdom by November 1, 1943, the Joint War Plans Committee, representing the three U.S. armed services, now declared it "unsound."

The chief of staff to Admiral King, Admiral "Savvy" Cooke, agreed with the JWP Committee. He'd never been convinced a cross-Channel assault could succeed, and thought that, if the Western Allies simply limited their future operations to the Mediterranean, more U.S. vessels and resources would be available to send to the Pacific.[10]

General Marshall was understandably aghast. Other planners like Brigadier General Wedemeyer, who was actually visiting American headquarters in the Mediterranean, vociferously protested, feeling it folly to divide and disperse impending Allied effort in Europe, when all logistical and fighting focus should be concentrated on an agreed *Schwerpunkt*, or focal point. Analyzing combat reports from Sicily — where German troops were fighting to the death to defend an Italian island that not even Italians were willing to defend — Wedemeyer recognized how tough it was going to be to defeat the German enemy; he felt "our [English] cousins" must somehow be made aware "that this European theater struggle will never be won by dispersing our forces around the Axis citadel," as he responded to General Handy, referring to Churchill's "closing the ring" policy. "Even though HUSKY is successful after a bitter struggle," he'd warned from Algiers the week before the invasion of Sicily, "we could never drive rampant up the boot, as the P.M. so dramatically depicts in his concept of our continued effort over here." Not only would an Italian campaign require "greatly increased resources than those now envisaged or available in the area," but to ensure success — or even security against German counteroffensive measures — the cross-Channel invasion "would be even more remote, in fact, maybe crossed off the books for 1944."[11]

But if not Rome, where next? Even Wedemeyer had to concede the Allies must continue to do *something* in the next nine months, before Overlord was mounted.

This, then, was the strategic conundrum facing the President as U.S. commander in chief in the summer of 1943, even as the war seemed, for the Allies, to be so nearly won.

36

A Fishing Expedition in Ontario

IT HAD BEEN agreed at the Trident Conference in Washington in May that another high-level military parley would probably have to be convened, once the invasion of Sicily was completed. Though Churchill had suggested Washington as the venue, once again the President had demurred. As one of the President's White House Map Room officers, Lieutenant Elsey — who encrypted and decoded almost daily signals between the White House and 10 Downing Street — recorded, "the President recommended to the Prime Minister that this Anglo-American conference be held in Quebec, a happier place in summer than Washington. Quebec offered the advantages of a delightful climate and appropriate and comfortable quarters at the historic Citadel and the Chateau Frontenac."[1]

Before meeting with Churchill and his chiefs of staff, however, Roosevelt still hoped to meet with Stalin. "By mid-July when it seemed unlikely that Marshal Stalin would be able to leave his armies, even briefly, during their first summer offensive, the President suggested to Mr. Churchill that time would be ripe for their conference around the first of September."[2]

The triumph of the Allied landings on July 10 had, however, made even this date seem too distant to Churchill, who now had the bit between his teeth — his wonderfully pugnacious head spinning with romantic excitement as he saw himself entering Rome like a victorious Caesar in the next few weeks. "The very rapid changes on the several fronts and, in particular, the overwhelming success of the Sicilian campaign made it imperative to hold the meeting earlier," Lieutenant Elsey recounted. "The degeneration of Italian resistance and the possibility of complete Italian collapse, greatly increased by the unexpected fall of Mussolini on July 25th, gave birth to new problems only faintly foreseen in the spring. As Mr. Churchill said, 'We shall need to meet together to settle the larger issues which the brilliant victories of our forces have thrust upon us about Italy as a whole.' The Prime Minister pressed for a very early date in August but the President replied that he would be unable to arrive in Quebec earlier than August 17."[3]

The tragedy of late 1943 was now to unfold, almost inexorably — Churchill seemingly blind to Hitler's likely response to the Allied invasion of Italy. As Hitler's war aims crystallized into a ruthless German defend-or-die strategy, without having to rely on weak allies, the Allies' conduct of the war fractured — with grave political as well as military ramifications. If Churchill was right, the Third Reich might, if the Allies put every man into the field in Italy, collapse — with vast political ramifications on top of military, since the Wehrmacht still held a solid front deep inside Russia. But what if Churchill and the generals like Hull in the Pentagon were *wrong*? What if Hitler meant to fight to the bitter end on all fronts — and was backed wholeheartedly by his Volk?

Holding the reins of global political as well as military unity on behalf of the Western Allies, at least, the President decided he must present to the people of America and the world a clear picture of the war's positive progress — and ultimate aims. Calling in Robert Sherwood, Judge Rosenman, and Harry Hopkins, he therefore spent many days at Shangri-la and in the White House working on a major new Fireside Chat.

Broadcast from the White House on the evening of July 28, 1943, the President's radio address certainly seemed a success: the President sounding confident, inspiring, and clear-minded: conveying to listeners a sense of wise direction in prosecuting the war to its appointed end — and beyond. ROOSEVELT HAILS "FIRST CRACK" IN THE AXIS; OUTLINES POST-WAR AID FOR ALL U.S. FORCES, ran the *New York Times* front-page headline on July 29, the newspaper giving extended coverage to every aspect of his speech — the President's first since February that year, "when he predicted invasion of the Continent of Europe." It was, the *Times* described, "a radio address as varied in its subject matter as the vast pattern of total war," one in which the President had "counseled against complacency, urged much greater efforts if Hitler and Tojo are to be defeated, as he promised, 'on their home grounds,'" — and one which, the *Times* added, "announced the end of coffee rationing due to the improved shipping situation."[4]

Was the war's direction really so clear, though? Was the speech not in truth window-dressing? Was not the "first crack" a split less in the Axis ability to wage war — given that German troops were reported moving ruthlessly into new, former Italian positions across the Mediterranean, and Field Marshal Rommel was reported to be preparing for the German defense of Greece — than in the Allies' *own* situation? Were not the Allies the ones with a problem?

At the State Department there were problems, as well. Former ambassador Bill Bullitt had been circulating throughout top circles in Washington a new paper urging an American invasion of the Balkans, before Soviet forces could reach central Europe, regardless of the military inanity of such a scheme. And to cap this, there were stories that Secretary of State Cordell Hull — at the insistence of his wife — was demanding the head of the President's right-hand man in postwar planning, Sumner Welles, on the grounds he was a homosexual — a story Bill Bullitt, who coveted Welles's job as assistant secretary of state, had been leaking to the press.[5]

And as if all this was not enough, there were indications that the Russians were exploring possible peace-feelers with the Germans — suggestions bruited in "official circles" that Stalin "may have forsaken President Roosevelt and Prime Minister Churchill on unconditional surrender" and was planning "to establish a European order on his own [communist] concepts and under the aegis of Moscow," as the *New York Times* reported.[6]

So much happening, so fast — and so many conflicting voices and calls in the great democracies of America and Britain!

It was small wonder the President felt, once again, exhausted. He longed to get away from Washington, and in cooler climes think things through, so that he could hopefully keep the Allied coalition together and pointing in the same direction.

On July 30, he thus went ahead with his latest plan. It would be another secret trip: this time "to Canada on a fishing and vacation expedition," as Admiral Leahy, his White House chief of staff, noted in his diary. On the beautiful lakes of Ontario, the weather would be less hot — and devoid of journalists, or anyone else. Away from the madding crowd the President could fish in peace, and think for a whole week.[7]

• • •

The *Ferdinand Magellan* duly pulled out from the Bureau of Engraving's special siding in Washington at 9:45 p.m.

The President was far from alone. In addition to Admiral Leahy he was taking his doctor, Vice Admiral McIntire; his naval aide, Rear Admiral Brown; his military aide, Major General Pa Watson; his two secretaries, Grace Tully and Dorothy Brady; twenty Secret Service men; his secret communications personnel; and Filipino crewmembers from the USS *Potomac* and Shangri-la.

The President had still heard nothing from Stalin, and thus knew as much or as little as the *New York Times* correspondent in Moscow concerning the dictator's intentions or thoughts. "The Stalin meeting is 'on,'" his cousin Daisy had noted in her diary on July 28 after speaking to the President on the phone[8] — which was to say the meeting wasn't off, and might still take place at Fairbanks, Alaska, to which he could fly from Ontario, using the nearest air base to his fishing expedition.

Daisy hated the idea. "It is much too dangerous," she recorded her anxiety about such "trips by air." "But he feels he has to, so he has to — His feelings are mixed about them, he told me — He doesn't want to go, but he has to put every possible effort into going because he thinks it will help in planning the future of the world — so — all we can do is wish him Godspeed and pray that all will go well."[9]

The fishing part of the plan, at least, went well — the bulk of it spent in McGregor and Georgian Bays, Ontario. "The days were interesting in providing fresh air and sunburn for all of us, and for me the nights were reasonably busy with messages to and from our British Allies in regard to the Italian campaign, the proposal to make Rome an open city which military authorities do not look with favor upon, and the general war situation," Leahy recorded.[10]

Harry Hopkins joined the party on August 4, in case they were to fly from there to meet Stalin, and though Leahy felt the vacation was a "success in giving all of us a change and exposure to the air and the sun," he did acknowledge "that on a vacation for relaxation we should have gone to bed earlier than midnight which was the usual hour."[11]

"For a week we lived in the train which remained a few yards from a landing from which we embarked each day on our daily fishing expeditions — each member of the party contributing a dollar a day for prizes," Leahy added. "The fish caught were small-mouth bass, wall-eyed pike, and what was either a pickerel or pike that the guides called snakes. In the final settlement of our pool at the weekend only the President and I were the winners."[12]

Air, sun, and pool winners, however, were not enough to solve the growing strategic crisis: one the President knew would be waiting for him once he got back to the White House.

37

The President's Judgment

To A CONSIDERABLE extent, the brewing Allied crisis was inevitable in a coalition, the President accepted, for each ally had its own concerns and war aims.

The President certainly did not take amiss Churchill's excitement over Mediterranean operations, or even the Prime Minister's loyalty to a decaying British empire. Churchill was, he felt, merely misguided — the product of high Victorian imperialism. As the President had discussed with former ambassador Davies, in a conversation that Davies had then related to Stalin, "British imperialism had contributed much to civilization, as well as to their people but, under modern conditions, there were now some aspects of it which did not conform to the American viewpoint. These variances in points of view were not such, however, as would or should be permitted to jeopardize a common effort for victory, and for the preservation of post-war peace. The Statute of Westminster [the Adoption Act of 1942, legally recognizing the independence of the Dominions] had given proof that modern England was conscious of the need for change, and with great courage and nobility had given independence of action in foreign affairs to the colonies and dominions."[1]

Stalin, looking up from his doodling pad, had queried the reason for excluding Churchill from the proposed meeting with the President, demanding to know "Why?"

"I replied," Davies recounted, "that Roosevelt and Churchill respected and admired each other, and although they did not always see eye to eye, they were always loyal. They were 'big' men, and on matters of difference, each could be relied upon. In fact, each would insist on finding common ground to win the war."[2]

This was, however, to tiptoe around the matter of the Second Front —

and the more the Italians caved in, the more brazen had become Churchill's call for exploitation in the Mediterranean—leaving the notion of Overlord as an Allied cross-Channel invasion to wither, the Prime Minister hoped, on the vine.

For the President this was not a surprise. He had gotten to know Churchill, on the Prime Minister's repeated visits to the White House, probably better than any American during the course of the war. The Prime Minister's moods, swinging from gravity to elation, were part and parcel of his colorful character as a leader. Churchill's approach to modern war was, the President accepted, wonderfully exuberant if often flawed. Certainly, with respect to what would now happen in Europe, the Prime Minister seemed to be giving way to a dangerous assumption: namely that Hitler might be toppled in the same way that Mussolini had been brought down.

Unhappily, despite a lifetime spent as a military officer and warrior-politician, Churchill seemed not to understand the nature of the problem confronting the Allies. This was not so much the Führer as the Germans themselves. The Prime Minister's abiding belief was that, once shorn of its allies, the men of the Third Reich would be unable to defend the vast territories they had so rapidly overrun when the Allies had been weak and disjointed. The Allies had now only to "close the ring," as the Prime Minister saw it, and sooner or later Germany would collapse, as it had in 1918—without the Western Allies having to take the great gamble of a cross-Channel assault and campaign in northern France. Churchill thus failed, in the President's view, to fully credit what had happened in Germany under Hitler—and how German forces, like the Japanese, would fight to the bitter end to defend the territory they had seized, *even without the Führer's orders;* that they would make the Allies pay for every meter of advance in blood, whether in the Balkans, Greece, Italy, or France.

Roosevelt's insistence on unconditional surrender had therefore been no aberration, or momentary thoughtlessness, as certain writers—even Churchill himself in a forgetful moment[3]—would later aver. Rather, it went back to the President's childhood sojourns in Germany, and spoke to the President's deep-seated cognizance of the collective German mentality. Roosevelt's unwavering judgment was that, whatever happened with the Italians, the Germans—like the Japanese—would go on fighting until beaten in battle; moreover, that their nations must be completely disarmed after the war's end and the world kept safe from any prospect of their military renascence. "The President believed also," Davies had told

Stalin on May 20, "that, despite differences in ideology and methods of government" between capitalism and communism, "it was entirely possible that our countries could live together in peace, in a decent world, with mutual respect, reciprocal consideration and joint safety, against a possible militant Japan, Germany or any other would-be disturbers of the Peace . . . Together, they could maintain and enforce law and order to preserve a just Peace, or there would be renewed disastrous wars."

Stalin had affirmed his complete agreement. "You can tell your President that so far as Germany is concerned, I will support him to any length he thinks necessary, no matter how soever, to destroy Germany's war potential for the future. Our people and our country have suffered immeasurably because of it. It is vital to us that Germany's war potential be destroyed. As to Japan, he said, the President already knew what their position was and needed no assurance."[4]

Goebbels's April announcement of *totaler Krieg*, in Roosevelt's view, had merely confirmed his judgment of Germany as the world's most dangerous nation, given the size and ruthlessness of its Wehrmacht and the abiding belief that *Macht ist Recht*: might is right. Any notion that the Germans would be easily pried from their conquests across Europe was therefore wishful thinking. The struggle to defeat the Germans and the Japanese would be hard and bloody, as he'd stated in his White House broadcast on July 18 — for there was no alternative to battle. And bloodshed.

What was important was for the Allies therefore to make no mistakes. To proceed methodically, building up command and combat experience, and trained, well-armed forces in order to defeat the Wehrmacht completely and relentlessly in combat, as Grant and his generals had done in the Civil War. Fantasies of victory merely by peripheral operations were seductive in terms of saving lives, but in the end they were idle. Only by relentless concentration of force, in focused application of America's growing output as the arsenal of modern democracy, would the Allies be enabled to win within a reasonable time frame.

The President's judgment of Wehrmacht intentions and abilities, moreover, was reinforced by reports he was receiving from his intelligence services. Access to the extraordinary riches of Ultra posed the danger that one sought in the decrypts for what one wanted to see. Churchill, who read Ultra decrypts every day and often "raw" ones — i.e., uninterpreted by his military staff — had fastened tightly on those indicating that

Hitler only intended his troops to stand in northern Italy, at the foot of the Alps. By contrast, the President was less beholden to that one source, and remained skeptical. On July 10, as the troops of the Western Allies had stormed ashore in Sicily, the latest OSS intelligence bulletin from Brigadier General Bill Donovan, who directed U.S. espionage services abroad, had been couriered to the White House Map Room. Rear Admiral Brown, the President's naval assistant, had himself brought it to the President — a report predicting the Italians would soon betray their Axis partner and sue for surrender. With stark realism, however, Donovan's report had also warned that the Germans "are quite prepared to treat the Italians as they would an enemy."[5] They would thus squash their former partners like cockroaches — and fight the harder once free of coalition allies they largely despised.

The President had agreed with Donovan — who had won the Medal of Honor and the Distinguished Service Medal fighting the Germans in France in World War I. The Allies, the President was sure, must not be complacent, or be swayed by armchair strategists. Italy's collapse would certainly be a political triumph for the Allies, and was certainly worth pursuing. It could also be dangerous, however, if it encouraged Churchill and like-minded peripheralists to jump to conclusions about Italian assistance, or German unwillingness to fight in southern Italy.

As the days of high summer unfolded, Donovan's prediction did indeed become reality. The Germans, it would become clear to even the most starry-eyed, were very, very different from their southern neighbors — neighbors the Germans had always held in suspicion but now began to treat with merciless, murderous contempt.

The profound cultural difference between the two Axis enemies would, in fact, climax in the summer and fall of 1943 — exposing the fault lines of what Churchill called the Grand Alliance, and threatening to sunder what had, in July, appeared to be the approach of Hitler's end.

PART TEN

Conundrum

38

Stalin Lies

As THE *Ferdinand Magellan* made its way back from Ontario to Washington, the President finally heard from Stalin. Once decoded, the cable — dated August 8, 1943 — was handed to him. It was a long message agreeing to a meeting. Not, however, the meeting Roosevelt was hoping for.

In surprisingly friendly English, the Russian marshal — who had gotten himself promoted as the first civilian to hold that rank by the Presidium of the Supreme Soviet of the USSR on March 6, 1943, in recognition of his role as supreme commander in chief of the armed forces of the Soviet Union — began by apologizing. His focus as a Russian marshal had had to be on his "primary duty — the direction of action at the front. I have frequently to go to the different parts of the front and to submit all the rest to the interests of the front," he kept repeating — blatantly lying, since he had only once ever gone near the front, and that only for a few hours. "I hope that under such circumstances you will fully understand that at the present time I cannot go on a long journey and shall not be able, unfortunately, during this summer and autumn to keep my promise given to you through Mr. Davi[e]s. I regret it very much, but, as you know, circumstances are sometimes more powerful than people who are compelled to submit to them." He was, however, willing to agree meantime to a later "meeting of the responsible representatives" of the United States and the Soviet Union at Archangel, on the north coast of Russia, or Astrakhan, on the south, Caspian, coast — i.e., on Russian territory, and terms.

If the President was unable to go to such a summit, so distant from Washington, Stalin continued, Mr. Roosevelt could send a "responsible and fully trusted person"; moreover, he was quite happy for Churchill to attend the get-together — thus making it a "meeting of the representatives of the three countries." In the meantime they should raise, in advance, the "questions which are to be discussed," and the "drafts of proposals which are to be accepted at the meeting." He added his belated congratulations to "you and the Anglo-American troops on the occasion of the outstanding successes in Sicily which are resulted [*sic*] in collapse of Mussolini and his gang."[1]

The dictator's excuses for not meeting the President might be specious, but what was clear, now that the battle of Kursk was over and Mussolini toppled, was that Stalin saw no need to travel to America or to Alaska, cap in hand. He could afford to play hard to get — or please.

The President was understandably disappointed, given the phenomenal amount of Lend-Lease equipment, food, chemicals, and metals being shipped to the USSR. Even Marshal Zhukov, Russia's greatest general, would admit after the war that "the Americans shipped over to us *materièl* without which we could not have equipped our armies held in reserve or been able to continue the war." As Zhukov explained, "We did not have enough munitions [and] how would we have been able to turn out all those tanks without the rolled steel sent to us by the Americans?"[2] — let alone the four hundred thousand trucks dispatched.[3]

"Drafts of proposals," meantime, made the President frown. Not only might it be more difficult to get agreement on the President's United Nations authority plan if preconference proposals had to go through the endless (and appropriately colored) red tape of Russian communist bureaucracy, but Churchill's presence might let the cat out of the bag — namely, that Churchill and his generals were once again tilting away from a cross-Channel Second Front in favor of exploitation in the Mediterranean. And dangerous overoptimism in London.

One American chaplain in London, Colonel Maurice Reynolds, had openly forecast that the war might be over in five months — that he would not be "surprised if we all went home for Christmas. The rats are beginning to leave the sinking ship — one [Mussolini] has left already," he'd been quoted in *Stars and Stripes,* the U.S. Army newspaper.

This was an almost tragic assumption, given the tough fighting that lay ahead with the Germans. Not only was Allied strategy in danger of being compromised by naive opportunism, but if the Western Allies pulled out of their commitment to a Second Front, the President recognized, there would be tough problems with America's Russian partner — with grave consequences for the peoples of central and even western Europe.

The disagreement between the U.S. generals at the Pentagon, and the growing continental divide between the Allies, was thus the unhappy scenario that faced the President when he finally entered the White House on the morning of August 9 for a whirlwind round of meetings. He'd agreed to meet Churchill and the British chiefs of staff in Quebec around August 15. This gave him only a few days to get his ducks back in a row.

He saw Secretary Hull for lunch, General Marshall at 2:00 p.m., Lord Halifax, the British ambassador, at 2:30, and dined with Hopkins that evening. He called his cousin Daisy to tell her what a great fishing trip he'd had — "a real success — the place much like the Maine Coast — rocky, wooded, 100s of islands, cool on the whole, very nice — He says he'll take me there, perhaps, next year!"[4] But he also confided to her his latest plan: that he was determined to do his best to head off another Trident-like battle royal in the Canadian capital. He would therefore see Churchill in private at Hyde Park *before* the Quebec meeting of the Combined Chiefs of Staff even began — and twist Churchill's arm there until the Prime Minister backed off.

39

War on Two Western Fronts

IN HIS FIRESIDE CHAT radio broadcast, the President had denied there was any disunity between the Allies. "You have heard some people say that the British and the Americans can never get along well together — you have heard some people say that the Army and the Navy and the Air Forces can never get along well together — that real cooperation between them is impossible." He'd denied the assertions, as U.S. president and commander in chief. "Tunisia and Sicily have given the lie, once and for all, to these narrow-minded prejudices. Ahead of us are much bigger fights. We and our Allies will go into them as we went into Sicily — together. And we shall carry on together," he'd claimed — lauding the achievements of the Soviet Union as America's ally, too.

Behind the façade of unity, however, the conduct of the coalition war was in grave peril. Moreover, with Stalin calling for a meeting of foreign ministers in the fall, before the Allied leaders or their representatives got together, it would become impossible to conceal British pressure to defer or abandon the Second Front in favor of further operations on the Southern, or Mediterranean, Front.

Even the President's postwar vision was in danger of unraveling — from within. Two *New York Times* journalists, John Crider and Arthur Krock, had now openly reported, while the President was fishing in Canada, on the growing rift between the secretary of state, Cordell Hull, and Undersecretary Welles — reports that had been carried in other newspapers, too.[1]

The President had therefore summoned both Welles and Hull to the Oval Office on August 10, the day after his return — a meeting at which

Hull declared he could not work with Welles, and that one of them must resign.

As if this was not enough, the President had read carefully his war secretary's "Brief Report on Certain Features of Overseas Trip," which Henry Stimson had sent over to the White House, following his return from London and North Africa — a report so alarming in terms of Allied strategy that the President had asked Stimson to lunch with him on August 10, immediately after his meeting with Hull and Welles. The lunch would precede the meeting he had convened with the Joint Chiefs of Staff at 2:30 in the Oval Office, to discuss "the attitude to be taken by the U.S. Chiefs of Staff at the coming conference [in Quebec] with our opposite members from London," as Admiral Leahy put it in his diary.[2]

An unfortunate breakdown in Allied war strategy was approaching — at the very moment when, in the Southwest Pacific, American destroyers had sunk all four Japanese destroyers of the "Tokyo Express" seeking to reinforce their troops on Kolombangara in the Solomons; a moment when, in the North Pacific, U.S. and Canadian troops were preparing to land on Kiska Island in the Aleutians; a moment when, in Sicily, the retreating German troops were beginning to evacuate their forces across the Strait of Messina to the Italian mainland; and when, in Russia, the Wehrmacht was being forced to retreat on a three-hundred-mile front, giving up Orel and Belgorod — cities occupied by German troops since October 1941.

Of one thing the President was absolutely certain at this strategic crossroads for the Allies, however: that whatever anyone said or posited, the war might very well *not* be over by Christmas — even by Christmas 1944. He must therefore redouble his efforts to keep the Allied coalition together, marching to the same tune.

And place. Berlin. Then Tokyo.

Reading over the materials the Joint Chiefs of Staff had sent him, prior to their meeting at the White House, the President appreciated their clear strategic reasoning, especially their August 9 memorandum, with its various enclosures.

The President was not, however, amused by the wording of one enclosure: a paper prepared by the Operations Division of the War Office, dated August 8, which stuck in his craw. In it the authors, headed by General Handy, painted the Torch invasion and year of victories since 1942 as wasteful and unnecessary — in fact as having set back the defeat of Germany by a year. A cross-Channel invasion in 1943 "was the one chance to end the war in Europe this year. If this had happened," General Handy claimed, "all that has been gained would be insignificant by comparison."[3]

Clearly the authors had never reflected on Dieppe. Or Kasserine. Or Sicily, for that matter, where the fighting had become remorseless. They had certainly never faced a German soldier in battle. It was, arguably, one of the most egregious underestimations of the enemy ever produced by a senior general of the U.S. military — neither *combat* nor *battle experience* ever appearing in the document. All arguments had merely been laid out in terms of numbers of men furnishable to the front.[4]

The President had shaken his head over that. Would these armchair planners never learn?

Fortunately, the Joint Chiefs of Staff had themselves prepared two far more mature papers, on August 7 and 9, attempting to "develop a strategic concept for the defeat of the Axis in Europe."[5] These papers concluded that, thanks to the Allied invasion of Sicily, the German offensive at Kursk had had to be curtailed; that the Wehrmacht would no longer be able to go on the attack or seek victory on the Eastern Front; and that therefore German strategy would now likely be one of fierce fighting to attain "a satisfactory negotiated peace."[6] As they warned, however, the Axis "still retains strong defensive power. A defensive strategy on the part of the Axis might develop into a protracted struggle and result in a stalemate on the Continent." Therefore, "the rapidly improving position of the United Nations in relation to the Axis in Europe demands an abrogation of opportunistic strategy and requires the adoption and adherence to sound strategic plans which envisage decisive military operations conducted at times and places of our choosing — not the enemy's."

This, at least, was sensible. "We must not jeopardize our sound over-all strategy," the memorandum argued, "simply to exploit local successes in a generally accepted secondary theater, the Mediterranean, where logistical and terrain difficulties preclude decisive and final operations designed to reach the heart of Germany."[7]

This new memorandum, Roosevelt felt, was far better argued than Handy's counterdocument. What it did not do was explain how the Western Allies could simply put major offensive operations against Germany on hold for nine months while they prepared Overlord. Not only would a nine-month hiatus be difficult to excuse to people at home, but it would be harder still to excuse to the Russians, currently facing three-quarters of the German Wehrmacht in combat on the Eastern Front. As the President chided Marshall, who had brought the memorandum to the White House for him to read on August 9, at 2:00 p.m., "the planners were always conservative and saw all the difficulties"; he was sure "more could usually be done than they were willing to admit," as Marshall noted on his return to the Pentagon. By 11:00 a.m. the next day Marshall therefore wanted new planning documents that would meet the President's concerns. As Marshall reported Mr. Roosevelt's wishes:

That between Overlord and Priceless [further major operations in the Mediterranean] he was insistent on Overlord but felt that we could do more than was now proposed for Priceless. His idea was that the seven battle-experienced divisions should be provided for Overlord but that an equal number of divisions from the U.S. should be routed to Priceless.

He stated that he did not wish to have anything to do with an operation in the Balkans, nor to agree to a British expedition which would cost us ships, landing craft, withdrawals, etc. But he did feel that we should secure a position in Italy to the north of Rome and that we should take over Sardinia and Corsica and thus set up a serious threat to southern France.[8]

Marshall was stunned — able only to protest that "we had strained programmed resources well to the limit in the agreements now standing." Moreover, though Overlord would have priority of resources, a multi-front strategy by the Western Allies, if adopted too heavily in the Mediterranean, would impose grave constraints on Overlord and its chances of success.

The President seemed unimpressed by Marshall's response — as the general was aware. Clearly the President saw Marshall as maintaining a kind of ideological focus on Overlord, which seemed not only bureaucratic but wooden and out of touch with political reality. The American people, furnishing the weapons and the soon-to-be eleven million soldiers for the war — as well as paying the taxes to fund it — could not be expected to condone *nine months* of a virtual cease-fire at this juncture, during which anything might happen — both positive and negative.

Rather, the President sounded determined the Allies should keep the initiative, now that they had the Germans on the run. General Brooke, the British CIGS, was right to see Italy as a major theater of war, where major German forces could be forced to fight, rather than switch divisions back to the Eastern Front. Once in Italy, moreover, the Allies could maintain the offensive initiative: possessing the airfields from which to bomb southern Germany, and bases for the troops from which to mount an invasion of southern France if it were deemed opportune, thus helping Overlord — indeed offering an alternative lodgment if Overlord did not succeed. The President, Marshall penned in the note he made at the Pentagon, therefore wanted to see him "at noon tomorrow" with the logistical implications of a two-front campaign on the European mainland. "Incidentally, he said he did not like my use of the word 'critical' because he wanted assistance in carrying out his conception rather than difficulties placed in the way of it — all of this in a humorous vein," Marshall reported to his staff.[9]

The President had spoken. He was U.S. commander in chief, and it was for Marshall, as U.S. Army chief of staff, to ensure the President's conception be carried out, not keep harping on "critical" insufficiencies, or jeopardy. Period.

Once the Joint Chiefs of Staff were seated in the Oval Office at 2:15 on the afternoon of August 10 — and with the secretary of war, Mr. Stimson, having been invited to witness the meeting, following his lunch with the President — Mr. Roosevelt held forth: explaining the political context behind the next decisions that must be made at Quebec, where they would be conferring with their British opposite numbers.

The "British Foreign Office does not want the Balkans to come under the Russian influence," he told them. Therefore, "Britain wants to get to the Balkans first" — understandably. However, he himself rather doubted the Russians wanted or were in a position to "take over the Balkan states" such as Yugoslavia, Bulgaria, Albania, and Greece. They would, he predicted, prefer rather to "establish kinship," or associative relationship, "with the other Slavic people" in southern Europe.[10] "In any event," he went on, he "thought it unwise to plan military strategy on a gamble as to political results," rather than what was possible or desirable militarily.[11] A major U.S. campaign in the Balkans would have no guarantee of succeeding, indeed might well fail. It would certainly distract from the cross-Channel invasion scheduled for May 1944 — a gamble the United States couldn't take.

General Marshall agreed wholeheartedly. If the shift of the seven battle-hardened Allied divisions designated for Overlord from the Mediterranean did not take place, it would, he pointed out, "simply invite having these extra divisions used for invasion in the Balkans. This would meet the Prime Minister's and Mr. Eden's desires, but would make the Mediterranean operation so extensive as to have a disastrous effect on the main effort from England"[12] — a warning that prompted Admiral King to suggest "to the President that if the British insist upon abandoning Overlord or postponing the operation indefinitely, we should abandon the project as in carrying it on we would simply waste our substance."[13]

Admiral King's disgust with the British prompted the President to reassert the crucial necessity of mounting Overlord as the number one priority. Indeed, to the amazement of his own advisers, the President then "said we can, if necessary, carry out the project ourselves. He was certain that the British would be glad to make the necessary bases in England available to us."[14]

The United States mounting the cross-Channel invasion *without* British participation?

In the long months since Pearl Harbor, there had been threats to switch military priority to the Pacific, but never such a gesture of scorn for British timidity and avoidance of decisive battle — certainly never before by the President.

In part the bleak picture of British cowardice was the result of Secretary Stimson's journey to London and Algiers. On his return he had painted a disturbing portrait of Churchill's intentions, but the President didn't think, in the end, it would come to a breach in the alliance. The British, he was certain, could not afford to let down, before the whole world, the major ally that had saved them from German and Japanese victory. Moreover, the United States was not averse, the President explained, to establishing air bases in southern Italy and opening a fighting front in Italy; it was just a matter of saying no to an advance further north than the capital, lest the Allies be drawn into Hitler's web.

"He was for going no further into Italy than Rome," Stimson noted with satisfaction that night, "and that for the purpose of establishing bases. He was for setting up as rapidly as possible a larger force in Great Britain for the purpose of Roundhammer [Overlord] so that as soon as possible and before the actual time of landing we should have more soldiers in Britain dedicated to that purpose than the British. He said he wanted to have an

American commander and he thought that would make it easier if we had more men in the expedition at the beginning. I could see that the military and naval conferees were astonished and delighted at his definiteness."[15]

They were. "The President stated that, frankly, his reason for desiring American preponderance in force," General Deane wrote in his minutes of the meeting, following discussion of the American divisions that could be shipped to England before D-day (fifteen in number), was "to have the basis for insisting on an American commander. He wished that preponderance of force to be sufficient to make it impossible for the British to disagree with the suggestion."[16]

The new strategy was thus clear. War on two western fronts — but the Italian front limited to a line just north of Rome. And an American supreme commander for Overlord, lest the British try to renege on their commitment to a cross-Channel invasion.

"The President then summed up the discussion by stating that our available means seem to fit in pretty well with our plans. He outlined these as insistence upon the continuation of the present Overlord buildup and carrying out that operation as our main effort," Deane recorded. Moreover, the President wanted to have enough Americans in Britain "in order to justify an American commander" for Overlord, he restated. Together with this, he was in favor of leaving Eisenhower with sufficient forces in the Mediterranean to establish U.S. air power in southern Italy (where weather conditions permitted takeoff and landing almost every day, compared to often prohibitive flying conditions over England). Such forces on the southern European front would give the Allies strategic flexibility if for any reason the Overlord operation was repelled, but the President was emphatically "opposed to operations in the Balkans."[17] Yes, it would be good to have an army able to stop the Russians from overrunning countries in south-central Europe as they advanced — but the Western Allies still did not have a single boot on the mainland of Europe, and the Balkans were in any case a nightmare in terms of terrain. Knowing the Germans, the Wehrmacht would contest every yard. It was, therefore, "unwise to plan military strategy based on a gamble as to political results."[18]

"I came away with a very much lighter heart on the subject of our military policy than I have had in a long time," Stimson dictated at home in his diary, delighted with his commander in chief's stance. "He was more clear and definite than I have ever seen him since we have been in this war."[19]

What pleased Stimson even more was that the President now wanted an American in charge of Overlord—something Stimson, in a letter he'd brought with him to the White House for the President, had also recommended. He'd shown his draft letter to Marshall before leaving the Pentagon that morning, pleading for Marshall to be the man, and Marshall had not demurred (though anxious that Stimson not tell the President he had seen the recommendation, lest he be seen to be pursuing personal ambition).

The loss of Marshall from Washington—were he to be Overlord's supreme commander—would be dire, but it was necessary, Stimson felt, to show the British that America meant business: Overlord the only way that "Germany can be really defeated and the war brought to an end."[20]

Whether the President would select Marshall as supreme commander, however, was quite another matter. As would be the British chiefs' reaction to the President's strategy, once they all reached Quebec.

And with that the President prepared to meet his counterpart, the Right Honorable Winston Churchill and his wife at Hyde Park on August 12, 1943.

The planning for the endgame in World War II in Europe was now coming to a climax.

40

The Führer Is Very Optimistic

THE PRESIDENT'S INSISTENCE that Churchill meet him at Hyde Park before the Quebec Conference was not motivated by politeness or hospitality. For good or ill, the President was aware the meeting with the British prime minister might well determine the course of World War II — and its aftermath.

Strategic flexibility or inflexibility — that was the question in Churchill's eyes. Opportunism or strategic determination — this was the question in Roosevelt's.

The question of who was right and who was wrong would vex political and military historians for the next seventy years. Time was certainly of the essence — the President having received reports of ever-increasing German atrocities in the occupied countries of Europe. The latest of these had come on August 10, the day he met with the Joint Chiefs at the White House. From London, the U.S. ambassador to the Polish government in exile, Tony Biddle, had reported German mass murder — genocidal pogroms — on a scale never seen before in human history.

The President, in his broadcast on July 31, had already warned neutral countries not to give asylum to war criminals, but Biddle felt this would not be enough. As he put it, "apart from the punishment of war criminals for the crimes they have committed, it has become more imperative than ever to restrain the Germans from committing further the mass murder of the Polish population in Poland. This becomes all the more urgent since it may be anticipated that the policy of exterminating the population of entire provinces, as is practiced in Poland, may also be applied by the Germans in the present final stages of the war to the people in other German-occupied territories, like the Czechs, Yugoslavs, French and those in the occupied parts of the U.S.S.R.," his report warned — noting the Germans had already "exterminated" the majority of the Jewish population, and were deporting to concentration camps hundreds of thousands of Poles, while men between the ages of fourteen and fifty were being taken to Germany as slave labor. "Women, children and old people are sent to camps to be killed in gas chambers which previously served to exterminate the Jewish population of Poland," he reported. As if this were not enough, it "may be presumed that the Germans are reckoning in the possibility of a defeat, and have consequently decided to exterminate the largest possible proportion of the Polish population" in a kind of apocalyptic conflagration — quoting Fritz Sauckel, the Reich minister of slave labor, saying as recently as June 19, 1943, in Kraków: "If the Germans lose the war, we shall see that nothing remains either here or elsewhere in Europe."[1] The Germans would, in other words, not only resort to a scorched-earth policy, but torch peoples as well.

It was thus imperative, Roosevelt considered, to end the Nazi nightmare in Europe as soon as could be achieved — something that would never be accomplished by opportunistic operations in the eastern Mediterranean and Aegean, however much Churchill and the British Foreign Office feared an eventual Sovietization in central Europe.

Churchill, too, was all for finishing the war as swiftly as possible; he merely saw the challenge differently. Imaginative, impetuous, and excitable, he was pulled in all directions, as General Brooke noted in his diary — but least of all in the direction of a cross-Channel landing and campaign. When writing his epic, six-volume memoirs of the conflict, Churchill would title his fifth volume *Closing the Ring*. The "Theme of the Volume" (a mantra he liked to insert in the frontispiece to each work) was the story of "How Nazi Germany was Isolated and Assailed on All Sides."

Could Hitler and his regime be swiftly toppled by being "isolated," however? In the excitement of the summer of 1943, Churchill was minded to think so. The Germans would surely cave in once they saw — like the Italians — the game was up, and only destruction faced their nation if they sought to fight on. His July 19 minute to his chiefs of staff maintained the "right strategy for 1944" would be to pursue the Germans "certainly to the Po," after Husky, with the option of attacking westward to the south of France or northeastward toward Vienna, "and meanwhile to procure the expulsion of the enemy from the Balkans and Greece." Moreover, rather than launch a costly cross-Channel assault, to prepare an Allied invasion of Norway, to be mounted "under the cover of 'Overlord.'" Encirclement around the fringes of mainland Europe, he'd considered, would lead to "Hitler and Mussolini" being "disposed of in 1944."[2]

It was this vision — tantamount to fantasy, unfortunately — that had come to obsess the Prime Minister, and which underlay his latest, enlarged mission to North America: some 230 men embarked on the *Queen Mary* to take Churchill's latest strategy to Quebec, which they reached on August 10.

It was a mission, however, that the President was determined to preempt by insisting on meeting Churchill first — in private. The British must be held to the only policy that would actually defeat Nazi Germany, rather than merely ringing it. This meant a spring 1944 cross-Channel invasion, with no holds barred — and no more backtracking by the British. Once the two men got together at Hyde Park, the President had decided, moreover, he would have to use his trump card.

As Roosevelt prepared to meet his recalcitrant ally, Hitler had meantime asked Dr. Goebbels to fly from Berlin to the Wolf's Lair to "discuss the whole situation from every point of view."[3]

The Führer, Goebbels found when he arrived on August 10, had decided to abandon his main Axis ally. The new Badoglio government would "betray" Germany, he was certain, despite its assurances of loyalty to the Axis Pact. A telephone conversation between Churchill and Roosevelt had been intercepted, and both Goebbels and Hitler were scornful. "These plutocrat leaders imagine things in Italy as being much more positive for them than they really are. The Führer knows every trick in the book, though," Goebbels noted with evil satisfaction in his diary. "German troops are now streaming into Italy" — in fact, German flags were already flying over Mantua and Genoa. "There's no danger of anything too terrible happening. The Führer is absolutely determined he's not going to surrender Italy as a battlefield. He has no intention of letting the Americans and the British get to northern Italy. The worthwhile part of the country, at least, will remain in our possession."[4]

Having overcome his initial panic and fury over Mussolini's arrest, Hitler now actually *welcomed*, he said, the impending capitulation of Italy: a nation that had no national will, he felt, beyond the popular fascist speeches of the Duce. Mussolini no longer impressed him, in retrospect. The Duce had failed to declare war in September 1939, when his intercession might have gotten England to back away from world war; moreover,

at home in Italy, Mussolini had failed to crush the monarchical, aristocratic conservative elements who considered him a fly-by-nighter.

To maintain his power, a dictator must be perceived by his own people
to be ruthless, Hitler understood—and by preparing to crush the forces
of Italy and move Wehrmacht troops immediately to occupy the entire
Italian peninsula, the Führer would be seen to be asserting his absolute
will—Aryan, egalitarian, merciless. Actions that would speak louder
than any words.

Was Hitler assuming too much of his *Volksgenossen*—his fellow citizens?

In 1943 Hitler would only appear in public twice—an isolation at his
headquarters that filled Dr. Goebbels, as a master of public relations, with
disappointment, even anxiety. Yet the Führer seemed to know better than
his chief propagandist that he had no need to show himself in public, or
even inspect his troops. With drums, banners, swastikas, and film and
press fanfare, he had as Führer given the German Volk what they yearned
for: order, authority, a new place—a supreme place—in the European
sun; a sense of belonging to a dynamic, productive community with ra-
tional if draconian goals—and sufficient pride in their country's history
and extraordinary military achievements to defend it and its conquests
now to the death, literally. He was therefore confident he had the willing, even enthusiastic, obedience of his troops—troops who would fight
all the harder and more effectively *without* the hindrance of an always-
unreliable Axis ally. Italy's military missteps in Greece and North Africa
in 1941 had dragged German forces into a southern theater of war that
had distracted from the Führer's main priority, the defeat of Russia—in
fact were now affording the Western Allies a possible stepping-stone into
Europe. Without the millstone of Italian allies, however, that stepping-
stone could be transformed into a *Sumpf:* a bog, where the Western Allies
could become enmeshed, ensnared, mired. If, that was, the Allies could
be tempted into further fighting in the Mediterranean and Aegean.

While always keeping the Atlantic Wall as strong as possible, ensuring
there were enough divisions stationed in France to defeat any attempt at a
Second Front, he would now lure the British and Americans to the south
of *Festung Europa,* Hitler told Goebbels. He would thereby buy time
without taking great losses, or facing a real threat to the Reich itself: the
Vaterland. True, in the probable event of Italian surrender to the Allies,
vital German divisions and air force groups would have to take over the

positions hitherto held by Italian units in the Mediterranean and Aegean, stretching from Sardinia to Samos — forces that could not then be used on the Eastern Front. But with no-nonsense German military control not only of Italy and of the eastern Adriatic — from Slovenia to Albania, Greece and Crete, with all their airfields — the Western Allies would be at a disadvantage. Given the mountainous terrain and the fighting efficiency of Wehrmacht and Luftwaffe units, the Americans and British would be hard put to form a Mediterranean front that had any hope anywhere of reaching Germany.

With every week and every month the Western Allies would be held in the Mediterranean *Sumpf.* Germany would thus have time, Hitler calculated, to finish the development of the Third Reich's secret weapons — long-range rockets and ballistic missiles — and to deploy them, from January 1944 onwards.

Roosevelt had boasted that America was the arsenal of democracy. But as Führer of the Third Reich he would show how, using not only slave labor in Germany but products manufactured in France and the occupied countries for the Third Reich, the Third Reich was the arsenal of Europe. Not even mass RAF night raids and U.S. Air Force daylight bombing could turn the tables. Allied air force losses in conducting mass raids of German cities were unsustainable in the long run. Under the leadership of Albert Speer, the production of German armaments was being dispersed away from big cities, while evacuation of families would deny the Allies the collapse of German civilian morale.

Hitler's fascination, in fact obsession, with the minutiae of weaponry might be mocked by some of his generals, but in a war of numbers, it was the quality of weapons that counted, along with the sheer discipline of German Wehrmacht soldiery in combat. U.S. and British industrial output might statistically outstrip that of the Third Reich, but the technical truth was, he sneered, their weapons were inferior, their soldiery less ruthless, and the demands of their various theaters of war too global. By contrast, now that Italy's ill-fated campaign in North Africa was over, the Third Reich had the advantage: cohesion. A single continent as its battlefield, with Germany at its epicenter — its high command able to furnish reinforcements in any direction, especially if Goebbels, Göring, and other senior officials could squeeze out still more military personnel from the workforce, and more slave labor from the occupied countries — including Italy now.

With the Japanese reaffirming their pact with Berlin, and drawing an

With hundreds of advisers and staff officers, Churchill arrives in New York in May 1943 aboard the *Queen Mary* (here bringing back U.S. troops two years later) to oppose agreed-upon U.S.-British strategy. On Capitol Hill he inveighs against a cross-Channel Allied invasion before 1945 or 1946, citing impossible odds.

Axis Surrender in North Africa

In Tunisia, a quarter million Axis troops in North Africa surrender to Eisenhower on May 12, 1943, the culmination of the President's "great pet scheme." For FDR this proves the Allies are on the road to military victory in Europe; for Churchill it means the Allies should stay in the Mediterranean.

Churchill is intransigent; the U.S. secretary of war accuses the British of cowardice. The President takes the Prime Minister to Shangri-la to fish, while the U.S. chiefs of staff work on Churchill's military team. Eventually FDR has to give Churchill a talking-to. Following the invasion of Sicily and southern Italy, U.S. troops will be withdrawn to England for a definite 1944 D-day. Churchill is furious.

Sicily — and Kursk

On July 10, 1943, the Western Allies take the war to Europe, invading Sicily. The magnitude of the landings stuns Hitler — who calls off Operation Citadel, his great summer battle on the Eastern Front to destroy Stalin's Soviet armies at Kursk.

The Fall of Mussolini

With Italian troops running from the Allies in Sicily, Hitler flies to Italy to encourage Mussolini to fight on rather than surrender. Six days later, the Duce is arrested by his own people. The Germans will have to fight for Italy instead.

Once again Churchill returns to Hyde Park, this time with his daughter Mary, to persuade FDR to abandon U.S. strategy for an Allied cross-Channel invasion in 1944. The Prime Minister is convinced it will be a disaster, and that better results will be obtained from Mediterranean operations.

The President refuses to listen to such defeatism. He threatens to withhold the Manhattan Project's atomic bomb discoveries from Britain. The two men join the Canadian PM and the Combined Chiefs of Staff in Quebec. There the D-day plans for spring 1944 will be cast in stone.

The First Crack in the Axis

In Ottawa, the President announces "the first crack in the Axis." The Allies suffer their own cracks, however. Churchill misunderstands German determination to fight, even in other people's countries, and Stalin — facing two-thirds of the Wehrmacht — loses faith in Allied willingness to defeat the Axis.

At Hyde Park (driving his own car), FDR tries to keep the Allies focused on the defeat of Nazi Germany, rather than become too embroiled in the Mediterranean. For all of Winston's faults, though, FDR needs the Prime Minister to help save western Europe from postwar Soviet domination once the Nazis are beaten.

At Salerno, south of Naples, on September 9, 1943, FDR's worst fears are realized. Churchill's vision of a "soft underbelly" is not soft. Fortunately, as Commander in Chief the President has stood firm, and U.S. preparations for D-day in 1944 will, he hopes, erase Churchill's near-fatal misjudgment.

ever more significant portion of U.S. and British military effort to the Far East and Pacific, the chances of the Western Allies mounting a Western Front — at least a successful Second Front — if they were tied down in the Mediterranean were, in Hitler's mind, distinctly dim.

Goebbels was thus delighted by the führer he'd met at the Wolfschanze. It was no mask of confidence Hitler was putting on for his generals, his headquarters staff, or his visitors in the high and late summer of 1943, the Reich minister judged: it was real.

The South Tyrol, annexed by Italy from the Austro-Hungarian Empire in 1918, would be occupied by German forces and henceforth become part and parcel of the Third Reich. "We just have to keep our nerve and not be distracted by the enemy's panic-machine," Goebbels noted. "Whatever they cook up in Washington and London, they won't find consuming as easy as preparing. It'll take quite a while for the Italian crisis to sort itself out." The Führer was determined to hold the Alps and Italy as far as the Po, but "the rest of Italy is worth nothing," intrinsically, Goebbels recorded — adding, though, that "in private and in the greatest secrecy," Hitler had stated he would not only try and arrest Marshal Badoglio, King Emmanuel, and "the whole baggage" in Rome, but was planning to "defend the Reich as far south in Italy as possible,"[5] as he'd confided to Goebbels already in June.[6]

This latter intention would have the gravest implications for the Allies — who could decode high-grade German communications from Hitler's headquarters, but not read Hitler's mind. "The fundamental principle of our war strategy is to keep the war as far as possible from the borders of the homeland," Goebbels noted on August 10. "It is absolutely the right principle," he reflected. "As long as we can master the war in the air" — especially with better *Flak* and new jet fighters — "the German people can be trusted to stick it out for a pretty long time." The harvest in Germany looked good, with more that could be brought in from occupied countries. Using slave labor, the outlook for the Third Reich was thus far more positive than the way the foreign press was depicting it. If the Western Allies could be lured to commit themselves to all-out war on the Southern Front rather than a Second Front, they could be savaged — perhaps even repelled — by the sheer professionalism and ruthless energy of the Wehrmacht. Certainly the Allies could be held at bay, far from the Reich, and in close combat — with London and the British Isles, meantime, under aerial bombardment by secret weapons: "our planned measures to be taken in the coming months."[7] "With regard to our counter-measures against the British," Goebbels confided, "the Führer thinks they can be launched in great numbers by January or February [1944] at the latest. He's going to set upon London with a fury never witnessed before. He's anticipating great things from our missiles. They've been fully tested; we just have to accelerate production to the level we need. So we have to be patient."[8]

As for the Eastern Front, moreover, Hitler seemed confident the Russians could be held — indeed had been beaten badly, in effect, at Kursk. As such they could be thrashed again that winter, if the Western Allies were kept at bay in the south.[9] "It will take time, and we have to be patient," Goebbels repeated[10] — Hitler interested in why Stalin had recently withdrawn his two ambassadors, Litvinov and Maisky, from Washington and London.

Puzzled, Hitler and Goebbels wondered if there was an opportunity to cleave the Allies apart. Stalin could not defeat the Wehrmacht without the Western Allies mounting a Second Front — something that, if the Allies still balked at such a mission, might well lead to a breakdown in the Allied alliance far more momentous than the looming collapse of the Axis Pact. "We have to let our apples ripen. It would be a real irony of world history if we were to be courted by both the Soviets and the Anglo-Americans in this situation — which is not inconceivable," Goebbels noted. "It sounds absurd, but it is a possibility. In any event we've got to do our best to work on the current difficulties between them. As long as we don't have a disaster on the Eastern Front, our situation will be secure."[11]

If Germany's Eastern and Southern Fronts were held, and the enemy's air offensive was parried, Germany would remain politically and militarily in the ascendant. "The Führer is very optimistic," Goebbels described, "perhaps too optimistic. But it's good to see him in such good form. Either way we're going to put everything we can, to the last breath, into the struggle." He hadn't seen Hitler looking so fresh and on such a high for ages — "he told me that as soon as things get dangerous, all his aches and pains disappear and he feels healthy as never before."[12]

A renewed German peace with Stalin, as in the Ribbentrop Pact of 1939? It didn't seem likely, as things stood. But over time?

Providing the Soviets were willing to leave Germany in control of the Ukraine — with its all-import grain harvest, and the Donets Basin, with its huge reserves of coal — the Führer seemed willing to parley. In the meantime 1943, far from being a *verlorene Jahr,* a lost year, the Third Reich would remain in almost complete military control of the whole of Europe — moreover able to deal with Jewish and Resistance problems more ruthlessly than ever.

This, then, was Hitler's strategy — one that was far more effective in the short term than his enemies or even his own generals admitted, then or later.[13] Mussolini's arrest and the probable defection of the Italians as his Axis ally were removing the biggest burden from Hitler's back — not increasing it, as so many assumed in their excitement. Winston Churchill and his British parliamentary colleagues, especially Anthony Eden, were known to be pressing for exploitation in the eastern Mediterranean. This was all to the good, as Goebbels had joyfully discussed with Hitler. Dissension among the Allies would make the Führer's task the simpler,[14] with no sign of Stalin willing to confer with his Western counterparts — only ever-increasing scolding in the Moscow press at the failure of the Western powers to mount a Second Front.

Just one thing could thus imperil the Führer's warplan: American insistence on the mounting of a massive, all-out cross-Channel invasion of northern France in 1944, in coordination with the Soviets, that would crush Germany between them — Hitler's age-old nightmare.

41

A Cardinal Moment

MRS. CHURCHILL HAD felt unwell, following the turbulent sea voyage from Scotland, so Churchill, summoned to stay a few days with the President at Hyde Park, arrived by train from Canada at the small railway halt near the President's home around midday on August 12, 1943, without her. He had, though, his twenty-year-old daughter, Mary, in tow, a bubbly, charming subaltern in the Women's Auxiliary Territorial (equivalent to National Guard) Service.

Contrary to General Brooke's sour mien in Quebec, where he was preparing to meet the U.S. chiefs, the Prime Minister was full of joy at the latest news of secret negotiations for Italian surrender with Marshal Badoglio's representative. Ever the historian in attempting to set current events within the larger picture of the past, he felt the coalition nations had reached "one of the cardinal moments" of the war, as he'd put it in a cable to the President when calling for a tripartite meeting with Stalin, rather than waiting for the President to meet with Stalin one-on-one. In his telegram he'd claimed "our Mediterranean strategy" had already gained all that Stalin had "hoped for from a cross-Channel second front" that year — dooming the German offensive at Kursk — and that a Big Three meeting "would be one of the milestones of history."[1]

The President, for his part, worried that, far from being a milestone of history, it would be a millstone, if the Russians learned Churchill and his 230-man entourage were all for pulling out of Overlord yet again. Worse, in fact, if the Russians — who were still facing some two hundred Wehrmacht divisions on the Eastern Front — lost all faith in the Western Allies. Stalin's unwillingness to meet before the fall had at least given the President time to reassert his role as leader of the Western nations. Roosevelt therefore arrived at Springwood ahead of Churchill on August 12, shortly after breakfast.

Rather than incurring an immediate contretemps, the President had decided to show no outward concern, but to treat Churchill and his daughter with his usual affable hospitality and respect. He'd therefore instructed that Winston's lovely painting of Marrakesh, which the Prime Minister had brought over in person in May, at the time of the Trident Conference, should be hung in the main room of the new Library at Hyde Park before the Prime Minister's arrival, as well as Raymond Perry Neilson's vibrant new canvas of the both of them at the Atlantic Charter meeting, on the deck of the *Prince of Wales,* flanked by their chiefs of staff.

Greeting Churchill and his daughter — who was in uniform — the President drove them in person to Hyde Park. Given the oppressive summer heat, he also arranged, once they were settled in, for swimming at Val-Kill, Eleanor's cottage: the President driving Churchill there in his special Ford, the swim to be followed by fish chowder from an old Delano family recipe, and hot dogs cooked by the First Lady herself.

The Prime Minister certainly showed no disappointment at the simple outdoors fare, indeed he entered into the spirit of the country weekend as to the manor born — even eating the hot dogs he was served. "Mr. C. ate 1 & ½," Daisy Suckley recorded with amusement in her diary, "and had a special little ice-pail for his scotch."

Daisy thought Churchill "a strange little man," though. "Fat & round, his clothes bunched up on him. Practically no hair on his head" — a fact that compelled him to seek shelter from the sun's harsh glare under "a 10-gallon hat."[2] When he undressed, Daisy was even more amused. "In a pair of [swimming] shorts, he looked exactly like a kewpie," she described.

Returning to her own family mansion at Wilderstein that evening, Daisy noted that "Churchill adores the P" — "loves him, as a man, looks up to him, defers to him, leans on him. He is older than the P. but the P. is a bigger person, and Churchill recognizes it. I saw in Churchill, too, an amount of real greatness I did not suspect before. Speaking of South Africa, Ch.[urchill] said General Smuts is one of the really great men of the world — a prophet — a 'seer' — his very words — He wants to get him to London, for his 'mind on post war Europe' . . ."[3]

The President, too, was an admirer of Jan Christiaan Smuts.

Smuts's support for Roosevelt's vision of the United Nations had certainly been encouraging. But in terms of military strategy, Smuts's over-optimism was as worrying as Churchill's, the President felt — seemingly unaware, despite or perhaps because of his great reputation as a guerilla fighter in the Boer War, just how difficult it would be to fight the Wehrmacht head-on, and thus, like Churchill, now contesting the feasibility of Overlord.

To add to the British Commonwealth preference for peripheral rather than head-to-head combat, also, there was Anthony Eden, the British Balkanist — who would be attending the Quebec Conference and clashing horns with Secretary Hull. This would make the President's task doubly difficult. The President gave no hint of anxiety, however, even to Daisy.

"The P. was relaxed and seemingly cheerful in the midst of the deepest problems," she described. As the President explained to Churchill, the imminent surrender of Italy was a most welcome development — but it would not win the war against Germany. Nor could it be counted upon, in all likelihood, to keep Russia as an ally in the war against the Axis. Germany would arguably be more powerful alone than burdened by an ally like Italy. This could have serious ramifications — not only in the event that Stalin sought a separate peace with Hitler or an alternative German government, but in terms of Russian cooperation in the war against Japan, slated to follow the defeat of Germany.

There was also the question of whether Russia would agree to be a participant in a United Nations security system thereafter, if the Western Allies failed to carry out Overlord — and instead put their energies into a doomed campaign in the Dardanelles, to spite the Russians. As Secretary Stimson had put it in the memorandum he'd brought with him to lunch with the President two days before, the "Prime Minister and his Chief of the Imperial Staff," General Brooke, were still "frankly at variance with" Overlord. "The shadow of Passchendaele and Dunkerque still weigh too heavily over the imagination of these leaders of his government. Though they have rendered lip service to the operation, their hearts are not in it." Nor were their heads — though it was difficult to understand British reasoning that "Germany can be beaten by a series of attritions in northern Italy, in the eastern Mediterranean, in Greece, in the Balkans, Rumania and other satellite countries, and that the only heavy fighting which needs to be done will be done by Russia. To me, in the light of the post-war problems which we shall face, that attitude towards Russia seems terribly dangerous," Stimson had written. "None of these methods of pinprick warfare can be counted on by us to fool Stalin," he'd warned. And he'd pointed to the year 1864, "when the firm unfaltering tactics of the Virginia campaign were endorsed by the people of the United States in spite of the hideous losses in the Wilderness, Spottsylvania [*sic*], and Cold Harbor."[4] Overlord was the only way "Germany can be really defeated and the war brought to an end."[5]

Stimson was certainly right to question the Prime Minister's loyalty to the Trident agreement. The day after his first talk with Churchill in London, on July 13, the Prime Minister had minuted his chiefs of staff with an immortal phrase that would come to personify his irrepressible but often unrealistic spirit. In the minute he had scorned the notion of landing merely on the toe of Italy, across the narrow Sicilian strait at Messina; "why should we," he'd asked his generals, "crawl up the leg like a harvest bug, from the ankle upwards? Let us rather strike at the knee" — an amphibious assault north of Naples, "thus cutting off and leaving behind all Axis forces in Western Sicily and all ditto in the toe, ball, heel and ankle. It would seem that two or three good divisions could take Naples and produce decisive results if not on the political attitude of Italy then upon the capital. Tell the planners to throw their hat over the fence," the Prime Minister had declared in July, adding it was "of the utmost urgency."[6]

Two or three whole divisions, to be transported by sea, put ashore by landing craft, and reinforced more than two hundred miles behind the current German-Italian frontline?

The feasibility of this was something that had not concerned the Prime Minister. He'd seemed on the Mediterranean warpath, delighted with Smuts's supportive cable, and responding to it with excitement. "I believe the President is with me: Eisenhower in his heart is naturally for it. I will in no circumstances allow the powerful British and British-controlled forces in the Mediterranean to stand idle." He would bring a Polish division from Persia, he would use Canadians and Indians — all rushed in to exploit the imminent "collapse" of Italian forces. "Not only must we take Rome and march as far north as possible in Italy but our right hand must give succour to the Balkan Patriots." If the Americans declined to cooperate "we have ample forces to act by ourselves."[7]

Churchill's claim, in retrospect, was as ridiculous as the President's remark to his chiefs that U.S. troops could mount Overlord on their own, if the British reneged on the operation. The two statements were, however, an alarming indication as to how much the two Allies were now separating, not converging, in their war strategy. It was therefore up to the President to stitch them back together — if he could.

In the circumstances, the President felt he had no option but to play his biggest card: the atom bomb.

42

Churchill Is Stunned

BEFORE LEAVING WASHINGTON, the President had rehearsed over lunch with Stimson the latest position over U.S. atomic bomb research — which he'd placed under the war secretary's direction the previous year.

When swift development of research had been in danger of stalling for lack of sufficient funding, early in January, 1943, Roosevelt had found the necessary money. Critical Canadian supplies of the necessary raw materials, moreover, had been contracted with the cooperation of the President's friend, Prime Minister Mackenzie King — leaving the British, essentially, with only a cadre of theoretical physicists and no possibility of producing such a weapon by themselves. For months Churchill had been pressing for a bilateral agreement to pool research and its dividends — the U.S. authorities refusing to cooperate, however, on grounds of American national security. Only the President had the authority to decide.[1]

If Churchill would not adhere to the American Overlord strategy, as per the Trident agreement reached in May, the President thus quietly indicated to the Prime Minister that the United States would have to withhold an agreement to share development of the atomic weapon. If, by contrast, the British were willing to stand by the agreed Anglo-American Overlord strategy, then the President would go ahead and sign an agreement to share its atomic research program with the British — *and not the Russians.* This would, in itself, assure the Western Allies of a reserve weapon that could, if indeed it worked, stop the Soviets from spilling into western, perhaps even central, Europe.

The Prime Minister was shocked by the President's proposed deal. For Churchill personally, it would be a climbdown even more embarrassing than at the climax of the Trident Conference. Before leaving for Hyde

Park on August 10, Churchill had gaily assured Prime Minister Mackenzie King in Quebec that the "president is a fine fellow. Very strong in his
views, but he comes around."[2] This had not only been smug but clearly
presumptuous, it seemed.

The President's firmness certainly surprised Winston. How would he
explain backing off his opposition to Overlord, in Quebec, after bringing
230 staffers to argue his case? An agreement on the atomic bomb project
must, of necessity, remain as secret as the research itself; he would thus
not be able to reveal, let alone explain, the quid pro quo arrangement,
save to a handful of his British team back in Quebec. It would also be
politically problematic at home in England. A groundswell of resentment
was already forming there against the United States, given that America
was so clearly becoming the dominant partner in the Western Alliance.
It might well affect the Prime Minister's support in Parliament, and room
for maneuver in the War Cabinet.

In his heart of hearts, Churchill therefore continued to hope events
on the ground in Europe would make Overlord unnecessary: that if the
Allies' fall and winter operations against the Germans prospered in Italy
and the Mediterranean, they would find Overlord unnecessary. Or if German defense forces in northern France swelled to an even greater extent,
threatening disaster for Overlord, then he could always request the right
to cancel the Overlord landings . . .

In any event, after swallowing the bitter pill, Winston Churchill recognized he would have to agree to the President's terms — for the moment.
He thus gave his assent.

Overlord would go ahead as the number one Allied operation — the
decisive Allied operation — with priority over all other commitments.

Churchill was disappointed, but took his defeat graciously.

There was one further potion, however, Churchill must take before the
two men left Hyde Park, the President made clear.

Churchill waited to hear it.

The supreme commander of Overlord must be an American, since
the largest contingent in the cross-Channel invasion would ultimately be
from the United States. This decision, too, the Prime Minister would have
to convey to General Brooke.

Churchill was shocked — the President's insistence an understandable
blow to his patriotic British pride.

In the circumstances, though, there was nothing he could say, other than: Yes, Mr. President.

The historic deal, then, was struck.

Churchill was not happy with the outcome — indeed, he woke in the night "unable to sleep and hardly able to breathe." He got up and "went outside to sit on a bluff overlooking the river," where he "watched the dawn," he later recalled.[3]

The worst, at least, was over, however — leaving the Western Allies with a clear, unified timetable and strategy for defeating Hitler's Third Reich. Considering that, at the Oval Office on August 10, Admiral King had suggested switching U.S. priority to the Pacific, Churchill had been skating on very thin ice — with the gravest consequences for world history.

Fortunately the President had gotten the Prime Minister to concur. And with their new accord, the brief Hyde Park summit came to a happy end — the Western Allies on the same page.

Churchill tried to persuade the President they should both now go straight to Quebec to meet with the Combined Chiefs — and thus spare Winston the humiliation of reporting his change of stance alone. The President said no, however.

Mrs. Roosevelt was about to tour American forces, hospitals, and installations in the Pacific theater for six weeks, and the President wanted to see her off. He wished, in particular, to give her a personal letter for General MacArthur in order to facilitate her tour once she arrived in Australia. Though they conducted more or less separate lives, Roosevelt was more proud of Eleanor as First Lady, and guardian of his social conscience, perhaps, than ever. He also wanted to have lunch with Secretary Hull in Washington and concert their approach to Italian government after unconditional surrender, before they both went to Quebec.

Taking Churchill to the station, meantime, the President bade him and his daughter farewell. The following evening, August 15, Roosevelt himself boarded the *Ferdinand Magellan* together with Harry Hopkins, who did not look at all well — "white, blue around the eyes, with red spots on his cheek bones," Daisy Suckley commented[4] — and set off, southwards. Traveling through the summer night the little presidential party made its way back to the White House. It had been quite a weekend.

PART ELEVEN

Quebec 1943

43

The German Will to Fight

IN THE GENERAL narrative of the Second World War, the famous Quebec Conference of August 1943 would be seen as the moment when the Allies — the Western Allies — laid down their D-day strategy and timetable — an Overlord operation scheduled to take place on May 1, 1944.

In reality, however, the decision had already been taken in May 1943, at the Trident Conference — and in writing. Overruling Churchill — and General Hull's brief planning revolt at the Pentagon — the President had thereafter stuck to his guns. There was therefore no reason for Churchill to have brought his 230-man team to the Canadian capital, from a military point of view — or for them to stay. General Eisenhower was handling the secret Italian surrender negotiations with Marshal Badoglio's representative, and the decision to appoint an American, not a British, supreme commander for Overlord had been agreed by Churchill at Hyde Park, in deference to the President's wishes. Had Churchill simply told his British team of the new deal — trading partnership in the atomic bomb's development for British commitment to a clear American D-day strategy — and had they returned to their ship, the *Queen Mary*, the Quebec Conference need not have taken place.

Instead, of course, it did take place — bringing the British and American military teams almost to blows. At one point the noise of a revolver being fired in the conference room — which had been cleared of clerks and junior officers — would be thought to be the start of a gunfight.[1]

The British, in short, acted at Quebec with extraordinary ill grace — loath to accept a policy in the Mediterranean that did not envisage or permit exploitation of what they saw as a unique opportunity, after the toppling of Mussolini, to strike at the outer pillars supporting the Third Reich. In his war memoirs Churchill would title this section of his account "Italy Won." But as the historian of Churchill's *opus magnum* would later point out, Italy was *not* won.[2]

Instead, the Allied campaign in Italy would arguably prove the most ill-conceived Allied offensive of the war thus far: a sad reflection, in all truth, of Churchill's misconception of modern combat. Far from being a victory, it would drag on for almost two years, never putting the Allies anywhere near a breakthrough, and causing the deaths of hundreds of thousands of Italian civilians long after their government had surrendered unconditionally. It would incur almost a third of a million Allied casualties — killed and wounded — for no other gain than could have been made at virtually no cost in September 1943. And this largely because Churchill and his military team completely underestimated the German will to fight, not for their homeland but for every inch of other people's territory as if it was their own: a demonstration of blinkered yet also professional approach to battle that had few parallels in the history of war.

The difference between Germans and Italians in their response to the Allied onslaught would say it all. On July 19, 1943, the largest single bombing raid of the war had taken place in Italy. More than five hundred B-17s and B-24s of Major General James Doolittle's North African Strategic Air Forces had pounded Rome's railway marshaling-yards and nearby airfields.

The raid had destroyed the equivalent of two hundred miles of railway track, and — in spite of millions of warning leaflets dropped the previous day — had resulted in some seven hundred civilian deaths:[3] enough, when rumors of vast casualties spread among the Italian population, not only to frighten the Italian government to end Mussolini's long reign as Duce, but to begin surrender negotiations with the Allies under a different leader, Marshal Badoglio, in order to avoid more destruction of their Italian homeland.

The Italians had not reckoned on the German response to their imminent capitulation, however — not only German forces in Italy, but Germans at home in the Fatherland, where German cities faced the same, indeed far worse, bombing than Rome experienced. Five days after the U.S. bombing of the Rome railway network, there had taken place an even bigger air raid, or series of raids: this time the combined heavy bombers of the RAF and USAAF attacking from airfields in Britain the northern German city of Hamburg — Operation Gomorrah. Employing not hundreds but thousands of bombers in rolling attacks, night and day for an entire week, the Allies created a literal firestorm — with temperatures of 1,000 degrees Celsius, hurricane winds of 150 miles per hour, and melting asphalt in the streets. By its end, Operation Gomorrah had killed some forty-two thousand people — the majority, civilians — injured thirty-seven thousand more, left the center of Hamburg in utter ruin, and had caused a million people to evacuate the burning city. Yet the result was the very opposite of reaction in Italy.

Instead of calls for the arrest of their country's dictator and immediate unconditional surrender to the Allies, as in Italy, there was reported to be an even more relentless determination in Germany to continue to prosecute war to the death. It was as if any hope of conscience — *Gewissen* — had now been incinerated in Germany. Certainly it removed any sense of guilt at having been the first to launch such a war of ruthless conquest by *Blitz* and *Blitzkrieg*. The Allied raid on Hamburg — which would soon be replicated on Berlin — merely reinforced German stoicism: a collective will that was expressed in yet deeper loyalty to the nation's leader and calls for the Führer, in their fury, to exact German revenge. In particular, for him to use, finally, the secret weapons he and Goebbels had publicly alluded to.

At his Wolfschanze headquarters near Rastenburg, far from Hamburg and Berlin, Hitler thus viewed the Allied bombing raids on those cities as more inherently counterproductive than his own earlier raids on London and Coventry in 1940 and 1941. Bombing would not bring Germany to its knees. The fact was, the Allies could not defeat the Third Reich, Hitler reasoned, unless they could defeat his primary weapon, the Wehrmacht. The German armies embodied the highest Teutonic virtues of obedience, courage, group loyalty, and self-sacrifice — and as he studied his maps and daily Abwehr intelligence reports, he rightly saw no signs whatever of an Allied intention to follow up the mass bombing of German cities with a ground offensive on Germany via the beaches of northern France — at least not for another year.

To the extent that, if they did attempt to breach the Atlantic Wall in the late summer of 1943, the Allied invasion forces would be crushed by his German divisions in France, the delay was disappointing to the Führer — and to Goebbels. However, if the Allies didn't dare launch such an assault in 1943, as Hitler pointed out to his panicky generals, then there was no cause for alarm. The German Volk and the German Wehrmacht were too unified and imbued with too much resolve to simply collapse;

rather, they would hold fast at home, despite the bombing, and fight hard and harshly abroad. They would treat every attack on German forces in the occupied countries as if it was an assault on the Vaterland — in fact on the very honor and courage of the German nation. Meantime, German scientists and engineers would make available the new, secret weapons they had devised that would give Germany the wherewithal, if not to win the war, then to negotiate favorable armistices with Germany's enemies.

The war was not over, Hitler thus made clear. There was everything to gain by continuing to fight, implacably and fearlessly, to preserve the Third Reich they had so heroically created out of the ashes of World War I and the stupid Weimar Republic. Once he overcame his fury over Italy's imminent defection, in fact, Hitler was seen to regain his composure — and confidence. Fall weather was approaching; it would soon make conditions for an Allied cross-Channel assault impossible. For all their superiority in the air, at sea, and on land, the Western Allies were, in sum, *in no position to invade Germany* — and without such an invasion there was little chance the Russians could, either. In fact, judging by the American and British performance against modest numbers of German troops defending Sicily — where only sixty thousand Wehrmacht troops had been committed — the Allies might not be able to seize control of much of the Italian mainland, whether or not the post-Mussolini government surrendered unconditionally.

By stamping on the Italians and by using the Italian mainland — with its mountain ranges that would provide good defensive positions — as a Hindenburg Line of the Third Reich, the Germans had nothing to lose, Hitler reckoned. And much to gain scientifically in the meantime.

For all his mistakes — holding on in North Africa, despite Rommel's recommendation of evacuation after Alamein and Torch; holding on at Stalingrad rather than a calculated withdrawal; launching Operation Citadel instead of using his armored forces to entice and then crush a Russian offensive — Hitler was about to show that he had, in fact, a better grasp of the German war machine he'd built up over the past decade than his own generals. He was backed loyally and enthusiastically by the spirit of a whole nation, he felt, and was in a position to fight the war to the bitter, bitter end.

That Hitler was not wrong was certainly the view later taken by German official historians, in a kind of bemused, retrospective awe.

In fanning the flames of *Volksgemeinschaft,* involving a profound sense of national German community, identity, and destiny, Hitler had built upon quite the opposite of what most observers — even the Nazi elite, on occasion — assumed. The "belief that under National Socialism the Germans were, so to speak, subjected to total communicative and ideological brainwashing" by Hitler and his Nazi accomplices was simply not fact, the official historians concluded. "The widespread view that systematic government propaganda kept the population ready and willing for war, or even created a unified 'national' feeling among them, ignores reality," the historians pointed out. "Identification with the nation could not be produced on command, and as a rule propaganda was convincing only to those already converted."[4]

German nationalism, stretching back decades before Hitler, was in truth "the precondition for propaganda being successful, not the other way around." Hitler and Goebbels's propaganda had succeeded so well, in other words, because it hinged upon "established nationalist beliefs." The "spreading of racist, xenophobic, or authoritarian stereotypes" had, as instanced in the conquest of Poland and huge swaths of the Soviet Union, worked so effectively because such propaganda was directed at "soldiers already predisposed to them."[5] In a country like Germany, given the country's warring history since ancient times, Hitler had understood as an Austrian outsider that the very concept of democracy was foreign. German intellectuals had for centuries sneered at it — and had avoided practical politics, preferring philosophy, the arts, and science. With its rich history of land warfare at the epicenter of Europe, and its distaste for thinking through or dealing with the necessary compromises involved in civilized society, Germany's people could therefore, in the wake of deep economic depression and defeat in World War I, be encouraged to focus on a supposedly egalitarian, simplistic expression of nationalist German identity: one that, in order to cohere and remain strong, must see others — whether foreigners or Jews, communists or non-Aryans — as enemies: enemies to be excluded, disrespected, defeated. And where deemed necessary, simply liquidated, without remorse or compunction.

Anyone who objected to the nationalistic program in Germany was "othered," while "in foreign affairs" the "seed was planted for the future offensive war of extermination," the German official historians concluded. "War, established as a permanent component of German politics as an inheritance from the First World War, from then on became the natural means of achieving political ends both at home and abroad."[6] Far from becoming a nation of warrior-serfs obeying a draconian führer, in other words, nationalistic Germans had become loyal and obedient members of a community — proud and arrogant citizens of a revived empire: a third Reich, a *Volksgemeinschaft*, a "master race" of individuals each cognizant at some level and largely supportive of the genocide being directed against Jews in Germany as well as outside Germany on their behalf; supportive, too, of barbarous treatment of enemies such as Russian *Untermenschen*, since the denigration of "others" only increased and inflamed this powerful sense of national German identity.

What Hitler had intuited, then, as Italy's new leaders prepared to defect from the Axis Pact, was what many of his own generals did not: namely that the war would not be won or lost by cleverness or better tactical strategy in the East, the South, or the West, per se — tactics such as the fighting withdrawals that these German generals suggested, or the marshaling of armored reserves using the latest panzers in German counterstrikes. The war could only be won, in the end, by employing Germany's national *spirit*: the amazing solidarity of its people, bonding in a nationalist saga that Hitler saw as mythic in the noblest, Nibelungen sense: a demonstration of national pride and unity by seventy million people at home, but especially so abroad when acting as military overlords — an achievement unmatched, in many eyes, since the Romans.

This national German unity that the Führer had channeled and directed would never be broken by aerial bombing or by peripheral Allied operations, let alone by the cowardly defection of Germany's partners. It was not, in the end, a matter of winning or losing; it was a matter of hunkering down and asserting German moral and military strength, in dark days as well as fair ones. German forces had won, in the shortest time, almost unimaginable victories and territories. All genuine Germans were participants, implicated in its sins and a part of Germany's new trial by fire. No one would be spared. There was thus no talk of the future, the postwar world, because the concept no longer existed — only the current defend-or-die struggle.

By fighting offensively in the Mediterranean in the hopes of German collapse, then, the Allies might well, Hitler recognized, play into German hands. Wehrmacht forces would be operating closer to home, the Allies further away from theirs. Moreover, German forces would have the advantage of mountainous terrain, easily defensible lines, highly disciplined and well-armed troops who would fight *even better* when shorn of their weak, former ally, Italy, once the Italian government capitulated. Moreover, by continuing — in fact expanding — its massed daylight and night-time bomber attacks that inevitably killed so many German civilians, the Allies could truthfully be portrayed as barbarians — giving Hitler not only the "right" to use new weapons of mass destruction in reply, but impelling the German Volk to *demand* he use them: *Vergeltungswaffen,* as the secret weapons were soon called — weapons of revenge. Winged but pilotless flying bombs, launched from easily constructed concrete ramps and aimed to fall indiscriminately on Allied cities. And also ballistic missiles, with even greater range — and so high and fast they were impossible to shoot down.

As Hitler had assured Mussolini at Feltre, there was no need to fear the Allies — especially the British: their cities would, the Führer forecast, be "razed to the ground," as they deserved. And unless the Allies dared take the risk of attacking Germany proper with ground troops, the Allies could not win. Moreover, if they tried to do so by launching a cross-Channel invasion, they would be easily repelled. Ergo, the Third Reich was bound, the Führer predicted, to prevail.

This, then, was the challenge facing the Allies even at the very moment when they seemed to be winning the war, both in Russia and the Mediterranean in the high summer of 1943. By underestimating German determination to fight on mercilessly in southern Europe, the Allies were heading toward disaster.

Only the President could now steer the Allies through these rapids, and to his great credit Roosevelt tried. Yet in truth he failed — forcing him to paper over the true military debacle, which now, as in a Greek tragedy, unfolded.

44

Near-Homicidal Negotiations

AFTER A HECTIC day at the White House on August 16, 1943, the President prepared to set off by train to Canada — hoping Churchill had done as he'd promised: getting his chiefs of staff to back off proposals for more extensive operations in the Mediterranean, once southern Italy was in Allied hands. And to start putting all British efforts into Overlord under an American commander.

Churchill certainly did the latter — to the consternation of General Brooke, who took the news badly. As Brooke noted in his diary, the Prime Minister "had just returned from being with the President and Harry Hopkins" at the President's home in Hyde Park. "Apparently the latter pressed very hard for the appointment of Marshall as Supreme Commander for the cross Channel operations and as far as I can gather Winston gave in, in spite of having promised me the job!!"[1]

Since Churchill still did not believe, in his heart of hearts, that Overlord would ever really be mounted, he had shown no sympathy when speaking with Brooke on his return to Quebec. Nor did he tell Brooke that it was the President's decision, not Hopkins's. More importantly, however, he did not tell Brooke what had been agreed with the President regarding the prioritization of Overlord over all other opportunistic operations — hoping that the redoubtable Brooke would fight hard in the Combined Chiefs meetings for maximum possible interim American support in the Mediterranean.

As the Prime Minister admitted to General Marshall, when dining with the general in Quebec on the evening of August 15, he'd "changed his mind regarding Overlord," and now agreed "that we should use every opportunity to further that operation." But when Marshall said the first meeting of the Combined Chiefs of Staff that day had been pretty contentious over the issue of Overlord priority, and that the U.S. chiefs were adamantly opposed to prejudicing the success of a spring 1944 Overlord by overambitious "bolstering" operations in Italy in the coming months, the Prime Minister had "finally dropped the subject, saying 'give us time.'"

In relaying Churchill's comment to his fellow American chiefs the next day, General Marshall assumed Churchill meant time for the British chiefs to swallow the inevitable, and put their energies behind Overlord rather than Italy. Marshall was wrong, however. Churchill was not one to give up so easily — and one way or another, the Prime Minister remained bent on pursuing his "soft underbelly" strategy, whether or not it prejudiced the success of Overlord.

Marshall had, after all, agreed to an amphibious American landing south of Naples, at Salerno, in two or three weeks' time, as Churchill knew — in fact the operation, codenamed Avalanche, had filled Churchill with excitement. If all went well, not only would the amphibious assault secure the unconditional surrender of Italy but it would cut off German troops in the foot of Italy and open the road not only to Naples but to Rome. The consequences were irresistible. Once the Italians — who were still occupying positions all across southern Europe, from the south of France to Greece and the Balkans, on behalf of the Axis Pact — came over to the Allies, the soft underbelly of Europe would, Churchill remained certain, become the gateway to central Europe, promising to make a cross-Channel assault either unnecessary or pro forma. And a Russian inundation of central and western Europe impossible.

Churchill's duplicity, in other words, arose not from a perfidious British effort to extend British imperial influence, as some U.S. generals such as Admiral Leahy posited at the time, but from a genuinely held belief that Overlord would fail. And, conversely, out of a genuine belief that opportunistic Allied operations in the Mediterranean — especially if Turkey could be persuaded to join the Allies — would succeed.

In both matters Churchill would be proved utterly wrong. As the historian of Churchill's memoirs, David Reynolds, would write, Churchill was profoundly if understandably deceitful in writing his fabled account of that fateful summer and autumn[2] — but the Prime Minister was not insincere in his faith in a Mediterranean rather than a doomed Normandy strategy. His was a faith based not only upon fear of failure in northern France, but also a deep and abiding fear of Russian motives and intentions — and in this respect the President was just as concerned. It was certainly something that he was taking very, very seriously as on August

16, 1943, Roosevelt set forth from the secret siding near the White House at 8:20 p.m. to join the Prime Minister in Quebec.

By the time the President's train arrived in Quebec, via Montreal — where Fala's presence on the platform banished any attempts by the Secret Service to maintain secrecy[3] — on the evening of August 17, 1943, the Combined Chiefs of Staff of the United States and Britain had been at loggerheads for three days, and were getting close, he was informed, to homicide.

General Brooke, chairing the Combined Chiefs of Staff meetings (since they were being held on "British," or non-U.S., soil), felt he was being driven almost out of his mind by American unwillingness to see the connection between operations in the Mediterranean and Overlord. "I entirely failed to get Marshall to realize the relation between cross Channel and Italian operations, and the repercussions which the one exercises on the other," Brooke noted in exasperation on August 15. "It is quite impossible to argue with him as he does not even begin to understand a strategic problem."[4]

This was the pot calling the kettle black. If anything, the reality was the reverse. Brooke's obstinate insistence, along with that of his irrepressible prime minister, upon overambitious Allied operations in Italy would, just as Marshall had feared, become a near-fatal drag on trained Allied manpower and logistical support for Overlord, as well as incurring a far higher Allied death toll than was necessary. Had Brooke devoted himself to how best to achieve the maximum German commitment of troops and reserves in the Mediterranean by the minimum of effective Allied operations, the course of World War II for the Allies would have been far better served. Far from later acknowledging his mistake, Brooke — who was promoted to the rank of field marshal in 1943 and then raised to the peerage as Lord Alanbrooke in 1946 — would go to his grave in 1963, arguing he'd always been right: that the German defense of Italy and the casualties the Werhmacht suffered by the summer of 1944 had contributed mightily to Overlord's success.

This was ridiculous. The Western Allies were to suffer 312,000 troops killed, wounded, and missing — including 60,000 Allied deaths — in the eighteen-month Italian campaign, without ever getting much further than the Po. The Wehrmacht would suffer 434,000 casualties, including 48,000 men killed in Italy by May 1945[5] — but though it did keep German divisions from the Eastern Front, it had little or no effect upon Overlord, since the Germans would have been forced to keep troops stationed across southern Europe (as they did in Norway) in fear of invasion, whatever happened in Normandy. It would become a heavy price in blood, destruction, and civilian misery to have paid for British strategy—a strategy based on a fatal illusion, or delusion: that the Allies would be able to achieve great things in a country that was ideally suited to defense, not offense.

The fact was, as Churchill's military biographer, Carlo D'Este, would write, Churchill and Brooke had utterly failed to predict "the casualties that would be incurred" by their obsession with warmaking in Italy. "During their twenty months in Italy the Allies fought one bloody battle after another, for reasons no one ever understood," D'Este would lament. "Allied strategy in Italy seemed to be not to win, but rather to drag out the war for as long as possible," he would write in retrospective frustration, a tragedy that "simply distracted the Allies from their real task: crossing the English Channel and opening the endlessly delayed second front."[6]

Nor was this hindsight. Marshall's understanding of the "strategic problem," far from being ignorant, as Brooke described it, was prophetic—and Marshall's unrelenting argument with the British chiefs of staff was greatly to his credit in counseling caution before sending tens, even hundreds of thousands of men—American, British, Canadian, French, Polish, and others—to their deaths in Italy and southern Europe. In this respect Brooke's diary gave but a glimpse of the fierce altercations and traded accusations coloring their meetings.

Brooke was implacable. "Dined by myself as I wanted to be with myself!" he noted on August 15, after hearing he was no longer to command Overlord, and having learned from Field Marshal Dill that General Marshall, now the presumed supreme commander-to-be, was "threatening to resign if we pressed our point" on overambitious Mediterranean operations. The next day Brooke himself was near resignation—"Marshall has no strategic outlook of any kind, and [Admiral] King has only one thought and that is based on the Pacific," he penned in his special green ink—the traditional color reserved for chiefs of the Imperial General Staff in Britain. The Combined Chiefs had had to ask all secretaries, stenographers, and planners to leave the room, and had argued for three hours without agreement. "This is the sixth of these meetings with the American chiefs that I have run," Brooke noted, "and I do not feel that I can possibly stand any more!"[7]

Admiral Leahy was certainly stunned by the extreme acerbity. "The

British and U.S. Staffs today got into a very frank discussion of a difference of opinion as to the value of the Italian campaign to our common war effort against Germany," Leahy recorded in his diary that night. He felt Marshall's willingness to go ahead with occupation of southern Italy to secure the Foggia airfields, from which the U.S. Army Air Forces could bomb southern Germany and the Ploesti oil fields in Romania, was "very positive in his attitude toward the Mediterranean committment [*sic*]," but Brooke seemed ungrateful, and dissatisfied. When Brooke suggested the Combined Chiefs divert Allied forces on their way out to the Far East and the Pacific to mount a bigger campaign in Italy, King's language lit the borealis lights. "Admiral King was very undiplomatic to use a mild term for his attitude," Leahy confided.[8]

Admiral King was once again reaching the end of his tether. If the British devoted too much effort to Italy, then the "build up in England would be reduced to that of a small Corps" for Overlord, as Brooke mocked King's approach — in which case King would favor "the whole war [being] reoriented towards Japan."[9]

It was small wonder. Ignoring King, Brooke had argued for an immediate, major Allied campaign in Italy to reach as far north as Turin and Milan. Not content with those objectives, Brooke had even pressed to "retain" in the Mediterranean three of the seven battle-hardened divisions earmarked for Overlord, and perhaps all seven, if German resistance in Italy was fierce . . .[10]

Marshall was almost apoplectic at this, causing Brooke to grudgingly admit, under pressure, that "'battle experienced' troops were required for Overlord" if it was to succeed.[11] Brooke remained furious, however, noting that night, "It is not a cheerful thought to feel that I have a continuous week of such days ahead of me!"[12]

The American chiefs felt the same.

As the Combined Chiefs of Staff discussions became ever more strident, Brooke had descended into the foulest of moods. He later confessed that "it took me several months to recover" from what he called the "blow" at being passed over for the cross-Channel supreme command[13] — something doubly disappointing since he had begun to yearn to get away from the Prime Minister, he confessed, and be able to command troops in battle once again.

The imminent arrival of the President had made it imperative that the chiefs come to an accord, however. Though the British team pushed the struggle over strategy to the very brink on August 16, 1943, they finally and reluctantly gave in. The decisions made at the Trident Conference in May would stand. Overlord would, they confirmed, be top Allied priority — and the seven battle-hardened divisions the President wanted would be transferred from the Mediterranean to Britain by November. Whatever could be achieved in Italy in the interim would be undertaken jointly by the Allies with remaining forces in the Mediterranean, on an ad hoc basis, to keep as many German forces away from France and Russia as possible — but under no circumstances were operations to be considered in the Balkans or elsewhere in the eastern Mediterranean.

There were, besides, equally important decisions still to be reached concerning Southeast Asia and the Pacific. The difference of opinion over strategy in Europe was therefore papered over at the conference. It was not a perfect result, but better than an outright split.

Meeting the President on his arrival in Quebec and bringing him up to speed regarding the recommendations of the Combined Chiefs of Staff, Admiral Leahy told him of the long days of contention — and the result.

As Lieutenant Elsey later recalled, Leahy was very much the President's lynchpin. "He was already at Quebec, and Roosevelt looked to him, in the summer residence of the governor general, the Citadel, as the top dog. Roosevelt looked to him rather than reaching out to King, Arnold, and Marshall. Leahy was the channel of communication from the chiefs to FDR. He, Leahy, really *was* the chief of staff to the President, and was dealt with as such, and Roosevelt saw relatively little of the Joint Chiefs during the Quebec Conference. Things came to him from Leahy, their views."[14]

The President, after all, had not come to Quebec to do their job. In truth he'd come for a very different reason.

45

A Longing in the Air

PRIOR TO THE President's arrival in Canada, a team from his White House Map Room had traveled to the Citadel in Quebec to set up a map room there, as Lieutenant Elsey afterward explained. They were "standing by the President's map room on his arrival at the Citadel to acquaint him with all the latest developments of the war. War reports had been radioed to the train during our trip up from Washington, but a more complete picture was available here for the President. The Prime Minister had his own map room in another part of the Citadel."[1] Special telephone communications with Washington and the White House had also been set up, "so that the President was never out of instantaneous communication with Washington." "Direct telegraph wire service," also, "was available between the Citadel and the White House."

Once the President was established in the Citadel, the wires grew hot with new cables — for the President was found to be batting drafts of a big speech back and forth with Judge Rosenman and Robert Sherwood, his speechwriters in Washington. On August 14, before leaving, he'd told them he wanted something he could broadcast to the whole world from Ottawa, on the eve of what looked like imminent Italian collapse and surrender. As he'd explained, he'd set the strategy and the timing of Overlord in stone. Though there would be much fighting still to be done, the war was moving into a new gear, political as well as military — and it was time to speak to the people of the United Nations: to make sure the moral aims and objectives of the Western Allies were clear and noble, before their first soldiers set foot on the mainland of Europe, early in September.

Before the President could give his speech, however, his Map Room received a very different kind of cable — this time from Moscow.

• • •

The telegram was from Marshal Stalin, dated Kremlin, August 22, 1943. It was not friendly.

Having refused every invitation to meet with the President for the past ten months, the Soviet dictator now declared he was fed up with the Soviet Union being treated as "a passive third observer" of agreements made by the United States and Britain with liberated countries, as well as with others "dissociating themselves" from Hitler. "I have to tell you that it is impossible to tolerate such a situation any longer," the quasi-emperor cabled. "I propose to establish," he declared, a three-power military-political "Commission" to handle such matters, immediately, "and to assign Sicily as the place of residence of the Commission."[2]

Stalin's arrogant new signal from Moscow made the President "mad," Harriman recalled, as it did Mackenzie King.[3] When, two days later, Stalin sent *another* cable, yet again turning down the President's invitation to meet at Fairbanks, Alaska, but demanding that a "Soviet Representative" be part of Eisenhower's secret negotiations with the Badoglio government for unconditional Italian surrender, the President became doubly incensed.

Except for his epistolary relationship with Stalin, the President had come to feel proud of the way his war strategy since Pearl Harbor had played out — thus far. He'd even treated Churchill with extraordinary patience and good humor when the Prime Minister had gotten into an interminable argument over Sumatra, after the President's arrival.

Sumatra?

"Mr. Churchill strongly advocated the establishment of an allied aviation base on the north end of Sumatra instead of the west coast of Burma," Leahy had protested, amazed at the Prime Minister's chutzpah. Instead of helping reestablish Burmese road communications with China — which Chiang Kai-shek considered vital for U.S. supplies — Sumatra would offer the prospect of air cover for a British invasion of Singapore, Churchill had argued: an objective that had never hitherto been raised before the Combined Chiefs. Even General Brooke had cringed. The Prime Minister's latest obsession had led to distracting arguments that continued for three long days — leaving Brooke furious and ashamed of his boss. An assault on Sumatra had never been seriously examined by the British chiefs — in fact the idea had only come to Churchill on the transatlantic voyage to Canada, Brooke railed in his diary, "in a few idle moments," yet here was the Prime Minister "married to the idea that success against Japan can only be secured through the capture of the north tip of Sumatra" — and "wants us to press the Americans for its execution!" The Prime Minister was acting like "a peevish temperamental prima donna," and proving "more unreasonable and trying than ever this time."[4]

Churchill would not give up his bone of contention, however — as if in lockjaw. Not even the President had been able to silence him on the subject. When the two leaders went on a quick fishing trip for the day in Laurentides Park, forty miles from Quebec, on August 20, and in the governor-general's cabin were eating the small trout they'd caught, Averell Harriman witnessed the sight of Churchill *still* going at the subject hammer and tongs with the President — who responded with glass and silverware.

There was simply insufficient shipping for such a venture, the President patiently pointed out to Churchill, even if they wanted such a strategy — which they didn't. Reopening the supply route to China was the real priority. The President "used most of the glasses and salt-cellars on the table making a 'V'-shaped diagram to describe the Japanese position" from western China to the South Pacific, "indicating the advantages of striking [Japan] from either side." Instead of laboriously trying to "remove the outer ones," such as Singapore and Sumatra, "one by one," the Allies should, the President said, simply go for the enemy's jugular — "thereby capturing the sustaining glasses" behind the outliers — Roosevelt corralling the glassware with a sweep of his hand.[5]

Churchill had remained unpersuaded, though — the argument mirroring, Harriman later reflected, their earlier "disputations over striking across the Channel or in the Mediterranean. Roosevelt once again favored the straight-line approach," Churchill the peripheral.[6] As the President shared with Mackenzie King, however, Winston's military misjudgments might be truly appalling, but they were vastly outweighed by Churchill's profound *political* wisdom: wisdom that would be crucial in the next phase of the war — especially when both men saw the tone of Stalin's cable. The war against Hitler, and then Hirohito, was set — but avoiding future war with Russia was not.

Despite the war of words traded by the chiefs of staff at the Château de Frontenac, then, the irony was this: that an extraordinary measure of harmony seemed to persist between the President and the Prime Minister — both of them staying in the Citadel, where they lunched and dined together every day.

What the President, in contrast to his chiefs, recognized was that the very unity of the Allies was being tested — not merely by the challenge of defeating the forces of Hitler and Hirohito in battle, but by the need to deal with Stalin. *And that the Western Allies must not fail this test.*

To the world, the Allied summit at Quebec in the summer of 1943 thus held a symbolic importance far outweighing any recommendations the Combined Chiefs of Staff might make: an alliance that must be seen by the world as growing closer and closer, not further apart. Though it could not be revealed to the public, possession of an atomic bomb, if nuclear fission worked, would give the Western Allies huge authority in ensuring a world free of German- or Japanese-style militarism and aggression — or Russian. The President had even gotten British acceptance of the draft Joint Four-Power Declaration he'd asked Sumner Welles to draw up in writing before his meeting with Churchill at Hyde Park, together with a suggested United Nations Protocol document.[7] All in all, this was a tremendous achievement for such an alliance between the Old World and the New: an achievement the President was determined to emphasize in the speech he intended to deliver in Ottawa, the capital of Canada. And Stalin's rude new cables only made him the more determined to make it strong.

To outsiders, the President thus appeared in an even more confident frame of mind than usual on August 25, as Mr. Roosevelt and the governor-general, the Earl of Athlone, were driven to the seat of Canadian government, having traveled to Ottawa by train from Quebec. "It was estimated that there were a crowd of approximately 30,000 people on hand at Parliament Hill and its vicinity to welcome President Roosevelt and to hear his address," the official chronicler of the President's trip noted. "This was said to be the largest crowd ever to welcome a distinguished visitor to Ottawa, even exceeding the welcome accorded to King George VI and Queen Elizabeth" in 1939.[8]

"The setting of the ceremony was one of the finest if not the finest ever provided for a Presidential speech," the *New York Times* agreed the next day. "Through streets packed with people and lined with sailors, soldiers, airmen and uniformed women in all services, the President drove from the railroad station into the parliamentary grounds in his open car." As people swarmed over the lawn, the President, "looking down on the waving crowd, turned to Prime Minister King and said, 'I shall never forget this sight.' The crowd in turn looked up at the magnificent Gothic building with its tower stretching up into the blue sky, as imposing a monument to parliamentary government as exists in the world. Carved over the portal are the lines by a Canadian poet descriptive of this great country: 'The wholesome sea is at her gates, her gates both east and west.'"⁹

The President was determined to give no hint of weakness — physical or moral. He "stood throughout the ceremony," Mackenzie King recorded in his diary. "Quite an effort as one could see, and shaking a good deal as he held on a chair and the stand" — kept upright by his steel leg braces.¹⁰

Robert Sherwood and Rosenman — "the firm of Sherwood and Rosenman, astrologers," as they signed their first draft — had been tasked with helping the President compose an address that would encompass his political philosophy, as well as his vision of the war's purpose — and the future. The two speechwriters had thus done their best and had arranged for the first finished draft to be flown to Canada, along with a plea that they be invited to Quebec to incorporate the new military decisions being made there. "It was signed with a drawing (by Sherwood) of a tall thin man — Sherwood; and a short fat man," Rosenman recalled humorously.¹¹

The President had turned down their request, however — for he had no intention of announcing the military decisions he'd made, either to the Germans or to the Japanese. He liked the "astrologers'" initial draft, however, which he then worked on "very carefully, making many changes in language here and there, which strengthened it," Rosenman later recalled. Most significantly he'd added a whole new section relating to the postwar. "The Ottawa speech was not a major policy speech in any sense of the word," Rosenman explained its tenor. "It was, however, important," for in it the President declined to mention the Russians — at all.¹²

What Roosevelt had decided to do, instead of talking about the things his military advisers were discussing with their counterparts, was to raise instead, at a critical moment in the prosecution of the war, a rallying cry for the democracies. A call for the United States and the United Nations to put isolationism finally and forever behind them, and embrace his larger, moral vision of the future. He therefore "discarded the last few pages of our draft," Rosenman recalled, "and wrote a new conclusion with an optimistic note."¹³ A note that would follow his grimmer picture of the turmoil that Hitler and the Japanese had brought to mankind. "We did not choose this war," the President reminded his audience — "and that 'we' includes each and every one of the United Nations. War was violently forced upon us by criminal aggressors who measure their standards of morality by the extent of the death and destruction they can inflict upon their neighbors."

With war forced upon them, the United Nations were now pulling harder and harder *together,* the President emphasized. He mocked the panickers who, after Pearl Harbor, had "made a great 'to-do' about the invasion of the continent of North America" — especially the Aleutian Islands. "I regret to say that some Americans and some Canadians wished our Governments to withdraw from the Atlantic and the Mediterranean campaigns and divert all our vast supplies and strength to the removal of the Japs from a few rocky specks in the North Pacific" — from which the Japanese had now wisely retreated, he pointed out. America was, he made clear, taking upon itself a much, much larger challenge. "Today, our wiser councils have maintained our efforts in the Atlantic area, and the Mediterranean, and the China Seas, and the Southwest Pacific with ever-growing contributions." It was in this context he himself had come to Canada — "Great councils are being held here on the free and honored soil of Canada — councils which look to the future conduct of this war and to the years of building a new progress for mankind."

> During the past few days in Quebec, the Combined Staffs have been sit-
> ting around a table — *which is a good custom,*

the President explained,

> — talking things over, discussing ways and means, in the manner of
> friends, in the manner of partners, *and* may *I* even say in the manner of
> members of the same family. (applause)
>   We have talked constructively of our common purposes in this war —
> of our determination to achieve victory in the shortest possible time — of
> our essential cooperation with our great and brave fighting allies.
>   And we have arrived, harmoniously, at certain definite conclusions. Of
> course, I am not at liberty to disclose just what these conclusions are. But,
> in due time, we shall communicate the secret information of the Que-
> bec Conference to Germany, Italy, and Japan. (applause) We *will* (shall)
> communicate this information to our enemies in the only language their
> twisted minds seem capable of understanding. (laughter and applause).[14]

As the *New York Times* reporter described, "Thirty thousand persons had gathered on the lawns in front of the building to welcome the President and to hear him speak and their cheers rolled up in a storm when he uttered that warning."[15]

> Sometimes I wish that that great master of intuition, the Nazi leader, could have been present in spirit at the Quebec Conference — I am thoroughly glad that he wasn't there in person. (laughter) If he and his generals had known our plans they would have realized that discretion is still the better part of valor and that surrender would pay them better now than later.

Hitler and his Volk were, however, unlikely to surrender without a great deal more bloodshed.

> The evil characteristic that makes a Nazi a Nazi is his utter inability to understand and therefore to respect the qualities or the rights of his fellowmen. His only method of dealing with his neighbor is first to delude him with lies, then to attack him treacherously, then beat him down and step on him, and then either kill him or enslave him. *And* the same thing is true of the fanatical militarists of Japan.
>
> Because their own instincts and impulses are essentially inhuman, our enemies simply cannot comprehend how it is that decent, sensible individual human beings manage to get along together and live together as (good) neighbors.
>
> That is why our enemies are doing their desperate best to misrepresent the purposes and the results of this Quebec Conference. They still seek to divide and conquer allies who refuse to be divided just as cheerfully as they refuse to be conquered. (applause)
>
> We spend our energies and our resources and the very lives of our sons and daughters because a band of gangsters in the community of Nations declines to recognize the fundamentals of decent, human conduct...
>
> We are making sure — absolutely, irrevocably sure — that this time the lesson is driven home to them once and for all. *Yes,* we are going to be rid of outlaws *this time*. (applause)

Under the heading "Much Post-War Discussion," the *Times* reporter noted the President's speech then addressed a much bigger challenge than merely winning the war. "There was much talk" in the speech, he added, "of the post-war world."

Every one of the United Nations believes that only a real and lasting peace can justify the sacrifices we are making,

the President claimed,

and our unanimity gives us confidence in seeking that goal.

It is no secret that at Quebec there was much talk of the postwar world. That discussion was doubtless duplicated simultaneously in dozens of nations and hundreds of cities and among millions of people.

There is a longing in the air. It is not a longing to go back to what they call 'the good old days.' I have distinct reservations as to how good 'the good old days' were. (laughter) I would rather believe that we can achieve new and better days.

Absolute victory in this war will give greater opportunities to the world, because the winning of the war in itself is certainly proving to all of us up here that concerted action can accomplish things. Surely we can make strides toward a greater freedom from want than the world has yet enjoyed. Surely by unanimous action in driving out the outlaws and keeping them under heel forever, we can attain a freedom from fear of violence.

I am everlastingly angry only at those who assert vociferously that the four freedoms and the Atlantic Charter are nonsense because they are unattainable. If those people had lived a century and a half ago they would have sneered and said that the Declaration of Independence was utter piffle. If they had lived nearly a thousand years ago they would have laughed uproariously at the ideals of Magna Carta. And if they had lived several thousand years ago they would have derided Moses when he came from the Mountain with the Ten Commandments.

We concede that these great teachings are not perfectly lived up to today, but I would rather be a builder than a wrecker, hoping always that the structure of life is growing — not dying.

May the destroyers who still persist in our midst decrease. They, like some of our enemies, have a long road to travel before they accept the ethics of humanity.

Some day, in the distant future perhaps — but some day, it is certain — all of them will remember with the Master, "Thou shalt love thy neighbor as thyself."[16]

Mackenzie King, standing behind the President, was deeply moved. "I noticed that he had the speech in a ring binder so as to prevent the leaves slipping away. He followed what he was saying by running his little finger along the lines as he spoke. He was given a most attentive hearing and a fine ovation at the close."[17]

It was small wonder. Rosenman was both right and wrong in writing that the Ottawa address was not a "policy speech." In its deeply personal way, using the simplest of language, it was perhaps the most heartfelt moral speech the President would ever give, cutting to the essence of what he believed: spoken to an audience in the open sunshine and through microphones and radio to the world, on behalf of a country that was rapidly becoming the most powerful nation on the earth: a nation that, with enough determination, would be able with its democratic allies to safeguard at war's end the future of humanity.

46

The President Is Upset — with the Russians

FOLLOWING THE PRESIDENT'S speech, there was lunch at Government House, following which Mr. Mackenzie King took FDR on a drive through the city, and showed him his two homes, Kingsmere and Laurier House, where they had tea.

On the drive Roosevelt confided to King how glad he was to have gotten from Churchill the now firm, formal British commitment to launch "an attack from Britain to the North of France," and that "he believed he could get a million men across [to England] during the remainder of the summer and on in the autumn," that very fall, 1943, ready for D-day on May 1, 1944. He felt, in retrospect, that the Quebec discussions had been, despite the fierce arguments, ultimately satisfactory and boded well for the successful prosecution of the war. Was that all, though?

"The most important of all he told me," King dictated that night, "was in answer to the question which I asked him: how satisfied he was with the conclusions of the conference."

Expecting the President, from what he'd shared, to say that he was — especially in view of his rapturously received speech that day — the Canadian prime minister was stunned. "He replied instantly that everything was most satisfactory until last night — just after 6. A telegram came from Stalin at that time which was most disconcerting; very rude and wholly uncalled for. It was the reply to the invitation that had been sent him to meet Winston and himself somewhere, the suggestion having been made in particular of Nome, Alaska. Stalin had replied that he, himself would arrange a conference, and it would be in Sicily" — but not between leaders, only "on a lower level." He, Stalin, had other things to attend to, of "greater importance."[1]

"I asked the President what it meant. He said there were only two interpretations. The most charitable one is that [just] like the Russians, they are one day with you, and the next day, they are prepared to take a very opposite course and be against you. You never feel sure of them. They may one day be very cheerful on your side; later, very down against you."[2]

And the other?

"The other interpretation — which is a very serious one and which is quite possible — is that Stalin is trying to work up a record against us" — in order to have an excuse "to make a separate peace with Germany. In this way, get us out of the war [with Hitler], leaving it to us to bring the war to a conclusion. He said that would be a very serious matter as the German armies would then be quite free of the Russian attack from the rear and," as King noted with alarm, "could devote all their energies to fighting against our forces."[3]

Certainly, the two leaders of North America agreed, the very threat of making a separate peace with Germany would give Stalin more leverage in making further demands for American aid and for more Allied operations in the West — as well as more concessions in terms of the end-of-war/postwar. Demands, amounting to blackmail, that Stalin "could not hope to get out of a peace conference," as King noted.

The President was clearly upset — as was Churchill, who had received the same cables. Roosevelt "then said: Winston was terribly annoyed. Was all for sending him [Stalin] a sharp answer. That he, the President, had strongly urged him to do nothing of the kind but to wait a day or two." Instead of responding, he himself would arrange for a message to be sent to Stalin by his secretary that he was traveling back to Hyde Park and would be in touch again in a few days. "'In the meantime, Winston and I will have a chance to think over what is best to say in reply.'"

"We talked a good deal of the conference," King summarized; "of what had been achieved. He was greatly pleased that all had been so harmonious" with the British, in the end. But the President "made no bones about telling me how deeply concerned he was" — about Russia.[4]

The President's concern was palpable — and understandable. Not only was Stalin an unreliable ally, constantly refusing to get together to discuss the prosecution of the war, but more worryingly still, refusing to get together to discuss either the endgame or postgame.

Roosevelt found himself amazed not only by the arrogance of the Soviet leader, after refusing to attend the summit meetings, but at his shameless hypocrisy. Cocooned in secrecy and almost pathological security in the Kremlin, Stalin was still forbidding any but the barest information about Russian forces and operations to be shared with the United States or Britain, his allies, and had declined to meet with the President and Prime Minister — yet was now fiercely decrying them for not including him in their deliberations. Given that the Soviets would permit virtually no Allied access to Russian cities, organizations, or individuals, his sudden demand that Soviet politico-military representation be set up in Sicily, an island thousands of miles from Moscow and which the Western Allies had only captured a few days previously, was significant. Stalin, clearly, was flexing his muscles: dictator of a power or quasi-empire now boasting two hundred army divisions in the field, on the Eastern Front — and the Western Allies still without a single division on the mainland of Europe.

It was, in other words, Stalin taking stock of the resolve of the Western Allies — a test that would best be met by a demonstration of Allied unity, not irritation.

Mackenzie King and Harriman — who had few illusions about the nature of the Soviet police state — seemed nevertheless surprised by how offended the President seemed to be over Stalin's two cables, once they heard their content. As Harriman put it, at the time, surely "one can't be annoyed with Stalin for being aloof and then be dismayed with him because he rudely joins the party."[5]

The President *was* dismayed, however — and not merely at Stalin's gatecrashing with regard to imminent Italian surrender negotiations. There was the question of how Stalin would behave, once he arrived at the bigger "party," when German surrender was in sight: a dictator running an impenetrable police state at home, yet announcing he wished to be treated as a controlling presence in Western councils: even dictating where the political-military surrender commission should be located.

However dismaying, it was clear that the balance of power within the United Nations was changing. In the spring of 1943, nervous about Hitler's impending Kursk offensive, Stalin had felt compelled to make certain concessions to his capitalist allies, such as closing down the egregious Comintern — which he'd finally done in May 1943. As the dictator explained to a Reuters correspondent, "the dissolution of the Communist International" as the purveyor of world communist revolution since 1919 would, once effected, increase the "pressure by all peace-loving nations against the common foe, Hitlerism, and expose the lie of the Hitlerites that Moscow allegedly intends to interfere in the life of other states and to 'bolshevize' them."[6]

Now, in late August, 1943, Stalin sounded quite different. With the great German offensive at Kursk called off thanks to the Allied invasion of Sicily, and with Russian armies pushing the Wehrmacht out of Orel and Kharkov — moreover with a huge Russian battle in the offing to move forward their forces from the Dnieper River in the south — Stalin clearly felt he could bang the Allied drum without having to leave Russia to meet with the President or Prime Minister.

Far from intimidating the President, however, let alone hammering a wedge between the President and British prime minister, Stalin's outburst now served to bring the leaders of the Western alliance closer to each other than Stalin could ever have imagined.

Behind the scenes at Quebec and Ottawa a deep and consequential *political* shift began to take place — a "sort of changed attitude," as Roosevelt put it to Mackenzie King on the way back to Quebec.[7] The President and his Joint Chiefs of Staff might hold Churchill's fantasies of defeating the Wehrmacht via the Mediterranean — whether through Italy, Yugoslavia or Greece, Turkey or the Balkans — to be just that: fantasy. But in terms of Soviet intentions, the President was very much on the same page as the Prime Minister. Stalin might make outward concessions to the Western Allies, such as closing down the Comintern, and even easing Soviet restrictions on religion — which the Soviet leader now also did. But the dictator himself remained a godless Russian psychopath — "Ivan the Terrible," directing two hundred divisions on the field of battle.

It was at this point that the President — who still nursed serious qualms not only about Churchill's military judgment but his backward, Victorian views on colonial empire and postwar social reconstruction — paused to reconsider his approach to the Grand Alliance. He still hoped he could come to a military understanding with Stalin, since neither he nor Stalin could defeat Hitler without the other. Moreover he still hoped he could come to a political understanding with the Russians, where the two powers — who clearly would be the dominant world powers at the war's end — could agree to disagree in terms of their own ideologies. But he needed, he recognized, a Plan B if Stalin did not cooperate in the postwar world the President envisioned — or even failed to cooperate in the end-of-war scenario that would come either in 1944 or 1945.

Winston Churchill might be the most infuriating partner in terms of his military obsessions, his impetuous whims, and his failure to follow a consistent strategy. He was, nevertheless, a political partner of huge and possibly historic importance in the world that was fast approaching: a democratic partner more important, in terms of dealing with Russia, than Harriman, or Hopkins, or former ambassador Davies — all of whom had been to Moscow and had firsthand knowledge of Stalin — perhaps realized.

What, though, was Stalin's real plan — if indeed he had one? Stalin was refusing to meet the President, either one-on-one or with the Prime Minister. Clearly the dictator wanted to conceal and safeguard Russian intentions behind a wall of paranoid secrecy, using a front of apparatchiks and spokesmen who never dared speak with authority, but referred everything to Stalin, on pain of dismissal or death.

For his part, Churchill didn't necessarily believe that Stalin would conclude a separate peace with Germany, despite the 1939–1941 Ribbentrop Pact, since "the hatreds between the two races" — the millions killed — "have now become a sanitary cordon in themselves," as Churchill told the President, and cabled his deputy prime minister in London that night. To Mackenzie King Churchill said the same: that the Russians and the Germans had "come to hate each other with an animal hate." So conscious were the Germans of their crimes against humanity in Russia and the likely repercussions, in fact, that they would probably "prefer to open their Western front to British and American armies and have them conquer Germany rather than Stalin," Churchill thought (and hoped), if "Stalin went on winning."[8] But the tone of Stalin's message boded ill for agreement between the Allies themselves in prosecuting the war. Which raised the question: what *was* Stalin's version of the endgame?

Without a single American or British boot on the mainland of Europe, the Western Allies were in a weak position, still, to inhibit Stalin. Would he use the new power of his many hundreds of Russian divisions — four hundred in total, it was calculated, stationed across the entire Soviet Union — to dictate the territorial and political outcome of the war in Europe?

To both Harriman and Mr. Roosevelt, the Prime Minister said he "foresaw 'bloody consequences in the future'" — "using 'bloody' in the literal sense," as Harriman noted. "'Stalin is an unnatural man. There will be grave troubles,'" Churchill declared — and openly rebuked Eden, who, like Harriman, considered the cable from Stalin "not so bad." "There is no need for you to attempt to smooth it over," he snapped, "in the Foreign Office manner."[9]

The President felt the same as Churchill — the Soviets a strange yet brave people, in the service of another psychopath.

Some historians would later resent and question Churchill's anti-Soviet stance,[10] but there can be little doubt in retrospect that, though Churchill would be proven completely wrong about Hitler, the Wehrmacht, and the progress of the war in Italy, he was extraordinarily prescient about Stalin and the Russians — and that the President was of like mind. Where Roosevelt and Churchill differed, however, was in how to deal with the Russian threat to freedom and democracy, as the Western Allies understood those ideals.

With no American or British forces yet on the mainland of Europe, the Western Allies were hamstrung. By the same token, however, without an Allied Second Front the Russians could not defeat the forces of the Third Reich. Ergo, if the Third Reich was to be defeated and the Nazi nightmare brought to an end, there would *have* to be a military agreement between the three countries, irrespective of political considerations. It would be up to the President and the Prime Minister, if possible, to turn that military agreement into a political accord, setting out a road map for postwar Europe and the world that both sides could live with. It might not prove possible to reach, but it would be worth trying to. The example of the disastrous Versailles Peace Conference in 1919, which had been tasked with solving end-of-war issues that had not been discussed or agreed in advance, was too awful to contemplate.

Encouraging Russia, then — a country or empire that had not been a party to the 1919 peace talks, but which had been the elephant in the room there — to take a responsible role in the postwar world was now the biggest challenge for Roosevelt and Churchill.

Both men had been present at Versailles, and both knew the task of an enduring postwar security settlement would be no easier. Also that Russia would be, together with the United States, the key player. In spite of the terrible losses the Soviets had suffered since Hitler's invasion in 1941, the USSR still comprised more than 170 million people: the largest nation, or union of so-called republics, in Europe. It was more than twice the size of Nazi Germany in population — and many times its size in territory. Its wartime economy might be a disaster, its industry dependent largely on slave labor, its military dependent on American Lend-Lease aid, and its society ruled by fear, incarceration, deportation, and execution; nevertheless, it now boasted the largest number of troops in the world — in excess of thirteen million men in 1943. After utter disarray and retreat in the summer of 1941, Soviet forces had finally turned the tables on the mighty Wehrmacht: by numbers, willingness to take casualties, determination to fight for the homeland, fear of what further atrocities the dreaded Nazis would commit if they were not repelled; and younger, better, nonpolitical professional military leadership on the field of battle. Patriotic pride, moreover, had swelled and grown as the Soviet armies successfully defended Mother Russia — the Communist Party taking a secondary, background role. Stalin's Great Terror and his Purges of the 1930s had been set aside — for the moment at least. As supreme commander in chief of the Soviet Armed Forces, Joseph Stalin was not only the effective, single ruler and dictator of the USSR, but he was in a position to begin moving Russia toward a less repressive future, *if he so chose:* something his ambassador to Washington, Maxim Litvinov, had begged him to do, before Stalin had recalled him from America.

Would Stalin dare — or want — to take that course, though?

It seemed unlikely, as Churchill intuited — especially after reading the latest, more detailed investigation of the Katyn massacre.[11] Behind Soviet propaganda, directed and controlled from Moscow, Marshal Stalin remained an arguably certifiable psychopath: a mass murderer living with his own terror, namely that of being assassinated. And of flying. His refusal to meet with the President, as well as his recent decision to withdraw his highly experienced Soviet ambassadors from Washington and London and replace them with apparatchiks, offered little hope of an open, democratic future for the Russian-dominated world — at least one based on the four freedoms to which the President referred in his Ottawa speech.

Stalin's latest cables to Quebec were thus dispiriting, at a moment of Allied joy and hope, on the eve of Italian surrender. The telegrams convinced both Churchill and the President that the defeat of the Third

Reich and Japan — which would still entail a vast military effort — would be but the first act in a new struggle for control of those occupied nations: nations such as Poland, currently ruled by the Germans, whose people innocently hoped for independence, self-determination, free elections, and freedom from fear.

This was, in actuality, the saddest of prospects, even as the unconditional surrender of Italy loomed.

Churchill, too, saw the moment as a watershed. He had earlier favored Sumner Welles's notion of grand regional or hemispheric councils, representing "spheres of influence" across the postwar world; now, suddenly, it became clear to him — as to the President — that there would, essentially, be but two such spheres: Anglo-American versus Russian. A rivalry, moreover, that would not necessarily be confined to central Europe, if Stalin's talk of southern Europe — of Sicily and Italy — was anything to go by.

In many ways it was a tragedy: a road not taken. Had Stalin been a different leader, a statesman willing to rise to the challenge of advancing and protecting a postwar world based upon the four freedoms, the challenge of the future could, in the aftermath of Hitler and Hirohito's demise, have been that of a secure, spirited, economic, social, and cultural opportunity for the progress of all nations. Instead, a very different prospect arose: a darker world of communist dictatorships and puppet states, modeled on the Soviets, answering to Moscow.

Unless Stalin were assassinated, or the Allies could somehow prevail upon the Russians to abandon the notion of tyrannous rule by fear, the postwar future thus suddenly looked bleak to Churchill and the President — despite the grandeur of a United Nations coalition that had successfully turned the tide against two empires, German and Japanese, still committing crimes against humanity on a scale of mass murder not seen for centuries, if ever.

All therefore now seemed to depend on a Russian dictator: a Soviet supreme commander in chief who was, as Averell Harriman later remarked, "the most inscrutable, enigmatic and contradictory person I have ever known."[12] It was a sobering prospect.

The Canadian prime minister accompanied the President to the station at 7:00 p.m. on August 25. "As the last word," King recorded in his diary, "I reached over to the President and said quietly God bless and help you."[13]

Roosevelt's talks with the Canadian prime minister had left Mackenzie King at once awed and anxious. In his library at Laurier House, the Canadian premier had shown the President and Grace Tully, the President's secretary, not only his private library but a "photograph of Hitler." The President had "instantly reacted to it with a shudder at the appearance of the man." King had also "pointed out the handbill of the time of Lincoln's assassination" — a reminder how seldom violence was separable from politics, their chosen profession.

"I was unfortunately pretty tired and unable to take in or contribute to the conversation as much as I would have liked, but I felt throughout how real was the affection the President had for myself and felt drawn more closely to him than ever," King recorded that night. "I confess, too, one came to feel he had a much more profound grasp of the situation than I had, at times, believed him to have. By that, I mean not a knowledge of the facts but the understanding of history and places and the like which are so essential to the understanding of great movements. The kind of thing that Churchill possesses in so great a degree."[14]

In his pedantic, cautious way the Canadian had come to see, increasingly, just how blessed was the free world in having such titans of humanity as their two great leaders — and how vital it was to create a durable system of international security and development *while they were still in office*. Moreover one that would survive them — since, "unhappily, we could not rely on having the President and himself at the head of affairs for all time," as King remarked to Churchill. "That any post-war order would have to take account of the persons who might take their places, and that each nation would want its say."[15]

Winston Churchill, Mackenzie King reflected, was "not so democratic at heart as the President. He still remains a monarchist and a Conservative," whereas "Roosevelt is clearly for the people and they know it." To be sure, "Churchill is for his country and its institutions" — including its "great Empire," King allowed. Thinking especially of India, though, King deplored continuing colonialist complacency at high levels in England, where "less believe in the abilities of people to govern themselves" than was the case in the United States and Canada.[16]

The future shape and peace of the world, however, was at stake: leading inexorably to the question of whether the President would stand for an unprecedented fourth term. "We talked," King had already noted, "of the next elections," which would take place the following year, in November. Health was a factor, the President had acknowledged. "He quite clearly has it in mind to run again but says he will not travel about; will not do any speaking over the radio and not make many speeches. He dislikes Willkie" — his Republican opponent in the 1940 presidential election — "but says he has been encouraging Willkie's renomination in order to get more or less a split in the Opposition [Republican] party which he believes will come if Willkie is nominated. He said that Willkie was all right on foreign policy which was important, but it would be dangerous if a Republican isolationist were to get the nomination."[17]

American participation, even leadership, in the new world order was quite clearly the President's goal — thus redeeming the failure of President Woodrow Wilson to get Senate ratification of U.S. membership in the League of Nations in 1920. As Churchill pointed out, it was not the League of Nations that had failed; rather, it was the nations who had failed the League of Nations — something the President was determined would *not* be the case this time.

Thus arose, at Quebec in the summer of 1943, the greatest irony of the war: that the United States and its Western Allies were, in effect, faced with two potentially competing struggles. The first, to pursue the fight against the odious, genocidal Axis powers to obtain their unconditional surrender; the second, to achieve a global postwar democratic system that would not be prejudiced or sundered by the emerging power of a Russian-directed Soviet Union — a communist quasi-empire ruled by a psychopath scarcely less dangerous to humanity than Adolf Hitler.

PART TWELVE

The Endgame

47

Close to Disaster

THE PRESIDENT HAD laid down the strategy and timetable of the war to defeat the Third Reich and then Japan, on behalf of the Western Allies; Churchill, for all that he feared a bloodbath in northern France, had had to comply. Yet to achieve the political results of the war that he wanted — a new world order — the President had need of Stalin. And in dealing with Stalin, he also had need of Winston Churchill, as a demonstration of unity between the U.S. and British governments. Roosevelt therefore asked the Prime Minister to come stay with him in Washington after Quebec. They would be together when the Italians, as seemed likely, surrendered. Above all, though, they would be together in showing Stalin there was no rift in the Western Allies: that the U.S.-British coalition was inviolable, and would remain so.

Early on August 26, 1943, the *Ferdinand Magellan* pulled into the little halt at Highland, north of New York, and the President was driven up to his family home. "The P. came from Ottawa, looking well," Daisy Suckley noted in her diary, "but tired. He said he would try to get rested before Churchill comes to Wash.[ington] next Wednesday. The Quebec Conference was a success but Russia is a worry — the P. said a message had come from Stalin which was 'rude — stupidly rude.' Churchill wanted to send back an answer — even ruder!"[1]

Stalin was not the only problem. There was the question of how Hitler would react, once the Italians surrendered and U.S. and British armies landed on the mainland of Europe, as they planned to do in the coming days. Though in a sense it was only a diversion in order to keep the Germans from beating the Russians and away from the eventual beaches of Normandy, the Allied assault on Italy would reveal whether Churchill was right, or the President: whether the Germans would collapse, or whether Italy would turn out to be a hornet's nest.

All too soon they would find out.

In the domestic comfort of his Hyde Park home, Roosevelt meantime took things easy — with Admiral Leahy at his side. "Today ends a three day restful visit with the President at Hyde Park, where there were no demands on any of us at any time," Leahy noted in his diary on August 29, 1943, "and where we were completely relaxed after our strenuous Staff Conference in Canada."[2] "The P. was very cheerful & seemed relaxed," Daisy recorded. Taking the sun at his cottage he "sent for some eggs & bread & butter — He toasted the bread on the electric toaster, sitting by the fire on the sofa," and to unwind "talked about a good many phases of the present situation."[3]

The first landings in mainland Italy would begin on September 3, 1943: a crossing of the Strait of Messina by troops of Montgomery's British Eighth Army, which would hopefully draw Axis forces into close combat — and away from the primary invasion site: Salerno, where the major Allied assault would take place a week later. The Salerno landings would be a massive three-division invasion in the Gulf of Salerno, 270 miles north of Montgomery's army; it would plant major Allied forces close to Naples under U.S. general Mark Clark, and hopefully cut off German forces facing the British. Not content with this sweeping plan, Marshall had urged Eisenhower to use his Eighty-Second Airborne Division — not to ensure the success of the Salerno landings but to mount a yet more ambitious landing, 200 miles further north still. On Rome, from the air.

This operation would be called Giant II — perhaps the most misguided military undertaking of the war thus far. Churchill thought it a masterstroke, which would enable the Allies to seize Rome, the Italian capital, by coup de main. Were Rome to fall to the Allies, and the Italians turn against their former partners, who knew what might then transpire? The Third Reich might collapse like a house of cards.

The President remained doubtful; taking Rome would be nice in terms of morale and publicity, but it led nowhere, strategically, given the terrain in northern Italy. And Hitler, he was sure, would not fold his hand that easily. He thus left the campaign to Marshall and the chiefs of staff, confident that General Eisenhower would not be pressed into doing anything too foolish.

As it turned out, however, Eisenhower *was* so pressed — and the Allies, in the days that followed, came very close to disaster in Italy.

48

A Darwinian Struggle

HITLER, FOR HIS part, was contemptuous of Roosevelt's call for Allied unity in Quebec, as was Goebbels. The President's speech in Ottawa was dismissed as rhetoric. "It consisted of dull, stupid scolding and lacked any political substance," Goebbels sniffed in his diary. "It's not worth bothering about. One can see from the speech, and the terrific reception it was given by Canadian members of Parliament, though, just how half-witted the public is over there. Roosevelt threatens military operations, but refrains from being specific, because he probably can't be. He ends by quoting Jesus, which is all-of-a-piece with his bizarre and misbegotten character."[1]

For both the Reich minister and the Führer, the world was now entering the vortex of a great Darwinian struggle of survival — a struggle in which only the strongest would emerge. Italy was exhibiting weakness, would most likely crumble, and would have to be sacrificed on an altar of blood; Germany, by contrast, would only grow stronger, more savage — and more ruthless once unencumbered by allies.

Those among the Allies who hoped Germany's generals or Wehrmacht soldiers would lose heart in their leader were to be disappointed. Hitler and Goebbels's *Weltanschauung,* including their *Nibelungentreue,* was to be largely replicated among German civilians across the Third Reich — and among German troops across the occupied countries. Goebbels noted, for example, how contented were German soldiers, returning on leave from the frontline to their relatives in the German homeland — yet how angry, stunned, and surprised they were at the effects of RAF and U.S. Air Force bombing on the civilian population.

The question, then, arose for Goebbels as the propaganda genius of the Third Reich: could the war be prolonged for another six months or a year by stubborn German defense of the nations the Wehrmacht had conquered in western, southern, and eastern Europe — keeping the enemy as far as possible from Germany until the Führer's *Vergeltungswaffen,* or V-bombs, were ready to be launched?

On his last visit to the Wolf's Lair, Goebbels had found the Führer disinclined to think Kharkov as being in danger — at least, if it was in danger, there should be no mention of it in public. "Wir kämpfen an allen Fronten, im Süden wie im Osten, möglichst weit vom heimatlichen Boden entfernt, um den Krieg vom Reichsgebiet fernzuhalten" — "We are fighting on all fronts — in the South as well as the East, as far from home ground as possible — in order to keep the war as far as we can from the Reich," Hitler had declared — while doing everything in his power as führer to counter Allied air power, from expediting German antiaircraft guns to greater priority for jet-engined Messerschmitt fighters, better radar, and new interception tactics.[2]

As this was ordered, the question of a political solution had meantime become more and more tempting. How could Goebbels and the German Foreign Ministry exploit the widely suspected split between the Western Allies and the Soviets? Could they persuade either Churchill or Stalin to negotiate an armistice with the Third Reich, and thus avoid war on two fronts?

"I ask the Führer whether he thinks we might be able to make an accommodation with Stalin, over time," Goebbels noted on his next visit to the Wolf's Lair. "For the moment, however, the Führer thinks not," he recorded, disappointed. Moreover, the Führer was unwilling to surrender, if negotiations could be started, the Ukraine: the breadbasket of Europe and crucial for Germany's food needs. "In general," Goebbels noted, "he thinks it more likely we would have more success in doing something with the British rather than the Soviets." As the British came to realize that fighting the Wehrmacht on European soil was very different from war in faraway North Africa, they would surely "come to their senses" — especially once German V-bombs began to rain down on London.

"It's true Churchill is an absolute anti-Bolshevist," Goebbels agreed with Hitler — a Churchillian stance that might be manipulated to get him to abandon his antifascist rhetoric and agenda in favor of anticommunism. Given Churchill's Mansion House speech, in November 1942, warning that he would never allow the dissolution of the British Empire, the Prime Minister might well be open to new peace feelers, Hitler intimated, if convinced Britain could not win the war militarily. Churchill was "naturally pursuing British imperial objectives in this war, as in the last. Now that he has Sicily in his pocket he's in a good position," Goebbels recorded their conversation. "The Italians will never get Sicily back, for with Calabria and Sicily in British hands Churchill will control the whole Mediterranean as an English ocean, for all time . . . So the Führer thinks the English rather than the Russians will be more willing to come to an arrangement in the end."[3]

Knowing Churchill, Goebbels was skeptical, however. "I don't see any sign of this happening," he admitted in the privacy of his diary, whatever Hitler might think — though he did not dare say so to the Führer. Besides, the matter of an armistice either with the British or the Russians was academic, since the split between the Allies had not reached the point where they could be prised apart — yet. Nevertheless, the "controversy between the Soviets and the Anglo-Americans is really serious," Goebbels noted with satisfaction. "Our information from Quebec is quite clear about that." However, "the Führer doesn't think the crisis in the enemy camp is ripe enough to exploit at the moment. So we have to wait, and make sure we get both our fronts back under control. That is a sine qua non: that we have to stand firm where we are. A faltering military power can't be looking for an arrangement."[4]

September 1943, then, would reveal whether the Allied coalition was going to hold together, or could be brought to stalemate on the battlefield and either the Western Allies or Russia be persuaded to sue for an armistice with Germany.

49

A Talk with Archbishop Spellman

"I LEFT QUEBEC by train, and arrived at the White House on September 1," Churchill recorded in his memoirs. "I deliberately prolonged my stay in the United States in order to be in close contact with our American friends at this critical moment in Italian affairs."[1]

News had come from General Eisenhower that the post-Mussolini government of Italy, under Marshal Badoglio, had secretly agreed to surrender, once American and British troops were established on the mainland of Italy — and two days later, on September 3, Montgomery's troops crossed the Strait of Messina to Reggio, where they encountered negligible opposition. Italian forces simply abandoned their posts, in anticipation of imminent surrender, while Wehrmacht forces laid mines, detonated bridges, and staged a fighting withdrawal from Calabria.

Staying in Washington with the President, the Prime Minister seemed dangerously overconfident about impending victory in Italy. "Churchill does not think," Mackenzie King had already noted in his diary on August 31, as the British prime minister set off from Quebec, that "the further fighting in Italy will occasion anything like the loss of life that the fighting in Sicily has occasioned."[2]

The President certainly wished Winston to be by his side when the Italian surrender took place. But in truth, there was a more important, underlying reason for Churchill to stay at the White House — a purpose both men had agreed was vital not only to the winning of the war, but the postwar. For whatever happened on the ground in Italy, it was understood by the two leaders, the unity of the *Western* Allies must be further symbolized, beyond the conference in Canada, and an incontrovertible message of common purpose be sent not just to Hitler and the world, but to Stalin in Moscow.

The Western Allies, this message went, would hold together in pursuing the defeat of Germany — *and beyond.*

Though he could barely contain his excitement over Montgomery's crossing at Messina and Clark's impending invasion at Salerno, Churchill made every effort to be patient and good company to the President. Mrs. Roosevelt was still on her tour of the Pacific, requiring Daisy Suckley to stand in for her as White House hostess, and at Hyde Park. In her diary she noted the "intensely interesting" conversations at table — the President "full of charm, always tactful, even when he has to be 'painfully' truthful & perhaps harsh. He is harsh, but with a smile which tells you you are wrong, but there is no ill-feeling toward you because of the wrong — It's more that you are mistaken — in all probability because you don't know the facts. I've never known a person who so consistently tries not to hurt people."[3]

Churchill, by contrast, "snaps out disapproval. They say he fights with everyone" — not just Hitler; "jumps all over them. One person alone he doesn't jump on," Daisy added, however, "& that is the P.! The P. laughs about it: he says that if the P.M. ever did jump on him, he would just laugh at him! As I have said before, the P.M. loves F.D.R." Moreover, Daisy had had this confirmed, from the highest authority, for "Mrs C[hurchill]. told me that, too, out of a clear sky."

"The P.M. recognizes in the P. a man with a greater soul & a broader outlook than his own — It is very evident to a person who has had such wonderful opportunities to see them as I have. I consider W.S.C. a 'great man,' also, but he has not yet achieved the spiritual freedom of F.D.R. . . . They get along beautifully, and understand each other. The P. is all for the Democratic ideal because he loves it & believes in it. The P.M. is working for it because he thinks it is inevitable . . ."[4]

Daisy was naturally biased, but she was also perspicacious — and one of the only people, other than the President's White House doctor, who was watching Roosevelt's health. Churchill's daughter Mary, traveling now with her mother, Clementine, found "the pres magnetic & full of charm" as she wrote in her own diary; "his sweetness to me is something I shall always remember — But he is a raconteur," she noted, and in all honesty, aged only twenty, she found his stories "tedious" at times, though "at other times it is interesting & fun" — a "cute, cunning old-bird — if ever there was one. But I still know who gets my vote," she added loyally — her father probably the most eloquent raconteur alive. "Every evening FDR makes extremely violent cocktails in his study. Fala attends — & it is all very agreeable & warm. At dinner Mummie is on his right, & several nights no other guests being there I've been on his left. I am devoted to him & admire him tremendously — He seems to have fearless courage & an art of selecting the warmest moment of the iron."[5]

Still so young, Mary thought both her father and the President indestructible. She did, however, find herself intrigued, as was Daisy Suckley, by the "contrast" between their two characters. "To me," she noted in her diary, Roosevelt "seems at once idealistic — cynical — warm hearted & generous — worldly-wise — naïve — courageous — tough — thoughtful — charming — tedious — vain — sophisticated — civilised — all these and more for 'by their works ye shall know them' — And what a stout hearted champion he has been for the unfortunate & the battling — and what a monument he will always have in the minds of men. And yet while I admire him intensely and could not but be devoted to him after his great personal kindness to me — yet, I must confess [he] makes me laugh & he rather bores me."[6]

The truth was, the President had had other things on his mind, despite doing his best to keep the Churchills and their daughter entertained. He'd dined on September 2 with Winston and Averell Harriman — who was to be his new ambassador to the Soviet Union — to discuss Russia. Also present at the meal was Francis Spellman, the archbishop of New York, who was returning after a long inspection tour of American units overseas, as the vicar military responsible for all Catholic priests in the United States.

The next morning — the day Montgomery's troops crossed onto the mainland of Italy — Spellman came to see the President privately at the White House for another hour. The Archbishop was concerned about the Allied bombing of Rome — where he'd spent the greater part of his adult life. Spellman had shown as little concern about the alleged extermination of European Jews as his mentor who had promoted him to the top American see in 1939: the pope, Pius XII. Now that Rome itself was threatened with heavy bombing, however, Spellman was deeply worried. Moreover, he was becoming concerned over Russian designs on European countries yet to be liberated — especially Catholic Poland.

As Spellman had found on his tour overseas, American officials in Iran (where the majority of U.S. Lend-Lease supplies were now being delivered) were disgusted at the way the Russians behaved. It was as if every

Russian lived in terror of being accused of cooperation with their allies, or worse: sharing secrets with a quasi-enemy. Spellman's "information is that two of the four freedoms as we understand them, — freedom of expression and freedom of religion, — do not exist in Russia."[7]

The President was all too aware of this. What to do, though? Spellman had hitherto raised no protest over the President's conduct of the war, and at the White House he now found the President extraordinarily frank about the chances of American forces being able to stop two hundred Russian divisions from doing whatever Stalin pleased, at a time when the United States did not yet have a single boot on mainland Europe. The President certainly hoped to "get from Stalin a pledge not to extend Russian territory beyond a certain line," but there was little the United States could do when Stalin "had the power to get them anyway" — "them" being Finland (which had been a Russian duchy from 1809 through 1917), the Baltic States (a part of the Russian Empire from the eighteenth century until 1917), the eastern half of Poland (partitioned by Russia, Prussia, and Austria in the wake of the Russo-Polish war of 1792, and much of it a czardom until 1918), and Bessarabia (a czarist governorate from 1812 until 1917). Such countries might *want* to retain their recent independence, but the President was sanguine. "There is no point to oppose these desires of Stalin, because he has the power to get them anyhow. So better give them gracefully."[8]

"Give" them?

In later years — especially once the United States became a nuclear superpower, with global military reach — Roosevelt's acceptance of the inevitable would be seen as shocking, even immoral, especially for a president who was so idealistic.[9] Right-wing American critics of Roosevelt such as Senators Robert A. Taft and Arthur H. Vandenberg, fired by American exceptionalism, would deplore such a "giveaway," but the criticism reflected their historical ignorance and lack of realism.[10] No one at that time had any idea how the United States could have approached the matter differently, given U.S. military weakness, with no soldiers yet in mainland Europe — and little idea how effective those soldiers would be, once they reengaged with Wehrmacht forces on European soil.

At a moment when the Third Reich still extended from the shores of France to the Ukraine, and when Hitler, Goebbels, and Ribbentrop seriously hoped to split the Allied alliance and compel the British to negotiate an armistice in the manner of Munich in 1938, or get Stalin to renew the Ribbentrop Pact, the President saw his main priority in avoiding a premature collapse of the Grand Alliance before the Western Allies even landed in force on the European mainland. As he made clear to Spellman, one had to be realistic. Over time, he was sure, the Russians would become more civilized — especially when having to interact and compete with Western economies. Unless they somehow remained a closed society, under lock and key, they would eventually be forced to adapt to Western cultural influences.

Such a long-term view left open the question of the imminent fate of western European nations, however — nations the United States *could,* realistically, hope to save, as long as the President could get Churchill and the British to throw themselves wholeheartedly into the cross-Channel assault the following spring. Once these nations were liberated, however, would the American public support tough American peacekeeping, in countering Russian influence, after the war? Taking soundings nationwide, Judge Rosenman had warned the President that, politically, he would have to be more careful in his speechmaking with regard to postwar security, if he or any Democratic nominee wished to prevail in the 1944 election. "People are almost twice as much interested in domestic affairs as international affairs," Rosenman passed on to the President the conclusion of a recent opinion poll. Two-thirds of those polled did not wish even to provide "aid to foreign countries after the war," let alone have to keep the peace in Europe.[11]

Such findings did not stop the President from pursuing his vision of a United Nations authority, with the Four Policemen acting on the UN's behalf. It did, however, cause him to wonder how far he could single-handedly change or guide American public opinion to back such a vision. What would be the fallout, the President and the Archbishop wondered, if the United States did *not* take the leading role? Would Britain — virtually bankrupt and, pace Churchill, far more concerned with avoiding the dissolution of its colonial empire than maintaining European peace — be able to marshal sufficient will and force of arms to do the job: namely holding the Soviets at bay, if and when they began to "Bolshevize" the continent after the fall of Hitler?

From reports of communist governments in exile in Moscow it was evident Stalin intended, if possible, to install communist puppet regimes beyond Russia's borders: in Germany, Austria, and probably other bordering states. This would make it unnecessary for the Soviets to keep their forces there, beyond establishing bases. Roosevelt "agreed this is to be expected. Asked further, whether the Allies would not do something from their side which might offset this move in giving encouragement to the better elements, just as Russia encourages the Communists, he declared that no such move was contemplated [by the United States]. It is therefore probable that Communist Regimes would expand, but what could we do about it?"[12]

Archbishop Spellman was disappointed — but could see the problem: namely the American electorate. Although, in the wake of the President's State of the Union speech and his Casablanca summit, there had been a growing acceptance in Republican circles of the idea of American involvement in international decision-making once the war was won, there was still a deep core of the American public wedded to isolationism.

To push through American membership in a United Nations organization, given President Wilson's failure in 1920 with respect to the League of Nations, would already be a tremendous challenge. To achieve this, Roosevelt was ready to stand for a fourth term in 1944. But offering a platform of American intercession in European politics, with the possibility of yet another war to be fought there — this time with the Soviet Union, which not even Hitler's two hundred divisions had been able to defeat — was unlikely to fly.

The President sounded, for once, almost defeatist. "France might possibly escape" such a puppet fate, if its people elected a sufficiently socialist government, so that "eventually the Communists might eventually accept it. On the direct question whether the odds were that Austria, Hungary or Croatia would fall under some sort of Russian protectorate, the answer was clearly yes." Hopefully, with the Soviets industrializing their economy, the outlook would not necessarily be so terrible in terms of European people's standard of living. "It is natural that the European countries will have to undergo tremendous changes in order to adapt to Russia, but he hopes that in ten or twenty years the European influences would bring the Russians to become less barbarian."[13]

The President's hopes on this score would, in the end, take more than forty years to be met — not ten or twenty. Spellman, however, did not contest the President's crystal ball after his own foreign trip, for it seemed too grounded. The archbishop was only disappointed that Mr. Roosevelt, normally such a figure of moral as well as physical courage, should be so laissez-faire. As the President put it: "The European people will have to endure the Russian domination, in the hope that in ten or twenty years they will be able to live well with the Russians" — the Russians gradually becoming more civilized, while the Europeans became more egalitarian. "Finally he hopes, the Russians will get 40% of the Capitalist regime, the capitalists will retain only 60% of their system, and so an understanding will be possible. This is the opinion of Litvinoff," too, the recent Soviet ambassador to Washington, the President averred.[14]

Litvinov had been recalled to Moscow, however, not simply for talks, but to be replaced in October by a "barbarian" apparatchik: Andrei Gromyko.

Spellman, who had spent so many years at the Vatican earlier in his career, wondered at the almost dispirited view of the President regarding the future of Europe: the very cradle of civilization, and the home of so many Christians. Roosevelt had always been against "spheres of influence" in the world, but was now talking of "an agreement among the Big Four. Accordingly the world will be divided into spheres of influence: China get the Far East; the U.S. the Pacific; Britain and Russia, Europe and Africa. But as Britain has predominantly colonial interests it might be assumed that Russia will predominate."[15]

It was an unenviable scenario for Europe. "Although Chiang Kai-shek will be called in on the great decisions concerning Europe, it is understood that he will have no influence on them," the President explained. "The same thing might become true — although to a lesser degree — for the U.S.," in terms of meager American "influence on decisions concerning Europe." The President "hoped, 'although it might be wishful thinking,' that the Russian intervention in Europe might not be too harsh."[16]

Stalin "not too harsh"?

Was the President serious? American knowledge about the Soviet regime, thanks to Russian secrecy, was admittedly minimal, but from the head of U.S. foreign intelligence, General Donovan, the President had received an all-too-real picture of Stalin's system of mass deportation, arrests, executions, and rule of fear. The President's realism concerning Russia, in fact, went way back to his instructions when sending Ambassador Bullitt to Moscow to establish the first U.S. embassy in Soviet Russia: "You will be more or less in the position of Commander Byrd — cut off from civilization."[17]

The President's view of communist Russians as "barbarians" had not changed since then. Tragic though it might be, Stalin the Barbarian had survived as dictator of the USSR. As had communist Russia itself, despite facing the greatest war-assault ever mounted in military history.

Was Russian nationalist barbarianism reason enough, though, for the United States to hold back and watch while the struggle for Europe was — as in the 1930s — left to others? Could a near-bankrupt Britain be expected to master events in western Europe any better than it had in 1940, let alone in central or eastern Europe? Its military forces had been evacuated from the continent in Norway and at Dunkirk in 1940, been trounced in North Africa and rebuffed with ease at Dieppe in 1942, and even in 1943 its prime minister was really only backing a 1944 cross-Channel attack in deference to the President's will — Churchill concerned, still, that it could be a disaster if indeed it took place . . .

Britain, in short, could not be depended upon as a military power in Europe in its own right.

If Soviet domination of Europe was to be the ultimate price of defeating the Nazis, then, should American sons be sent to Europe at all? Here the President sounded more positive, for he was by no means defeatist about the larger, global picture. The League of Nations had been "no success, because the small states were allowed to intervene," he said — leading to a state of anarchy that Hitler had exploited, allowing him to conquer most of Europe by force. The lesson was therefore simple. Once Hitler was defeated, it had to be assumed postwar peace could only be guaranteed by "the four big powers (U.S., Britain, Russia, China)." The United States would be supreme in its own hemisphere, and across the Pacific. But did that mean that the security of the heartland of modern civilization — a civilization built on the foundations laid by the Greeks and the Romans — should be handed over to the British, who were weak, and the Russians, "because they are big, strong and simply impose themselves"? the vicar military asked.[18]

The President shrugged — unsure how the future would play out, and whether American voters would support a permanent American presence in Europe. All that could be said with certainty at this juncture was that, after waging two vast and destructive wars in Europe in the space of thirty years, Germany was clearly too powerful a nation to be allowed to threaten world peace again. It should, he thought, be divided up into numerous states — "Bavaria, Rhineland, Saxony, Hesse, Prussia," and "disarmed for forty years," he asserted. "No air force, no civilian aviation, no German would be authorized to learn flying." Austria, though

Catholic, could not be saved from a "Russian dominated Communist Regime." Hungary, by contrast, might be saved — "He likes the Hungarians. He wants them to come over," Spellman quoted the President's view. "He would be ready to accept them on the Allied side as they are, if they come over." The only states where self-determination would actually be guaranteed — presumably by Britain — would be in western Europe: "Plebiscites would be held in the following countries: France, Italy, Netherlands, Belgium, Norway, Greece" — but not even Czechoslovakia, which he doubted could be saved in time.[19]

Western Poland, on September 3, 1943, went unmentioned.

The Allied "side."

Hungary coming "over" . . .

It was clear the President foresaw a division of Europe into an Allied West and a Russian-dominated East in the not-too-distant future, now that British Eighth Army troops, having crossed onto mainland Italy, were beginning to fight their way north.

Spellman, who had supported Roosevelt against the bitter denunciations of Father Charles Coughlin in 1936, as well as in confronting the Axis powers after Pearl Harbor, was made acutely aware by the President of the domestic political challenge: how to get the American public to endorse, after the fall of the Third Reich, even the remotest possibility of another war to "save" specific nations in central Europe, and push back the Soviets, once they established themselves there.

Leaving the conundrum up to the President, the Archbishop focused, for his part, on pressing for Rome — as well as its environs in a twenty-mile safe zone — to be considered an "open city" in order to protect the Vatican and Rome's historic churches: "what to do for Holy See," as he put it.[20]

Nevertheless, the President's somewhat dispirited "realism" worried him. Was the President ailing?

50

The Empires of the Future

THOUGH NOT PRIVY to the President's discussions with the British prime minister, young Mary Churchill was aware that, though almost a decade younger than her father, Mr. Roosevelt was not one hundred percent well.

Decades older than Mary, Daisy Suckley was noticing the same — and was concerned. The President had returned from Canada in apparent good health, yet sported "dark rings under his eyes" — and was finding it more difficult to exhibit the abiding confidence and humor that were his trademark as a leader.

For his part Harry Hopkins seemed ill — but that, at least, showed in public. In Roosevelt's case, the President refused to show weakness, let alone signs of illness. "This is one noticeable way in which the P. is so outstanding," Daisy noted. Others seemed positively "shell-shocked" by the pace and demands of government and command in war, whereas the President "is completely normal mentally & spiritually, although he has in a way, more responsibility than anyone," she described.[1] Roosevelt would not even permit Ross McIntire, his doctor, to accompany him to Hyde Park — nor would he allow McIntire to bring in a medical consultant to assess his cardiac and circulatory health, lest word leak out he might not be up to the trials of a fourth presidential election, were he to stand.

Daisy thus worried that Churchill's extended stay at the White House, with his wife, daughter, and immediate staff — military, clerical, private — to boot, was simply too demanding at a time when the First Lady was still away: leaving the President to have to take care of even the most basic aspects of hospitality.

What she did not quite understand was that Churchill was now the only man in the world who could help the President not only shoulder his great burdens, but stop the "barbarians" from occupying too much of eastern, central, and western Europe as the war progressed.

The responsibilities of being a national leader, and on top of that commander in chief in a world war, were almost literally crushing — and Daisy was certainly right to be anxious.

Hitler, for his part, was unwell, living in isolation, intimate only with his mistress, Eva Braun, and his dog, Blondi; Stalin associated only with those in literal terror of him — even instructing the NKVD to "investigate" his son and daughter by his second wife, Nadezhda Alliluyeva, who had allegedly committed suicide in 1932.[2] (Of his first wife, Ekatarina, who had died of tuberculosis in 1907, a year after their marriage, Stalin had reportedly said: "With her died my last warm feelings for humanity."[3])

Given that the Quebec Conference was over and that its military decisions would henceforth be carried out by the Combined Chiefs of Staff, twelve days of entertaining the Churchills did seem rather long, however, to Daisy. It appeared so even more to the press, who wondered why Churchill needed to spend so much time in Washington with the President. What was Churchill busy plotting now, if the big decisions had supposedly been made at Quebec? skeptics wondered.

It was in this respect that Dr. Goebbels was more insightful than Allied journalists. The fact that Churchill was spending so much time with the President in America spoke volumes to him. The Reichsminister and Führer might still hope for signs of a split in the Allied coalition, one that might help preserve the Third Reich and its armies. The President, however, seemed still master of world opinion. Hitler had spent only a few hours with Mussolini at Feltre, before the Duce's arrest. By contrast, hosting Churchill for almost two weeks, the President was demonstrating to the world the *solidarity* of the Western Allies — an even more symbolic demonstration, in fact, than the Quebec Conference.

Taking his cue, Churchill had settled in and talked to the President at length about the Russian menace, in front of Cardinal Spellman and others. As a result of those conversations, in fact, a new idea of Western unity began to emerge in the Prime Minister's fertile brain.

At 10:00 p.m. on September 5, Winston Churchill left the President and with his wife, Clemmie, and his daughter Mary, departed the White House and took the train to Boston.

The Prime Minister had cabled Field Marshal Smuts, the South African prime minister, writing: "I think it inevitable that Russia will be the greatest land power in the world after this war which will have rid her of the two military powers, Japan and Germany, who in our lifetime have inflicted upon her such heavy defeats. I hope, however, that the 'fraternal association' of the British Commonwealth and the United States together with sea and air power, may put us on good terms and in a friendly balance with Russia at least for the period of re-building. Further than that I cannot see with mortal eye, and I am not as yet fully informed about celestial telescopes."[4]

Unrecognized by most historians, however, this was in fact a new turning point in the war, as Churchill now sought not only to wed Britain to the United States in terms of defeating Hitler, but beyond that in dealing with the Soviet Union.

The truth was, without the help of the United States there was little hope Britain could, on its own, do much of anything to halt the advance of Soviet forces in Europe, or even combat Soviet communist "influence" there. *In partnership with the United States,* however, it could — possibly. It would require girding up the people of the United States to the challenge, but it was perhaps for this reason, rather than to perpetuate British colonialism, that he had been put on this earth. Churchill had earned huge respect for his moral courage in confronting Hitler, when Britain stood alone; as Prime Minister he now felt he must, as far as possible, use that continuing respect and public support to buck up the President; to help Americans, not simply Britons, embrace a new, quasi-imperial global role as the guarantors, as far as possible, of democracy and the four freedoms.

It was a tragedy the present war could not end as the triumph of democracy over fascism and tyranny, but as the President said, it could take a generation or more before the Russians cast off communist dictatorship and embraced anything like the four freedoms.

Distinct from Western norms of civilization, the Soviet Union remained a tyranny based on fear, paranoid secrecy, incarceration, deportation, mock justice, xenophobia, and ruthlessly Russian — as opposed to international — self-interest. How much better would history have been served had Stalin never been born! Stalin had, however — and his tough, dictatorial leadership had at least ensured the Soviet armies succeeded in halting Hitler's mad invasion, just as Napoleon's invasion army had been destroyed in the heart of Russia. Somehow, Churchill mused, it would be for the United States not only to create a United Nations authority that would help preserve the peace after the defeat of Hitler and the Japanese but—in partnership with the British—face up to the Russians . . .

Fortunately the Prime Minister liked to work long and late. No sooner had the train pulled out than "he started to compose his speech," his secretary, Elizabeth Layton, wrote home,[5] and together with Churchill's shorthand stenographer, Patrick Kinna, she took down his words over four hours of nighttime railroad dictation: his speech to be given at Harvard University on September 6, on the acceptance there of an honorary degree.

Churchill had already given some of the most memorable, indeed historic, speeches in the annals of rhetoric—rich in metaphor and in the sheer magnitude of his historical perspective. His Harvard University address, however, was to be special in that, three years before his famous "Iron Curtain" speech, Churchill now made an open appeal to the youth of America to assume responsibility not only to help win the war against current tyranny but to continue to do so thereafter: safeguarding democracy on behalf of those who could not, by virtue of their weakness, do so on their own.

To the "youth of America, as to the youth of Britain, I say 'You cannot stop,'" Churchill declared the next day in Harvard's famous Yard. "There is no halting-place at this point. We have now reached a stage in the journey where there can be no pause. We must go on. It must be world anarchy or world order." As he put it, "We do not war primarily with race as such. Tyranny is our foe, whatever trappings or disguise it wears, whatever language it speaks, be it external or internal, we must forever be on our guard, ever mobilized, ever vigilant, always ready to spring at its throat. In all this," he emphasized as a British prime minister speaking in America, "we march together. Not only do we march and strive shoulder to shoulder at this moment under the fire of the enemy on the fields of war or in the air, but also in those realms of thought which are consecrated to the rights and dignity of man." The British Commonwealth and the United States were now joined at the hip—not only in their common language, but in their willingness to fight alongside, even subordinate to, one another.

The Combined Chiefs of Staff was the clearest manifestation of this development: acting not only as the transatlantic advisory body to the two elected leaders, but as the de facto strategic command center of the forces of the United Nations. Churchill was therefore unapologetic in claiming it would be a "most foolish and improvident act on the part of our two Governments, or either of them, to break up this smooth-running and immensely powerful machinery the moment the war is over. For our own safety, as well as for the security of the rest of the world, we are bound to keep it working and in running order after the war — probably for a good many years, not only until we have set up some world arrangement to keep the peace but until we know that it is an arrangement which will really give us that protection we must have from danger and aggression" — a protection "we have," as Britons, "already had to seek across two vast world wars."

In all but name this was a warning not only to Hitler, but to Stalin: that the English-speaking democracies of the world should — and would — hold together to confront and defeat tyranny and the evils of a police state. "Various schemes of achieving world security while yet preserving national rights, tradition and customs are being studied and probed," the Prime Minister acknowledged: a search to develop a system more durable and effective than the League of Nations. "I am here to tell you," he declared, though, "that whatever form your system of world security may take, however the nations are grouped and ranged, whatever derogations are made from national sovereignty for the sake of the large synthesis, nothing will work soundly or for long without the united effort of the British and American peoples."

"If we are together," Churchill declared, "nothing is impossible. If we are divided all will fail," he warned. How proud Americans and Britons could be, then, "young and old alike" to live at a time in the story of man when "these great trials came upon it" — and had found, he declared, "a generation that terror could not conquer and brutal violence could not enslave."[6]

The speech even contained the most stunning suggestion: that not only should Britons and Americans continue their military alliance after the war, but even resume a "common citizenship."[7]

While there was little enthusiasm expressed in America for common citizenship — the United States, after all, having waged a revolutionary war to achieve independence from the British Empire — Churchill's remarks, at the very moment when cables were being exchanged between the President's Map Room and the Kremlin regarding the need for high-level U.S., British, and Soviet meetings, were welcomed by newspapers in

America, England, and United Nations countries. An initial meeting of the Big Three's foreign ministers was in the works for October; then a Big Three summit to be held hopefully in November or December, 1943 . . .

Beyond the imminent amphibious Allied assault at Salerno and airdrop on Rome, then, there were larger issues at stake.

The United States was at last entering upon its manifest destiny not only as a world power, but as *the* leading power of the free world, Churchill accepted — and while no one knew which way France and other occupied countries would eventually turn, there was no doubt as to where he, the President's "ardent lieutenant" and "representative of the British War Cabinet," stood.

It would not be easy. "The price of greatness is responsibility," Churchill solemnly warned at Harvard. "Let us go forward in malice to none and good will to all. Such plans offer far better prizes than taking away other people's provinces or lands or grinding them down in exploitation. The empires of the future," the once-implacable British imperialist maintained, "are the empires of the mind."[8]

Such a bold assertion of Anglo-American solidarity would not stop Stalin from controlling those eastern and central European countries the Soviet armies might well overrun, as they combined with the United States and Britain to defeat the forces of the Third Reich. It left no doubt, however — whether in Hitler's mind, Goebbels's, or Stalin's — that the Western Allies, led by the United States and Britain, would not rest until the evils of the Third Reich were ended, and in the aftermath that they would remain united: intent upon blocking any attempt by Stalin to expand into western Europe a Soviet empire of gulag and fear.

51

A Tragicomedy of Errors

WHILE CHURCHILL GAVE his support to the notion of a new, internationalist America, General Eisenhower faced the problem of the military and political prosecution of the current war in the Mediterranean.

It did not go quite as planned. Indeed, blame for the near-catastrophe that befell the Allies in Italy ultimately rested with the two commanders in chief in Washington, historians would rightly aver[1] — for the failure to make clear to Eisenhower that his task was merely to occupy southern Italy while the Overlord invasion of northern France was prepared permitted the most dangerous optimism and false hopes to spread among the senior ranks of U.S. and British forces in the Mediterranean.

Thus the tragedy unfolded.

Churchill, so magnificent in his appreciation of the larger forces of history and tyranny, once again demonstrated an impetuous military opportunism — an aspect of his character he had never been able to control. Without General Brooke at his side in Washington to restrain him, he yearned for the Allies to swiftly seize Rome, as in the days of the Caesars — rightly seeing in it a prize whose capture would electrify both the free and the occupied countries of the world. The image across the world evoked by Italian unconditional surrender and the Allied occupation of Rome would be the second "crack in the Axis" that the President had spoken of in Ottawa.

These were understandable political and moral ambitions for the Allies — achievements that would impress the Soviets (who were still nowhere near evicting the German armies from the USSR).

Unfortunately, neither agenda took account of the Wehrmacht's likely response. Nor did it account for the invidious dilemma into which it placed Badoglio's Italian government: whether the country was to be destroyed alongside the Germans — or by the Germans.

As the days of early September passed, then, the various headquarters in the Mediterranean suffered a fatal lack of clear strategic direction from the President, the Prime Minister, and the Combined Chiefs of Staff. The President favored only a limited Allied military campaign, but was less than clear where it should end — whether in the south of Italy, in order to secure the important all-weather Foggia airfields, or as far as Rome. In fact, in a moment of levity, having summoned the chiefs to the White House to discuss the "strategic situation in light of Italian collapse," he suggested that "a new slogan should be adopted" for the campaign in Italy: "Save the Pope"![2] He was not anxious to go further, however, lest the buildup for Overlord be compromised.

By contrast the Prime Minister wanted to drive right up to the mountains of Tuscany, and there "establish a fortified line to seal off the north of Italy; a line prepared in depth which Italian divisions should help us man and so strong that it would make it very costly for the Germans to do anything effective against us." In the meantime, he urged, the Allies should do everything in their power to seize the Dodecanese islands such as Rhodes and put pressure on Turkey to enter the war.[3] The Allies would then possess a huge staging post in southern Europe to strike, in the event of a German collapse, toward southern France, the Balkans, Greece, or even northern Italy through the so-called Ljubljana Gap and Austria.

Behind the rejoicing over the recent conquest of Sicily and the first Allied boots on the mainland of Europe, across the Messina Strait — where Italian forces simply fled, and British Eighth Army troops had only to follow retreating Wehrmacht survivors of the Sicilian campaign — the real situation for the Allies began, in all truth, to border on the farcical.

"He is host & hostess & housekeeper all in one," Daisy reflected of her hero, the President — for it seemed really amazing with what ease Roosevelt had switched from a meeting of the Joint Chiefs of Staff at the White House to arranging trips of his English guests to Williamsburg, Virginia, or from reviewing British Eighth Army progress with General Ismay, at Hyde Park, to showing his guests his library before they finally left. Major military forces — land, sea, and air — were being committed to battle in the Mediterranean, but without clear and realistic strategic objectives passed down the Allied chain of command, the situation in the Mediterranean became daily more complicated.

Tasked with obtaining, if possible, the unconditional surrender of all Italian forces in Italy, southern France, the Balkans, and Greece, General Eisenhower had begun parleys with the emissaries of Marshal Badoglio, while having to decide what to do about General Patton's latest scandal (a report by the U.S. chief medical officer in the Mediterranean claiming Patton was psychologically and behaviorally unfit to command U.S. forces after striking battle-traumatized soldiers);[4] planning and commanding an invasion of Italy with limited resources (since Overlord was now to have logistical priority) and unclear strategic objectives; and having to meld as supreme commander in the Mediterranean the international ground, navy, and air force contributions to that uncertain challenge.

In the Torch invasion and campaign, the Allies had made a plethora of errors — errors that had taken place in an area occupied only by Vichy troops. This had permitted the U.S. and supporting British troops to establish themselves in overwhelming force before Hitler could react. In Husky, again, only two German divisions were on hand to repel boarders — even Hitler conceding it would be impossible to hold Sicily for more than a few weeks. But now, as the Allies prepared to invade the mainland of southern Europe in considerable force and from two different directions, the challenge changed. Montgomery had already complained on August 19 that his "Baytown" landing across the Messina Strait had no strategic objective; when pressed, Eisenhower's land forces commander, General Alexander, could only say Montgomery was to "engage enemy forces in the southern tip of Italy," and thus give "more assistance" to "Avalanche" — the four-division assault on Salerno, three hundred miles away on Italy's west coast, near Naples.

Three hundred miles, Monty had whistled! "If Avalanche is a success, then we should reinforce that front for there is little point in laboriously fighting our way up Southern Italy," his headquarters staff had protested — vainly. For his part, Montgomery, having faced the cream of the Afrika Corps since the battle of Alamein, was deeply skeptical whether Avalanche, south of Naples, would be the sort of walkover that Eisenhower and Alexander's headquarters assumed. Or Mark Clark — the as-yet-untested commander of the U.S. Fifth Army, tasked with the amphibious assault there. "The Germans had some 15 Divisions in Italy and at least four could be concentrated fairly quickly against the 5 American Army," Montgomery wrote in his diary after listening to Clark's presentation of the Avalanche plan.[5] He vigorously disputed, as the Allies' most professional if slow field commander, any idea of an easy run. So did the swifter Patton, when shown the task given to Clark. Given the hills surrounding the beautiful beaches, the "avalanche" might well come to a halt on the shore without chance of reaching Naples — let alone Rome.

As if this was not all, the plan — pressed by General Marshall — to land U.S. airborne troops on Rome was even less prudent; indeed Giant II, as it was code-named, was arguably one of the most ill-conceived near-blunders of the entire war.

General Eisenhower later confided that he "wanted very much to make the air drop on Rome," and was so "anxious to get in there," at Marshall's urging, that he removed the Eighty-Second Airborne Division from Mark Clark's Avalanche invasion force for the purpose. Somewhat surprised, General Matt Ridgway was thus ordered by the Allied commander in chief Mediterranean to drop his Eighty-Second Airborne Division on the Italian capital instead.[6]

Eisenhower's chief of staff, General Bedell Smith — a brilliant staff officer, but wholly ignorant of combat — proved equally naive, not only then but even after the event. He considered it would have been a "bold move, and it would have caught the Germans off balance" — causing Field Marshal Kesselring to retreat "immediately . . . Caught by the surprise of the American airborne landing in Rome and with his communications cut, Kesselring would have been compelled to retire to the North, and to abandon all southern and central Italy," Smith later asserted.[7]

At West Point, such boldness might have been lauded — in theory. Would the Italians, even if they were ordered to surrender to the Allies by Marshall Badoglio, actually lift a finger, however, to challenge let alone fight the Germans, who had two armored divisions surrounding Rome, and more approaching? Although General Alexander had browbeaten General Castellano, Badoglio's secret representative, into promising four divisions of Italian troops to aid Ridgway's assault from the sky, Montgomery certainly remained deeply skeptical. The "Italians won't do anything" he predicted — and Ridgway and his artillery director, General Max Taylor, feared the same. Indeed — though trashed after the war by both Bedell Smith and general Eisenhower's intelligence chief, Brigadier Kenneth Strong — Ridgway and Taylor refused to commit thousands of their paratroopers' lives to a wild plan, concocted in an "all night session" in a tent in Sicily, without further research.[8] General Taylor and a companion—Colonel William Gardiner—were therefore authorized to go behind the enemy lines, in advance of the airborne drop, to interview the commander of all Italian forces in Rome.

Transported in disheveled uniforms—posing as POWs being taken from the coast at Gaeta to the outskirts of the capital, then in an ambulance with frosted windows to the Italian War Office in Rome—Taylor and Gardiner only got to see General Carbonari at 9:30 p.m. on September 7, roughly twenty-four hours before the 150 C-54 paratroopers' planes of the Eighty-Second Airborne Division were due to take off from Sicily. A draft Instrument of Surrender—approved by President Roosevelt and by Prime Minister Churchill—had been signed on behalf of Badoglio on September 3, but had been held back in order to give the Germans no chance of preempting the Eighty-Second Airborne's drop on Rome, or Clark's invasion at Salerno, at dawn on September 9.

The paratroopers, however, did not go in—mercifully. Once Taylor reached Rome, General Carbonari explained that there were twelve thousand German paratroopers and twenty-four thousand men of the German Third Panzer Grenadier Division, with tanks, encircling the city. The American landing area was *twenty miles* from Rome; only two U.S. battalions could be airlifted in the first wave, and the Italian divisions had ammunition for only a few hours fighting—if that.

Taylor and Gardiner were agog. General Alexander, a Brit, had predicted Clark's land forces would reach Rome from Salerno, hundreds of miles away, in only three—five, at maximum—days, to relieve them.[9] It was a prediction near-criminal in its credulity—and cavalierness. Without genuine Italian assistance from the four Italian divisions, Taylor foresaw, the Eighty-Second's airdrop would be a bloodbath: an American one. He rightly demanded to see Marshal Badoglio—who, when roused from his bed, was even more defeatist, Taylor found.[10]

Badoglio had seen no fighting since 1940, and now disavowed the very Instrument of Surrender he had authorized by cable—saying he had not signed it, and had only given way to temporary telephone agreement when General Alexander threatened his emissary to destroy Rome by bombing. His representative in the negotiation "did not know all the facts," he told Taylor; "Italian troops cannot possibly defend Rome." In fact he predicted grave "difficulties" for the Allies if they landed at Salerno, given the number of German troops in the area and those streaming down with more tanks from the north. When Taylor tried the same tactic as General Alexander — threatening to bomb the Eternal City, unless the Italians carried out the proposed surrender — Badoglio merely looked at him. "Why would you want to bomb the city of the people who are trying to aid you?"[11]

Trying — but not very hard. Certainly not hard enough to save the Eighty-Second Airborne Division from extinction.

There followed a veritable tragicomedy of errors as Taylor's secret wireless signals to Eisenhower's headquarters and to General Ridgway, in Sicily, failed to get through. By the time Eisenhower called off the operation — sending Alexander's American deputy, General Lemnitzer, in person to Sicily to stop it — more than fifty C-47s with their paratroop companies were already in the air, circling the departure airfield. Firing an emergency warning flare, Lemnitzer — crammed behind the pilot in a British Beaufighter — managed to land with the cancel order, and the planes were instructed by radio to return to base.

It was a near-run thing.

But for Mark Clark's Fifth Army there was no cancellation or reprieve as, like the cavalry in the famous Charge of the Light Brigade, they were convoyed through the night toward the beaches of Salerno, and a most unwelcome welcome.

52

Meeting Reality

TOUCHING DOWN AT dawn on September 9, 1943, the Western Allies finally met reality. It was to be the most venomously contested amphibious invasion since Dieppe — contested by major Wehrmacht forces.

With the assent of the President and the Prime Minister, the "unconditional surrender" of all Italian forces had finally been announced on Allied radio in Algiers by General Eisenhower at 6:30 p.m. on September 8, in order to give the Germans the least possible time to man the beaches at Salerno. There was no confirming announcement on Rome radio by Marshal Badoglio, however — and for ten minutes it looked as if the Allies would have egg as well as blood on their faces.

All Eisenhower could do was continue to bluff — by reading aloud on Allied radio in Algiers the text of Marshal Badoglio's supposed surrender proclamation — which the Marshal was still refusing to confirm. This proclamation ordered the Italian military on the mainland and abroad to "cease all acts of hostility against the Anglo-American forces wherever they may be."[1]

Badoglio's hand was thus forced. After much handwringing, the seventy-one-year-old marshal — fearing arrest, even execution, by stalwart Italian fascists — felt he had no option but to confirm the surrender on Rome radio and seek to save himself. At 7:20 p.m. he did so — and immediately made himself scarce. Together with the royal family in the capital he fled the city on the only still-open road, in a convoy of carabinieri-protected vehicles, and bearing boxes of lire to bribe loyal fascists at roadblocks.

It was an ignominious end to the Pact of Steel: the final act of Italy's venal participation in the war — first as Hitler's partner in world crime, then as partner to the approaching Allies, which Badoglio now offered, on behalf of the Italian government, to become.

Others were skeptical. "The House of Savoy never finished a war on the same side it started, unless the war lasted long enough to change sides twice," a Free French newspaper commented sarcastically.[2] The inheritors of Rome's great empire in ancient times, the Italians now merely blew with the wind. "If you analyze the matter in cold blood there is no doubt the Italians have carried out a really good double-cross; they change sides on one day!!!" Montgomery wrote the next day to friends in England. "I wouldn't trust them a yard, and in any case they are quite useless when it comes to fighting."[3]

This was the real issue — for the Germans, by contrast, were very good when it came to fighting. And merciless. As Field Marshal Kesselring remarked of the Italians, "I loved these people. Now I can only hate them"[4] — hate that was now authorized to be channeled into vengeance on an unsparing scale, not only against Italian military units, but women, children, and the elderly. "No mercy must be shown to the traitors," Kesselring instructed General von Vietinghoff, his Tenth Army commander. Nor was it: the Italian general commanding the Salerno coastal division was executed in his headquarters even before the Germans turned on the approaching Allies — and the same fate befell tens of thousands of Italian troops across the country, as well as partisans, indeed anyone who challenged German military occupation or was seen to be aiding the Allies.[5]

General Sir Harold Alexander had willfully overestimated Italian assistance while utterly underestimating German resistance — fatally misleading the Allied commander in chief, General Eisenhower, as well as the Fifth Army commander, General Mark Clark.[6]

As the ground-forces commander of the assault, Clark had meantime hourly become more anxious. He'd thought the removal of his airborne division a terrible mistake, and had not been amused by Eisenhower's offhand dismissal of his doubts. "'Well, Wayne' — he always called me Wayne," Clark recalled Eisenhower's words, "When it drops [on Rome], it passes to your command!' And I said, 'Thanks, Ike, that's five hundred miles away!'"[7]

With the belated decision to call off the airdrop on Rome, Clark had no airborne division to worry about in Rome — indeed, no airborne division at all.[8] "As dusk came I was on the bridge. I could see the silhouettes of a hundred ships with my men in them. And I had never had such a forlorn feeling in my life," he later recounted. Shorn of the Eighty-Second Airborne, the fifty-five thousand men (British and American) of his Fifth Army thus sailed into a trap — "spitting right into the lion's mouth."[9]

Alerted that an Allied armada of almost a hundred ships was anchoring twelve miles offshore in the Gulf of Salerno, Kesselring had sent out his orders. The enemy "must be completely annihilated and in addition thrown into the sea. The British and Americans must realize that they are hopelessly lost against the concentrated German might."[10] Facing a barrage of Luftwaffe planes, lethal 88mm guns, and dense machine-gun fire, the Allied invasion force went into battle — the scene soon resembling something out of Dante's *Inferno* as both the clear Italian water and the sandy beaches ran with blood. As the veteran AP reporter Don White-head heard someone remark, "Maybe it would be better for us to fight without an [Italian] armistice."[11]

With operations now in the hands of General Eisenhower, there was nothing President Roosevelt, as the U.S. commander in chief in Washington, could do but leave the battle to the men in combat.

Late in the evening of September 9, once his meeting with the Joint Chiefs of Staff was over, the President therefore set off in the *Ferdinand Magellan* for Hyde Park with his British guests, the Prime Minister and his family. He had delivered another Fireside Chat the previous night, from the Diplomatic Reception Room, to announce the armistice with Italy — and to warn his listeners against complacency or idle assumptions. He welcomed the Italian people, who were "at last coming to the day of liberation from their real enemies, the Nazis." But "let us not delude ourselves that this armistice means the end of the war in the Mediterranean. We still have to drive the Germans out of Italy as we have driven them out of Tunisia and Sicily; we must drive them out of France and all other captive countries; and we must strike them on their own soil from all directions. Our ultimate objectives in this war will continue to be Berlin and Tokyo," he made clear.

"I ask you to bear these objectives constantly in mind — and do not forget that we still have a long way to go before we attain them," he'd warned. "The great news that you have heard today from General Eisenhower does not give you license to settle back in your rocking chairs and say, 'Well, that does it. We've got 'em on the run. Now we can start the celebration.' The time for celebration is not yet. And I have a suspicion that when this war does end, we shall not be in a very celebrating frame of mind. I think that our main emotion will be one of grim determination that this shall not happen again.

"During the past weeks," he continued, "Mr. Churchill and I have been in constant conference with the leaders of our combined fighting forces. We have been in constant communication with our fighting allies, Russian and Chinese, who are prosecuting the war with relentless determination and with conspicuous success on far distant fronts. And Mr. Churchill and I are here together in Washington at this crucial moment. We have seen the satisfactory fulfillment of plans that were made in Casablanca last January and here in Washington last May. And lately we have made new, extensive plans for the future," he added — a coded reference to Overlord. "But throughout these conferences we have never lost sight of the fact that this war will become bigger and tougher, rather than easier, during the long months that are to come.

"This war does not and must not stop for one single instant. Your fighting men know that. Those of them who are moving forward through jungles against lurking Japs — those who are landing at this moment, in barges moving through the dawn up to strange enemy coasts — those who are diving their bombers down on the targets at roof-top level — every one of these men knows that this war is a full-time job and that it will continue to be that until total victory is won."[12]

At Hyde Park, once the party arrived, the Prime Minister found himself on tenterhooks. Though the President tried as far as possible to keep the Churchills, including young Mary, entertained, Winston remained anxious. Giant II had been canceled; fearing savage Wehrmacht reprisals, Badoglio had reportedly attempted to renege on the Italian surrender.

The news that did come through was not good — indeed, with more German troops racing toward the battle zone at Salerno in succeeding days, Clark not only asked Eisenhower's authority to use troops of the Eighty-Second Airborne Division, but to drop them on the very beaches of Salerno, to bolster the infantry — and even ordered contingency plans be made for possible evacuation, á la Dunkirk.[13]

Daisy Suckley, watching the President, was amazed at his sang-froid. "Sunday, September 12, 1943," she wrote in her diary, three days into the invasion. "Sitting on his wheelchair, with all the Churchill party standing around, he sent for Jennings, and, in two minutes arranged for the visit, next week-end," of his son John Roosevelt and John's wife, Anne, "with two children & a nurse, and 6 Norwegians with a maid."[14]

The President had spent the morning driving his visitors about the estate, "at the wheel, his dog Fala beside him," and had arranged for lunch to be served for them all "at his own cottage (higher up the hillside than Mrs R's Val-Kill)." Following this they'd lain on the veranda — Churchill telling his daughter Mary the colors he would use, were he painting the scene, and commenting with a smile on "the wisdom of God in having made the sky *blue* & the trees *green*. 'It wouldn't have been nearly so good the other way round.'"

"To me these moments with Papa are the golden peaks of my life," Mary noted in her diary — aware that, between them, the President and the Prime Minister had it in them to protect and preserve civilization as they knew it. Then, after dinner, where the President had proposed the health of his guests Winston and Clemmie, who were celebrating their thirty-fifth wedding anniversary, "FDR drove us down to the train," the subaltern jotted in her diary.[15]

"God Bless You," Daisy heard Churchill say, leaning into the President's car. "I'll be over with you, next spring."

"Next spring" had meant before D-day. There was a long way to go before Overlord, however. Behind the bonhomie, the war in Europe was now entering a critical time for the Western Allies.

Churchill's moral and political sturdiness had certainly bucked up the President, but his military judgment, once again, was of a different order. The campaign in Italy upon which he'd so set his heart would now, inexorably, prove the very quagmire that General Marshall and the U.S. chiefs had foretold.

Even Churchill's doctor recorded how anxious, at the White House the week before, Winston had become: his thoughts "wandering to the coming landing at Salerno. That is where his heart is. As the appointed day draws near, the P.M. can think of nothing else. On this landing he has been building all his hopes. There are no doubts in his mind; anyway he admits none. It must succeed, and then Naples will fall into our hands. Last night, when the stream of his conversation was in spate, he talked of meeting Alex [General Alexander] in Rome before long — the capture of Rome has fired his imagination; more than once he has spoken about Napoleon's Italian campaign."[16]

At Hyde Park, three days after Clark's landings, Dr. Wilson had then noted the effect on Winston when the troops landed on the Salerno beaches and "it did not prove to be a walk-over. On the contrary, the news that filtered into Hyde Park, where we had followed the President, was disquieting: the Germans had launched a strong counter-attack and the situation was very uncertain."[17]

This was the reverse of what Churchill had so confidently forecast. There would be heavy casualties and loss of life, it seemed — American as well as British. "These things always seem to happen when I am with the President," the Prime Minister confided to Wilson, thinking of Tobruk the previous year — Sir Charles noting: "Poor Winston, he had been so anxious to convince Roosevelt that the invasion of Italy would yield a bountiful harvest at no great cost." Now that the first bill had come in, it was proving almost prohibitively expensive — both in human life and in the very vessels and logistical backup the U.S. chiefs wanted transferred to Britain for D-day. "When we left Hyde Park tonight, on the long journey to Halifax," Wilson recorded in his diary, "the situation was still very obscure."[18]

Churchill was embarrassed — and as his train bore him back to Canada, where he was to embark for Britain, the news from Italy only became more forbidding. Instead of seemingly effortless victory initially — the Italian fleet having sailed south from Taranto to join the Allies, pursued by German U-boats and Luftwaffe that sank many of them — Eisenhower's ground campaign turned sour. By September 16, Eisenhower was admitting to his naval aide that, if the Salerno battle ended in disaster," he himself would "probably be out."[19]

For his part, Churchill saw his once-glorious predictions for an Allied campaign in southern Europe exposed as wishful thinking. He'd earlier called upon his British chiefs of staff to be much bolder in their plans, and to "use all our strength against Italy," even without American help. He'd even recommended making plans for British assault landings as far north along the coast of Italy as possible, in order to "cut off" as many Germans as they could. Far from throwing their proverbial hats further over the fence, as Churchill had urged his military team, the Prime Minister was now faced with having to eat his own. Though from his train he cabled directly Eisenhower's field deputy, General Alexander, urging him to go ashore in person at Salerno and avoid another Dardanelles fiasco, it could not alter the bitter, bitter truth: namely that the Allied campaign in Italy, as planned, had been based upon a false premise: not only that the Italians would help, but that the Germans would fail to offer a serious defense of Italy south of the Po.

The next day, as Churchill's train bore him to Halifax, where HMS *Renown* would take him across the Atlantic, things sounded "no better,"

Sir Charles noted. "I have never seen him more on edge during a battle. Three 'bloodys' bespattered his conversation, and twice, while I was with him, he lost his temper with his servant, shouting at him in a painful way. He got up and walked down the train." Without information he seemed bereft. "'Has any news come in?' he kept demanding. In truth, "the reports that are reaching him only leave him more anxious," his doctor noted. "There is a dreadful hint, though it is carefully covered up, that we might be driven into the sea. It appears, as far as I can tell, that the P.M. is largely responsible for this operation; if anyone is to blame, he is the man; and, from the way things seem to be going, I suppose he is beginning to think that there might be a good deal to explain."[20]

Without the President to calm him, Churchill was metaphorically at sea — and soon was in reality, where he remained "immured in his cabin"[21] the whole voyage home, firing off telegrams to General Alexander to do more, and other wild cables, too, such as to General Maitland Wilson to accelerate a British seizure of the Dodecanese islands in the Aegean — without the agreement of the President — and be ready for potentially war-altering operations in the Balkans, where the Germans might, following the Italian surrender, be forced to withdraw to the Danube . . .

To Sir Charles Wilson this was all of a piece: the Prime Minister a bundle of nerves when things did not go in the way he had optimistically and impetuously planned.

At Hyde Park, however, the President neither blamed Winston nor worried unduly. He'd gotten to talk at length with young General Mark Clark during his stay in Casablanca, and was confident the U.S. troops — many of them in their first battle — would acquit themselves well. Moreover that General Eisenhower would recognize the gravity of the crisis and commit all he could to rectify the situation.

Neither Rome nor even Naples was the point, after all. Even if Clark failed to make much headway, the Italians had surrendered — unconditionally. All the Allies had to do, now, was secure the vital Foggia airfields, and bring the Germans to battle in Italy over the next months, until D-day was launched.

If Clark was forced to evacuate, after all, Allied troops could be sent to reinforce Montgomery's Eighth Army in Calabria. All would be well. Most importantly, the United States had demonstrated to the Soviets an absolute determination to fight on the mainland of Europe — first in southern Italy, then across the Channel. He and Churchill would show Stalin they meant business, and would follow through on their promises — moreover, that it would be best for the Russians to maintain civil discourse with the Western Allies in the fight to defeat the Third Reich.

The President thus slept a full ten hours after Churchill's train left the Hudson railway halt. He would spend only three days out of the next two weeks in Washington.

The fact was, he had bigger things on his mind than Salerno: his meeting with the Russian dictator, who in a flurry of new cables had finally agreed to a meeting of the Big Three — though not outside Russia. His tone had been, however, more "civil," as the principal private secretary to King George VI had noted in his diary at Buckingham Palace in London; "he re-iterates his wish to have a three-party meeting," Sir Alan Lascelles aptly put it, "but he won't go outside Russia, and I don't see how the President is to be got inside it."[22]

What had changed the Russian dictator's attitude?

There was much speculation — though few were sure. Certainly, in terms of public attention, the Allied conference at Quebec, coming on top of the summit at Casablanca, had monopolized the attention of the free world. Russia was losing the very respect it was looking for, internationally — Stalin conspicuous by his absence at such conferences, a fact that, in view of the many invitations to take part, began to suggest an ominous Russian agenda rather than genuine commitment to the anti-Axis cause and the Atlantic Charter/Declaration of the United Nations.

Above all, though, the war had moved into a new phase: the endgame. American, British, and Canadian troops were now on the mainland of Europe, only eight hundred miles from Berlin — while Russians were still fighting deep in the Soviet Union, more than a thousand miles from the German capital. As a result, Russian media calling for an immediate Second Front, instead, sounded silly — however strategically necessary a cross-Channel assault might be in terms of the military defeat of the Third Reich. The President and Mr. Churchill, in short, appeared to be in control of the moral and political dimensions of the war, even the military — leaving the Russians out on a limb, despite the almost obscene casualties they were suffering in their struggle to evict the Germans from their country.

In the new cables, Stalin still speciously claimed his presence was needed on a daily basis to control the battles raging on the Eastern Front ("where more than 500 divisions are engaged in the fighting in all"), but he now went out of his way not only to compliment the President on the "new brilliant success in Italy" but to acknowledge, for the first time, something even more significant. As Stalin put it, in his telegram to the President on September 11, "the successful landing at Naples and break between Italy and Germany will deal one more blow upon Hitlerite Germany and will considerably facilitate the actions of the Soviet armies at the Soviet-German front."[23]

This latter acknowledgment was, for Roosevelt, especially gratifying. Not only was the President relieved that his long, patient striving to convene a Big Three summit seemed about to pay off, but for the first time since Torch, Stalin had conceded that the President's strategy of landing in Sicily and then the mainland of Italy was having a major military impact on the war on Stalin's own Eastern Front. First at Kursk — where the Germans had called off the battle early — and now in the helter-skelter Russian advance in the Ukraine, where the Wehrmacht was being defeated in battle largely because Hitler simply had insufficient reserves to put into the line. The initiatives taken by the Western Allies had effectively spoiled any chance of the Wehrmacht defeating the Soviets that year.

"Everything turns on Italy at the moment," Goebbels had himself acknowledged on September 11, while staying with Hitler. Granted, "the enemy hasn't the faintest idea of the real situation in Northern and Central Italy. They are still imagining we'll pull back our divisions over the Brenner to the homeland, and they'll be able to unleash a huge aerial attack on Berlin from airfields in southern Italy." Clearly the Allies hadn't reckoned on the German genius for combat. The ruthless German occupation of Rome and other Italian cities was being greeted with applause in the Third Reich, evoking shades of 1940 and the German occupation of Paris: the German Volk expressing "rage against the Italians," who had nefariously betrayed them[24] — a people who would now be treated with the same remorseless cruelty that the Wehrmacht had shown their former Ribbentrop Pact partners when launching Barbarossa in 1941.

At the Wolf's Lair, the Reichsminister for Propaganda had even gotten Hitler to deliver the speech he'd desperately wanted the Führer to give, in order to bolster morale in Germany. It had been recorded at the OKW headquarters and relayed by radio in Berlin to the nation on September 10: a speech given in measured tones without the usual Hitler histrionics. Instead, it had soberly denounced those Italians who had failed their

Duce and who were now giving an example of cowardice and treachery that would go down in the annals of dishonor. Germany had consistently been compelled to bail out its ailing partner, in the Balkans and in North Africa — "the name of Field Marshal Rommel will forever be attached to this German effort" — but the Reich had now been "betrayed" by reactionary elements in Italy. "Italy's defection will have little military impact," the Führer claimed, "since the battle in that country has primarily been carried and conducted by German forces. We'll now be freed of all restrictions and constraints."[25]

Hitler's calm, measured tone would be balm to those in Germany wondering at the massive Allied air raids, the arrest of Mussolini, and then the unconditional surrender of the Italian government — his speech worth "seven divisions," as Goebbels put it. Hitler even made open mention of his secret weapons program. With Germany's enemies a thousand kilometers from the Reich, only their bombers could seek to "terrorize" the German population — and in that connection "there are," the Führer announced, "technical and organizational measures now being developed not simply to completely stop the terror bombing attacks, but to repay them with other, more effective measures" — his *Vergeltungswaffen,* or V-1 and V-2 weapons.[26]

The Führer's speech worked "like a refreshing thunderstorm," Goebbels noted — "one of the best," he reflected, "he has delivered in the whole war."[27]

Still and all, Goebbels acknowledged, the Allied invasion of the European continent was now a game changer. Though the Führer was confident the Wehrmacht could hold back the Allied armies south of Rome if they were fortunate, the divisions required for such a campaign would make it impossible to restrain the gathering Soviet tide on the Eastern Front: thus starving the German line of the reserves they desperately needed, especially on the line of the Dnieper, where little had been done to prepare solid defensive positions.

As Goebbels dictated in his diary, not only was the Allied invasion of Italy a lance in the German flank, but the situation in the East was "absolutely critical,"[28] with German troops pulling further and further back. "We see here what the unexampled betrayal of the Italians has caused us. If we'd had at hand the divisions we've had to send to Italy since the fall of Mussolini available to go into action on the Eastern Front, the current crisis would never have arisen. The superiority the Russians have over us is not that big — you can see that in the way we've slowed their advance."[29]

It was, for the Reich, a tragedy, he wrote. "We have about eight divisions in northern Italy and in southern Italy another eight, so about sixteen divisions, fitted out with first-class personnel and equipment. The Führer is convinced that with these sixteen divisions we'll be able to deal with the crisis in Italy," with a further fifty thousand troops in Sardinia and four thousand in Corsica who could be switched to Italy — battle terrain that would be "tabula rasa," with no concern about civilian casualties or destruction.[30] Yet the absence of those very divisions from the Eastern Front was now galling. "If we only had fifteen or twenty intact first-class divisions to put into battle, we'd be able to throw back the Soviets without any doubt whatsoever. But we're having to send those fifteen, twenty divisions south to the Italian theater," Goebbels wailed.[31]

For German leaders accustomed to seize whatever they wished from weakly defended European neighbors, the arrest of Mussolini, the defection of Italy as an ally, and the arrival of the Western Allies on the mainland of Europe now threatened, in other words, to stretch and bring down the whole Axis edifice — with the Allies possessing the upper hand.

If only the Western Allies would have launched a Second Front that year, Goebbels mused. A cross-Channel invasion by the Anglo-Americans would have given the Wehrmacht and Luftwaffe a real chance to defeat the Allies using the forces the Germans had in France, while retaining sufficient first-class divisions to deal with Stalin's forces on the Eastern Front. "But that would be too good to be true," Goebbels lamented.[32] Instead, the Western Allies had brought the war to the mainland of *Italy:* not only obtaining the unconditional surrender of its government at very little cost to themselves, but opening the floodgates, in the east, to Stalin's armies, against whom the Wehrmacht would now have insufficient reserves. And with the Führer too anxious about a fall invasion of France or even the Netherlands by the Allies to dare withdraw German divisions from the Atlantic Wall.

It would be up to valiant German troops both on the Eastern Front and the Southern Front, then, to show the Soviets and the Anglo-Americans the true mettle of the Wehrmacht. In Italy, Goebbels noted with a kind of sneering satisfaction, Allied troops would now face a ruthless German military machine unencumbered by Italians — and with more German divisions streaming down from the north, they would demonstrate their prowess in killing, without question or remorse. Italians who did not lay down their arms, or who sought to impede the German military occupation of Italy in any way, would simply be shot or slaughtered — as would civilians who aided partisans. Ruthlessness had gotten the Third Reich to its hitherto unimaginable string of imperial conquests — and would now be applied as mercilessly as in Russia. *Totaler Krieg.*

"The main purpose of my visit to the High Command Headquarters is fulfilled," Goebbels thus noted with satisfaction, on September 12. "I think Göring was right when he said to me that we have thereby won a battle. The Führer's speech will be worth whole divisions on the Eastern Front and in Italy. I spend a little time chatting with the Führer. He himself seems pleased he's gotten the speech out of the way. He wishes me all the best in my work and for my health . . . He promises to give another speech in the Sportpalast [in Berlin], to start the Winter Assistance Program. I'll make sure he'll get to taste once more just what it's like to be in touch with the Volk. Our farewell is very warm. I wish the Führer all the best."[33]

At 8:00 p.m. the Reich minister heard the latest news on the radio of "our operations in Italy, which are going very well," at Salerno, on top of the Führer's recorded speech — which the Russians had failed to jam. "A little more work, a little more talk. Then I fall into bed, dead tired. There'll be a mountain of work waiting for me in Berlin."[34]

53

A Message to Congress

GOEBBELS WAS, HOWEVER, misinformed about the Italian campaign. Though the Allied assault landings at Salerno came close to the very "brink of obliteration," as the American campaign historian Rick Atkinson recorded six decades later, the line held.[1]

It was touch-and-go, however. According to Rommel's son, Manfred, Hitler — buoyed by early reports of Wehrmacht victory at Salerno — "discussed with my father the possibility of launching a counter-offensive to retake southern Italy and possibly Sicily."[2] Ordered in panic by General Alexander to cease dawdling and save Clark, however, General Montgomery — who feared just such a Rommel riposte, as the Desert Fox had attempted at Medenine — finally renewed his advance. As Clark himself related, years later, "we had a hard time . . . Monty was sending me messages: 'Hang on, we're coming!' And I'd send back: 'Hurry up — I'm not proud, come and get me.' So it was really something."[3]

In truth it was Clark himself who saved Fifth Army, since his U.S. VI Corps commander, Major General Ernest Dawley — another protégé of General Marshall's — proved a broken reed. Clark himself went ashore to take personal command, in a magnificent display of courage and leadership in battle. He persuaded General Ridgway to drop airborne troops on the beaches, and with U.S. and Royal Navy vessels firing almost as many shells as at Iwo Jima and Okinawa, later,[4] Clark's men fought off the German counterassault.

Eisenhower had meantime warned the chiefs of staff of the possible need to evacuate the landings — a message passed on to the President and to Churchill — but the crisis eventually passed. Necessity — the need to fight harder or die at Salerno — had proven the ultimate mother of virtue.

Hitler was furious, as was Goebbels, but the President was relieved.

"You know from the news of the past few days," the President began his Message to Congress on September 17, 1943, as the Allied situation at Salerno seemed to stabilize, "that every military operation entails a legitimate military risk and that occasionally we have checks to our military plans — checks which necessarily involve severe losses of men and materials.

"The Allied forces are now engaged in a very hard battle south of Naples," he admitted. "Casualties are heavy. The desperation with which the Germans are fighting reveals that they are well aware of the consequences to them of our occupation of Italy. The Congress and the American people can rest assured that the landing on Italy is not the only landing we have in mind. That landing was planned at Casablanca," he claimed — bending the truth somewhat, since post-Husky operations had not actually been discussed in more than principle. Still and all, such planning had certainly taken place during the early summer. At Quebec, he explained, "the leaders and the military staffs of Great Britain and the United States made specific and precise plans to bring to bear further blows of equal or greater importance against Germany and Japan — with definite times and places for other landings on the continent of Europe and elsewhere."

Congress should be aware, then, that even though reverses lay ahead, the story of the Allied prosecution of the war was proceeding according to a genuine timetable and a larger, overall strategy — a strategy that was American, not British, but one calculated to succeed on behalf of the United Nations.

The President also pointed to the difference between Allied liberation and Nazi occupation — the "food, clothing, cattle, medicines, and household goods" systematically stolen by the Germans in "satellite and occupied Nations," whereas the Allies had a "carefully planned organization, trained and equipped to give physical care to the local population — food, clothing, medicine." He lauded the advance of the Allied armies from Sicily to the mainland of Italy on September 3 — stating: "History will always remember this day as the beginning of the answer to the prayer of the millions of liberty-loving human beings not only in these conquered lands but all over the world." However, "there is one thing I want to make perfectly clear. When Hitler and the Nazis go out, the Prussian military clique must go with them."

Unconditional surrender — without negotiation. "The war-breeding gangs of militarists must be rooted out of Germany — and Japan — if we are to have any real assurance of future peace," he asserted. Surrender negotiations with the Italian government, of necessity, had had to be conducted in secret, in order that the Nazis not be able to seize Marshal Badoglio or his associates in Rome, but he wanted Americans and Congress to know "that the policy which we follow is an expression of the basic democratic tradition and ideals of this Republic. We shall not be able to claim that we have gained total victory in this war if any vestige of Fascism in any of its malignant forms is permitted to survive anywhere in the world."

Bearing a banner of American democracy, the United States was, in other words, on the move — producing planes, tanks, and matériel on a scale that beggared description: fifty-two thousand airplanes, twenty-three thousand tanks, forty thousand artillery guns in the first six months of 1943 alone, he reported. American shipyards were launching "almost five ships a day."

The war had become "essentially a great war of production. The best way to avoid heavy casualty lists is to provide our troops with the best equipment possible — and plenty of it," the President asserted. Although the nation had come a long way since his State of the Union address just before the Casablanca Conference, he now cautioned that "we are still a long, long way from ultimate victory in any major theater of the war." It would entail "a hard and costly fight up through Italy — and a major job of organizing our positions before we can take advantage of them.

"Likewise," in the British Isles "we must be sure we have assembled the strength to strike not just in one direction but in many directions — by land and sea and in the air — with overwhelming forces and equipment." Moreover, to "break through" the Japanese defensive ring stretching from the "mandated islands to the Solomons and through the Netherlands East Indies to Malaysia and China" would be a challenge. "In all of history, there has never been a task so tremendous as that which we now face," he stated candidly. And warned: "Nothing we can do will be more costly in lives than to adopt the attitude that the war has been won — or nearly won. That would mean a letdown in the great tempo of production which we have reached, and would mean that our men who are now fighting all over the world will not have that overwhelming superiority of power which has dealt so much death and destruction to the enemy and at the same time has saved so many lives."[5]

"Overwhelming superiority of power" — directed at the right time and at the right place — to produce the necessary outcome: the unconditional surrender of the Third Reich and the Empire of Japan. Their total disarmament. And a "national cooperation with other Nations" in order that "world aggression be ended and that fair international relationships be established on a permanent basis"[6]: these were the military and political objectives the President was pursuing on behalf of the United States — on a global scale.

Aware there were those who resented him in his role as U.S. commander in chief as much as they had resented him as president in tackling the Great Depression and New Deal, Roosevelt dismissed the narrow-minded critics who, "when a doughnut is placed in front of them, claim they can only see the hole in it" — people who lacked "war-winning ideals." "Obviously," he added, "we could not have produced and shipped as much as we have, we could not now be in the position we now occupy in the Mediterranean, in Italy, or in the Southwest Pacific or on the Atlantic convoy routes or in the air over Germany and France, if conditions in Washington and throughout the Nation were as confused and chaotic as some people try to paint them" — paintings "eagerly sought by Axis propagandists in their evil work." For himself he remained proud of the "amazing" job that "the American people and their Government" were doing "in carrying out a vast program which two years ago was said to be impossible of fulfillment."[7]

Nothing, the President claimed, could now halt the Allies, whatever the Germans and Japanese threw at them.

54

Achieving Wonders

In BERLIN, THE master of Axis propaganda read the text of the President's latest Message to Congress carefully.

"The American struggle isn't just against Nazism," Dr. Goebbels noted, "it's also against militarism. We know these words. The British and the Americans have always used them to try to carve the Reich into little pieces," he sneered. "More significant was what he says about American output. The numbers are way behind their needs; nevertheless," he confessed, "as far as airplane production goes, the U.S. has achieved wonders."

In proof of what he saw as his own analytic intelligence, however, the Mephistopheles of public relations and propaganda thought he could discern Roosevelt's deeper motive behind his Message to Congress — and the free world. "It's quite clear," Goebbels noted, "that the whole enemy press is being brought to bear to distract attention from Soviet successes on the Eastern Front — and make sure their own public isn't made uneasy."[1]

At a time of unease in Washington political circles over ultimate Soviet intentions, there was considerable truth in this. The President was certainly banging a proud American drum to remind the American public of the war's *global* dimensions — the manner in which control of the Mediterranean would release naval vessels for the Far East, closing the gap between Northwest Australia and Ceylon, thereby forcing "General Tojo and his murderous gang" to "look to the north, to the south, to the east, or to the west," where he would only see "closing in on them, from all directions, the forces of retribution under Generalissimo Chiang-Kai-shek, General MacArthur, Admiral Nimitz, and Admiral Lord Mountbatten,"[2] the new supreme commander of Allied forces in the Indian Ocean. But the President's target audience went beyond American or even English shores. Published not only in nearly every newspaper in America and abroad, the President's long congressional address was once again directed at Moscow.

Whether at Hyde Park, Quebec, Ottawa, or the White House, the President had taken great pains to demonstrate over recent weeks just how solid was the U.S.-British alliance. Now he wished to back that image, in writing, with quotable numbers: statistical proof of new, global American power that would not be content with Hitler's fall, but was to be harnessed to a postwar democratic agenda.

His conversation with Archbishop Spellman had reflected his unusually despondent mood; two weeks later, though, with American and British troops having established a hard-won lodgment on the mainland of Italy, and U.S. air forces already beginning to bomb factories in southern Germany, he seemed to have recovered his confidence: a confidence he would certainly need if he was to bring the American electorate, via his own efforts and the Congress, to ditch isolationism for good and take responsibility for the survival and development of a democratic postwar world.

Churchill's stay, in other words, had acted as a tonic, despite the crisis at Salerno — and the President was fired up.

Ranked seventeenth in the table of world military strengths in 1939, the United States was now primus inter pares, with an all-American military, economic, and political agenda, based on the clear goals of the four freedoms, that the President was determined to fulfill come hell or high water — with or without Soviet participation.

Exactly what would happen if the Soviets did *not* participate in an endgame agreement — indeed, what exactly such a political agreement should comprise — was still to be decided.

As Churchill had said to Mackenzie King before leaving Quebec to join the President in Washington, it was impossible to predict whether the "Germans will give up this autumn." It was, as Winston put it with characteristic wit, "like trying to bet on the Derby. No one could tell exactly what would happen. He spoke of the small numbers the British and Americans have in armies compared with the Germans" — and with the Russians.[3]

The President had been "very mad" at Stalin at the time, and had deliberately refrained from responding to the Russian's rude cables — ignoring him and working with Churchill to show the strength of the Western, Anglo-American coalition. Somehow, though, in the interests of postwar peace, agreement would nevertheless *have* to be obtained on the "post-war order," however powerful the Russian land armies. Compromise would be necessary, involving sad concessions — ones that would hope-fully preserve, at least, the western nations of Europe within an Allied, democratic embrace: the "Allied side." While meantime encouraging the Soviets to join an international security system, not stand outside it.

Could such a system of postwar security be negotiated with the inscru-table Russians? Would it be effective? Would the American public even support security guarantees of foreign countries on another continent, in another hemisphere, at the risk of a further war? It was small wonder that, in relation to the "post-war order," Churchill had given to Mackenzie King a "desultory sort of account of the scheme that he, himself, had in mind, and what the President had talked of, but there was nothing very definite about it. Nothing is to be published at present as coming out of the [Quebec] Conference. Some months will be needed to consider the matter."[4]

With Stalin's sudden willingness to tackle "the matter" — first through a preliminary meeting of foreign ministers, then a summit of the Allied leaders, perhaps — planning for the future of the world was, however, be-coming hot: red hot.

In the hopes therefore of obtaining formal Russian participation — participation in a four-power postwar security structure; participation in a global United Nations authority; and formal international agreements to be made on the future of Germany and the countries that had aided Hitler militarily, from Austria to Bulgaria and Rumania — the President thus authorized Secretary Hull to attend the preliminary Moscow Con-ference of foreign ministers of the Big Three, plus a representative from China.

The President had wanted Sumner Welles to attend, despite his recent resignation as undersecretary of state, but Hull was insistent that *he* should represent the United States as secretary of state, and the Presi-dent — needing congressional support for the mission and its outcome — had acquiesced. The war was moving toward a climax, as even the Rus-sians were aware. After almost a year of pressure to get together and get with a formally agreed Allied program, the Russian dictator had, it ap-peared, finally seen the light. The foreign ministers' conference would begin in only four weeks' time — on October 11, 1943 — and might last as long as a month.

There in Moscow, the President hoped, the secretary would pave the way for the leaders of the Four Policemen to sit down together and discuss postwar security — and how to avoid the fate of the League of Nations. The President, Churchill, Stalin, and Chiang Kai-shek would also have to decide the war's endgame: how, exactly, Nazi Germany was finally to be defeated and its military disarmed. Following which, the Empire of Japan.

With that vast challenge looming, the President wheeled himself from the Oval Office to the mansion, stopping by the Map Room to check on messages from London, Moscow, and Chungking. Where the national leaders would meet, when exactly, how he would travel — by air or sea — and how they would get along, Roosevelt had little idea, but he was suddenly supremely confident.

"Of course he knew better than anyone else what was good for the United States," Lieutenant George Elsey remembered the spirit the President conveyed. "That was the attitude at that point. He was supreme in every respect!" — the Map Room off-limits to all but five people in the world, not only to safeguard the most sensitive and secret military information, including Ultra, but because it enabled the President to be the only person with a complete picture of the war's progress — and perils. "'I'm in control; this is the way it's going to be — it's going to be the way I want it' — this was the sense I had of his perception of himself as the war went on," Elsey recalled.[5]

Franklin Roosevelt had every reason to feel supreme. As president he had not only brought America out of the Great Depression without resorting to the kind of tyranny that had been occasioned in Germany and elsewhere, but he had subsequently become — in the least dictatorial yet most dominating manner — a most successful U.S. commander in chief in war. A global "war for civilization," as he rightly called it.

The President's generals and admirals had "no reason to challenge or contradict his leadership,"[6] Elsey pointed out, since in setting the ongoing strategy of the war — at times against their dissenting voices — he had so ably brought the United States now within sight of eventual victory.

Many great battles still lay ahead, as well as further disagreements with Churchill and the British over military operations and policy. Churchill's obsession with war in the Mediterranean would continue, despite disastrous expeditions in the Greek islands that would drive his own generals as mad as it did the American military in the next weeks[7] — Churchill resisting to the bitter end the British commitment to the mounting of Overlord the following spring.[8]

For all his faults as quasi–commander in chief of British Empire forces, however, Winston Churchill's loyalty to the President, as the de facto commander in chief of the forces of the Western Allies, had never snapped; nor had Churchill's acumen in terms of Stalin and the Russians, and his moral courage. This would be of inestimable value in the coming months.

There would be dire problems of agreement with the Soviet Union, the President was all too aware — Russians who would have no gratitude to the United States for having helped save them, nor genuine interest in the Four Freedoms in a postwar world. There was also the matter of a fourth presidential election, and the President's always-precarious health. Moreover, what exactly should be done with Nazi Germany in the aftermath of victory — disarmament or dismemberment. How best to help the Chinese, and plan the defeat of Japan. And how best to then turn Japan from aggression to peaceful coexistence . . .

These were but some of the politico-military challenges remaining, as the President began planning his second trip to North Africa later that fall — hopefully there to meet with Chiang Kai-shek, Churchill, and Stalin.

The road from Torch had certainly been rocky, over the past year, but what a year of achievement it had been!

His secretary of war and Joint Chiefs of Staff were now finally on the same page — *his* page. So was Churchill — if he could be kept there. From faltering first offensive combat in Tunisia, the United States had in less than one year moved to the brink of what would become the greatest global military performance in its history: a massive American-led invasion and campaign in 1944 that would hopefully win the Second World War in Europe. And after that, Japan.

With that, the President left the Map Room and went up to bed.

Acknowledgments

Readers of *The Mantle of Command: FDR at War, 1941–1942* will know how indebted I am to those who have helped me in recounting, afresh, one of the most important stories of the twentieth century.

My task was to challenge the widely held perception of Franklin Delano Roosevelt as a hands-off U.S. commander in chief in World War II, and to demonstrate, rather, just how important was his role in directing U.S. and Allied strategy, even though he did not live to record it. Now, with publication of *Commander in Chief: FDR's Battle with Churchill, 1943*, I am in debt again to a number of people. First off, I'd like to thank my commissioning editor, Bruce Nichols, without whose guidance, editing, and support this book could not have been published. And his assistant, Ben Hyman; my copyeditor, Melissa Dobson; and the indefatigable manuscript supremo, Larry Cooper — indeed the whole team at Houghton Mifflin Harcourt. At a time when my longtime London publisher had rejected the manuscript of *The Mantle of Command* and pulled out of the project completely, claiming there was insufficient interest in Franklin Delano Roosevelt in Britain or in the British publishing territories (Australia, New Zealand, South Africa, India, the West Indies, etc.) for a multivolume work on FDR as commander in chief in World War II, Bruce's encouragement meant the world to me — and something, I think, to the many readers who have enjoyed *The Mantle of Command*. I hope this sequel will again repay Bruce's faith in my project.

Second, I'd like to thank Dr. Hans Renders, Professor of Biography at Groningen University in the Netherlands, who has not only been a stalwart supporter and colleague of my work in biographical studies, but who encouraged me to include *Commander in Chief* as part of my submission for a doctorate at the Biografie Instituut, Research Faculty of Arts, Groningen University. For his and Professor Dr. Doeko Bosscher's suggestions, corrections, and support I am deeply grateful.

Writing history and historical biography is a process of research and constant iteration — factual, interpretive, selective, and architectural — before a book is finished and goes to press. Many fellow historians have assisted me; in particular I'd like to thank Carlo D'Este, Roger Cirillo, James Scott, Mark Schneider, David Kaiser, Douglas Brinkley, David Reynolds, and Ron Spector. I'd like to acknowledge my debt as a historian also to Gerhard Weinberg, Rick Atkinson, Mark Stoler, Warren Kimball, Michael Schaller, H. W. Brands, Andrew Roberts, David Woolner, Evan Thomas, Douglas Porch, Michael Howard, and the late Martin Gilbert, Stephen Ambrose, and Forrest Pogue, for their many works on World War II and FDR's role. Over the years as a military and presidential historian I have learned not only from them but from many hundreds of veterans, from generals to GIs, as well as other students of World War II, ranging from professors to archivists in the United States, Britain, and Germany. Without those years of grounding, going back to the decade I spent as official biographer of Field Marshal Bernard Montgomery, I could not have undertaken such an ambitious project, and I will always be grateful to them.

At the FDR Presidential Library I'd like to thank the Deputy Director, Bob Clark, as well as the staff of the Research Room and Photographic Records. At the Warm Springs Presidential Museum I'd like to thank the Manager, Robin Glass, and his staff. At the Eisenhower Presidential Library in Abilene I'd also like to thank the Deputy Director, Timothy Reeves, and the Research Library staff. In New Orleans, where I winter, I'd like to thank Nick Mueller, the President and CEO of the National World War II Museum, as well as his Director of Research, Keith Huxen, and Conference Director, Jeremy Collins. At the Churchill Society of New Orleans I wish to thank the President, Gregg Collins, and his colleagues. In Washington, D.C., I'd like to thank especially Jeff Flannery, Head of Reference in the Manuscript Division at the Library of Congress, and his staff, as well as the staff of the National Archives in College Park, Maryland. Also John Greco and his colleagues at the Operational Archives of the U.S. Naval History and Command, Washington Navy Yard.

At the Imperial War Museum in London I'd like to thank particularly the Keeper of Documents, Anthony Richards. At the Churchill Centre in Chicago I'd like to thank Lee Pollock and David Freeman. At the Churchill Archives Centre in Cambridge, England, the Director, Allen Packwood.

Closer to home, at the University of Massachusetts Boston I'd like to thank Ira Jackson, the former Dean of the McCormack Graduate School of Policy and Global Studies, where I am Senior Fellow; the new Dean, David Cash; and my many colleagues at the university, especially Provost Winston Langley. My thanks also to the staffs of the Widener Library, Harvard University, and its Microfilm Department, and the staff of Boston College Library.

In Boston I'm indebted, also, to my fellow members of the Boston Biographers Group, whose monthly meetings have offered the kind of support that only fellow biographers can, in the end, offer: collegial understanding, sympathy, advice, and reassurance in our necessarily often lonely biographical profession. I'd like also to acknowledge the friendship and intellectual fraternity of my fellow members of the Tavern Club — as well as my fellow members of Biographers International Organization (BIO), whose annual conference is both an inspiration to biographers and a chance to share a common passion for the study of real lives.

My literary agent, Ike Williams, has been once again my stalwart champion, together with his colleagues Katherine Flynn and Hope Denekamp. To my brother Michael and to my children, my thanks; and to my wife, Raynel, much more than thanks can ever repay.

As in the writing of *The Mantle of Command*, I have kept a portrait of my father, Lieutenant Colonel Sir Denis Hamilton, DSO, above my desk during the writing of *Commander in Chief*—for it is the memory of his service as a fighting infantryman, first at Dunkirk and then at D-day and the grim Battle of Normandy, that cautions me never to forget the men who had to carry out, in combat, the strategies laid down by the "brass hats" in World War II—and pay the price of their decisions, for good or ill.

Finally, to those readers of *The Mantle of Command* who wrote me with corrections as well as expressions of gratitude, my great appreciation.

NIGEL HAMILTON
*John W. McCormack Graduate School of Policy
and Global Studies, UMass Boston*

Photo Credits

Total War. FDR addresses Congress, Jan. 7, 1943: FDR Library; boarding the *Dixie Clipper* at U.S. naval base, Trinidad, Jan. 12, 1943: National Archives

En Route to Casablanca. Stopover at Bathhurst, Gambia: National Archives; aboard the USS *Memphis* with Captain John McCrea: National Archives; FDR aboard C-54 with pilot, Captain Otis F. Bryan, Jan. 11, 1943: FDR Library; President's C-54 and ramp, North Africa, Jan. 1943: FDR Library

Casablanca. The President's villa, Dar es Saada: FDR Library; FDR dines with sons Elliott and Franklin Jr., and Harry Hopkins, Jan. 16, 1943: FDR Library; with Joint Chiefs of Staff, Jan. 20, 1943: FDR Library

Directing World Strategy. At the President's villa, hosting Winston Churchill and the Combined Chiefs of Staff, Jan. 1943: FDR Library; FDR with Admiral Ernest King: National Archives; with Generals Henri Giraud and Charles de Gaulle: National Archives

Visiting Troops on the Battlefield. FDR with General Dwight Eisenhower (seen flying together in December 1943): National Archives; with Generals Mark Clark and George Patton, Jan. 21, 1943: FDR Library; reviewing a U.S. armored division, Jan. 21, 1943: FDR Library; reviewing U.S. troops, Jan. 21, 1943: FDR Library

Unconditional Surrender. FDR and Churchill with Combined Chiefs, Jan. 1943: FDR Library; with Churchill at press conference, Jan. 24, 1943: FDR Library; press conference, Jan. 24, 1943: FDR Library

End of Empires. FDR with son Elliott, Jan. 1943: FDR Library; dining with the Sultan of Morocco, Jan. 22, 1943: National Archives; with Churchill at top of tower of Villa Taylor, U.S. vice consulate, Marrakesh, Jan. 24, 1943: FDR Library; with President Edwin Barclay of Liberia, Jan. 27, 1943: FDR Library

Totaler Krieg. Goebbels at the *Sportpalast:* Bundesarchiv, Federal Archives of Germany; FDR reviews military training camp: National Archives; Admiral Yamamoto saluting Japanese plane, ca. 1942: Corbis; group of U.S. Army Air Forces P-38 Lightning fighter planes, June 1, 1943: Associated Press

Churchill on the Wrong Warpath. The RMS *Queen Mary* in New York harbor, June 20, 1945: Interim Archives / Getty Images; Churchill addresses Congress, May 19, 1943: Corbis

Axis Surrender in North Africa. Roundup of German and Italian soldiers in Tunisia, June 11, 1943: Associated Press; soldiers in a prison camp: The Print Collector / Getty Images

Reading Churchill the Riot Act. FDR fetching Churchill from train, Washington, May 11, 1943: Bettmann / Corbis; fishing with Churchill at Shangri-la: FDR Library; U.S. Chiefs of Staff (Generals Arnold and Marshall, Captain Royal [deputy secretary], Admirals Leahy and King) at a Combined Chiefs Conference, facing British counterparts, 1943: Three Lions / Hulton Archive / Getty Images

Sicily — and Kursk. Allied landing in Sicily, July 10, 1943: IWM © Sgt. Frederick Wackett / Getty Images; retreat from Kursk: Bundesarchiv, Federal Archives of Germany

The Fall of Mussolini. Mussolini greets Hitler upon arrival in Italy, July 19, 1943: ullstein bild / Getty Images; on their way to Feltre, Italy: ullstein bild / Getty Images; before the meeting at Feltre: ullstein bild / Getty Images

Churchill Returns — Yet Again. Churchill with daughter Mary, Aug. 16, 1943: Toronto Star Archives / Getty Images; FDR with Churchill, Canadian Prime Minister McKenzie King, and Combined Chiefs in Quebec, Aug. 18, 1943: FDR Library

The First Crack in the Axis. FDR addresses crowd outside Canadian parliament, Ottawa, Aug. 25, 1943: FDR Library; Stalin with Foreign Minister Molotov (seen later, Feb. 1, 1945): Keystone / Getty Images

The Reckoning. FDR drives Churchill at Hyde Park, Sept. 12, 1943: Associated Press; Allied invasion of Italy, Salerno, Sept. 9, 1943: SeM / UIG / Getty Images

Notes

PROLOGUE

1. Lieutenant Commander George Elsey, interview with author, September 12, 2011.
2. See this volume, chapter 32, 257.
3. Entry of Tuesday, November 10, 1943, in Alan Lascelles, *King's Counsellor: Abdication and War: The Diaries of Sir Alan Lascelles,* ed. Duff Hart-Davis (London: Weidenfeld & Nicolson, 2006), 75.
4. Ibid., entry of Thursday, May 13, 1943, 129.
5. David Reynolds, *In Command of History: Churchill Fighting and Writing the Second World War* (New York: Random House, 2005).

1. A CRAZY IDEA

1. "Exclusive of the President's own car, the train comprised one compartment car, one Pullman sleeper, one combination club-baggage car, and the special Army radio car": "Log of the Trip of the President to the Casablanca Conference, 9–31 January, 1943," Papers of George M. Elsey, Franklin D. Roosevelt Presidential Library, Hyde Park, NY.
2. Entry of January 9, 1943, Leahy Diary, William D. Leahy Papers, Library of Congress.
3. "Because of his infirmity he [the President] could walk only briefly on two canes. It was much easier for him to use one cane and the right arm of an escort" for balance and support while swinging the fourteen-pound steel irons encasing his legs, from his thighs to his shoes, McCrea explained: John McCrea, "Handwritten Memoirs/Recollections," McCrea Papers, FDR Library.
4. Ibid.

2. ABOARD THE MAGIC CARPET

1. "Marriage of Hopkins to Louise Macy," miscellaneous files for "Roosevelt & Hopkins," Robert E. Sherwood Papers, Houghton Library, Harvard University.

2. Robert Sherwood, *Roosevelt and Hopkins: An Intimate History* (New York: Harper, 1948), 669.

3. Entry of January 8, 1943, in Geoffrey C. Ward, ed., *Closest Companion: The Unknown Story of the Intimate Friendship Between Franklin Roosevelt and Margaret Suckley* (Boston: Houghton Mifflin, 1995), 194.

4. Ibid.

5. Entry of January 9, 1943, in Ward, *Closest Companion,* 194.

6. Ibid., entry of January 10, 1943, 196.

7. Sherwood, *Roosevelt and Hopkins,* 669.

8. Ibid.

9. McCrea, "Handwritten Memoirs/Recollections."

10. Letter of January 11, 1943, in Ward, *Closest Companion,* 196.

11. Ibid.

12. Ibid.

13. Ibid., letter of January 12, 1943, 197.

14. Ibid., letter of January 13, 1943.

15. Related to John McCrea by the President: McCrea, "Handwritten Memoirs/ Recollections."

16. Letter of January 13, 1943, in Ward, *Closest Companion,* 197.

17. Ibid.

18. Letter to Eleanor Roosevelt, January 13, 1943, in Elliott Roosevelt, ed., *F.D.R.: His Personal Letters, 1928–1945* (New York: Duell, Sloane, and Pearce, 1950), vol. 2, 1393.

3. THE UNITED NATIONS

1. Nigel Hamilton, *The Mantle of Command: FDR at War, 1941–1942* (Boston: Houghton Mifflin Harcourt, 2014), 138 et seq.

2. Ibid.

3. Christopher D. O'Sullivan, *Sumner Welles, Postwar Planning, and the Quest for a New World Order, 1937–1943* (New York: Columbia University Press, 2008), 65 and 72.

4. Sumner Welles, *Seven Decisions That Shaped History* (New York: Harper, 1951), 182–83.

5. Christopher Thorne, *Allies of a Kind: The United States, Britain, and the War Against Japan, 1941–1945* (London: Hamish Hamilton, 1978), 221. Christopher O'Sullivan argued that such foot-dragging was deliberate. "The imperial powers faced growing demands for independence" among colonial and mandated countries — exposing "a paradox at the heart of empires: progress in the political and economic sphere would encourage self-rule, whereas a lack of progress justified continued European rule": *FDR and the End of Empire* (New York: Palgrave Macmillan, 2012), 4.

6. O'Sullivan, *Sumner Welles,* 67.

7. Ibid., 74, quoting Gladwyn Jebb.

8. It was not only the British Empire that was having to face the prospect of dismantlement; Queen Wilhelmina of the Netherlands gave a broadcast on the first anniversary of Pearl Harbor, December 7, 1942, promising that the Dutch colonies in Southeast Asia would be given home rule — see Thorne, *Allies of a Kind,* 218.

9. David Reynolds, *In Command of History: Churchill Fighting and Writing the Second World War* (New York: Random House, 2005), 334.

10. Letter of November 24, 1942, in Elliott Roosevelt, ed., *F.D.R.: His Personal Letters, 1928–1945* (New York: Duell, Sloane, and Pearce, 1950), vol. 2, 1371–72.

11. Ibid.

12. Entry of December 4, 1942, Diaries of William Lyon Mackenzie King, Library and Archives Canada, Ottawa, ON (hereinafter Mackenzie King Diary). The Democrats lost the election in the House of Representatives by over a million ballots in the popular vote. To Roosevelt's relief they nevertheless retained a majority of 222 seats to 209. In the Senate, Democrats lost 8 seats and 1 independent — as well as the popular vote, in ballot numbers cast. Again, however, they held on to their majority, 58 seats to 37.

13. Ibid.

14. Ibid.

15. Susan Butler, ed., *My Dear Mr. Stalin: The Complete Correspondence Between Franklin D. Roosevelt and Joseph V. Stalin* (New Haven, CT: Yale University Press, 2005), 98.

16. Ibid., 99.

17. Ibid., 99–100.

18. Ibid., 101.

19. Entry of December 5, 1942, Mackenzie King Diary.

20. Ibid.

21. Ibid.

22. Ibid.

23. Ibid.

24. Ibid.

25. Roosevelt's speechwriter and later editor of his presidential papers, Sam Rosenman, later pointed out that "it was not at Appomattox but at Fort Donelson that Grant demanded unconditional surrender; it was not of Robert E. Lee but of S. B. Buckner — in 1862": Samuel I. Rosenman, *Working with Roosevelt* (New York: Harper, 1952), 372.

26. Entry of December 5, 1942, Mackenzie King Diary.

27. In June 1941, prior to the war, Roosevelt had set up an Office of Scientific Research and Development to direct science for military purposes. The OSRD was soon tasked with atomic research. The notion that an atomic weapon would have to be launched by ship, given the necessary volume, quickly gave way to the idea of a small, bomb-size weapon that could be flown and dropped on a target. A so-

called S-1 Committee was therefore set up to report directly to the President at the White House, chaired by the president of Harvard University, James Conant. Robert Oppenheimer was made director of fast-neutron research, and by the summer of 1942 the need for substantially more fissionable material was reported to FDR. To accelerate development, General Brehon Somervell, the U.S. Army's senior officer for logistics, appointed Lieutenant Colonel Leslie Groves to take charge of the Manhattan Project — which was moved to Los Alamos, in New Mexico. The 60 tons of Canadian uranium ore, already ordered in March 1942, was judged insufficient. After consultation with the U.S. government, Mackenzie King's Canadian government nationalized the Eldorado Mining and Refining company in June 1942, and another 350 tons of uranium was immediately ordered by the U.S. government — followed by another 500 tons later that year, and 1,200 tons of stored Congolese ore to be refined by the Canadians.

28. Entry of December 5, 1942, Mackenzie King Diary.
29. Ibid.
30. Ibid.
31. Ibid.
32. Churchill referred to the plan as "airy visions of Utopia and El Dorado" (Martin Gilbert, *Winston S. Churchill*, vol. 7, *Road to Victory: 1941–1945* [London: Heinemann, 1986], 292), while Harold Laski, professor of political science at the London School of Economics, wrote to President Roosevelt, hoping he would "teach our Prime Minister that it is the hope of the future and not the achievement of the past from which he must draw his inspiration" (Thorne, *Allies of a Kind,* 144).
33. Entry of Saturday, January 9, 1943, "Secret Diary" of Lord Halifax, Papers of Lord Halifax, Hickleton Papers, Borthwick Institute of Historical Research, University of York, Yorkshire, England.
34. Entry of December 5, 1942, Mackenzie King Diary.
35. Ibid.
36. Ibid.
37. Ibid.

4. WHAT NEXT?

1. Ibid., entry of December 6, 1942.
2. Ibid., entry of December 4, 1942.
3. Ibid., entry of December 5, 1942.
4. Ibid.
5. Ibid.
6. David Kaiser, *No End Save Victory: How FDR Led the Nation into War* (New York: Basic Books, 2014).
7. Entry of December 5, 1942, Mackenzie King Diary.
8. Ibid., entry of December 4, 1942.

9. Ibid., entry of December 6, 1942.
10. Ibid.
11. Ibid.

5. STALIN'S *NYET*

1. Cable of December 6, 1942, in Butler, *My Dear Mr. Stalin,* 102.
2. Ibid., cable of December 8, 1942, 103.
3. Ibid., cable of December 14, 1942, 103.
4. Ibid.
5. Ibid., 103–4.

6. ADDRESSING CONGRESS

1. Rosenman, *Working with Roosevelt,* 366–68.
2. Entry of November 29, 1942, in William D. Hassett, *Off the Record with F.D.R., 1942–1945* (New Brunswick, NJ: Rutgers University Press, 1958), 145.
3. "The Spirit of This Nation Is Strong" — Address to the Congress on the State of the Union, January 7, 1943, in Franklin D. Roosevelt, *The Public Papers and Addresses of Franklin D. Roosevelt,* comp. Samuel I. Rosenman, 1943 vol., *The Tide Turns* (New York: Russell and Russell, 1969), 21–34.

7. A FOOL'S PARADISE

1. Entry of January 7, 1943, Halifax Diary.
2. Entry of November 20, 1942, Stimson Diary, Henry L. Stimson Papers, Yale University Library, New Haven, CT.
3. Ibid, entry of December 11, 1942.
4. Ibid., entry of December 12, 1942.
5. Ibid.
6. Ibid.
7. Henry Stimson and McGeorge Bundy, *On Active Service In Peace and War* (New York: Harper & Brothers, 1947).
8. Entry of December 14, 1942, Stimson Diary.
9. Ibid.
10. Nigel Hamilton, *The Full Monty,* vol. 1, *Montgomery of Alamein, 1887–1942* (London: Allen Lane, 2001), 467–68.
11. Because of its five fortress-like side walls, President Roosevelt referred to the Pentagon as the "Pentateuchal Building," after the first five books of the Bible: Steve Vogel, *The Pentagon: A History* (New York: Random House, 2007), 297. The U.S. Navy was offered space to ensure a combined-services headquarters; "He was very much pleased," Stimson had noted the President's satisfaction with the offer

in his diary, "and told us to go ahead": Ibid., 281. The Navy bureaus declined to integrate their activities, however — as they did racial integration in the seagoing Navy, other than small numbers of black sailors as messmen or glorified bellhops. Even onshore, the Navy insisted their installations be strictly segregated, with no black officers — causing the National Urban League's journal *Opportunity* to declare Japan was not wrong in claiming "the so-called Four Freedoms in the great 'Atlantic Charter' were for white men only": Morris J. MacGregor, *Integration of the Armed Forces, 1940–1965* (Washington, D.C.: Government Printing Office, 1985). The Pentagon saga would epitomize the President's difficulties as commander in chief in a democracy — the U.S. Navy refusing, in fact, to move in with the Army and U.S. Air Force until 1948, under protest, while the Marine Corps held out another four decades, until 1996.

12. Entry of January 7, 1943, Stimson Diary.
13. Entry of December 28, 1942, Leahy Diary, William D. Leahy Papers, Library of Congress.

8. FACING THE JOINT CHIEFS OF STAFF

1. "Joint Chiefs of Staff Minutes of a Meeting at the White House," Washington, January 7, 1943, *Foreign Relations of the United States: The Conferences at Washington, 1941–1942, and Casablanca, 1943* (hereinafter *FRUS I*) (Washington, D.C.: Government Printing Office, 1968), 511.
2. Ibid., 509.
3. Ibid.
4. Ibid.
5. Ibid., 509–10.
6. Ibid., 510.
7. Ibid.
8. Ibid.
9. Ibid.
10. Ibid.
11. Ibid.
12. Ibid.
13. Ibid.
14. E.g., Albert Wedemeyer, *Wedemeyer Reports!* (New York: Henry Holt, 1958), 95, and John McLaughlin, *General Albert C. Wedemeyer: America's Unsung Strategist in World War II* (Philadelphia: Casemate, 2012), 31, referring to "the utter failure of 'Unconditional Surrender.'" For the view that it was a sop to the Soviets, see Frank Costigliola, *Roosevelt's Lost Alliances: How Personal Politics Helped Start the Cold War* (Princeton, NJ: Princeton University Press, 2012), 179–81. The classic condemnatory statement on unconditional surrender was, however, by Hanson Baldwin: "Unconditional surrender was an open invitation to unconditional

resistance: it discouraged opposition to Hitler, probably lengthened the war, cost us lives, and helped to lead to the present abortive peace": Hanson Baldwin, *Great Mistakes of the War* (New York: Harper, 1950), 13.

15. Wedemeyer, *Wedemeyer Reports!*, 186–87.

16. In the House of Commons on July 21, 1949, Labor Minister Ernest Bevin claimed the British War Cabinet had not been consulted over "unconditional surrender," prompting Churchill to claim he "had never heard the phrase until the President suddenly uttered it at the Casablanca press conference": David Reynolds, *In Command of History: Churchill Fighting and Writing the Second World War* (New York: Random House, 2005), 323.

17. Ibid., 506.

9. THE HOUSE OF HAPPINESS

1. John McCrea, "Handwritten Memoirs/Recollections," McCrea Papers, FDR Library.

2. Letter of January 14, 1943, in Geoffrey C. Ward, ed., *Closest Companion: The Unknown Story of the Intimate Friendship Between Franklin Roosevelt and Margaret Suckley* (Boston: Houghton Mifflin, 1995), 198.

3. McCrea, "Handwritten Memoirs/Recollections."

4. Letter of January 14, 1943, in Ward, *Closest Companion*, 198.

5. Letter of December 17, 1942, Elsey Papers, FDR Library.

6. S. E. Morison, "Memorandum For the President," December 18, 1942, Elsey Papers, FDR Library.

7. David Stafford, *Roosevelt and Churchill: Men of Secrets* (Woodstock, NY: Overlook, 1999), 197–98.

8. Letter of January 14, 1943, in Ward, *Closest Companion*, 198.

9. Elliott Roosevelt, *As He Saw It* (New York: Duell, Sloan, and Pearce, 1946), 65.

10. Letter of January 14, 1943, in Ward, *Closest Companion*, 198.

11. Ian Jacob, unpublished Casablanca account, Churchill College Archives, Cambridge, UK.

12. Elliott Roosevelt, *As He Saw It*, 62.

13. Ibid., 67.

14. Ibid., 66.

15. Ibid., 66.

16. McCrea, "Handwritten Memoirs/Recollections," McCrea Papers, FDR Library.

17. Robert Sherwood, *Roosevelt and Hopkins: An Intimate History* (New York: Harper, 1948), 673.

18. "A Gleam of Victory: A Speech at the Lord Mayor's Luncheon at the Mansion House, November 10, 1942," in *The War Speeches of the Rt. Hon. Winston S. Churchill*, ed. Charles Eade (London: Cassell, 1952), vol. 2, 342–45.

19. Entry of 10.11.1942, Joseph Goebbels, *Die Tagebücher von Joseph Goebbels* [The

diaries of Joseph Goebbels], ed. Elke Froehlich (Munich: K. G. Saur, 1995), Teil II, Band 6, 273 (hereinafter *Die Tagebücher 6*). Quotes from this source have been translated by the author.

20. Ibid., entry of 10.11.1942, 265.
21. Ibid., entry of 11.11.1942, 273.
22. Ibid., entry of 15.11.1942, 294.
23. Quoted in Winston S. Churchill, *The Second World War,* vol. 4, *The Hinge of Fate* (London: Cassell & Company, 1951), 583.

10. HOT WATER

1. Martin Gilbert, *Winston S. Churchill,* vol. 7, *Road to Victory: 1941–1945* (London: Heinemann, 1986), 269.
2. Ian Jacob, unpublished Casablanca account, Churchill College Archives, Cambridge, UK.
3. Ibid. The ship, which had been the headquarters ship for the landing at Algiers, had "a complete set of wireless instruments." It could be "placed in Casablanca harbor, & our cipher staff could live aboard and all our telegram traffic with London could thus be handled without the necessity for any elaborate machinery ashore. All that was necessary was a constant carrier service between ship & hotel, and a Defense Registry organization in the latter" — "exactly as" if they were operating out of the War Rooms in London. The *Bulolo* sailed for Casablanca on January 5, arriving on January 10, 1943. Jacob, unpublished Casablanca account.
4. Ibid. See also Brian Lavery, *Churchill Goes to War: Winston's Wartime Journeys* (London: Conway, 2007), 160–64.
5. Jacob, unpublished Casablanca account.
6. Gilbert, *Road to Victory: 1941–1945,* 294.
7. Jacob, unpublished Casablanca account.
8. Ibid.
9. Ibid.
10. Ibid.

11. A WONDERFUL PICTURE

1. McCrea, "Handwritten Memoirs/Recollections," McCrea Papers, FDR Library.
2. Jacob, unpublished Casablanca account.
3. McCrea, "Handwritten Memoirs/Recollections."
4. Sherwood, *Roosevelt and Hopkins,* 673.
5. Elliott Roosevelt, *As He Saw It,* 66.
6. Entry of January 14, 1943, John W. Huston, *American Airpower Comes of Age: General Henry H. 'Hap' Arnold's World War II Diaries* (Maxwell AFB, AL: Air University Press, 2002), vol. 1, 464.

7. Entry of January 14, 1943, Arthur Bryant, *The Turn of the Tide: A History of the War Years, Based on the Diaries of Field Marshal Lord Alanbrooke, Chief of the Imperial General Staff* (New York: Doubleday, 1957), 446.

8. Elliott Roosevelt, *As He Saw It*, 67.

9. Entry of January 14, 1943, Huston, ed., *American Airpower Comes of Age*, 464.

10. Ibid.

11. Entry of January 14, 1943, Bryant, *The Turn of the Tide*, 446.

12. Elliott Roosevelt, *As He Saw It*, 71.

13. Ibid., 73.

14. Ibid., 74.

15. Ibid., 76.

16. Ibid..

17. Ibid., 77.

12. IN THE PRESIDENT'S BOUDOIR

1. Albert Wedemeyer, *Wedemeyer Reports!* (New York: Henry Holt, 1958), 192.

2. Andrew Roberts, *Masters and Commanders: How Four Titans Won the War in the West, 1941–1945* (New York: Harper, 2009), 337.

3. Wedemeyer, *Wedemeyer Reports!*, 337, quoting Brigadier General J. E. Hull of the War Department's Operations Division.

4. Wedemeyer, *Wedemeyer Reports!*, 191–92.

5. Joint Strategic Survey Committee, January 8, 1943, Map Room Files, FDR Library.

6. "Meeting of Roosevelt with the Joint Chiefs of Staff, January 15, 1943, 10 a.m., President's Villa," *Foreign Relations of the United States: The Conferences at Washington, 1941–1942, and Casablanca, 1943* (hereinafter *FRUS I*) (Washington, D.C.: Government Printing Office, 1968), 559.

7. Ibid.

8. Ibid.

9. Ibid.

10. McCrea, "Handwritten Memoirs/Recollections."

11. Harry C. Butcher, *My Three Years with Eisenhower: The Personal Diary of Captain Harry C. Butcher, USNR, Naval Aide to General Eisenhower, 1942 to 1945* (New York: Simon and Schuster, 1946), 237.

12. Entry of January 15, 1943, Brooke, *War Diaries*, 351. Also "Meeting of the Combined Chiefs of Staff, January 15, 1943, 2:30 pm., Anfa Camp," *FRUS I*, 567.

13. Entry of December 28, 1942, Brooke, *War Diaries*, 351.

14. Jacob, Casablanca Diary, Churchill Archives.

15. Butcher, *My Three Years with Eisenhower*, 243.

16. Entry of January 14, 1943, Martin Blumenson, ed, *The Patton Papers, 1940–1945* (Boston: Houghton Mifflin, 1974), 154.

17. "Meeting of the Combined Chiefs of Staff, January 15, 1943, 2:30 pm., Anfa Camp," *FRUS I*, 568–69.

18. Elliott Roosevelt, *As He Saw It,* 79.
19. Ibid.
20. Ibid.
21. "Meeting of the Combined Chiefs of Staff with Roosevelt and Churchill, January 15, 1943, 5:30 p.m., President's Villa," *FRUS I,* 573.
22. Entry of January 15, 1943, Brooke, *War Diaries,* 359.
23. Elliott Roosevelt, *As He Saw It,* 83.
24. Ibid.
25. Ibid., 84.

13. STIMSON IS AGHAST

1. Entry of January 19, 1943, Stimson Diary, Henry L. Stimson Papers, Yale University Library, New Haven, CT.
2. Ibid., entry of January 21, 1943.
3. "Meeting of Roosevelt with the Joint Chiefs of Staff, January 16, 1943," *Foreign Relations of the United States: The Conferences at Washington, 1941–1942, and Casablanca, 1943* (hereinafter *FRUS I*) (Washington, D.C.: Government Printing Office, 1968), 594.
4. Entry of 16 January 1943 and annotation, *War Diaries, 1939–1945: Field Marshal Lord Alanbrooke, War Diaries, 1939–1945,* ed. Alex Danchev and Daniel Todman (Berkeley: University of California Press, 2001), 360.
5. "Meeting of the Combined Chiefs of Staff, January 16, 1943," *FRUS I,* 591.
6. Brooke: "We should definitely count on reentering the Continent on a large scale" — "Meeting of the Combined Chiefs of Staff, January 16, 1943," *FRUS I,* 591.
7. "Meeting of Roosevelt with the Joint Chiefs of Staff, January 16, 1943," *FRUS I,* 597.
8. Ibid.
9. Martin Gilbert, *Road to Victory: Winston S. Churchill, 1941–1945* (London: Heinemann, 1986), 299–300.
10. See, for example, Mark Stoler and Melanie Gustafson, "Creating a Global Allied Strategy," in their *Major Problems in the History of World War II: Documents and Essays* (Boston: Houghton Mifflin, 2003), 74–108.
11. John McCrea, "Handwritten Memoirs/Recollections," McCrea Papers, FDR Library.
12. Mark Clark, *Calculated Risk* (London: Harrap, 1951), 148–49.
13. Letter of Thursday, January 21, 1943, to Daisy Suckley, in Ward, ed., *Closest Companion: The Unknown Story of the Intimate Friendship Between Franklin Roosevelt and Margaret Suckley* (Boston: Houghton Mifflin, 1995), 199.
14. Unpublished autobiography, chapters 12 through 22, Private Papers of Brigadier G.M.O. Davy, PP/MCR/143, courtesy of Documents Department, Imperial War Museum, London.
15. Elliott Roosevelt, *As He Saw It* (New York: Duell, Sloan, and Pearce, 1946), 106.
16. Ibid., 106–7. General Mark Clark, later recalling the episode, confessed that by

the time the President had asked for the mess kit, it had already been washed and mixed with others. Clark had demanded "any mess kit" from the kitchen staff, "And make it fast." The President had been delighted, and had said, "I'll have them put it in the Smithsonian Institution": Mark Clark, *Calculated Risk,* 149.

17. Harold Macmillan, *War Diaries: Politics and War in the Mediterranean, January 1943–May 1945* (London: Macmillan, 1984), 8.

14. DE GAULLE

1. McCrea, "Handwritten Memoirs/Recollections," McCrea Papers, FDR Library.
2. Ibid.
3. Letter to Daisy Suckley, January 20, 1943, in Ward, *Closest Companion,* 199.
4. Ibid., January 21, 1943.
5. Kenneth Pendar, *Adventure in Diplomacy* (New York: Dodd, Mead & Co, 1945), 161.
6. Robert Murphy, *Diplomat Among Warriors* (New York: Doubleday, 1964), 168.
7. Ibid.
8. McCrea, "Handwritten Memoirs/Recollections."
9. Friday, January 22, 1943, "The President's Log, January 14–25, 1943," *FRUS I,* 531.
10. Elliott Roosevelt, *As He Saw It,* 111.
11. Murphy, *Diplomat Among Warriors,* 173.
12. Elliott Roosevelt, *As He Saw It,* 112.
13. Pendar, *Adventure in Diplomacy,* 145.
14. McCrea, "Handwritten Memoirs/Recollections."
15. Elliott Roosevelt, *As He Saw It,* 112.
16. Entry of January 14, 1943, *The Patton Diaries II,* ed. Martin Blumenson (Boston: Houghton Mifflin, 1974), 154.
17. Ibid., entry of January 17, 155.
18. Ibid., entry of January 19, 157.
19. Ibid., entry of January 21, 158–59.
20. Ibid., 158.
21. Ibid.
22. Ibid., entry of January 22, 158.
23. Elliott Roosevelt, *As He Saw It,* 112.

15. AN ACERBIC INTERVIEW

1. Robert Sherwood, *Roosevelt and Hopkins: An Intimate History* (New York: Harper, 1948), 678–79.
2. McCrea, "Handwritten Memoirs/Recollections."
3. McCrea Notes: "Roosevelt–De Gaulle Conversation, January 22, 1943," *FRUS I,* 694.
4. Ibid., 695.

5. Immediately following the Allied Torch invasion, Hitler had ordered Operation Anton, the German and Italian occupation of all Vichy-administered France and Corsica.

6. "Roosevelt De-Gaulle Conversation, January 22, 1943," *FRUS I,* 696.

7. Charles de Gaulle, *The Complete War Memoirs of Charles de Gaulle,* vol. 2, *Unity* (New York: Simon and Schuster, 1964), 388–89.

8. Henri Giraud, *Un seul but, la victoire: Alger, 1942–1944* (Paris: R. Julliard, 1949).

9. De Gaulle, *The Complete War Memoirs,* vol. 2, 392–93.

10. Ibid., 384.

11. Elliott Roosevelt, *As He Saw It,* 113.

12. Ibid., 113–14.

13. De Gaulle, *The Complete War Memoirs,* vol. 2, 384.

14. Elliott Roosevelt, *As He Saw It,* 114.

15. Ibid., 114–15.

16. Ibid., 115.

17. Ibid.

18. Ibid., 115–16.

19. Ibid., 121.

20. Ibid., 122.

21. François Kersaudy, *Churchill and De Gaulle* (London: Collins, 1981), 252.

22. Ibid., 253.

23. Ibid., 254.

24. Ibid., 255.

25. Sherwood, *Roosevelt & Hopkins,* 693.

26. Kersaudy, *Churchill and De Gaulle,* 255.

16. THE UNCONDITIONAL SURRENDER MEETING

1. "Historic Meeting Informal in Tone: Reporters Sit on Garden Grass at Leaders' Feet to Hear of Momentous Talks," *New York Times,* January 27, 1943.

2. Ibid.

3. De Gaulle, *The Complete War Memoirs,* vol. 2, 399.

4. Giraud, *Un seul but,* 96.

5. "Historic Meeting Informal in Tone," *New York Times.*

6. Ibid.

7. "875th Press Conference. Joint Conference by the President and Prime Minister Churchill at Casablanca, January 24, 1943," in Franklin D. Roosevelt, *The Public Papers of Franklin D. Roosevelt,* comp. Samuel Rosenman, 1943 vol., *The Tide Turns* (New York: Russell and Russell, 1969), 37–44.

8. McCrea, "Handwritten Memoirs/Recollections."

9. Ibid.

10. *Roosevelt Presidential Press Conferences,* No. 875, 90–91.

11. Entry of Wednesday, January 27, 1943, in Alan Lascelles, *King's Counsellor:*

Abdication and War: The Diaries of Sir Alan Lascelles, ed. Duff Hart-Davis (London: Weidenfeld & Nicolson, 2006), 93.

12. Entry of 27.1.1943, Joseph Goebbels, *Die Tagebücher von Joseph Goebbels* [The diaries of Joseph Goebbels], ed. Elke Froehlich (Munich: K. G. Saur, 1993), Teil II, Band 7 (hereinafter *Die Tagebücher 7*), 203. Quotes from this source have been translated by the author.

13. Ibid., entry of 26.1.1943, 197.

14. Ibid., entry of 27.2.1943, 203.

15. Ibid., entry of 28.1.1943, 208.

16. Ibid., entry of 26.11943, 197.

17. Ibid., entry of 28.1.1943, 209.

18. Max Domarus, ed., *Hitler, Speeches and Proclamations 1932–1945: The Chronicle of a Dictatorship,* vol. 4, *The Years 1941 to 1945* (Wauconda, IL: Bolchazy-Carducci, 1997), 2671–85.

19. Entry of 28.1.1943, Goebbels, *Die Tagebücher 7,* 209.

20. Albert Speer, *Inside the Third Reich* (New York: Macmillan, 1970), 258.

21. Ian Kershaw, *Hitler, 1936–1945: Nemesis* (London: Allen Lane, 2000), 552.

22. Entry of 29.1.1943, Goebbels, *Die Tagebücher 7,* 216.

23. Domarus, ed., *Hitler, Speeches and Proclamations 1932–1945,* 2749.

24. David Irving, *Goebbels: Mastermind of the Third Reich* (London: Focal Point, 1996), 421.

25. "*Nun, Volk steh auf, und Sturm brich los! Rede im Berliner Sportpalast,*" *Der steile Aufstieg* (Munich: Zentralverlag der NSDAP, 1944), 167–204. Translated by the author.

26. Irving, *Goebbels,* 422–23.

27. Ralf Georg Reuth, *Goebbels* (Munich: Piper Verlag, 1990), 563.

17. KASSERINE

1. Ian Kershaw, *Hitler, 1936–1945: Nemesis* (London: Allen Lane, 2000), 550.

2. Ibid., 548.

3. Entry of January 19, 1943, Robert Ferrell, ed., *The Eisenhower Diaries* (New York: Norton, 1981), 86.

4. Ibid.

5. Rick Atkinson, *An Army at Dawn* (New York: Henry Holt, 2002), 308.

6. Ibid., 317.

7. Ibid., 322.

8. Entry of 18.2.1943, Joseph Goebbels, *Die Tagebücher von Joseph Goebbels* [The diaries of Joseph Goebbels], ed. Elke Froehlich (Munich: K. G. Saur, 1993), Teil II, Band 7 (hereinafter *Die Tagebücher 7*), 366.

9. Ibid., entry of 19.2.1943, 370.

10. Ibid., entry of 21.2.1943, 389.

18. ARCH-ADMIRALS AND ARCH-GENERALS

1. Atkinson, *An Army at Dawn*, 390–91.
2. Nigel Hamilton, *Master of the Battlefield: Monty's War Years, 1942–1944* (New York: McGraw Hill, 1984), 142.
3. Letter of February 23, 1943, in Martin Blumenson, ed, *The Patton Papers II, 1940–1945* (Boston: Houghton Mifflin, 1974), 175.
4. Entry of February 15, 1943, Stimson Diary, Henry L. Stimson Papers, Yale University Library, New Haven, CT.
5. Ibid., entry of February 17, 1943.
6. Entry of 20.2.1943, *Die Tagebücher 7,* 377.
7. Entry of February 18, 1943, Stimson Diary.
8. Ibid.
9. Entry of 20.2.1943, *Die Tagebücher 7,* 377.
10. Ibid., entry of 23.2.1943, 398–99.
11. Ibid., 398.
12. Blumenson, *The Patton Papers,* vol. 2, 183.
13. "'Memorandum' to Admiral Leahy and General Marshall, Copy to the Secretary of the Navy," November 17, 1942, King Papers, Naval Historical Archives.
14. Letter of November 19, 1943, in Alfred Chandler, ed., *The Papers of Dwight David Eisenhower,* vol. 2, *The War Years* (Baltimore: Johns Hopkins, 1970), 964–65.
15. Ibid., 965.

19. BETWEEN TWO FORCES OF EVIL

1. Report to the President, January 10, 1943, Bullitt File, Safe and Confidential Files, FDR Library.
2. Ibid.
3. Henri Giraud, *Un seul but la Victoire: Alger 1942–1944* (Paris: R. Julliard, 1949), 93–94.
4. Report to the President, January 10, 1943, Bullitt File, Safe and Confidential Files, FDR Library. See also Michael Cassella-Blackburn, *The Donkey, The Carrot, and the Club: William C. Bullitt and Soviet-American Relations, 1917–1948* (Westport, CT: Praeger, 2004), 213–14.
5. Report to the President, January 10, 1943, Bullitt File, Safe and Confidential Files, FDR Library.
6. Ibid.
7. C-259-A/1, From the Prime Minister to the President, February 2, 1943, in Warren Kimball, ed., *Churchill & Roosevelt: The Complete Correspondence,* vol. 2, *Alliance Forged* (Princeton, NJ: Princeton University Press, 1984), 129–30.
8. S. E. Morison, *The Two-Ocean War* (Boston: Little Brown, 1963), 272.
9. Entry of January 8, 1943, in "Secret Diary" of Lord Halifax, Papers of Lord Halifax,

Hickleton Papers, Borthwick Institute of Historical Research, University of York, Yorkshire, England.

10. Ibid., entry of January 11, 1943.
11. Ibid.
12. Ibid., entry of January 18, 1943.
13. Ibid., entry of January 26, 1943.
14. Ibid., entry of January 28, 1943.
15. Ibid., entry of February 2, 1943.
16. Ibid., entry of February 15, 1943.

20. HEALTH ISSUES

1. Elie Abel and Averell Harriman, *Special Envoy to Churchill and Stalin, 1941–1946* (New York: Random House, 1975), 183.
2. R. H. Ferrell, *The Dying President* (Columbia: University of Missouri Press, 1998), 10.
3. Entry of December 4, 1943, Diaries of William Lyon Mackenzie King, Library and Archives Canada, Ottawa, ON (hereinafter Mackenzie King Diary).
4. Entry of February 3, 1943, Stimson Diary.
5. Entry of February 1, 1943, Stimson Diary.
6. Diary entry of February 7, 1943, in Geoffrey Ward, ed., *Closest Companion: The Unknown Story of the Intimate Friendship Between Franklin Roosevelt and Margaret Suckley* (Boston: Houghton Mifflin, 1995), 201.
7. James A. Farley, *Jim Farley's Story* (New York: Whittlesey House, 1948), 108–9.
8. Jean Edward Smith, *FDR* (New York: Random House, 2007), 442, quoting Orville Bullitt, ed., *For the President, Personal and Secret: The Correspondence Between Franklin D. Roosevelt and William C. Bullitt* (Boston: Houghton Mifflin, 1988), 398. Also Will Brownell and Richard Billings, *So Close to Greatness: A Biography of William C. Bullitt* (New York: Macmillan, 1987).
9. Diary entry of February 7, 1943, in Ward, *Closest Companion*, 201.
10. Ibid.
11. Ross McIntire, *White House Physician* (New York: Putnam's Sons, 1946), 159.
12. Ferrell, *The Dying President*, 29.
13. Diary entry of February 14, 1943. Ward, *Closest Companion*, 201.
14. Ibid.
15. R-262/1, letter of March 17, 1943, in Kimball, ed., *Churchill & Roosevelt*, vol. 2, 156.
16. Diary entry of February 27, 1943. Ward, *Closest Companion*, 203.
17. Entry of April 8, 1943 (relating March 26, 1943, visit to White House), Butcher Diary, A-292–3, Eisenhower Library; also Harry Butcher, *My Three Years with Eisenhower*, 278–79.
18. Ibid., A-293.
19. Ibid., A-294.

20. Michael Burleigh, *The Third Reich: A New History* (New York: Hill & Wang, 2000), 740.

21. INSPECTION TOUR TWO

1. Entry of April 16, 1943 (regarding Fort Benning), in Ward, *Closest Companion,* 210.
2. Ibid., entry of April 24, 1943, 219.
3. Ibid., entry of April 16, 1943, 211.
4. Ibid., entry of April 17, 1943, 211.
5. Ibid., entry of April 18, 1943, 214.
6. Ibid., entry of April 24, 1943, 219.
7. Ibid., entry of April 25, 1943, 220–21.
8. Ibid., entry of April 19, 1943, 214.
9. Entry of February 24, 1943, Stimson Diary.
10. Ibid., entry of March 30, 1943.

22. GET YAMAMOTO!

1. George Kenney, *George C. Kenney Reports* (New York: Duell, Sloan, and Pearce, 1949), 52–53.
2. Entry of April 8, 1943 (relating March 26 visit to War office), Butcher Diary, A-287, Eisenhower Library.
3. Samuel Morison, *The Two Ocean War: A Short History of the United States Navy in the Second World War* (Boston: Little, Brown, 1963), 272–73.
4. Kenney, *George C. Kenney Reports,* 215.
5. See Christopher Andrew, *For the President's Eyes Only: Secret Intelligence and the American Presidency from Washington to Bush* (New York: HarperCollins, 1995), 123–24.
6. William Rigdon, *White House Sailor* (Garden City, NY: Doubleday, 1962), 19. For an account of how Ultra/Magic messages were relayed to the President, see David Stafford, *Roosevelt and Churchill* (Woodstock, NY: Overlook, 1999), 118–19; Andrew, *For the President's Eyes Only,* 103–11; and David Kahn, "Roosevelt, Magic, and Ultra," *Cryptologia* 16, no. 4 (October 1992).
7. Signal NTF131755, in Japanese Naval Cipher JN-25D, decoded by the U.S. Fleet Radio Unit Pacific in Hawaii: Ronald Lewin, *The American Magic: Codes, Ciphers and the Defeat of Japan* (New York: Farrar Straus Giroux, 1982), 182–83.
8. John Prados, *Combined Fleet Decoded: The Secret History of American Intelligence and the Japanese Navy in World War II* (New York: Random House, 1995), 453–58; Edward J. Drea, *MacArthur's ULTRA: Codebreaking and the War Against Japan, 1942–1945* (Lawrence: University Press of Kansas, 1992), 73.
9. Donald A. Davis, *Lightning Strike* (New York: St. Martin's, 2005), 220.

10. Ibid., 222.
11. Ibid., 227.
12. Rear Admiral Matome Ugaki, chief of staff to Admiral Yamamoto, in Burke Davis, *Get Yamamoto* (New York: Random House, 1969), 207.
13. Lewin, *The American Magic*, 185.
14. Burke Davis, *Get Yamamoto*, 128; Carroll V. Glines, *Attack on Yamamoto* (London: Orion Books, 1990), 9; Thomas Lanphier, "I Shot Down Yamamoto," *Reader's Digest*, December 1966, 48.
15. According to subsequent Japanese accounts, U.S. code breakers may have misinterpreted Admiral Yamamoto's flight schedule, which had the airfield of Buin, not Ballale, as its destination. "In the end it didn't matter," given the proximity of the two: Prados, *Combined Fleet Decoded*, 462.
16. Donald Davis, *Lightning Strike*, 273. Admiral Yamamoto was widely thought to have said, before Pearl Harbor, that he would take the surrender of America riding down Pennsylvania Avenue on a white charger; in truth he had pointed out that the United States would never surrender to Japan unless Japanese forces reached Washington, D.C., and the White House — which, having earlier studied at Harvard and having twice served as naval attaché in Washington, Yamamoto thought unlikely to eventuate.

23. "HE'S DEAD?"

1. Donald Davis, *Lightning Strike*, 304–8.
2. The airfield at Ballale was constructed in November 1942 by the Japanese, using forced labor of British artillery officers and men who had surrendered at Singapore. All 517 men were murdered by the Japanese on completion of the air base, in March 1943. See Don Wall, *Kill the Prisoners!* (Cambridge, UK: Peter Moore, 1996). Also Australian War Memorial Archives.
3. Burke Davis, *Get Yamamoto*, 196.
4. Ibid.
5. Donald Davis, *Lightning Strike*, 306–8.
6. Ibid., 309.
7. Ibid., 289–90. See also Andrew, *For the President's Eyes Only*, 138, and Walter Borneman, *The Admirals: Nimitz, Halsey, Leahy, and King — the Five-Star Admirals Who Won the War at Sea* (New York: Little, Brown, 2012), 315.
8. Burke Davis, *Get Yamamoto*, 210.
9. Presidential Press Conference No. 891, April 19, 1943, FDR Library.
10. In the first three weeks of March, 1943, more than three-quarters of a million tons of Allied shipping were still being sunk in the North Atlantic gap "not yet covered by air search," War Secretary Stimson complained to the President: Henry Stimson and McGeorge Bundy, *On Active Service in Peace and War* (New York: Harper and Brothers, 1948). For the best summary of the interservice controversy

see Samuel Eliot Morison, *The Battle of the Atlantic: September 1939–May 1943* (Boston: Little, Brown, 1947), 237–47.

11. Presidential Press Conference No. 898, May 21, 1943, FDR Library.
12. Grace Tully Archive, Franklin D. Roosevelt Papers, Box 11, Yamamoto (joke letter to), May 23, 1943, FDR Library.
13. Donald Davis, *Lightning Strike,* 315.
14. John C. Fredriksen, *The United States Air Force: A Chronology* (Santa Barbara, CA: ABC-CLIO, 2011), 104.

24. SAGA OF THE NIBELUNGS

1. Rick Atkinson, *An Army at Dawn* (New York: Henry Holt, 2002), 489–90.
2. Ibid., 484.

25. A SCENE FROM *THE ARABIAN NIGHTS*

1. Kenneth Pendar, *Adventure in Diplomacy* (New York: Dodd, Mead & Co, 1945), 43.
2. Ibid., 147.
3. Ibid., 148.
4. Ibid., 149.
5. Ibid., 152.
6. Ibid., 150.

26. THE GOD NEPTUNE

1. Entry of May 2, 1943, Leahy Diary, William D. Leahy Papers, Library of Congress.
2. Entry of May 7, 1943, Stimson Diary, Henry L. Stimson Papers, Yale University Library, New Haven, CT.
3. Ibid., entry of May 10, 1943.

27. A BATTLE ROYAL

1. Entry of May 11, 1943, Diaries of William Lyon Mackenzie King, Library and Archives Canada, Ottawa, ON.
2. Entry of May 9, 1943, Leahy Diary, William D. Leahy Papers, Library of Congress.
3. Ibid., entry of May 9, 1943.
4. Ibid., entry of May 11, 1943.
5. Entry of May 11, 1943 in Alan Brooke, *Field Marshal Lord Alanbrooke, War Diaries, 1939–1945,* ed. Alex Danchev and Daniel Todman (Berkeley: University of California Press, 2001), 402.
6. Ibid.

7. Entry of May 12, 1943, Stimson Diary.

8. The figure of 150,000 Axis troops who had already surrendered by May 12 was announced to the press the next morning, May 13, 1943, by the secretary of war: see entry for May 13, 1943, Stimson Diary.

9. "Meeting of the Combined Chiefs of Staff, May 13, 1943, 10:30 A.M.," in *Foreign Relations of the United States: The Conferences at Washington and Quebec, 1943* (hereinafter *FRUS II*) (Washington, D.C.: Government Printing Office, 1970), 24–25.

10. Entry of May 12, 1943, Brooke, *War Diaries*, 402.

11. Entry of May 13, 1943, Leahy Diary.

12. Ibid.

13. Ibid.

14. Lord Ismay, *The Memoirs of General Lord Ismay* (London: Heinemann, 1960), 296.

28. NO MAJOR OPERATIONS UNTIL 1945 OR 1946

1. Letter of May 13, 1943, in Mary Soames, *Speaking For Themselves: The Personal Letters of Winston and Clementine Churchill, Edited by Their Daughter* (New York: Doubleday, 1998), 479–80.

2. "A Global Strategy: Memorandum by the United States Chiefs of Staff," in *FRUS II*, 222–23.

3. "Conduct of the War in 1943–44, Memorandum by the British Chiefs of Staff," in *FRUS II*, 223–27.

4. "Meeting of the Combined Chiefs of Staff, May 13, 1943, 10:30 A.M.", *FRUS II*, 39–40.

5. Ibid., 41.

6. Ibid., 43.

7. Ibid., 44.

8. Ibid.

9. Ibid.

10. Ibid.

11. C-294, Churchill cable to Roosevelt, May 10, 1943, in Warren Kimball, ed., *Churchill & Roosevelt: The Complete Correspondence*, vol. 2, *Alliance Forged* (Princeton, NJ: Princeton University Press), 212.

12. Richard Breitman and Allan J. Lichtman, *FDR and the Jews* (Cambridge, MA: Harvard University Press, 2013), 206–10.

13. Robert E. Sherwood, *Roosevelt and Hopkins: An Intimate History* (New York: Harper, 1948), 728.

14. Winston S. Churchill, *The Second World War*, vol. 4, *The Hinge of Fate* (London: Cassel & Company, 1951), 713.

15. Ibid.

16. Ibid.

17. Lord Moran, *Winston Churchill: The Struggle for Survival, 1940–1965* (Boston: Houghton Mifflin, 1966), 95.
18. Ibid., 95–96.
19. Ibid., 96.
20. Ibid.
21. Ibid.
22. Entry of May 17, 1943, Stimson Diary.
23. Ibid.
24. Ibid.
25. Letter of May 12 (on "Office of the Secretary, Department of the Navy" notepaper), Bullitt Files, FDR Library.

29. THE DAVIES MISSION

1. "This is a situation full of ugly possibilities, and engendering it is a triumph for Goebbels": entry of Monday, April 26, 1943, in Alan Lascelles, *King's Counsellor: Abdication and War: The Diaries of Sir Alan Lascelles,* ed. Duff Hart-Davis (London: Weidenfeld & Nicolson, 2006), 126.
2. Walter Reich, former director of the Holocaust Museum in Washington, "Remember the Women," *New York Times Book Review,* April 12, 2015, 23.
3. Roosevelt to Stalin, Document 88, March 16, 1943, in Susan Butler, ed., *My Dear Mr. Stalin: The Complete Correspondence of Franklin D. Roosevelt and Joseph V. Stalin* (New Haven, CT: Yale University Press, 2005), 121.
4. Elizabeth MacLean, *Joseph E. Davies: Envoy to the Soviets* (Westport, CT: Praeger, 1992), 100.
5. "Meeting of the Combined Chiefs of Staff, May 18, 1943, 10:30 A.M.," *Foreign Relations of the United States: The Conferences at Washington and Quebec, 1943* (hereinafter *FRUS II*) (Washington, D.C.: Government Printing Office, 1970), 101.
6. Sir Alan Brooke, Proceedings of the Conference, "Defeat of the Axis Powers in Europe: discussion, Combined Chiefs of Staff," *FRUS II,* 101.
7. Entry of May 19, 1943, Stimson Diary.
8. Ibid.
9. Ibid.

30. A DOZEN DIEPPES IN A DAY

1. Entry of May 18, 1943, Diaries of William Lyon Mackenzie King, Library and Archives Canada, Ottawa, ON (hereinafter Mackenzie King Diary).
2. Ibid.
3. Ibid.
4. Ibid., "Conversation with Hon. L. McCarthy, at Canadian Legation after luncheon, Washington."

5. Ibid., "Conversation Mr. Mackenzie King had with Mr. Winston Churchill, Tuesday, May 18, 1943 — White House, Washington, 6.00 p.m."
6. Ibid., "Meeting of the Joint Chiefs of Staffs, May 20, 1943."
7. Ibid., "Conversation Mr. Mackenzie King had with Mr. Winston Churchill, Tuesday, May 18, 1943 — White House, Washington, 6.00 p.m."
8. Ibid.
9. Ibid., "Memorandum re questions asked Mr. Churchill by members of the Senate of the U.S. and representatives of the Foreign Committee and answers given by Mr Churchill, Washington, May 19, 1943."
10. Ibid., entry of May 19, 1943, "Quotations and answers, members of Senate of the U.S. — 19.v.43."
11. Ibid.
12. Meeting of the Combined Chiefs of Staff, May 19, 1943, 10:30 A.M., in *FRUS II*, 113.
13. Ibid., 114.
14. Entry of May 19, 1943, in Arthur Bryant, *The Turn of the Tide: A History of the War Years, Based on the Diaries of Field Marshal Lord Alanbrooke, Chief of the Imperial General Staff* (New York: Doubleday, 1957), 509.
15. Meeting of the Combined Chiefs of Staff with Roosevelt and Churchill, May 19, 1943, 6 P.M.," in *FRUS II*, 122–23.

31. THE FUTURE OF THE WORLD AT STAKE

1. Entry of May 19, 1943, Mackenzie King Diary.
2. Ibid.
3. Ibid., "Meeting of the Joint Staffs — May 20, 1943."
4. Prime Minister's Personal Telegram, 21 February 1943, in Martin Gilbert, *Road to Victory: Winston S. Churchill, 1941–1945* (London: Heinemann, 1986), 343.
5. E.g., entry of Wednesday, May 26, 1943, Mackenzie King Diary.
6. Entry of May 20, 1943, in "Secret Diary" of Lord Halifax, Papers of Lord Halifax, Hickleton Papers, Borthwick Institute of Historical Research, University of York, Yorkshire, England.
7. "Meeting of the Joint Staffs, May 20, 1943," Mackenzie King Diary, Library and Archives Canada.
8. Under the Canadian constitution, command of Canada's all-volunteer forces to serve overseas (conscription was confined to service in Canada only) was vested in the British monarch, and exercised by the Canadian federal Cabinet, who deferred largely to the authority of Winston Churchill in his role as minister of defense and prime minister of Great Britain.
9. "Meeting of the Joint Staffs, May 20, 1943," Mackenzie King Diary.
10. Ibid.
11. Ibid., entry of Friday, May 21, 1943.

12. Ibid., "Conversation with Mr. Churchill, White House — May 21, 1943."
13. Ibid.
14. Ibid.
15. Ibid.

32. THE PRESIDENT LOSES PATIENCE

1. Entry of May 24, 1943, in Bryant, *The Turn of the Tide*, 513.
2. Ibid.
3. Entry of May 24, 1943, Leahy Diary, William D. Leahy Papers, Library of Congress.
4. Ibid.
5. Entry of May 25, 1943 in Lord Moran, *Winston Churchill: The Struggle for Survival, 1940–1965* (Boston: Houghton Mifflin, 1966), 97.
6. Entry of May 24, 1943 Moran, *Winston Churchill*, 97–98.
7. Entry of May 25, 1943 (400c), Mackenzie King Diary.
8. Entry of May 28, 1943 Moran, *Winston Churchill*, 99.
9. Entry of 25 May, 1943, Bryant, *The Turn of the Tide*, 514.
10. Entry of May 27, 1943, Stimson Diary.
11. Ibid., entry of May 25, 1943.
12. Ibid.
13. "He thought the time might be in August . . . He then said: if, by any chance, something should prevent Stalin making the trip, what I would like to do is to come to Ottawa just the same though perhaps this might be in July" — "Conversation with Pres. Roosevelt, White House — May 21, 1943," Mackenzie King Diary.
14. Entry of May 25, 1943, Leahy Diary.
15. Entry of May 24, 1943, Bryant, *The Turn of the Tide*, 512–13.
16. Entry of Tuesday, January 26, 1943, in Lascelles, *King's Counsellor*, 93.
17. Entry of May 31, 1943, Diary of Harry C. Butcher, Eisenhower Presidential Library, Abilene.
18. Ibid.
19. Entry of 26 May, 1943, Bryant, *The Turn of the Tide*, 517.
20. Kershaw, *Hitler 1936–1945*, 606.

33. SICILY — AND KURSK

1. Entry of July 9, 1943, in Geoffrey C. Ward, ed., *Closest Companion, The Unknown Story of the Intimate Friendship Between Franklin Roosevelt and Margaret Suckley* (Boston: Houghton Mifflin, 1995), 225.
2. Entry of July 9, 1943, Leahy Diary, William D. Leahy Papers, Library of Congress.

3. Entry of July 9, in Ward, *Closest Companion,* 226.

4. Ben Macintyre, *Operation Mincemeat: The True Story That Changed the Course of World War II* (New York: Random House, 2010), 294.

34. THE FÜHRER FLIES TO ITALY

1. Erich von Manstein, *Lost Victories* (London: Methuen, 1958), 448.

2. Ibid., 449. Manstein's view has been much contested, especially by Russian military historians anxious to honor the Soviet defense of Kursk and the start of a major counteroffensive by Russian forces at Orel: see, inter alia, Chris Bellamy, *Absolute War: Soviet Russia in the Second World War* (New York: Palgrave, 2007), 586–87. However, it is clear from Joseph Goebbels's private conversations with Hitler at Berchtesgaden before the battle that Hitler was far more worried by the next moves of the Western Allies in the Mediterranean than by what would happen at Kursk — essentially a "show" offensive to write down Soviet armies using the latest German firepower. "The Führer has decided to stay where we are," on the Eastern Front, Goebbels recorded. "We have to keep our reserves up our sleeves. His old plan of seizing the Caucasus and fighting in the Middle East is redundant, thanks to last winter's crisis . . . Under no circumstances is he prepared to give up the Italian mainland — he has no intention of pulling back to the Po, even if the Italians abandon the front. We will simply take over the running of the war in Italy. That is the overriding principle of German strategy: to keep the war as far from the German homeland as possible": entry of 25.6.43, in Goebbels, *Die Tagebücher von Joseph Goebbels,* ed. Elke Froehlich (Munich:K. G. Saur, 1993), Teil II, Band 8, 531–34.

3. Entry of July 14, 1943, Ward, *Closest Companion,* 226.

4. Ibid., entry of July 13, 1943, 226.

5. Ibid., entry of July 19, 1943, 227.

6. Entry of 17.7.43, in Joseph Goebbels, *Die Tagebücher von Joseph Goebbels* [The diaries of Joseph Goebbels], ed. Elke Froehlich (Munich: K. G. Saur, 1993), Teil II, Band 9 (hereinafter *Die Tagebücher 9*), 116.

7. Ibid., 114.

8. Ibid., 116.

9. Ibid., 114.

10. Despite being made aware of Soviet rather than Nazi responsibility for the massacre back in April 1943, both Roosevelt and Churchill had been unwilling to raise the issue in public — or even encourage others to do so, when continued Soviet resistance on the Eastern Front was crucial. General Sikorski, the commander in chief of all Polish forces in the West, on April 15, 1943, was thus begged not to make Katyn, however awful, a matter of contention, just before Hitler opened his expected summer offensive: Martin Gilbert, *Road to Victory: Winston Churchill, 1941–1945* (London: Heinemann, 1986), 385.

11. Entry of 19.7.43, Goebbels, *Die Tagebücher 9*, 126.

12. Ibid.

13. Ibid., entry of 20.7.43, 132.

14. Ian Kershaw, *Hitler 1936–1945: Nemesis* (New York: Norton, 2000), 594.

15. Ibid., 597.

35. COUNTERCRISIS

1. See inter alia Trumbull Higgins, *Soft Underbelly: The Anglo-American Controversy over the Italian Campaign, 1939–1945* (New York: Macmillan, 1968), 91–124; Douglas Porch, *The Path to Victory in World War II: The Mediterranean Theater in World War II* (New York: Farrar, Straus and Giroux, 2004), 459–76; Mark Stoler, *The Politics of the Second Front: American Military Planning and Diplomacy in Coalition Warfare, 1941–1943* (Westport, CT: Greenwood Press, 1977), 97–129; and Mark Stoler, *Allies in War: Britain and America Against the Axis Powers, 1940–1945* (New York: Hodder Arnold, 2005), 123–28.

2. Davies Papers, mss for May 20, 1943, 9, Library of Congress.

3. Entry of June 3, 1943, "Arrival in Washington and Report to the President," Davies Papers, Library of Congress.

4. Davies Papers, mss for May 20, 1943, 9.

5. Entry of July 22, 1943, Stimson Diary, Henry L. Stimson Papers, Yale University Library, New Haven, CT.

6. Ibid.

7. Ibid.

8. Maurice Matloff, *Strategic Planning for Coalition Warfare* (Washington, D.C.: Center of Military History, 1959), 165.

9. Ibid.

10. Ibid., 167.

11. Ibid., Letter to Handy, July 4, 1943, 164.

36. A FISHING EXPEDITION IN ONTARIO

1. George M. Elsey, Introduction to "The Log of the President's Visit to Canada, 16 August 1943 to 26 August 1943," p. 3, FDR Library.

2. Ibid.

3. Ibid.

4. "Will Punish Duce; President in His War Report Demands Total Surrender," *New York Times*, July 29, 1943.

5. FDR finally told Daisy Suckley "the whole story, which is unsavory," later that summer, including Bullitt's part. "The P. never wants to speak to Bullitt again": entry of September 22 and 29, 1943, in Ward, ed., *Closest Companion*, 244.

6. "Warning by Stalin to Allies Is Seen; U.S. Observers in Moscow Said to View German Manifesto as Russian Declaration," *New York Times*, July 29, 1943.

7. Entry of July 29, 1943, Leahy Diary.

8. Entry of July 28, 1943, Ward, *Closest Companion,* 227.
9. Ibid.
10. Entry of August 9, 1943, Leahy Diary.
11. Ibid.
12. Ibid.

37. THE PRESIDENT'S JUDGMENT

1. Davies Papers, mss for May 20, 1943, 9, Library of Congress.
2. Ibid.
3. David Reynolds, *In Command of History: Churchill Fighting and Writing the Second World War* (New York: Random House, 2005), 322–23.
4. Davies Papers, mss for May 20, 1943, 10, Library of Congress.
5. OSS Numbered Intelligence Bulletins, No. 39, 10 July 43, Roosevelt Map Room, Military Subject Files, Box 72, Section 2, MR 203 (12), FDR Library.

38. STALIN LIES

1. From Premier J. V. Stalin to President Franklin D. Roosevelt, August 8, 1943, in Susan Butler, ed., *My Dear Mr. Stalin: The Complete Correspondence of Franklin D. Roosevelt and Joseph V. Stalin* (New Haven, CT: Yale, 2005), 151.
2. Albert Weeks, *Russia's Life-Saver: Lend Lease Aid to the United States* (Lanham, MD: Lexington Books, 204), 1.
3. Ibid, 146–47. By the end of the war, over 30 percent of Russian wheeled vehicles had come from the United States, as also aircraft; almost 60 percent of aviation fuel, and more than 50 percent of Russian ordnance (ammunition): Ibid., 8–9.
4. Entry of August 9, 1943, in Geoffrey C. Ward, ed., *Closest Companion, The Unknown Story of the Intimate Friendship Between Franklin Roosevelt and Margaret Suckley* (Boston: Houghton Mifflin, 1995), 228.

39. WAR ON TWO WESTERN FRONTS

1. Entry of September 29, 1943, in Ward, *Closest Companion,* 244.
2. Entry of August 10, 1943, Leahy Diary, William D. Leahy Papers, Library of Congress.
3. "Memorandum: Subject: Conduct of the War in Europe, 8 August, 1943," in *Foreign Relations of the United States: The Conferences at Washington and Quebec, 1943* (hereinafter *FRUS II*) (Washington, D.C.: Government Printing Office, 1970), 467–72; also Maurice Matloff, *Strategic Planning for Coalition Warfare* (Washington, D.C.: Center of Military History, 1959), 176.
4. Even in the President's meeting with the Joint Chiefs of Staff at the White House, General Marshall was more concerned with logistical waste than vital combat

experience, chiding the President that it was "impossible to calculate the wastage that has accrued to the United Nations war effort from changes made to basic decisions" — i.e., the cross-Channel invasion, planned in 1942. "The first instance was carrying out TORCH which involved moving troops set up from the United States to England and thence to Africa" — "Minutes of Meeting Held at the White House Between the President and the Chiefs of Staff on 10 August at 1415," in *FRUS II*, 503.

5. "Memorandum by the Joint Chiefs of Staff: Strategic Concept for the Defeat of the Axis in Europe, 9 August, 1943," *FRUS II*, 472–81.
6. Ibid., 473.
7. Ibid.
8. "Memorandum for General Handy," August 9, 1943, in *The Papers of General George Catlett Marshall*, vol. 4 (Baltimore, MD: Johns Hopkins University Press, 1996), 85–86.
9. Ibid.
10. "Minutes of Meeting Held at the White House Between the President and the Chiefs of Staff on 10 August 1943 at 1415," *FRUS II*, 499.
11. Ibid.
12. Ibid., 500.
13. Ibid., 500–501.
14. Ibid., 501.
15. Entry of August 10, 1943, Stimson Diary, Henry L. Stimson Papers, Yale University Library, New Haven, CT.
16. "Minutes of Meeting Held at the White House Between the President and the Chiefs of Staff on 10 August 1943 at 1415," *FRUS II*, 501.
17. Ibid., 502
18. "Minutes of meeting held at the White House at 1415 between the President and the JCS, 10 Aug 43, with JCS Memo 97 in ABC 337 (25 May 43)," in Matloff, *Strategic Planning for Coalition Warfare*, 215.
19. Entry of August 10, 1943, Stimson Diary.
20. "Dear Mr. President" letter, August 10, 1943, attached to Stimson Diary.

40. THE FÜHRER IS VERY OPTIMISTIC

1. "The Polish Ministry for Foreign Affairs to the American Embassy Near the Polish Government in Exile," in *FRUS II*, 410.
2. "Prime Minister's Personal Minute," July 19, 1943, in Gilbert, *Road to Victory*, 445.
3. Entry of 10.8.1943 in Joseph Goebbels, *Die Tagebücher von Joseph Goebbels* [The diaries of Joseph Goebbels], ed. Elke Froehlich (Munich: K. G. Saur, 1993), Teil II, Band 9 (hereinafter *Die Tagebücher 9*), 250.
4. Ibid.
5. Ibid., 254.

6. "Er denkt nicht daran, bis zum Po zurückzuziehen" ["He has no intention of retreating to the Po"], entry of June 25, 1943, Goebbels, *Die Tagebücher von Joseph Goebbels* [The diaries of Joseph Goebbels], ed. Elke Froehlich (Munich: K. G. Saur, 1993), Teil II, Band 8, 532.

7. Entry of 10.8.1943, Goebbels, *Die Tagebücher 9*, 255.

8. Ibid.

9. Ibid., 260.

10. Ibid.

11. Ibid.

12. Ibid., 261.

13. See Karl-Heinz Friezer et al., *Das Deutsche Reich und der Zweite Weltkrieg* (Stuttgart: Deutsche Verlags-Anstalt, 2007) Band 8, 1192–1209.

14. "die schon erwähnte Spekulation auf wachsende und letztlich bündnisprengde Divergenzen innerhalb der Feindkoalition": Ibid., 1194.

41. A CARDINAL MOMENT

1. Cable of June 25, 1943, in *Foreign Relations of the United States: The Conferences at Cairo and Tehran 1943* (hereinafter *FRUS III*), 10.

2. Entry of August 14, 1943, in Ward, *Closest Companion*, 229.

3. Ibid.

4. "Dear Mr. President" letter, August 10, 1943, attachment to entry of August 10, 1943, Stimson Diary.

5. Ibid.

6. Personal Minute of July 13, 1943, in Martin Gilbert, *Road to Victory: Winston S. Churchill, 1941–1945* (London: Heinemann, 1986), 442.

7. Ibid., Cable T.1043/3, July 16, 1943, 443.

42. CHURCHILL IS STUNNED

1. In London, Secretary Stimson had told Churchill that with regard to the sharing of atom bomb development (code-named S-1), "I could only promise to report the matter to the President for the final decision": "Brief Report on Certain Features of Overseas Trip," August 4, 1943, Stimson Diary.

2. Entry of August 10, 1943, Mackenzie King Diary, Library and Archives Canada, Ottawa, ON.

3. Winston Churchill, *The Second World War*, vol. 5, *Closing the Ring* (London: Cassell, 1952), 73.

4. Entry of August 14, 1943, in Ward, *Closest Companion*, 228.

43. THE GERMAN WILL TO FIGHT

1. Vice Admiral Mountbatten used his pistol to demonstrate the toughness of ice

floes — his latest brainwave for floating harbors in the invasion of Normandy: Andrew Roberts, *Masters and Commanders: How Four Titans Won the War in the West, 1941–1945* (New York: Harper, 2009), 405.

2. David Reynolds, *In Command of History: Churchill Fighting and Writing The Second World War* (New York: Random House, 2005), 363.

3. Philip A. Smith, *Bombing to Surrender: The Contribution of Air Power to the Collapse of Italy, 1943* (Maxwell Air Force Base, Alabama: School of Advanced Airpower Studies, 1997), 63.

4. Sven Oliver Mueller, "Nationalism in German War Society 1939–1945" in *Germany and the Second World War,* ed. Jörg Echternkamp (Oxford: Clarendon Press, 2014), vol. 9, no. 2, p. 32.

5. Ibid., 34.

6. Ibid., 30.

44. NEAR-HOMICIDAL NEGOTIATIONS

1. Entry of August 15, 1943, *Field Marshal Lord Alanbrooke: War Diaries, 1939–1945,* ed. Alex Danchev and Daniel Todman (Berkeley: University of California Press, 2001), 441.

2. Reynolds, *In Command of History,* 374–82.

3. "The Log of the President's Trip to Canada, August 16–August 26, 1943," 2, FDR Library.

4. Entry of August 15, 1943, Arthur Bryant, *The Turn of the Tide: A History of the War Years, Based on the Diaries of Field Marshal Lord Alanbrooke, Chief of the Imperial General Staff* (New York: Doubleday, 1957), 578.

5. Carlo D'Este, *World War II in the Mediterranean, 1942–1945* (Chapel Hill, NC: Algonquin, 1990), 196. Since over 200,000 Germans were reported "missing," these may include many who surrendered at the war's end.

6. Carlo D'Este, *Warlord: A Life of Winston Churchill at War, 1874–1945* (New York: Harper, 2008), 626.

7. Entry of August 16, 1943, Brooke, *War Diaries,* 443.

8. Entry of August 15, 1943, Leahy Diary, William D. Leahy Papers, Library of Congress.

9. Entry of August 15, 1943, Brooke, *War Diaries,* 442.

10. *Foreign Relations of the United States: The Conferences at Washington and Quebec, 1943* (hereinafter *FRUS II*) (Washington, D.C.: Government Printing Office, 1970), 865.

11. Ibid., 866.

12. Entry of August 16, 1943, Brooke, *War Diaries,* 443.

13. Annotation to entry of August 15, 1943, in Brooke, *War Diaries,* 442.

14. Commander George Elsey, interview with the author, September 11, 2011.

45. A LONGING IN THE AIR

1. "The Log of the President's Trip to Canada, August 16–August 26, 1943," compiled by Chief Ship's Clerk William Rigdon, 4, FDR Library.
2. Cable of August 22, 1942, in Susan Butler, ed., *My Dear Mr. Stalin: The Complete Correspondence of Franklin D. Roosevelt and Joseph V. Stalin* (New Haven, CT: Yale University Press, 2005), 155.
3. Averell Harriman and Elie Abel, *Special Envoy to Churchill and Stalin, 1941–1946* (New York: Random House, 1975), 225; and entry of August 31, 1943, Mackenzie King Diary, Library and Archives Canada, Ottawa, ON.
4. Entry of August 23, 1943, Brooke, *War Diaries*, 447. Lieutenant General Henry Pownall, who became one of Churchill's many assistants in writing his memoirs, claimed in his 1943–1944 diary that the Sumatra idea, code-named Operation Culverin, was "a typically Winstonian project, advanced with his usual fatuous obstinacy": David Reynolds, *In Command of History*, 404.
5. Harriman and Abel, *Special Envoy*, 224.
6. Ibid.
7. *FRUS II*, 691ff.
8. "The Log of the President's Trip to Canada, August 16–August 26, 1943," compiled by Chief Ship's Clerk William Rigdon, 15, FDR Library.
9. P. J. Philips, "President Is Grim: Only Long Peace Could Justify Sacrifices," *New York Times*, August 26, 1943.
10. Entry of August 25, 1943, Mackenzie King Diary.
11. Samuel I. Rosenman, *Working with Roosevelt* (New York: Harper, 1952), 387.
12. Ibid.
13. Ibid.
14. Text in "The Log of the President's Trip to Canada." (President's own copy. The alternative wording gave the President a choice, for extra emphasis, as he spoke.) Also as "Address at Ottawa, Canada, August 25, 1943," in *The Public Papers and Addresses of Franklin D. Roosevelt*, vol. 12, *The Tide Turns*, comp. Samuel Rosenman (New York: Russell & Russell, 1950; reissued 1969), 365–69.
15. Philips, "President Is Grim," *New York Times*.
16. "Address at Ottawa, Canada, August 25, 1943," in *The Public Papers and Addresses of Franklin D. Roosevelt*.
17. Entry of August 25, 1943, Mackenzie King Diary.

46. THE PRESIDENT IS UPSET — WITH THE RUSSIANS

1. "Memorandum of conversation Mr. Mackenzie King had with President Franklin D. Roosevelt — Ottawa, Wednesday — August 25, 1943," Mackenzie King Diary.
2. Ibid.
3. Ibid.

4. Ibid., "Conversation with Mr. Roosevelt, Ottawa — August 25, 1943."
5. Martin Gilbert, *Road to Victory: Winston S. Churchill, 1941–1945* (London: Heinemann, 1986), 482.
6. Dmitri Volkogonov, *Stalin: Triumph and Tragedy* (Rocklin, CA: Prima, 1991), 486.
7. "Conversation with Mr. Roosevelt, Ottawa, August 25, 1943," Mackenzie King Diary.
8. Ibid., entry of August 22, 1943.
9. Gilbert, *Road to Victory*, 482.
10. E.g. Susan Butler, *Roosevelt and Stalin: Portrait of a Partnership* (New York: Knopf, 2015).
11. Gilbert, *Road to Victory*, 484–85.
12. Harriman and Abel, *Special Envoy*, 536.
13. Entry of Wednesday, August 25, 1942, Mackenzie King Diary.
14. Ibid., "Conversation with Mr. Roosevelt. Ottawa — August 25, 1943."
15. Ibid., entry of August 31, 1943.
16. Ibid., "Conversation with Mr. Roosevelt. Ottawa — August 25, 1943."
17. Ibid.

47. CLOSE TO DISASTER

1. Entry of August 26, 1943, in Geoffrey C. Ward, ed., *Closest Companion: The Unknown Story of the Intimate Friendship Between Franklin Roosevelt and Margaret Suckley* (Boston: Houghton Mifflin, 1995), 231.
2. Entry of August 29, 1943, Leahy Diary, William D. Leahy Papers, Library of Congress.
3. Entry of August 28, 1943, Ward, *Closest Companion*, 231–32.

48. A DARWINIAN STRUGGLE

1. Entry of 27.8.1943, Joseph Goebbels, *Die Tagebücher von Joseph Goebbels* [The diaries of Joseph Goebbels], ed. Elke Fröhlich (Munich: K. G. Saur, 1993), Teil II, Band 9 (hereinafter *Die Tagebücher 9*), 369. Quotes from this source have been translated by the author.
2. Ibid., entry of 10.8.1943, 260.
3. Ibid., entry of 10.9.1943, 464. Interestingly, addressing reporters' questions in Washington, "Churchill said Britain wants no more territory: such as Sicily, Pantelleria, etc," but that "islands of chiefly strategic value probably should be held by the Allies." However, he also made clear the "British did not propose to give up any territory" they considered theirs — "this in answer to a question about Hong Kong": "Churchill Luncheon with Correspondents, September 3, 1943," in Raymond Clapper Papers, Personal File, 1942–43, Box 23, Library of Congress.
4. Ibid.

49. A TALK WITH ARCHBISHOP SPELLMAN

1. Winston Churchill, *The Second World War*, vol. 5, *Closing the Ring* (London: Cassell, 1952), 109.
2. Entry of August 31, 1943, Mackenzie King Diary.
3. Entry of September 6, 1943, Ward, *Closest Companion*, 236–37.
4. Ibid.
5. Mary Soames, *A Daughter's Tale* (New York: Random House, 2011), 275–76.
6. Ibid, 276–77.
7. Robert I. Gannon, *The Cardinal Spellman Story* (Garden City, NY: Doubleday, 1962), 218.
8. Ibid., 223.
9. "To many historians, especially but far from exclusively those writing in the first years of the Soviet-American Cold War that followed World War II, Roosevelt was exceptionally naive and foolish to believe he could collaborate with Stalin": Mark Stoler and Melanie Gustafson, eds., *Major Problems in the History of World War II: Documents and Essays* (Boston: Houghton Mifflin, 2003), 378.
10. John Morton Blum, *V Was for Victory: Politics and American Culture During World War II* (New York: Harcourt Brace Jovanovich, 1976), 271–73.
11. Ibid., 255.
12. Ibid.
13. Gannon, *The Cardinal Spellman Story*, 223.
14. Ibid.
15. Ibid.
16. Ibid.
17. Susan Butler, *Roosevelt and Stalin: Portrait of a Partnership* (New York: Knopf, 2015), 153.
18. Gannon, *The Cardinal Spellman Story*, 223.
19. Ibid.
20. Ibid., 227.

50. THE EMPIRES OF THE FUTURE

1. Entry of September 2, 1943, Ward, *Closest Companion*, 234.
2. Simon Sebag-Montefiore, *Young Stalin* (New York: Knopf, 2007), 193.
3. Ibid., 193.
4. Martin Gilbert, *Road to Victory: Winston S. Churchill, 1941–1945* (London: Heinemann, 1986), 492.
5. Ibid.
6. "Anglo-American Unity: A Speech on Receiving an Honorary Degree at Harvard University, September 6, 1943," in *The War Speeches of Winston Churchill*, ed. Charles Eade, vol. 2 (London: Cassell, 1952), 510–15.

7. Ibid.
8. Ibid.

51. A TRAGICOMEDY OF ERRORS

1. E.g., Douglas Porch, *The Path to Victory: The Mediterranean Theater in World War II* (New York: Farrar, Straus and Giroux, 2004), 459–61.
2. "Review of the Situation in the Light of Italian Collapse," in RG 218: Records of the U.S. Joint Chiefs of Staff, Box 307, National Archives.
3. Ibid.
4. Carl D'Este, *Patton: A Genius for War* (New York: HarperCollins, 1995), 533–55; Rick Atkinson, *The Day of Battle: The War in Sicily and Italy, 1943–1944* (New York: Holt, 2007), 147–49.
5. Nigel Hamilton, *Monty: Master of the Battlefield, 1942–1944* (New York: McGraw-Hill, 1986), 390.
6. Ibid., 398–402.
7. Ibid., 399.
8. Ibid., 388.
9. Atkinson, *The Day of Battle*, 190.
10. General Mark Clark to author, interview of October 26, 1981, in Hamilton, *Monty: Master of the Battlefield*, 414.
11. Atkinson, *The Day of Battle*, 192.

52. MEETING REALITY

1. Atkinson, *The Day of Battle*, 195.
2. Ibid., 196.
3. Hamilton, *Monty: Master of the Battlefield, 1942–1944*, 393.
4. Atkinson, *The Day of Battle*, 197.
5. On the island of Cephalonia, for example, more than five thousand Italian troops were massacred by invading German forces, who were told to take no prisoners: Alexander Mikaberidze, ed., *Atrocities, Massacres, and War Crimes: An Encyclopedia* (Santa Barbara, CA: ABC-CLIO, 2013), 326 and 750.
6. See Hamilton, *Monty: Master of the Battlefield*, 404; and Atkinson, *The Day of Battle*, 190.
7. General Mark Clark to author, interview of October 26, 1981, in Hamilton, *Monty: Master of the Battlefield*, 414.
8. Ibid.
9. Atkinson, *The Day of Battle*, 199.
10. Ibid., 203.
11. Ibid., 205.
12. "Fireside Chat Opening Third War Loan Drive, September 8, 1943," *The Public Papers and Addresses of Franklin D. Roosevelt*, 377–80.

13. See Hamilton, *Monty: Master of the Battlefield,* 405–6 and footnote 403.
14. Entry of Monday, September 13, 1943, Ward, *Closest Companion,* 237.
15. Soames, *A Daughter's Tale,* 278.
16. Entry of September 7, Moran, *Winston Churchill: The Struggle for Survival, 1940–1965* (Boston: Houghton Mifflin, 1966), 118.
17. Ibid., entry of September 12, 1943, 119.
18. Ibid.
19. Entry of September 16, 1943, Diary of Harry C. Butcher, Eisenhower Library.
20. Entry of September 13, 1943, Moran, *Winston Churchill,* 119–20.
21. Ibid., 120.
22. Entry of Friday, August 27, 1943, in Alan Lascelles, *King's Counsellor: Abdication and War: The Diaries of Sir Alan Lascelles,* ed. Duff Hart-Davis (London: Weidenfeld & Nicolson, 2006), 156.
23. Cable of September 11, 1943, in Susan Butler, ed., *My Dear Mr. Stalin: The Complete Correspondence of Franklin D. Roosevelt and Joseph Stalin* (New Haven, CT: Yale University Press, 2005), 164.
24. Entry of 11.9.1943, Goebbels, *Die Tagebücher 9,* 479.
25. Rede des Führers über den Zusammenbruch Italiens am 10. September 1943, http://de.metapedia.org/wiki/Quelle/Rede_vom_10._September_1943_(Adolf_Hitler). Translated by the author.
26. Ibid.
27. Entry of 12.9.1943, Goebbels, *Die Tagebücher 9,* 492.
28. Ibid., entry of 10.9.1943, 463.
29. Ibid., 464.
30. Ibid., 460.
31. Ibid., 464.
32. Ibid., entry of 7.9.1943, 438.
33. Ibid., entry of 12.9.1943, 486–87.
34. Ibid.

53. A MESSAGE TO CONGRESS

1. Atkinson, *The Day of Battle,* 212.
2. Hamilton, *Monty: Master of the Battlefield, 1942–1944,* 413.
3. Mark Clark to author, interview of October 10, 1981, in Hamilton, *Monty: Master of the Battlefield,* 405.
4. Atkinson, *The Day of Battle,* 207.
5. "Message to the Congress on the Progress of the War, September 17, 1943," in *The Public Papers and Addresses of Franklin D. Roosevelt,* comp. Samuel I. Rosenman, vol. 12, 388–406.
6. Ibid.
7. Ibid.

54. ACHIEVING WONDERS

1. Entry of 19.9.43, in Goebbels, *Die Tagebücher 9*, 533.
2. "Message to the Congress on the Progress of the War, September 17, 1943."
3. Entry of August 31, 1943, Mackenzie King Diary.
4. Ibid.
5. George Elsey, interview with the author, September 12, 2011.
6. Ibid.
7. Andrew Roberts, *Masters and Commanders: How Four Titans Won the War in the West, 1941–1945* (New York: Harper, 2009), 412–13.
8. Brooke was equally to blame, plotting with Churchill to postpone Overlord yet again beyond its planned spring 1944 target date, and to demand "another full-scale Combined Chiefs of Staff conference in early November," 1943, "to try to sell" the alternative Mediterranean-exploitation strategy to Roosevelt and Marshall: Roberts, *Masters and Commanders*, 418. "We should have been in a position to force the Dardanelles by the capture of Crete and Rhodes, we should have the whole Balkans ablaze by now, and the war might have been finished in 1943!!" Brooke lamented in one of his wildest diary entries of the war: November 1, 1943, in *War Diaries, 1939–1945: Field Marshal Lord Alanbrooke*, ed. Alex Danchev and Daniel Todman (Berkeley: University of California Press, 2001), 465. Even Roberts, who admired Brooke, was moved to harsh judgment regarding Overlord. "It had probably been the correct decision not to appoint him as its supreme commander after all," he considered — Roberts, *Masters and Commanders*, 419.

Index